THE PROFESSIONAL
SECRETARY'S HANDBOOK

THIRD EDITION

The Professional Secretary's Handbook

THIRD EDITION

HOUGHTON MIFFLIN COMPANY

Boston • New York

Library of Congress Cataloging-in-Publication Data
The Professional secretary's handbook. — 3rd ed.
   p.   cm.
  Includes index.
  ISBN 0-395-69621-6 (alk. paper)
  1. Office practice — Automation. 2. Secretaries. 3. Secretaries — Vocational guidance.
HF5547.5.P7 1995
651.3′741 — dc20   95-12835
                                       CIP

Manufactured in the United States of America

MP 10 9 8 7

Book design by Joyce Weston

For information about this and other Houghton Mifflin trade and reference books and multimedia products, visit The Bookstore at Houghton Mifflin on the World Wide Web at http://www.hmco.com/trade/.

ACKNOWLEDGMENTS

Airfone is a registered trademark of GTE Airfone, Inc. Amtrak is a registered trademark of National Railroad Passenger Corp. Anadex is a registered trademark of Anadex Instruments, Inc. Bufferin is a registered trademark of Bristol-Myers Products, a division of Bristol-Myers Squibb Company. Coke is a registered trademark of The Coca-Cola Company.

Dacron is a registered trademark of E. I. DuPont de Nemours & Co. Diablo is a registered trademark of Xerox Corporation. Express Mail is a registered trademark of the U.S. Postal Service. Hazeltine is a registered trademark of Hazeltine Corporation. Kleenex is a registered trademark of Kimberly-Clark Corporation. Lotus and 1-2-3 are registered trademarks of Lotus Development Corporation.

Mailgram is a registered trademark of Western Union Telegraph Co. MasterCard is a registered trademark of MasterCard International, Inc. Microsoft and Word are registered trademarks of Microsoft Corporation. Pepsi is a registered trademark of the Pepsi-Cola Co. Picturephone is a registered trademark of the American Telephone and Telegraph Company. Ping-Pong is a registered trademark of Parker Brothers. Railfone is a registered trademark of GTE Railfone.

Selectric is a registered trademark of IBM Corporation. Teletex is a registered trademark of Teledyne Industries, Inc. Visa is a registered trademark of Visa International Service Association. Xerox is a registered trademark of Xerox Corporation. Zilog is a registered trademark of Zilog, Inc.

CONTENTS

PREFACE

Like its predecessors, *The Professional Secretary's Handbook, Third Edition,* is a practical guide to the modern electronic office. This edition has been fully updated and expanded to include both current technologies, such as electronic mail, and new applications, such as the on-line information services available over the Internet. In addition to examining these aspects of contemporary business technology, the book reinforces the traditional practices and skills, such as human relations and communication, that are prominent in daily secretarial activities. These two objectives together comprise a total package for secretaries at every level of expertise employed in all types of business and professional enterprises.

Chapter 1, "The Electronic Office," takes you on a tour of the office of today and tomorrow, previewing the facilities where you will work and the systems and machines that you will use; subsequent chapters expand this introduction. Chapter 1 also summarizes the various types of computer systems and describes the components of a typical office workstation. Chapter 4, "Word Processing," expands this preview into a detailed examination of the systems, technologies, and procedures used to process text and other material.

Chapter 2, "Professional Career Development," follows up the introduction to modern technology in Chapter 1 by exploring the steps you will take to prepare for a successful secretarial career in the electronic office. Here you will read about discovering the right career path, taking advantage of available educational opportunities, preparing an effective resume, and fielding questions during a job interview, for example.

Chapter 3, "Human Relations," considers the important subject of getting along with people in a contemporary work environment. In matters of human relations, you will deal with a variety of concerns, such as the rules of proper office etiquette and the keen sense of diplomacy required when you work for more than one boss. This chapter also walks you through areas where your footing may be less secure, such as coping with sexual harassment and working with a boss in a remote office.

Chapter 4, "Word Processing," deals with both conventional and technical aspects of processing text and other data. First you will find a description of the word processing skills that are needed to handle this important part of your work successfully. Then you will read about using word processing equipment, such as electronic typewriters, computers, and desktop publishing equipment, and also discover practical word processing guides such as an actual dictation simulation.

Chapter 5, "Correspondence," deals with a crucial matter that can either build up or tear down a secretarial career: preparing effective and appealing domestic and international communications. Some secretaries compose and send many of their own letters; others spend substantial time polishing and typing letters for others. In either case, the desired result is the same. This chapter, therefore, has detailed formatting and style guidelines, as well as a comprehensive guide to the correct forms of address.

Chapter 6, "Business Documents," takes the descriptions and guidelines in Chapters 1 and 4 and applies them to the preparation of business documents such as press releases, reports, and proposals. Whether or not you are expected to prepare secretarial reports, you will most likely be required to help others prepare a wide variety of business reports. Hence this chapter gives step-by-step instructions on the planning, organization, typing, assembly, and duplication of such documents using both conventional and electronic processes and procedures.

Chapter 7, "Records Management," discusses something secretaries are doing almost every day: managing the massive accumulation of electronic and paper files, records, and databases. This ongoing accumulation threatens to overwhelm offices that lack effective records-management programs. It's not enough simply to cope with current filing; businesses need to decide what to do with an increasing collection of files and records. This chapter, therefore, discusses options and procedures for managing both active *and* inactive material.

Chapter 8, "Telecommunications," focuses on voice telecommunications technologies. (Chapter 9 looks at electronic mail, and Chapter 12 describes various forms of teleconferencing.) In this chapter you'll read about the current state of telecommunications systems found in the electronic office, as well as related concerns such as cost control and security precautions. You'll also learn the latest advice about the delicate matter of dealing pleasantly and effectively with incoming and outgoing calls.

Chapter 9, "Conventional and Electronic Mail," considers another aspect of handling electronic and paper material. This chapter explores the practices and procedures in processing both paper and electronic mail, including the available delivery systems. Here you'll find a necessary mix of conventional practices, such as maintaining a mail log, and modern practices, such as communicating by E-mail.

Chapter 10, "Business English," will be a favorite of many employers as well as secretaries. They both know that language skills play a part in nearly everything a secretary does, from writing a letter to searching a database to talking on the telephone. Therefore, this chapter has extensive information not only about parts of speech and other grammatical items but also about often misused words, such as *bimonthly* and *semimonthly,* and overused words and expressions, such as the cliche *easier said than done.*

Chapter 11, "Business Style Guide," considers the other type of language skill that secretaries must have — knowledge of proper punctuation, capitalization, spelling, and word division. A secretary cannot prepare correspondence or any other type of material without a sound grasp of business style. This chapter, therefore, gives specific rules and guidelines for the obvious aspects of writing style, such as capitalization, and also provides tips on handling a variety of other points of style, such as the proper use of italics, abbreviations, and symbols; and the formatting of mathematical expressions.

Chapter 12, "Meetings and Conferences," covers every possible type of meeting, including informal two-way conversations, company-wide videoconferences, and large off-site conventions. You will find out what types of conventional and technologically advanced meetings are held and how your duties will vary with each type. This chapter will also tell you how to handle many related tasks, such as sending meeting notices, working with a hotel coordinator, formatting meeting minutes, and making proper parliamentary motions during a meeting.

Chapter 13, "International and Domestic Travel," deals with planning and arranging business trips for destinations in this country and in other countries. Although travel agents assume a large portion of the burden in arranging business trips, secretaries must know how to work with an agent. With international travel there are numerous additional concerns, such as foreign currency, translation needs, and international security precautions. This chapter addresses all of those concerns and also lists essential information about nearly two hundred countries.

Chapter 14, "Accounting and Data Processing," addresses a common topic in many offices. Secretaries are frequently involved in some aspect of this subject, such as typing a balance sheet or cash flow statement, keeping a record of their employer's securities transactions, preparing a list of petty cash transactions, or reconciling the office checkbook with the bank statement. This chapter introduces essential accounting principles, the most common financial statements, and various records that secretaries may keep for their employers.

Chapter 15, "Business Law," deals with another essential topic that should concern all secretaries. However, not everyone is aware of the legal implications in everyday secretarial practices. Not everyone knows, for example, that if you are interviewing or hiring an assistant, you are considered an agent of your employer and that whatever you say will be binding on your company. This chapter, therefore, provides essential information that secretaries and others who perform work on behalf of a company should know.

To help you visualize the material described in these fifteen chapters, the book includes hundreds of in-text examples, as well as dozens of featured illustrations such as the following: Office Automation Configuration (Chapter 1); Body Language and the Messages It Conveys (Chapter 2); Tagged Document (Chapter 4); Forms of Address (Chapter 5); Letter-Report Format (Chapter 6); Lateral Files (Chapter 7); Dialing Codes and Time Differences (Chapter 8); Common Mathematical Operators (Chapter 11); Minutes (Chapter 12); Income Statement (Chapter 14); Uniform Commercial Code Financing Statement (Chapter 15).

Each chapter has been reviewed by both secretarial experts and authorities in specific disciplines, such as law and accounting, so the book promises to provide a reliable reference source for secretaries and other professionals working in today's electronic office. To locate specific topics that are of particular interest to you, check the table of contents in the front of the book or the detailed index at the back.

THE ELECTRONIC OFFICE

CHANGING SECRETARIAL FUNCTIONS IN THE ELECTRONIC OFFICE

Whenever technology changes, secretarial functions change as well, and in that respect, the secretarial profession has been evolving since its inception. Working in an electronic office is just one more step in this exciting, never-ending progression of changing functions.

Modern technology is transforming the whole basis of office work. In doing so, it is changing the secretarial role more dramatically than it has been altered since women began entering this formerly male field nearly a century ago. If secretaries are adequately prepared to recognize opportunities when they open up and if they are educated and trained properly to seize and capitalize on those opportunities, they should enjoy a wide range of challenging careers as information managers and professional information workers in the office of the future. See Chapter 2 for more about career opportunities.

The Impact of Office Automation

As more and more secretarial functions become automated, secretaries are spending more time managing the various technologies and less time performing manual tasks. Not only have certain tasks, such as answering the telephone, been taken over by automated equipment in some companies, but executives themselves are performing some of the tasks previously handled by secretaries.

Many executives now do a substantial amount of their own keyboarding and electronic filing. They often handle their own bookkeeping and report preparation through the use of accounting and spreadsheet software. They frequently transmit their own messages on electronic mail systems and pick up their own telephone messages from a voice mail system. All of these changes have had a significant impact on the way that secretaries function in the electronic office.

The On-Site Office

The most advanced electronic office is a computerized system, with its information set down in electronic bits rather than on paper. This type of office is freed from bulky filing cabinets and restrictive walls. You can enter such an office from any computer terminal that has a telephone line and a modem. The terminal could be in your home, in a hotel room halfway across the country, or in someone else's office. Instead of inserting a key into a door lock to enter the office, you key in your personal access number at a computer terminal and call up whatever information you need to do your work.

At the push of a key, your electronic mailbox, or in-basket, appears on the computer screen, listing its contents: mail, telephone messages, memos, reminders for meetings, and so on. You deal with what you can and then route material to various other people in the management group in which and for which you work. (These people also have desktop terminals, called *workstations*.) Next, you call up the electronic calendar to confirm the time for any meeting you're expected to attend, or you prepare material needed for that day. Then you call up the files on a research project you're involved in and settle down to work.

The Remote Office

As fax machines, computers, copiers, and other equipment have become smaller and more affordable, sophisticated home offices that rival business offices have been created, and telecommuting has become a viable alternative to working on-site in company facilities. This option has enabled more executives to work from homes or from other remote locations apart from the regular business facilities. Secretaries to such executives often assume more managerial, decision-making responsibilities to fill the gaps left by the executive's absence.

Secretaries, too, are handling certain functions from a remote location. Instead of visiting a company or other library and checking out books for in-house research or digging through the company files to locate information, they may be using their computers and modems to access a database in another city or state.

Factors Influencing Office Arrangements

Company Size and Information Volume   Company size and information volume are two of the most important determinants of the look and shape of the electronic office.

Large Companies. In large companies with massive amounts of paperwork, office automation most likely involves a major reorganization of work along the lines of specific tasks and functions. Large word processing and data processing centers may be established, as depicted in the example of possible office configurations on page 4, with the equipment arranged in a shared system to which all major information processing work is routed. Shared-logic and other computer systems are described in the section "Computers and Word Processors" beginning on page 9.

Although centralization was once widespread, a more diversified pattern is now common. In addition to a large central word processing pool, smaller satellite centers exist for more specialized or urgent work requirements in certain departments, as well as some stand-alone word processors for a management group or senior executive.

Medium-Sized Companies. Medium-sized companies tend to have one or two fairly small word processing centers, perhaps in a shared-logic configuration supported by a minicomputer. A stand-alone word processor or two and a few microcomputers or personal computers with word processing software may be found there as well.

Small Companies. In companies with a relatively small central office staff, drastic task reorganization is less common. Computer equipment is often installed in such companies on an ad hoc basis and gradually integrated with other equipment and upgraded as specific needs are identified over time.

A small company often starts by buying a stand-alone word processor and a couple of personal computers or microcomputers. After that, it acquires the components for integrating different offices through a local area network or private branch exchange. As office managers and secretaries become used to the system, they usually augment it with different applications software packages sold off the shelf.

Type of Information Work   The shape of the electronic office is greatly influenced by the type of information work that is performed. For example:

- A law office, a company involved in technical research, or a public relations firm will require a very sophisticated system, whereas

Office Automation Configuration in Small, Medium, and Large Organizations

Small

Other Desks or Offices

Word Processing
Equipment or Workstations

Medium

Large

a company processing vast volumes of similar information — an insurance company or a bank, for example — will need something simpler but more powerful.

- In some offices the emphasis may be on routing information to where it's needed as fast as possible — for example, to government policymakers and senior corporate executives. In this type of setting the communications components, such as the local area networks (LANs) and private branch exchanges (PBXs) described later in this chapter, are vital.

- In other offices the emphasis may be on effective record-keeping, as in a medical research facility or a library. Here the systems will be geared toward good database management and related systems software. These systems structure each record's content so that it is linked by logic to every other record in the system and thus can be retrieved instantly through a keyword search. This research, in turn, is facilitated through software designed for information retrieval, including content searches.

- Still other offices may need computer graphics capability. If computer graphics software is incorporated into a word processing unit, it will enable the user to display graphic information quickly, dramatically, and in a way that instantly communicates the desired message. Computer graphics capabilities combined with photocomposition enable companies to do more report formatting and printing work in-house. For secretaries this means the opportunity to do more artistically challenging work.

Centralized versus Decentralized Approach

One approach in the electronic office favors centralized planning and control. Another approach favors a decentralized, locally autonomous arrangement of computer users. Applied strictly to office automation and word processing, a centralized approach features a shared-logic setup with several dumb terminals (so called because they cannot function independently) linked to one central processing unit (CPU).

The decentralized approach could take one of two forms, depending on the size and nature of the setting: (1) a few stand-alone word processors distributed throughout the organization; or (2) a distributed-logic system, with some shared-logic features for high-volume word processing jobs as well as some distributed processing capabilities, thereby making each terminal smart and allowing for some local autonomy by the users. Whether a company has a centralized or decentralized approach will affect the physical layout of the electronic office.

The Workstation

Managing your workstation efficiently and sensibly will help you work effectively with your coworkers, assist your supervisor(s) competently, and make your duties proceed more swiftly and easily. Arranging the equipment and furniture properly and keeping your workstation well organized will yield benefits day after day.

Furniture   Your desk should be functional, compact, versatile, and, it is hoped, attractive. Space in an office is often limited — making it a valuable commodity — and virtually everything you need during the day should be no more than three to five feet from the focal point of your workstation. From a seated position on a swivel chair you should be able to swing around from left to right without any barriers or difficult maneuvering. Equipment and other items on the top of your desk ought to be organized for maximum efficiency.

Supplies   The best way to attack your work load is to be prepared for whatever may happen at any time. The basic supplies that every office worker needs include a stapler and staple remover, paper clips of several sizes, rubber bands, pens, pencils, markers, erasers, cellophane tape, small notepaper, ink pad, date stamp, diskettes, dictation belts or tapes, and rolls of paper for printing calculators.

You should also have equipment and operator instruction manuals, as well as a current edition of a collegiate-level dictionary or a dictionary specifically designed for your profession. A secretarial handbook is a valuable asset, too, and you will want to have an employee's manual, supply catalogs, and telephone books within easy reach.

Management of the Workstation   Once you have all the necessary furniture, equipment, and materials, you must be able to pool these resources and make them work effectively for you. Your system of generating documents should be managed so that you are able to receive the information or data at a moment's notice, produce a perfect document, and follow through with swift, intact delivery of the document to its correct destination.

The system will break down, for example, if you cannot use your fax machine because you forgot to call the repair service when the machine stopped working properly. But when you manage things well, paying attention to details, your office will run smoothly, and high productivity is the reward for having a functional workstation adequately supplied and efficiently managed.

Ergonomics

The term *ergonomics* refers to the incorporation of human factors design into a piece of equipment or furniture. An ergonomically designed system will be comfortable for the operator to use and will not cause eyestrain, hand fatigue, backache, and dozens of other possible discomforts.

A typical word processing system designed with user comfort in mind, for example, will be quiet, will not produce unnecessary screen glare, and will have a detachable keyboard. The system also should allow the user to adjust the monitor into a variety of positions, should be appealing to use, and should require only minimal physical effort to operate.

Health Concerns   The concentration of a person's time in a single location results in additional stress, especially with regard to eye fatigue, noise pollution, and neck, back, and hand strain. Any successful system must be designed with comfort and modularity in mind — factors allowing the user to modify and reconfigure the furniture and hardware to meet his or her own needs.

Computer-Display Health Problems. Video display terminal (VDT) operators have been the single largest group reporting health complaints to the U.S. National Institute of Safety and Health (NIOSH). Some of the health problems linked to the use of a VDT (a keyboard and monitor combined) include cataracts, birth defects and miscarriages, blurred vision, headaches, backaches, and neck and shoulder pain.

In recent years great concern has developed over the amount of radiation that humans become exposed to over an average life span. Modern word processing terminals, however, produce radiation below the government standards for safe radiation levels, and modern ergonomic workstation designs allow operators to sit back from the screen through the use of detached keyboards, further reducing the already minimal radiation exposure.

Furniture Health Problems. Eyestrain and back and neck pain are common health problems linked to the physical work environment. When the lighting is not right, an adjustable reading lamp is often recommended. Chairs that are not adjusted to the right height may not provide sufficient back support and may cause wrist and elbow strain while you are keyboarding. The unit generating the image on a screen may be inadequate or faulty, thus causing a slight flicker that will induce headaches and eye fatigue.

Repetitive-Motion Injuries. Injuries such as elbow tendinitis and carpal tunnel syndrome are serious disorders in the electronic office. *Elbow tendinitis* is similar to the sports injury known as *tennis elbow* and is commonly described as *computer elbow* in the business world. *Carpal tunnel syndrome* is a disorder that originates in the upper arm and spreads to the wrists and hands, causing pain and weakness in that region. Preventive measures include the following adjustments in workstation layout and practice:

- The chair's seat and back slant and height, its arm height, and the keyboard height and distance should all be adjusted so that your elbows are comfortably bent at a 90 degree angle while typing.

- The keyboard tilt should be adjusted so that your wrists remain nearly horizontally straight while typing.

- Wrist rests should be placed in front of the keyboard to help support your wrists.

- Other tools should be used as needed to ease strain, for example sliding elbow and arm supports and adjustable copyholders.

- Periodic rest and stretch breaks should be built into all keyboarding sessions.

MODERN OFFICE TECHNOLOGY

The electronic office depends on both computer and telecommunications technology, with the latter involving everything from telephones to satellites to private branch exchanges. Communications devices move information around and shift it from one medium to another. Computers, in turn, manipulate information. They add and subtract it, list it, process and combine it, and format and store it. Together, these technologies have revolutionized offices everywhere.

Forces Affecting Office Technology

Productivity The electronic office, with its changing roles for office workers, is being shaped by a number of forces, of which technology is but one. Those who are designing and installing automated information systems are driven by the pressure to improve productivity — the volume of work performed by one person in one day. Also responding to this pressure, companies are seeking ways to keep operating costs low and increase profits. These goals are being pursued by using computers to eliminate paperwork, legwork, and unnecessary finger work in running an office.

The productivity of secretarial work is increased enormously through office automation. For example, retyping is eliminated in word processing programs, and other software programs allow for information to be pulled from a variety of electronic files and databases and inserted into a text automatically. Still other software photocopies or prints texts automatically.

Decentralized Management   Other influences are evident also. A new management style, for example, has emerged to replace the bureaucratic, hierarchical approach of top-down administration. The new style is more decentralized, emphasizing involvement, teamwork, personal initiative, and entrepreneurship. As the new information technologies have moved into offices across the country, secretaries have come into their own as professional information workers: managers of information systems, packagers of information, and information brokers.

The Integrated Office   The integrated office is both a force affecting office technology and a result of the forces that are shaping office technology. Computer technology, for example, is not distinctly separate from telecommunications technology. Rather, the technologies are melding, and the integrated office directly links computers, telephones, fax machines, copiers, and other modern equipment.

Businesses no longer operate as entities isolated by time and distance. The electronic processes described throughout this book have made communication instant, and vast electronic networks link people and businesses around the globe.

The Internet, for example, is a giant web of individual computer networks that not only connects businesses but powers their growth. Companies of all sizes are signing onto the Internet's data link and becoming part of its vast marketplace. They are using it for everything from E-mail exchanges to file transfers to the advertising of goods and services. As legal, security, and other problems become less of a concern, the huge communications network will likely become as much a part of the modern office as the computer itself.

Computers and Word Processors

Computers and word processors (computers dedicated to text processing) are two of the most important components in the electronic office. However, they vary significantly in size and capability.

Types of Systems

- A *stand-alone system* for a computer or word processor is an independent, self-contained system providing all the essential hardware and software components required to create, edit, store, and print documents. The components usually include a keyboard, monitor, central processor, storage device, printer, and, possibly, telecommunications interface.

- A *shared-logic system* allows for a number of workstations and other peripherals to be attached to a central processing unit (CPU). The CPU, activated by commands sent from users at their individual workstations (sometimes called "dumb terminals"), controls all the handling and manipulation of data in memory, storage devices, printers, workstations, other peripherals, and communications equipment. The CPU, therefore, handles *all* system activity and performs *all* processing, with the peripherals being only extensions of the CPU.

- A *distributed-logic system* is similar to a shared-logic system in that both have multiple workstations connected to a large CPU. But the distributed-logic system provides the individual workstations, printers, and peripherals with *some* local memory and processing capabilities. The processing done inside the peripherals is handled by a microprocessor, which takes much of the burden off of the CPU. The printer, like the workstation, also can handle processing tasks for document printing.

- A *time-sharing system* consists of one or more workstations linked to a very large computer system, or mainframe, via telecommunications. This mainframe, in addition to providing data processing services for a number of remote users, also provides word processing software and supplies central processing power for each remote user. The user, therefore, pays for the use of someone else's CPU and the cost of communicating with it and shares the CPU with others who have also purchased time on the system.

- A *personal* or *microcomputer system* is a small stand-alone system designed for professionals, small businesses, and home users. Generally, a *microcomputer* is any computer that has both the arithmetic logic unit and the control unit contained on a single integrated circuit called a microprocessor. Such systems typically include a monitor, workstation with keyboard and some internal memory, and interfaces to options such as storage devices, printers, and telecommunications capabilities.

- A *notebook computer system* includes notebook computers that generally weigh four to seven pounds and are small enough to pack in a briefcase. In spite of their popularity for travel and the appeal of a small unit, they are more expensive and less sturdy than desktop models. In some features they resemble desktop units, for example having both hard disks and floppy drives; in other features they are inferior, for example having smaller display screens and keyboards, usually without a numeric keypad. However, it is sometimes possible to attach a separate monitor and numeric keypad. Batteries used in notebook computers are rechargeable. Most notebook units can be fitted with an external modem.

- An *integrated information system* offers the processing power and storage capability of a large computer system with the added advantage of having powerful word processing capabilities. This type of system is usually a mid- to large-size computer supporting a large number of workstations, a variety of printers and peripherals, and a multiple number of storage devices and accommodating the needs of the programmer and word processor user alike. The printers, CPU, and storage devices are located in a central area away from the operator's desk.

The Parts of a Computer   The principal parts of a computer system are the keyboard (input device), monitor, storage devices, and printer (output device). Miscellaneous other devices, such as a modem and a mouse, may also be part of the system.

Keyboard. The keyboard allows you to give the system commands to access text and data for editing and creation and to access and control the other system devices. Each key, when pressed, triggers an electrical pulse that is translated into a code the computer can accept. The most common code is ASCII (American Standard Code for Information Interchange).

The QWERTY keyboard is the industry standard (the first six alphabet keys spell *QWERTY*). In addition to the basic alphabet, numbers, and punctuation keys, some additional keys include an *execute* or *command* key, a *cancel* or *stop* key, and *direction* keys having arrows pointing up, down, right, and left. The *execute* or *command* key is used to begin a new process. The *cancel* or *stop* key is used to indicate that you want to terminate the current process. The direction keys are used to control movement of the cursor around the screen. Function keys, used to edit and revise a document, include *insert, delete, copy, move, indent, center,* and *previous screen.*

Keyboards may be permanently attached to the monitor or detachable/movable. Other input devices are described below under "Input Devices and Techniques."

Display Monitor. A display monitor is a televisionlike device with a screen used to view text, graphics, and numerical data. The best-known type of monitor is the cathode-ray tube (CRT) display.

Monitors are classified by their diagonal size, and common sizes for workstations are 12-, 13-, and 14-inch diagonal displays, which will display twenty-four or twenty-five lines of text by eighty characters wide, or about one third or one half of a page. Larger displays, such as 19- and 20-inch diagonal screens, are often used for desktop publishing and certain graphics applications.

Most monitors provide for contrast and brightness adjustment and are available in color or in green on black, amber on black, or black on white. Higher resolutions providing greater clarity are becoming increasingly common. Users who want greater clarity look for a high "refresh" rate, or the rate at which the screen is redrawn each second. In addition, a noninterlaced screen, unlike an interlaced screen, will scan each line in sequence, which provides a clearer image. The dot pitch — the spacing between the tiny dots making up the image — also affects clarity; the lower the dot pitch, the greater the clarity.

Optional features, such as foreign-language displays, are offered by some manufacturers.

Computer Memory. Program instructions and information that you are working on are held in the memory of the computer. The size of this memory is stated in *bytes*, and each byte is about the size of one typed character. One byte equals eight *bits*, and a bit is represented electronically as either 1 or 0. One *kilobyte* (K or KB) equals 1,024 bytes of information, and 1 megabyte (M or MB) equals 1,048,576 bytes.

The two basic types of memory are ROM (read-only memory) and RAM (random-access memory). *ROM* is permanent memory that you cannot alter, for example the instructions of your operating system. *RAM* is temporary memory that you can alter, for example a letter you are typing.

The size of the program you are using, such as a word processing program, and the document you are working on are limited by the amount of RAM that is installed in your computer. Hence it is important to have adequate RAM not only to handle current programs but to be able to use new ones that may require even more memory. When RAM is inadequate, you can usually add extra memory to the main system board (motherboard) of your computer.

Since RAM is temporary storage, documents being held in RAM while you work on them must be saved (transferred to disk storage) before you shut off the computer.

Storage Devices. Computer systems have several types of storage devices.

- *Diskettes:* Your software programs and the data you are working on are usually saved on removable floppy disks (diskettes) or on hard disks. A diskette is a magnetically coated disk enclosed in a protective jacket. It comes in 5¼- or 3½-inch sizes. The 5¼-inch diskette is available in double density (360K memory) or high density (1.2M memory), and the 3½-inch diskette is also available in double density (720K memory) or high density (1.44M memory). High-capacity disk drives can read and write to a lower-capacity disk, but a lower-capacity drive cannot read or write to a higher-capacity disk. Hence you cannot use a 1.44M diskette if your computer has only a 360K disk drive.

- *Hard disks:* Programs and documents can also be stored on high-capacity magnetic internal or external hard disks. The removable hard disk versions can be used for off-line permanent storage. To increase the storage space on a hard disk after removing all nonessential files, you can buy certain software programs that will allow you to compress the size of your files and gain additional storage space. In addition to providing for hundreds of megabytes of storage space, hard disks enable users to retrieve and store data at far greater speed than is possible with a diskette.

- *Optical disks:* Several types of durable nonmagnetic disks, which resemble diskettes, can be used for mass storage. The *magneto-optical disk* can be erased and reused. The *WORM (write once, read many times) disk* can be read as often as desired but cannot be erased and rewritten.

- *CD-ROMs (compact disk, read-only memory):* Compact disks can store both data and sound. Their exceptionally large storage capacity makes them suitable for large database storage or for the storage of encyclopedias and other extensive reference material.

- *Cassettes and cartridges:* Magnetic tape may be loaded onto reel-to-reel cassettes or onto either single or reel-to-reel cartridges. Up to 100 million characters can be stored on a single reel of tape.

- *Videodisks:* The videodisk is a laser-recording disk used for commercial products such as movies and audiovisual presentations.

Central Processor. The central processing unit (CPU) is the intelligence or brains of the computer. It includes a control unit, which controls what the computer system can do, and an arithmetic logic unit, which performs the calculations or processing of data. The CPU, therefore, contains the instructions that are necessary to allow input, processing, storage, and output of data.

The CPU is also the "engine" that determines how fast your computer will work. The CPU speed is measured in megahertz (MHz), and the higher the speed, the faster the computer will run. If your CPU power is inadequate for statistical work, it may be possible to add a co-processor to increase the speed of detailed mathematical calculations.

Printer. Depending on the need for speed and quality, businesses may select different types of printers.

- *Laser printers,* nonimpact devices that use a narrow beam of light to form images on light-sensitive paper, provide very high-quality print in a variety of fonts.

- *Ink-jet printers,* nonimpact printers that spray ink directly on the paper to form images, provide moderate- to high-quality print that approaches the quality of laser printers.

- *Thermal-wax printers,* which cause wax to melt on paper, provide reasonable quality print. They can use plain paper, although coated stock is available that is designed especially for the wax-transfer process.

- *Dot-matrix printers,* impact printers that project tiny pins, or dots, to form images, operate at a high speed and provide low- to moderate-quality print suitable for draft work. Those that have a 24-pin printhead matrix, rather than a 9-pin matrix, provide near-letter quality (NLQ) printouts, since the more dots in a matrix, the better the print quality.

- *Daisy wheel printers,* older impact printers that use a flat type device to type characters, are slow but provide high-quality print resembling typewriter type.

Modem. A modem (*modulator-dem*odulator) is an internal or external device that connects the computer to a telephone line and converts signals from digital to analog and back to digital at the destination.

Modems transmit information over the telephone lines at a rate of speed measured in bits per second, commonly called the *baud rate.* The faster the speed of the modem, the less telephone time it will use and hence the less a transmission will cost. See "Facsimiles" on pages 17–18 for a description of fax modems.

Input Devices and Techniques. In addition to the keyboard, described earlier, various other devices and techniques can be used to input data and manipulate the cursor.

- The *cursor* is a movable point on the screen that indicates the current place where you are working.

- *Directional keys* on the keyboard can be used to move the cursor up, down, left, or right.

- A *mouse,* which is a small, movable, hand-held device, can be rolled around on a hard surface to move the cursor to a different location on the screen.

- A *joystick* is a small lever that can be moved from side to side to reposition the cursor on the screen.

- A *light pen* is used to write or draw on the display screen.

- *Voice input* enables users to speak commands, which are converted into digital signals that in turn create characters.

- *Optical character reader* (OCR) devices scan or read printed or typed characters and digitally convert them into text or numerical data.

- A *touch screen* is a sensitized display screen that enables a user to select commands by touching the screen.

Refer to subsequent chapters for information on how to use computers for different functions and how to use the various software applications, such as word processing (Chapter 4) and records management (Chapter 7).

Desktop Publishing

In-House Composition   Desktop publishing (DTP), discussed in Chapter 4, is a computer-based form of composition that enables users to see a finished page on the display screen. Often used by companies as an in-house publishing system, it allows for the generation of different typefaces and sizes, multiple column formats, and both text and graphics combined. Page-layout software is used to incorporate graphics into the text pages. The graphics can be created by separate graphics software programs or manually and then scanned into the system or pasted onto the text-page printouts. Pages created on a DTP system are camera-ready (that is, ready to be photographed and printed).

DTP Equipment   A DTP system must have a large-storage-capacity computer, a monitor with a display screen able to show at least one entire page, and a printer with enough type fonts and sizes to create headlines and various other type features. A scanner, although optional for some applications, is necessary to bring outside graphics or other material into the system for manipulation.

Electronic Typewriters

Electronic typewriters are used to supplement computerized word processing activities in many offices. They are most often used to type envelopes, labels, index cards, fill-in printed forms, letters, memos, and short documents. Electronic typewriters vary from small portable units to add-on word processors, which have a separate monitor and disk drive connected to the basic unit. The high-end units rival small computers and can produce long documents containing several hundred pages, whereas the small portables are suitable only for occasional small jobs.

For more about typing procedures, see Chapter 4, "Word Processing."

Personal Word Processors   Memory typewriters are often called *personal word processors* (PWP) when they have additional capabilities. A PWP should have a screen showing at least a dozen lines of type or, ideally, about a half page; should have some type of disk storage; and should be able to perform a full range of text-editing functions on long, complex documents.

The Parts of an Electronic Typewriter   The principal parts of an electronic typewriter are the keyboard, visual display, storage device, and printer.

Keyboard. Most electronic typewriters have a standard QWERTY keyboard, either with separate function keys or with standard keys that can also be used as function keys. Although keybcards may differ depending on the manufacturer and the particular machine, many electronic typewriters have direction keys to manipulate the cursor, operation keys for instructions, format keys to format documents, and function keys for special editing operations.

Visual Display. Two types of display are available — cathode-ray tube or the more common liquid-crystal display (LCD). CRT displays are clearer and larger. On high-end models they may be similar to the displays used with a personal computer, which typically show twenty-four or twenty-five lines of text. The LCD displays require very little space since they show limited text; some of them display fewer than two dozen characters.

Memory. Electronic typewriters have limited memory for text storage ranging from a few hundred to sixty-four thousand (64K) characters, with the option of adding additional external memory to some models. *Correction memory* is the buffer that stores the characters you have typed and is intended for use in making lift-off corrections. *Text memory* is the storage capacity used for documents being retained for later revision and automatic retyping.

Storage Devices. A single disk drive for 3½-inch diskettes is common in most electronic typewriters. Additional storage can be purchased for some models. Unlike computer disks, the disks used in one kind of electronic typewriter are not compatible with those used in another manufacturer's machine.

Printer. The typewriter itself serves as the printer, although both printing and typing cannot be done at the same time. High-end models, however, may have separate printers. Most electronic typewriters use a daisy wheel impact printing device; some have thermal print devices, which can make corrections that generally escape detection.

Facsimiles

Facsimiles are standard features in the electronic office. A *facsimile* (*fax*) *machine* is a transmission device that operates by scanning pages and converting text and graphics into signals that will travel over the telephone lines to a destination fax machine where the signals are converted back again and a duplicate is printed out. A digital fax can be linked to a computer so that incoming signals may be viewed on screen, stored on disk, or printed out as hard copy. Color units will transmit and receive color material. Usually, all that is required for fax transmission is to insert the material into the machine, dial the number at the destination, and press a start button.

Chapter 9 describes proper procedures for handling incoming and outgoing mail, including fax transmissions.

Capabilities   Fax machines vary in size from small travel units to desktop models to large public machines. Capabilities vary from the less expensive low-end units to the more expensive high-end units. Low-end units usually require special paper, whereas high-end models will accept plain paper. Most machines today are digital units that will transmit a page in less than a minute, and some recent machines require only a few seconds per page.

Computer Interface   Special interfaces allow the fax machine to be connected to other equipment, such as an answering machine or a computer. With the proper interface, for example, a fax can send and receive messages from a personal computer. A *fax board* is an adapter that enables the computer to function like a fax machine when the material to be sent is either created on the computer or scanned into it.

A *fax modem* is a device that can be used with fax software to enable you to create documents on your computer and send them to another fax machine without first making a printout. You can also receive faxes on your computer, view them on the display screen, and print them out. However, you cannot fax material that isn't created on your computer, such as a photo. If you have a scanner, though, the material can be imported into your computer so that it can be faxed the same as a created document. An important disadvantage is that while the computer is being used for fax activity, it cannot be used for your regular work.

Photocopiers

Like fax machines, photocopiers are standard in the electronic office. Their principal function is to make duplicate copies. When vast quantities of copies are required, another form of duplication, such as offset printing, may be more appropriate, although some high-volume copiers can produce forty thousand or more copies per month. At the other extreme, some low-volume personal or convenience copiers (minicopiers), used in homes and small offices, may be designed to handle only five hundred or fewer copies per month. Speed also varies, with some high-speed units handling up to one hundred copies per minute and some low-speed units handling only five or six copies per minute.

Refer to Chapter 4 for information about the use of copiers and other duplication machines and processes in word processing.

Common Features Photocopier features vary greatly, although all new machines accept plain paper. Many will reduce or enlarge documents, copy on two sides of the paper (*duplexing*), and accept different color toner cartridges. The more expensive models may have some form of electronic cut-and-paste editing, job-sequence programming, a sorting and collating device, an automatic feed tray, an automatic stapling and binding device, and an automatic folding device.

Digital Copiers Digital units, which are more expensive and slower than the more common analog units, provide superior quality duplicates. Some of the digital models can double as a fax machine and a computer printer, and many have other capabilities and features linked to computer-telecommunications technology.

Scanners

Although less common than fax machines, scanners are becoming more common in the electronic office. A scanner is a peripheral device that digitizes images and stores them in a file that can be merged with word processing or DTP programs. In addition, scanners may be used in conjunction with fax modems, as described previously in the section "Facsimiles." Scanners may be color, black and white, or gray scale (for photographs). The higher the resolution of a scanner, the better the image that will be produced. These types of scanners are common:

- *Flatbed scanners* resemble a desktop photocopier. Images are placed face down on the scanning surface.

- *Sheetfed scanners* automatically feed a certain number of pages through the unit for scanning.

- *Overhead* or *copyboard scanners* scan documents, placed on the unit face up, from above.

Special scanning software is needed to operate a scanner. Usually, the software has a correction feature that allows you to correct errors introduced by the scanner. Most scanners have only a 95 percent accuracy rate.

Teletypewriters

While other machines, such as computers and fax machines, have become more prominent in the electronic office, teletypewriters have become less common. Nevertheless, they are still used in many businesses, particularly those that deal with European companies.

For more about procedures with telex messages, refer to Chapter 9.

Telex   Teletypewriters are used to send telex messages, one of the oldest forms of electronic mail. They were used more extensively in the United States before the introduction of the fax machine and are still very common in Europe. Unlike a fax machine, a teletypewriter can handle only text and cannot transmit graphics. Today, however, telex users can adapt their computers to provide higher-quality, faster telex communications.

Companies may have their own telex network, or they may use Western Union's Telex I or Telex II network. Through a Western Union conversion program, messages can be exchanged between Telex I and Telex II subscribers.

Telex messages that are prepared on a teletypewriter are of a lower quality than computer messages. Also, both Telex I and II are slower and more expensive forms of transmission than fax.

Teletex   Teletex, which is connected to the telex network, is faster than either Telex I or Telex II and, unlike them, allows lowercase letters and standard business formats to be used. Teletex messages can be prepared, sent, and received on computers modified and equipped for this purpose. Western Union offers Teletex service and provides interconnection with the telex network.

Dictation Equipment

Dictation equipment was an important part of the preelectronic office and remains common in the modern electronic office. It supplements computer equipment in the preparation of correspondence and other documents. Although many executives prefer to draft their material on a desktop or notebook computer and give their secretaries a diskette for final polishing and printout, some type of dictation equipment is often found in business and professional offices. Whether the executive uses a computer or dictation equipment, the secretary can be busy with other tasks while the executive is preparing a draft.

Types of Recording Media   Both endless-loop tape and discrete media are used to hold dictated material. An *endless-loop tape* is used over and over, with previous dictation erased after it is transcribed. *Discrete media,* such as a cassette, magnetic disk, or magnetic belt, can be removed from the dictation and transcription machines and stored for a limited time according to the life of the media.

Types of Recording Systems   The two types of recording systems are digital and analog. *Digital systems* use binary language like a computer and offer some of the same advantages. They enable users to access documents out of order (random access), to do some editing within a document, and to store more information in less space than is possible with an analog system. *Analog systems*, which use an older technology, do not allow for random access of documents. The transcriber must use fast-forward features to move through all the preceding documents until the desired document is reached. An audible tone or other type of signal alerts transcribers to the end of a document or to instructions concerning priorities and editing.

Types of Dictation Equipment   Three general types of dictation equipment are available: portable units, desktop units, and central systems.
Portable Dictation Units. The portable units, which are usually battery operated, are lightweight and small enough for travelers to carry with them. Some handheld units are small enough to fit in a pocket. Recording time ranges from fifteen to ninety minutes, depending on whether the medium used is a regular cassette, minicassette or microcassette, magnetic belt, or visible belt. Although the size of portable units limits the number of features that are possible, even the smallest units usually offer tape speed adjustments, digital counters that identify the amount of tape available, rewind and fast-forward buttons, pause buttons, and voice-activated recording.
Desktop Units. The desktop units are small machines that sit permanently on a desk. Most record on standard cassettes or minicassettes, which must be removed and taken to the transcription unit for typing. Some units combine both dictation and transcription capabilities. A handset and foot pedal are needed for the transcription. Other units are combined with a telephone, an answering machine, and an answering-recording device. Numerous features are available on desktop units, including speaker attachments (for conferences), speed control, tape counter or liquid-crystal display, and alarms for reminder functions.

Desktop units that are compatible with portable units provide an efficient total system for executives who are frequently away from the office.

Centralized Systems. The centralized systems have a single large recording device that usually consists of a multiple-cassette machine or uses an endless-loop tape. The endless-loop system enables numerous users to transcribe documents simultaneously. Those who are dictating access a centralized system from their individual offices and workstations using a handset or, from remote locations, a telephone. A supervisor frequently assigns the dictation to an operator, who transcribes material from a separate workstation or transcription center. Supervisors use a computer to monitor task assignments, task priorities, and other factors related to output and productivity.

Microfilm Equipment

Although computer filing is being used more and more in the electronic office to alleviate the pressure of finding space for paper storage, microfilm equipment is still used in some companies to reproduce documents with text and graphics on film for storage in a reduced size, a process known as *micrographics.* The rolls or sheets of film that contain color or black and white images of a document are called *microforms.* Since the images are recorded in a reduced size, they must be placed on a microform reader and enlarged in order to be read on a screen similar to a computer display screen; special printers are used to print out full-size paper copies.

Computer Interface   With the proper interface a reader can be linked to a computer so that a document can be called up and imported into the computer system. Computers can also be used to retrieve microfilm documents through a process called *computer-assisted retrieval* (CAR). Although computer disk storage has exceeded micrographics media storage in popularity, certain documents, such as a certificate, may not be suitable for disk storage. For more about the use of microforms for records storage, see Chapter 7.

Types of Microforms   Microforms can be produced in various ways. Special micrographics cameras can film the paper documents, or the microforms can be produced from machine-readable computer-processed data. In the latter method, known as *computer-output microfilm* (COM), the computer data are printed on the film, processed, and duplicated.

The best-known types of microforms are rolls, jackets, and fiche.

- A *microfilm roll* is a continuous roll of film capable of holding hundreds of pages in reduced image. Common sizes are 16mm, 35mm, and 105mm.

- A *microfilm jacket* is a double sheet of clear plastic that is sealed together to accommodate horizontal slots for holding film strips of microfilm.

- A *microfiche* is a sheet of film, about 4 by 6 inches, capable of holding several hundred pages in a reduced image form smaller than microfilm.

- An *ultrafiche* is an even smaller sheet of film capable of holding thousands of pages in a reduced image form. Ultrafiche is sometimes used to store directories, catalogs, and other large documents.

- An *aperture card* is a small card on which a frame of microfilm is mounted. The frame frequently holds one engineering drawing, map, or other large document.

Mass Storage and Retrieval Equipment

Large companies must routinely store massive amounts of information. This typically includes paper, electronic, and film storage (see Chapter 7). In paper storage documents that are released from active files for permanent storage as inactive film are indexed, placed in containers, and transferred to the appropriate storage facility. Computer-prepared documents are stored on magnetic or optical disks or tapes. Other material may be stored on microforms.

Storage and Retrieval Procedure   Mechanical or electronic devices are used to store and retrieve massive paper files. Motorized mechanical or electronic components physically transport shelf units or other containers from one location to another. To retrieve a document or folder, however, the user must first consult an index to determine the proper container number. Although such indexes may be maintained manually, they are usually prepared and maintained by computer. Once the correct index terms have been keyed into the system, a number of search commands must be entered to produce a list of relevant documents.

Computer-Assisted Indexing   The required hardware for computer-assisted indexing will vary with the application but typically includes a large-scale mini- or microcomputer, one or more video terminals or other input devices for the entry of index data, one or more video displays or printers to use in retrieval, and magnetic disks or other media for the storage of index data. The indexing itself may be done with a custom-developed software program or a commercial program. Any program used must allow for the entry of data about specific documents; the addition, deletion, or other modification of index data; and the identification of documents.

Chapter 7 discusses filing techniques and procedures and the steps required in effective records-management programs.

Accounting and Data Processing Equipment

In a fully electronic office the accounting and data processing equipment would be completely or primarily electronic. In many offices, however, accounting and data processing systems are a combination of manual, mechanical, and electronic but with increasing reliance on electronic systems.

Types of Systems   With *manual systems,* suitable only for very small businesses, accounting and data processing functions are performed by hand using limited equipment, such as a calculator and a typewriter or personal computer. With a *mechanical system,* other equipment is added, such as a cash register, an adding machine, and a posting machine. With an *electronic system,* most accounting and data processing functions are handled with computers and other electronic equipment.

Electronic Accounting and Data Processing   Electronic accounting and data processing require electronic calculators and computers of varying sizes and sophistication, from large mainframes to micro- and minicomputers, to process information. Electronic data processing equipment performs many functions that accounting activities require, such as arithmetic procedures, memory storage, memory recall, and information comparison. With the proper accounting and data processing software, numerous activities can be simplified, from payroll processing and record keeping to financial report preparation to a myriad of complex data calculations. For more about the principles and practices that apply to accounting and data processing, refer to Chapter 14.

Mailing Equipment

The mailing function in the electronic office is handled primarily with electronic equipment, although postal equipment has not advanced technologically at the same rate as other equipment, such as computers or fax machines. A small office may use an electronic typewriter or personal computer to prepare envelopes or labels, use a mechanical or electronic scale, and perform the folding, inserting, sealing, and postage-application steps by hand. Any organization that must maintain large address lists and prepare bulk mailings, however, will need a variety of modern electronic addressing and mailing equipment, including sorting, collating, and folding machines and postal scales and meters.

Electronic Mail Equipment   Electronic mail (E-mail) can be sent from one fax, teletypewriter, or computer to another through in-house direct wiring, over the telephone lines, or by satellite without the need to address, fold, stuff, and seal envelopes or other packages. E-mail users need a computer and for outside computer transmission a modem, as well as the proper software package.

Computer-based message systems can be based either on a central computer serving as a repository for all the messages or on a network of computers automatically transmitting messages to each other over the telephone lines, through a data network, or through a local area network. The illustration on page 26 indicates the difference between a central system and a network system.

If you are using a network, your computer should take care of all details of message transmission and reception. If you are accessing a central computer using an office computer as a terminal, your office computer may or may not be able to handle everything automatically.

A stand-alone E-mail system is really a computer that handles electronic transmissions and does nothing else. An integrated E-mail system combines the mail features with word processing and other capabilities. Chapter 9 describes procedures in the use of E-mail.

Addressing Equipment   Older forms of addressing equipment use metal, plastic, or paper plates that stamp addresses on envelopes or labels. The plates are maintained alphabetically, numerically, or according to some other file system. Electronic systems maintain addresses on tapes or disks, and sorting and printout on envelopes or labels are accomplished through the proper software program. Through a "merge" feature, the same addresses used on envelopes can be merged with the text of a letter in large mailings. Various other individual data can also be merged into the body of a standard letter. Unless the addresses in a mailing list are arranged alphabetically, a cross-index must also be maintained by computer.

Electronic Mail Systems

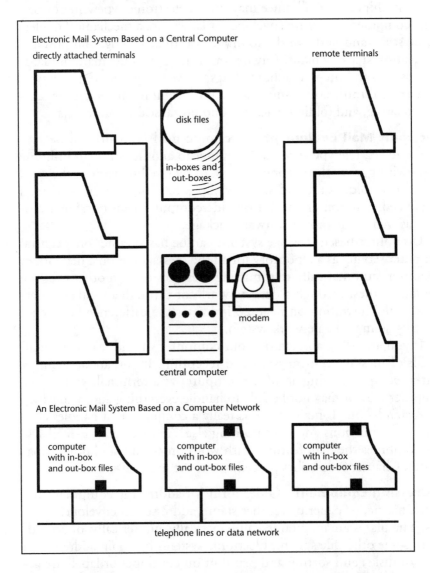

Electronic Mail System Based on a Central Computer

directly attached terminals · remote terminals · disk files · in-boxes and out-boxes · modem · central computer

An Electronic Mail System Based on a Computer Network

computer with in-box and out-box files · computer with in-box and out-box files · computer with in-box and out-box files · telephone lines or data network

Top: The computer's files serve as the repository for all messages, and users can get to them through terminals attached to the system, or by calling in from remote terminals. Bottom: The computers transmit messages to each other through the telephone lines or over a data network. The two methods overlap, since central computer systems also may exchange mail with computers in other offices.

Mailroom Equipment   Accurate electronic scales, meters, and a variety of other mailing equipment are part of the modern mailroom. Electronic postal meters are often enhanced with special features, such as an accounting function whereby mailing costs are automatically calculated according to customer, department, or some other designated category. Sophisticated collating, folding, and inserting equipment operating at high speed can prepare multiple pages for large bulk mailings. Because of the high cost of mailing, efficient modern equipment is essential for companies that handle large mailing lists and prepare numerous bulk mailings.

For more about procedures in handling conventional and electronic mail, refer to Chapter 9.

Telecommunications Equipment

Telecommunications equipment shares the spotlight with computer equipment in the electronic office. Together, they provide virtually instant communication around the globe.

Key Systems   Most offices have a key (pushbutton) telephone system or an exchange system. Although the distinction between the two is disappearing, *key systems* traditionally consist of interconnected telephones with various buttons, or keys, each of which represents a telephone line. To answer a call, you must push the button that is lit. With a key system anyone can use any telephone in the system to answer calls. Digital key systems, which use the discrete digital representations of computer technology, usually offer more features than the older analog systems, which use continuously variable quantities. Both types offer basic features, such as hold, call transferring, automatic dialing, last-number redial, remote-station answering, message-waiting, private access, and conference calling. See Chapter 8.

Exchange Systems   An *exchange* consists of equipment that switches calls among various telephone extensions. Most exchanges are broadly referred to as *PBX* (private branch exchange) systems. *PABX* refers to a private automatic branch exchange, and *CBX* refers to a computerized branch exchange.

PBX users share a limited number of outside lines. Although key systems may exist within a PBX network, the principal difference between the two is that all of a PBX's switching takes place in a central mechanism triggered by dialing code numbers instead of pushing buttons. Digital PBXs can carry digital sounds from computers as well as voice sounds. A PBX can support many more telephones than a key system and may have additional features, such as least-cost routing, long-distance control via access codes, and automatic message record-keeping.

Other Telecommunications Equipment   Companies that make extensive use of telecommunications may add other equipment or systems, such as voice mail and automated-attendant systems (see Chapter 8). Some common devices are speakerphones for conducting conversations without lifting the receiver, systems combining telephones and television for viewing the participants while talking, various answering and recording devices for handling incoming calls, pocket beepers for alerting users to incoming messages, security devices for ensuring confidential conversations, and mobile telephones installed in vehicles for placing and receiving calls while driving. Large companies sometimes rent or purchase large, sophisticated teleconferencing equipment (see Chapter 12), with either voice systems for audioconferences or video systems for videoconferences. Chapter 8 describes the proper procedure for using the different types of telecommunications equipment.

PROFESSIONAL CAREER DEVELOPMENT

SECRETARIAL DUTIES AND RESPONSIBILITIES

The modern technology described in Chapter 1 has changed the traditional role of the secretary just as it has changed the way that offices operate. The clerical worker of yesterday has become the information manager of today. Although information processing has always been at the center of secretarial work, this function is now combined with the management of the associated technologies.

In addition to handling basic office functions, such as greeting a visitor and sorting the incoming mail, secretaries must now direct and monitor the flow of information through advanced electronic and telecommunications systems. Also, in addition to having office proficiency, secretaries must now be able to work independently and make more decisions within the scope of their individual responsibilities. Instead of merely "taking care of" their supervisors, today's secretaries are taking on aspects of their supervisors' jobs. Secretaries, therefore, make an important contribution to business, academia, human services, and government, and the secretarial profession is unique in that its scope is as diversified as the number of businesses and agencies that require office workers.

Some secretaries are specialists and concentrate largely on a particular function, such as word processing; others are generalists, who do a little of everything in an office. The particular duties of a secretary must always be defined by the organization and the office in which he or she works. Nevertheless, the following are common duties and responsibilities:

- Place, answer, and route telephone calls
- Open, sort, and route incoming conventional and electronic mail

- Answer and initiate conventional and electronic correspondence
- Draft and edit letters and memos for executives
- Transcribe dictated material
- Supervise assistants and other clerical personnel
- Interview and train assistants and other personnel
- Schedule appointments and handle follow-ups and reminders
- Schedule and arrange meetings of all sizes
- Attend meetings
- Take and prepare minutes of meetings
- Make travel arrangements and plan itineraries
- Operate word processing equipment
- Operate telecommunications equipment
- Operate accounting, mailing, and other equipment
- Purchase equipment and supplies
- Use word processing, spreadsheet, and other software programs
- Set up and maintain conventional and electronic filing systems
- Set up and use on-line databases
- Develop and manage special projects
- Keep various books and records
- Set up and print out financial statements
- Conduct research
- Assist in report preparation
- Make photocopies and arrange for outside printing

Job Title

The dictionary definition of *secretary* ranges from a person employed to handle correspondence and filing and do clerical work to a corporate officer to an officer who presides over a governmental department to a type of desk. Today the job title also refers to an information manager, an information packager, and an information broker.

Within the secretarial position there are also many levels of responsibility, ranging from following instructions to bearing at least some responsibility for administration and office management. It is important to recognize these differing levels of responsibility, as well as the diverse secretarial functions that can be channeled into more specialized careers, and to formalize them into an occupational standard.

Table 2.1, using arbitrary job titles, illustrates how a series of occupations could be created. For example, secretarial services could become administrative services and, at the most senior level of responsibility, systems management services.

Table 2.1 Career Paths: Secretary to Information Worker

LEVEL	OCCUPATIONAL TITLE	WORK FUNCTION
Presecretarial	Information technician/ machine operator	Electrical technician fixing, testing equipment, etc. Computer operator Word processor operator Data-entry clerk
Secretarial	Information processor: Administrative systems assistant	Database maintenance Software support Programmer/assistant programmer
	Paraprofessional	Computer graphics Text composition Information brokerage
Postsecretarial	Information processor: Office systems administrator	Database management Computer-assisted administration Programming
	Professional	Manager, reference and research Manager, information display
Middle management	Systems administrator	Systems maintenance and management Systems analysis and design
	Executive team	Computer-aided research, analysis, planning, and decision-making

Job Descriptions

Entry-Level Positions   Clerk-typists and receptionists are entry-level positions in most companies because they require only basic communication skills and keyboarding. Often no substantive responsibilities are included in such positions. However, entry-level jobs are considered the first step toward a secretarial career in business.

Some secretaries begin their careers in "secretarial pools." There they start by handling a variety of clerical duties for executives who have no personal secretary. The range of duties and the challenge of preparing material for different executives usually proves to be excellent training for advancement.

Secretary   Certain basic competencies are required for any position labeled *secretarial*. Computer literacy and typing speed and accuracy are a must, as well as a good command of English. The specific level of the position may be defined by the complexity of tasks the secretary must perform without supervision.

Depending on the type of business, a secretary may be asked to transcribe or compose letters for the executive, manage and access databases, operate fax and other machines, order office supplies, make travel arrangements, plan on- and off-site meetings, write a company newsletter, screen callers and visitors, sort the executive's mail according to priority, and perhaps plan some of the company's recreational activities. Refer to the list at the beginning of this chapter for other common secretarial duties.

Some secretarial positions are specialized, such as the positions of legal secretary and medical secretary. Although the required training for specialized positions is very specific, many other positions rely just as much on experience in the field as they do on specialization, such as the positions of personnel secretary and advertising secretary. Some of these jobs require extensive experience in a particular field, and the employers equate such experience with a certain number of years in a secretarial school or college. For example:

- A *personnel secretary* should have prior experience with personnel record-keeping systems and should be able to work under rules of strict confidentiality.

- A *marketing secretary* should be familiar with different aspects of advertising, production, copywriting, and publicity; good research skills are especially desirable, and the ability to speak with many people on the telephone is an essential attribute.

- A *sales secretary* should be familiar with active lead follow-up and sales record-keeping as well as with customer files and correspondence; the ability to perform basic business mathematical operations is also important. The sales secretary must interact with various members of the company's sales force in a positive, organized manner; planning sales meetings and covering for the executive(s) when absent are important tasks.

- A *publishing secretary* should have an excellent command of the English language as well as some proofreading and copyediting experience, for the paperwork load in such a position is often heavy.

- An *advertising secretary* should be able to work under intense pressure and meet close deadlines. Excellence in communication is essential, for such a secretary is often called upon to assist in the preparation of ad copy or press releases; in addition, the ability to project a highly professional image through person-to-person contact and by way of manners and attire is requisite.

As you can see from these few examples, each field of specialization focuses on and demands particular abilities that can be honed and fine-tuned as you gain more and more experience in the workplace.

Executive Secretary   The executive secretary position is a step up from a general secretarial position and usually involves a high degree of confidentiality and formality. Working for a high-level executive often involves scheduling meetings, taking minutes at board meetings and transcribing them, doing public relations work, composing letters and instructions on your own initiative, and performing many other tasks such as screening calls and visitors and reading and evaluating mail with little or no supervision.

Interpersonal skills come into play in an executive secretarial position since it is highly visible and very political. You must be mature, honest, sophisticated, and diplomatic at all times.

Administrative Assistant   Companies have different definitions of *administrative assistant*. In many cases it refers to an administrative support job performed with little or no supervision, one that is a step higher than the executive secretary. For example, an administrative assistant may handle dissemination of contract information or work with the chief financial officer of a company in preparing corporate reports.

This position usually involves supervision of others and may require a college degree. A secretary is often promoted to administrative assistant when an executive decides to delegate additional responsibilities requiring more intensive effort than a strictly executive secretarial position requires. Since companies differ in the definition of administrative support positions, you should clearly understand the job description and the opportunities for advancement in the particular organization offering such employment.

Specialized Positions   Specialized positions, particularly those in a technical field, require very specific skills and abilities. This becomes clear when you examine the differences between the requirements for a medical secretary and a legal secretary.

Medical Secretary. A medical secretary requires training in medical terminology, medical office ethics and practice, and medical typing and transcription procedures. The medical secretary is often required to manage an entire office, and the position also requires a good knowledge of accounting procedures, financial record-keeping, and computerized data processing. The medical secretary must be able to understand and process many kinds of complex health insurance forms and must have excellent human relations skills.

Legal Secretary. The job opportunities for a legal secretary include private law offices, courts, and corporate law departments. The training is also highly specialized and requires knowledge of legal and court procedures and familiarity with a myriad of forms and legal documents and the software programs that are used to process these forms and documents. Often the legal secretary serves as office manager as well. If a secretary wants to achieve a higher level of specialization in the legal field, he or she may decide to become a paralegal aide, a position requiring further education.

Career Paths

When businesses were small and run by rule of thumb, the secretary was usually a generalist — an office manager, an administrator, an executive assistant, and a correspondence assistant. Promotion into management wasn't guaranteed, but it happened often enough to establish secretarial work as a premanagement training ground.

Today, when businesses are infinitely more complex and almost of necessity run by technical experts on productivity and scientific management, the secretary is at a crossroads. One route might lead to repetitive work as a machine operator in data or word processing. Another route might lead to a meaningful career in office management, information management, or some other professional information segment of the work force. The gateway to this latter route involves at least two things. It requires both specialization and personal initiative on the part of the women and men who either have or want to have careers in the secretarial field. Potential areas of specialization include computer graphics, systems analysis, and database management.

Most information work is of three kinds, each being a stepping-stone to new computer-assisted information work:

- Information management and administration
- Information formatting and packaging
- Information brokerage and research

The first career path, leading into administration and management, would be appropriate for those with strong organizational skills and a natural interest in that area. The second path could lead to work in companies specializing in computer-based information goods and services; it would appeal to someone with artistic talent and a flair for creating good layouts. The third specialization would be attractive to secretaries who relish research assignments, for as the number of commercially available databases increases, so will the scope for information brokerage increase, thus opening up another career path.

Information Management and Management/Administration

Although secretarial work involves many activities, information management is perhaps the most important, for it is on the success of this activity that the health and success of an organization depend. Capable secretaries know how to organize information according to subjects and priorities and route people and their information (verbal or written) through an organization with efficiency, tact, and grace.

Database Management. As office automation advances, there may be less paper and fewer people in transit to manage. Instead there will be electronic bits of information to route through hardware and software components. As a result, a possible first step in developing a career path in this area is specializing in database management.

Computer languages and systems specifically designed for this application already exist. Besides having a general knowledge of how organizations work and how information flows through them — knowledge that most secretaries acquire intuitively on the job — it would be helpful to study library referencing and indexing systems. The difference between running an ordinary filing system and running a library is largely one of degree; however, the larger systems associated with libraries require more formal systematized procedures for categorizing and cross-referencing information. Database management systems (DBMSs) are similarly formal and systematic in approach. A career path here might begin by helping a technical expert set up an electronic filing system or a corporate database.

The next step might involve working with the database — sorting and updating its files. Although many of the commercial database management systems are flexible enough to make it unnecessary for you to change the computer program, it would still be useful to master a programming language. This mastery would give you the option of modifying existing database software, to fine-tune it to your office's needs, and would give you the option of moving into the more technical areas of program analysis, systems design, and systems analysis.

In offices dealing with specialized information, such as law and medical offices, database management takes on an added dimension because the stored information therein can be vital to later research carried on in-house or by outsiders. A law office specializing in malpractice suits, for example, might make database information available to doctors wanting to avoid malpractice suits or to patients wanting to launch such suits. The database manager and administrative assistant would have to anticipate such ancillary uses when organizing the database and coding its information for future retrieval. The same law office also might use its database as the prime source for a short video course in malpractice law for insurance company in-house training.

General Management. If you want to get into more generalized management, it would be helpful to take courses in business and office administration, accounting, and computers. A secretary with a good knowledge of how the electronic office works could be employed as an assistant to a computer programmer, advising how to design the office system that would best harmonize with that organization's particular style, workflow, and procedures. After having taken some computer courses, such as introduction to computer systems, the principles of programming, and programming in BASIC or FORTRAN, the programming assistant could then advance to a job as office-systems administrator, a position that could later lead into middle management.

Middle management has become more technical. Although its human-resource aspect is by no means disappearing, the technical aspect of it demands that managers be able to control the technological resources of the electronic office, putting them to use both cost effectively and flexibly (according to the changing needs of the professional and executive personnel). Moving into this work doesn't require that you become a computer scientist or electrical engineer. But you must be aware of developments in office automation, be comfortable working with computer systems and technical experts, and have good knowledge of business administration and the systems theory associated with computer technology. Although occupational titles vary, the new middle manager is similar to a systems administrator.

Information Formatting and Packaging   This career path picks up where ordinary word processing leaves off. It involves the use of creative talent in conjunction with computer graphics and the color and typographic features associated with computer printers. It can lead to paraprofessional and professional information work within the company, most likely in the public relations or personnel departments, or in a new company expanding the horizons of the information sector. In this sector, employment involves creating and marketing new information goods and services.

Word Processing and Desktop Publishing. The path to a career in information formatting and packaging might lie in word processing. In any case, you should acquire a working knowledge of word processing and desktop publishing systems and their software and then find imaginative opportunities in which to apply that knowledge and those related skills. For example, there is software for creating columns and charts, software for drawing pictures and graphs, and software for underlining, coloring, and shading areas.

There are opportunities for applying this software in public relations, where the goal is to communicate information and a particular corporate image at the same time. Personnel offers possibilities, too, since personnel manuals and instructional materials are prepared in electronic form for display on employees' computer terminals at home or in the office. Public relations and personnel offices are only two examples of numerous possibilities.

Since the technology allows packaging of this material in a much more accessible and pleasing way, it raises the expectation that some real effort be put into the work of packaging and display. To augment your basic word processing and information-display skills, you could take courses in graphic arts and computer graphics. It might also be helpful to study public relations and advertising if you're interested in the media, or education and organizational behavior if you're interested in preparing training materials or in handling other aspects of personnel work.

Video-Based Opportunities. In addition to traditional organizational structures and occupations, there are video-based information industries. Through "teleshopping," for example, catalog-type items are relayed directly to the consumer's home television or computer terminal. Editing requires good organizational abilities, an ability to relate material to an intended audience, and a sense of communicating. In a bank wanting to prepare packages of financial information and how-to advice for customers using telebanking (that is, bank customers doing their banking via home computers), for instance, the editor would help design the overall package and rough out the information to be contained on each display. Some companies also use this process for in-house training programs. Secretaries employed by such companies could move into this challenging information field without ever leaving their companies.

Information Brokerage and Research　A third career path might concentrate on information usage. It could lead all the way to the executive ranks. From simply getting information according to given specifications, the work leads to taking on more and more research initiative and, from there, to analysis and decision-making. This work should attract those secretaries who are interested in finding answers, solving problems, and getting results — all essential attributes for success as an executive.

Entry-Level Research. At the beginning level the work would be little different from that of tedious secretarial tasks, such as finding information in the files or at the bottom of someone's in-basket. But instead of such file searches, the work involves dialing up a database to relay the specifications on information needed by a professional, such as a chemical or electrical engineer designing a new product and needing the latest data on the properties of a particular chemical or material.

Advanced-Level Research. At a higher level an information broker would be responsible for formulating keyword searches — the specifications on the basis of which information is pulled from a database and then relayed to a client company. It takes learning and experience to become proficient at formulating keyword search commands. Watch for articles in specialized trade journals dealing with commercial database services.

At this higher level a middle manager in charge of information brokerage would be responsible for keeping up with developments in the field of commercial databases, knowing their access protocols (call numbers), being able to advise senior management on the most useful databases to subscribe to on a regular basis, and budgeting for the company's research needs. Although research and information brokerage can become a full and rewarding career in itself, the option of moving beyond research into analysis work also exists, either in production planning, financial analysis, or marketing.

EDUCATION AND TRAINING

Many secretarial jobs require a college background as well as technical skills. For that reason, continuing education is a must for the secretary aspiring to advance to a higher professional level. Some companies have made tuition assistance available for employees at the secretarial level to encourage career advancement.

Education

When the Canadian philosopher Marshall McLuhan coined the phrase "learning a living" in the 1960s, few people knew what he was talking about. Today people are still only beginning to realize how clearly he understood that ongoing technological change was going to make continuous adult education a necessary component of our working lives. Office workers everywhere — whether they call themselves secretaries, information managers, systems administrators, or whatever — must keep up with new technological developments in their area of specialization: database management, electronic and voice messaging, financial spreadsheets, and computer applications in their field.

The New Basics   A good basic education is the foundation on which you can learn more relatively easily. But the traditional three Rs must be revised. Instead of reading alone, all forms of information intake should be stressed: good listening skills, the ability to read graphs, and so on. Instead of writing alone, techniques of preparing computer graphics, slides, transparencies, and oral presentations should be taught. Instead of arithmetic alone, there is a need for teaching good reasoning skills, which range from the discipline of thinking in a systematic way and being able to break down complex problems or projects into a logical series of discrete steps to, on a more technical level, the methodologies associated with higher mathematics and computer programming.

With the technology changing so fast, schools and colleges must scramble to understand what kind of education is required to master it, and they have barely begun to design the necessary additions to their curricula. It is a time, therefore, when individuals must take the initiative and almost custom-design their own educational agenda.

Recommended Courses   Secretaries interested in an information management career are advised to take courses in business administration from a secretarial or business administration school, as well as courses in computer systems theory and perhaps some courses in programming. Those interested in information packaging should take a course in graphic arts from an art school and a course in computer graphics. Those interested in information brokerage should take a course in research and reference systems at a school of library science along with a course in database management systems. In general, the secretary's education and training should include language skills, data processing, word processing, organizational skills, office technology, and business management.

Language Skills   You have to be able to write effectively, clearly, and correctly for both a domestic and a foreign audience. Since most business communications are read by a number of people inside and outside the organization, the content of any outgoing correspondence or other document must be grammatically correct, concise, and easy to understand.

Many guides designed to help you enhance your writing ability are available. Along with a basic writing guide, you should also have an up-to-date dictionary, a business style manual (see Chapters 10 and 11), and a thesaurus. In many ways, business writing is like newspaper reporting. If you follow the "who, what, where, when, and why" formula used by reporters, you will be able to cover every essential angle of a communication. If you have trouble with writing, many books and courses are available, some of which are geared specifically to the needs of the administrative assistant or secretary.

Business Math, Accounting, and Data Processing   Knowing basic arithmetic and how to use an electronic calculator, as well as accounting and spreadsheet software, is a necessity in a business environment. Many executives depend on the ability of administrative personnel to compile financial reports and to handle some or all of the office book-keeping. In many cases a knowledge of simple accounting techniques can mean the difference in job status between a secretary and an administrative or executive assistant. Chapter 14 has been written to help you understand basic on-the-job accounting and data processing principles and procedures.

Word Processing Speed on the typewriter and computer is a prerequisite for many secretarial jobs, and a knowledge of word processing software and computer operations is essential. Word processing skills should include formatting and editing capabilities, as well as an understanding of the use and care of dictation equipment, electronic typewriters, dedicated word processors, and computers. See Chapter 4.

Organization and Planning Organization and planning skills are solid ingredients for success in any secretarial position. The ability to set priorities and juggle several different tasks at once is necessary to command an efficient work flow. As secretaries assume more responsibility, the need will increase for better organizational abilities. Secretaries become more valuable to their employers to the extent that they can plan and organize not only routine tasks but also occasional special projects. Initiative and independent judgment are key assets. See also the section "Time Management" in this chapter.

Office Technology A working familiarity with the modern office technology described in Chapter 1 is important to ensure success in the electronic office. Secretaries should understand the purpose and general operations of the various electronic and telecommunications systems, as well as know how to use the associated equipment, such as computers, fax machines, copiers, postal equipment, and data processing equipment. They should understand office procedures that depend on modern technology, such as how to access an on-line database. For further information on practices and procedures in using the various systems and technologies, refer to the other chapters in this book describing word processing, accounting, and other office functions.

Business Management To work effectively and confidently in a business environment, it is necessary to be familiar with the principles and terminology associated with the various disciplines that affect business management and operations. Independent reading, seminars, and college-level courses in subjects such as accounting, law, economics, and business management are useful in providing an appropriate background.

Most companies will provide information to employees about continuing-education workshops, seminars, academic courses, and other career-development programs. Also refer to Chapters 14 and 15 and the following section on professional programs.

Other Forms of Education and Training

Although it is essential to keep up with technological developments and continue to learn and grow in your work, this doesn't mean you must spend the rest of your life in night school. In an age when learning and earning are intertwined, a host of educational options are available for continuing your education on formal and informal levels.

Formal Education   On a formal level many colleges, business schools, and correspondence schools offer courses to people in their homes or places of work, with the traditional classroom teacher replaced or augmented by an audio- or videotape, a computer disk, or a CD-ROM.

Information Channels   You can also learn through a variety of information channels, such as networking, whereby secretaries exchange practical information on a computer network or by mail or telephone. You can subscribe to journals specializing in computer applications in your own area of work. In addition, you can join associations in your occupational or professional group. Aside from general associations such as Professional Secretaries International, there are various technical associations focusing on law, medicine, information processing, database management, systems administration, and other fields.

Associations usually have information on networking opportunities and publish newsletters and magazines full of information useful in advancing your career. They often sponsor educational programs or at least can counsel members on the best local educational opportunities available. They hold annual or monthly meetings focusing on continuing education and self-improvement. You can learn by volunteering to organize meetings, by preparing and giving a talk, and so on. Having recorded these credentials on your resume, you can impress potential future employers with your talent, maturity, and intellectual flexibility.

Ongoing Career Development   Once you have found a comfortable niche in a company, however, it may be difficult to stay interested in your professional development. People often settle for job situations that are less than satisfactory because comfort has become a habit. Involvement in associations and networks helps you keep your eyes open to continuing educational opportunities and the need for ongoing career development. With the impact of high technology on the business world today, networking, continuing education, and intellectual flexibility will be crucial in your long-term efforts to use technology and the new career opportunities generated by it to your own advantage.

Professional Certification

Your professional development should involve the regular learning of new skills and the sharpening of those already acquired. This is the only way to survive and advance in the high-technology business world of today.

One way to enhance your professional status is by achieving certification through some of the examinations administered for professional secretaries. Certification is a valid goal for the career-oriented secretary. Among the organizations offering certification are the Professional Secretaries International, which offers the *Certified Professional Secretary* (*CPS*) rating; the National Association of Legal Assistants, which offers the *Certified Legal Assistant* (*CLA*) rating; and the American Association of Medical Assistants, which offers the *Certified Medical Assistant* (*CMA*) rating. Check the latest edition of a directory of associations in your local library for current addresses, and write to request information of certification-application requirements and an outline of subjects covered in the qualifying exam.

INTERPERSONAL RELATIONS

Communication

The American Heritage Dictionary of the English Language, Third Edition, defines communication as "the exchange of thoughts, messages, or information, as by speech, signals, writing, or behavior." Communication skills are needed in any profession, but they are especially crucial to the secretary since a major function of the job is handling communications, both oral and written. In addition to written communication and the need to be clearly understood when executing a well-written document (see the section "Language Skills"), oral skills, body language, and appearance are also important components in the communication process.

Oral Skills

You may have good ideas to contribute to your business environment, but if you can't articulate them effectively, they will be lost. Speaking well requires a command of English, good diction, and self-confidence. If you are shy and have little experience speaking in front of a group, take a course in public speaking. Such a course can help you overcome your fear of addressing a group. Other students in the class will be there for the same reason you are and will understand your own difficulties. If you are to take on a career role as a supervisor or trainer, you will probably have to speak in front of one or more persons regularly. The more you speak publicly, the easier it will become.

Body Language

The signals we use to communicate are often called *body language*. Your posture and gestures convey a number of attitudes and emotions. If you are nervous or jittery, for example, you will appear uncertain or insecure about your abilities. Try to be aware of your appearance without becoming self-conscious. If you want to send a self-assured, confident signal, look directly into the eyes of the person who is talking with you. A smile or nod will assure the person with whom you are speaking that you agree with or understand what he or she is trying to convey. Analyze some of the gestures and nuances of your nonverbal communication style and try to determine what kind of message you are conveying. It is easy to develop bad habits in conversation and in the gestures we use to support our speech. If you become more aware of what you are doing, it will be easy to correct bad habits. Table 2.2 on page 45 gives some examples of negative and positive body language habits.

Appearance

The way you look — cleanliness, hair style, care of fingernails, cosmetics, jewelry, and dress — are as important as your posture and gestures in nonverbal communication. Although vast differences in dress codes exist from one office to another, career-motivated secretaries pay special attention to appearance. To dress for success, strictly follow any company code for employees or imitate the styles of the firm's executives. A neat, clean, professional business appearance is always a safe guideline to follow. You should, therefore, look like you are dressed for a business meeting, not a nightclub or a camping trip. Table 2.3 on page 46 answers some general questions concerning common business style.

Table 2.2 Body Language and the Messages It Conveys

NEGATIVE ACTION/MANNERISM/ GESTURE/POSTURE	NEGATIVE MESSAGE/ IMPRESSION THUS CONVEYED
Hands tightly folded across chest	Insecurity; defensiveness
Clasped/unclasped hands; fiddling with rings, necktie, lapels	Nervousness; stress
Biting of fingernails	Deviousness and deceit; nervousness and general insecurity
Sitting with crossed legs, skirt hitched up; fiddling with hair (women)	Flirtatiousness
Lack of eye contact with the person to whom you are speaking	Disinterest in the other person, the conversation, or instructions being conveyed to you; deviousness
Slouching, either while standing or while sitting	Boredom; laziness; lack of interest in job or conversation
Holding hand over mouth while talking, especially during a meeting	Fear
Typing, filing, etc., while wearing a transistorized radio headset	Tuned completely out of the job and its responsibilities

POSITIVE ACTION/MANNERISM/ GESTURE/POSTURE	POSITIVE MESSAGE/ IMPRESSION THUS CONVEYED
Hands held loosely at sides, in jacket pockets, or behind back	Ease; confidence; relaxation; openness with others
Steady eye contact with the person to whom you are speaking	Interest in the other person, the conversation, or instructions being conveyed to you; straightforwardness, candor, and honesty
Erect yet relaxed posture while standing, walking, or sitting	Energy; control; self-confidence

Table 2.3   Dressing for Success: Questions and Answers

QUESTION	ANSWER
Do many companies have dress codes?	No, but they do have unwritten rules or standards of attire. Observe the dress of the executives — both men and women — and of their secretaries to discern the overall style of the company. Some companies state in their employee handbooks that personnel are requested to come to work in dress "appropriate to the business environment."
What is a typical business environment in which corporate style is important?	A typical conservative, or traditional, business environment might be that of a publishing house, a large TV network, a city newspaper, a law or accounting firm, or a government office where the general public, outside clients, and perhaps authors or public figures are often received. In such an environment the importance of a positive image is keenly felt.
Who is most influential with respect to dress and general style and manner in a company?	The chief executive and operating officers set the overall style and tone of the business environment. This style is often reflected in the dress of the employees at all levels. But in some companies studied informality in itself is an indicator of the desired image.
What attire is generally acceptable in a professional business environment?	The style commonly recommended for women and men is a conservative tailored suit (or dress) with easily mixed and matched separates, conservative sweaters, shirts, and ties. Jewelry, shoes, and hairstyles ought to convey an image of businesslike self-confidence and professionalism. The employee — not the clothes — should stand out.

TIME MANAGEMENT

Time management is a crucial factor in successful career development. A secretary who is highly skilled in planning and scheduling tasks for optimum productivity and one who is adept at controlling distractions and interruptions has a head start on a successful career.

Planning and Scheduling

Planning each workday and scheduling daily tasks are routine procedures for most secretaries. It's virtually impossible to handle a heavy work load combining short-term and long-term projects, rush jobs and low-priority jobs, without some type of planning and scheduling. To plan and schedule effectively, however, you also need to know other factors, such as how much time certain tasks usually take and what times during the day you have the fewest interruptions.

Analyzing Your Workday   Time-management experts recommend that you analyze your work load over a two- or three-week period. To do this, you need to list all the categories of work associated with your job and each day record both the total time spent on each category and the time of day when the work was done. For this record you could use a columnar accounting pad or any other sheet with columns and ruled lines. Down the left column, list the time of day in fifteen-minute increments from the time you begin work until the time you leave. For example:

> 8:00–8:15 a.m.
> 8:15–8:30 a.m.
> Etc.

Across the top of the page, head each of the other columns with a job category pertinent to your position. For example:

> Typing
> Handling outgoing mail
> Answering the telephone
> Supervising assistants
> Etc.

Make photocopies of this master sheet, one for each day. Then, throughout each day check off every time slot that applies to a task:

	TASKS			
Time	Typing	Filing	Telephone	Etc.
8:00–8:15 a.m.	X		X	
8:15–8:30 a.m.	X			
8:30–8:45 a.m.		X		
8:45–9:00 a.m.		X	X	
Etc.				

At the end of your record-keeping period, analyze the results. Is there a pattern? Did you do each job at the best possible time? Were high-priority jobs or rush jobs taken care of first? Were long jobs requiring a lot of concentration handled during periods of few interruptions? Should some similar tasks scattered throughout the day be combined at one time for greater efficiency? Make any adjustments that the record suggests in your future planning and scheduling.

Using "To Do" Lists   After you have a better idea of how you should group activities and in which time slot you should schedule them, you will be ready to begin each day with an orderly, intelligent plan. Start each morning by preparing a daily "to do" list on which you write every known job that you will likely handle. Also, at the beginning of each week and each month, make up weekly and monthly "to do" lists for long-term projects. Incorporate pertinent tasks from these lists onto the daily lists that you compile each morning.

After you have a list prepared, assign to each task an appropriate time to do it. If your daily desk calendar has fifteen-minute time slots, you may want to copy the "to do" list onto the calendar. If you use a computerized calendar or reminder program, key in the "to do" list and print out your schedule for the day, week, or month.

Controlling Interruptions

Your boss's work habits and the nature of business in your organization will determine the kind and frequency of interruptions you experience. Your daily schedule should take into account the normal pattern of these interruptions. If the period 10 A.M. until noon usually consists of endless interruptions, don't schedule work that requires uninterrupted concentration during those hours. Some interruptions, however, can be avoided. Although secretaries are expected to respond to their bosses' needs and schedules, through better time management you may be able to at least reduce the number of other, nonessential time-wasting interruptions. If necessary, make a conscious effort to change your work habits. For example:

- Make use of electronic or paper schedules and calendars. Computer software often has alarms, or reminders, to alert you to approaching deadlines.

- Develop goals and set deadlines for important tasks. Make a habit of putting your goals in writing.

- Arrange all tasks in order of importance. Schedule low-priority work after all rush jobs and high-priority tasks are completed.

- Be receptive to new timesaving procedures, and develop your own ideas on ways to save time. Keep assistants and coworkers informed about any changes that affect them.

- Be prepared with tools, supplies, reference materials, and so on before you start a job. Having to stop in the middle of a job for something you forgot wastes time and increases the possibility of introducing errors in your work.

- Use all available timesaving technology even if you must learn a new system or procedure to do so. Whenever possible, let your equipment do the work for you, and watch for newer versions of software that will increase your productivity.

- Schedule difficult jobs during periods when you are feeling fresh and have a reservoir of energy. You will be less likely to make mistakes and have to redo a job.

- Learn to delegate appropriate tasks to assistants. If you need additional help, discuss the needs with your boss.

- Work at a steady pace, rather than rush, so that you will do the job right the first time. It will only take more time if you have to redo it.

- Group similar activities, such as running errands, for maximum efficiency. Check your schedule for the rest of the week to see if certain tasks should be grouped and rescheduled.

- Find ways to deal with procrastination, such as starting with something you enjoy doing. Sometimes it helps to start with a short, easy task.

- Don't make personal visits or engage in social conversations during business hours. If others tend to waste your working hours with personal discussions, suggest that they call you after work to chat about any personal subjects.

- Be very specific and clear in your instructions and communications with assistants and coworkers to avoid time-wasting errors and misunderstandings. If there is something you don't understand, ask for clarification so that you don't waste time doing a job the wrong way.

- Avoid time-wasting disputes and personal confrontations. Reserve your energy for your job and the tasks you must complete.

- Learn to use downtime, such as when a telephone call is on hold or while you are waiting for a repairperson, to think about and plan future work. If the delay will be long enough, find a short task on your schedule to complete while waiting.

- Develop your power of concentration so that you can shut out noise and other distractions. Try various strategies, such as quietly reading your work out loud to drown out noise (if this won't disturb coworkers).

- Keep up with daily work, such as filing. If it piles up, it may become unmanageable later.

PERFORMANCE MEASURES

Companies of all sizes have some means to measure an employee's performance. They may use a standard program, such as Management by Objectives (MBO), or design their own performance-rating system. The purpose of any such program is to evaluate employee performance in regard to productivity, goal achievement, and standard of excellence.

Evaluation, which may occur at different times during the year according to company policy, is often linked to salary reviews and to budgetary considerations.

If your company has a performance-rating system, you may want to conduct your own self-evaluation in advance of each periodic company review or according to some other schedule that is convenient to you and will provide the information you need. To do this, prepare a list of performance factors and a set of performance measures. Ideally, you would use the same performance factors and measures that your company uses. If this information is not available, however, develop lists of performance factors and measures applicable to your job. Take a columnar pad similar to those used by accountants and list the performance factors you have chosen in the left column. Head the next several columns with the measures used by your company or those that you have selected, ranging from "well above average" to "well below average," for example:

PERFORMANCE FACTORS	WELL ABOVE AVERAGE	ABOVE AVERAGE	AVERAGE	BELOW AVERAGE	WELL BELOW AVERAGE

Depending on your job requirements, performance factors might consist of qualities and skills such as the following:

Personal qualities
   and abilities:

Businesslike appearance
Concern with accuracy
Concern with quality
Decision-making ability
Initiative
Interest in detail
Interpersonal relations
Leadership ability
Listening ability
Organizational ability
Personality
Reading comprehension
Retention ability (memory)
Supervisory ability
Temperament
Trustworthiness

Job skills and abilities: Accounting/bookkeeping
knowledge
Administrative skill
Arithmetic/math knowledge
Clerical skill
Computer literacy
Familiarity with software
Filing — conventional
Filing — electronic
Formatting skill
Keyboarding
Operation of copier
Operation of fax
Operation of telecommuni-
cations equipment
Operation of other equipment
Second language knowledge
Special field knowledge (e.g.,
advertising)
Technical subject knowledge
(e.g., physics)
Transcription
Typing — accuracy
Typing — speed
Use of databases
Use of grammar
Use of punctuation
Writing skill — correspondence
Writing skill — other

To rate yourself, put an *X* or a check mark in the appropriate column of performance measures. For instance, is your "concern with accuracy" well above average, above average, average, below average, or
well below average? Be ruthlessly objective and honest. No one will see
your ratings; they are meant only to let you develop a self-portrait so
that you can easily see what weaknesses you have and know which of
your qualities and skills need improvement — *before* your employer
uncovers them.

THE JOB SEARCH

Occupational Outlook

Before beginning your job search, examine your own marketability and your position in the job market. The U.S. Department of Labor publishes annually the *Occupational Outlook Handbook*, which describes major industries, including information such as growth potential, and general business trends. Hundreds of occupations are covered in it, along with information on salaries and working conditions. Visit your local library and ask the reference librarian to show you current directories and other publications about the job market. Study the "Help Wanted" advertisements in major newspapers and in your own community's local newspaper. Secretarial positions are available in all types of organizations, both private and public.

Opportunities in Other Countries   If you would like to live and work in another country, pay special attention to governmental and private organizations that have international interests. The United States Department of State, for example, offers positions in countries around the world to secretaries who meet the criteria for foreign service. You must be willing to work anywhere in the world and must pass a security check. If you pass the investigation, you will be assigned to the Foreign Service Institute for orientation and further training before receiving a posting. For further information on opportunities in the U.S. Foreign Service, contact the U.S. Department of State in Washington, D.C.

The government is not the only overseas employer, though. Large multinational corporations often recruit personnel in the United States for foreign assignments. Foreign job opportunities are advertised in major newspapers such as the *New York Times, Los Angeles Times,* and *Washington Post.*

Self-Evaluation   Before you apply for any job, assess your overall proficiency so that you can match your skill level with the available jobs. A realistic, objective assessment of your own qualifications (including your strong and weak points) will help you to avoid disappointments and failed expectations during the job search. Use the same type of self-rating system described in the previous section for employees.

Professional Assistance   For those of you who are career oriented and upwardly mobile, it is important to establish the right connections with people who can help you further your career. You may have been lucky enough to establish a relationship with a professional person whom you consider to be a role model. A mentor has the kind of professional wisdom gained through experience that is invaluable to another person who wants to improve his or her job status. When you want to make a career move, for instance, this person can advise you about the viability of the prospective move, explain its positive aspects, and counsel you about its negative aspects.

Having made a connection with a person you respect and admire, you should nurture the relationship. Counseling and guidance from an experienced person based on trust and mutual admiration is one of the most valuable elements for success in business. Connections often make the difference between a mediocre career and success in reaching your professional goals.

Your First Job

If you have recently graduated from secretarial school or have a certificate for business training, you should have some idea of your performance level in the most basic areas, such as filing, transcription, word processing, and office machine technology. But if you have little or no job experience, it may be difficult to decide what kind of job will suit your abilities and personality. Ask yourself the following questions:

- Am I a people-oriented person? If so, would I enjoy a job where I will be dealing with the public on a regular basis, such as a job in a sales or customer service department?

- Would I rather work in a large, midsize, or small company?

- Is there a profession or business that I find particularly fascinating? If so, what is it?

- What are my salary requirements? (If you are a recent graduate of a secretarial school, your placement office may provide you with information on salary levels that you should pursue. Many employment agencies can provide current salary surveys and job classifications useful to you in assessing your own marketability.)

- Where do I want to work? In the city? In the suburbs? Overseas?

If you have no idea of the kind of job you are looking for or where to start, a temporary employment agency may be the answer. With basic secretarial training you can usually find work in a temporary agency.

Contract work, whereby you are hired for a specific period or a specific project, is another option. Both of these alternatives are excellent ways to try different types of jobs without making a commitment until you are ready to decide where you want to work permanently. With temporary employment and contract work you have the advantage of being able to observe the diverse jobs in different businesses.

In addition to familiarizing yourself with contemporary practices in the business world, temporary employment or contract work will provide you with some recent work history to be included on your resume. Also, temporary employment is a means of building up the self-confidence that may be lacking after a long absence from the work force. (See "Returning to the Work Force.")

Companies require temporary help or contract work when there is an overload of work to be done or when someone has left the company unexpectedly or is on vacation. If you are filling in for someone who has left the company and you make a favorable impression, you may be offered a permanent job.

Temporary agencies usually charge a fee to an employer who hires a temporary worker on a permanent basis. Since the fee is often less than the ones charged by most permanent placement agencies, more and more companies are hiring temporaries with permanent jobs in mind if the people do well. Use of temporary employment services gives the employer a chance to observe a candidate in action and to see if that person fits in well with the company.

Returning to the Work Force

Many people want to return to the work force after being out of work because of illness or some other reason or after their children have left home or are old enough to attend school. Often this is necessary when extra part-time or full-time income is needed. If you are returning to the work force after considerable time has passed, the first step is to renew your skills through independent reading and study. A good investment is a computer course or a course in basic word processing. Although you may have a better idea of the kind of job you want from previous work experience, you may want to try temporary work, described in the previous section.

The Job Change

If you are presently working at a job and feel it is time for a change, consider several things before looking elsewhere:

- What conditions do I expect to improve or change in another job?

- Have I been at my present job long enough to have exhausted all possibilities of increased responsibilities or promotion?

- Have I considered seeking employment in another part of my company?

- Does my company encourage career-pathing? If so, have I talked with my supervisor or with the personnel office to determine what my next step for advancement would be?

If you have done all of these things and still believe you need a change, set some goals for yourself to achieve the kind of change that will be beneficial to your career. When you already have a job, you have the financial security that affords you time to search out another position that meets all of your needs and standards.

The Resume

Your resume should be used as a marketing tool to sell yourself to a prospective employer. Before preparing the resume, however, take an inventory of your present abilities and all of the responsibilities you have had in your present job and any previous jobs. After completing the inventory, decide which tasks you like the most and which ones you like the least. By doing this you will have a basis for comparing what you want to do with what is available to you when looking for your new job. It will also help you to avoid getting into a pattern similar to the one causing you to want to leave your present job. When you have completed an accurate ability and task analysis, you will then be ready to prepare your work history.

Since you will have limited page space on which to present everything relevant about your work history, you must be concise and clear in your presentation and format. Many people are looking for jobs, and all of them have resumes. An employer may have to look through as many as one hundred resumes of applicants for the same job before selecting the people to be interviewed. Therefore, your resume must be eye-catching and brief so that a person scanning a page can immediately pick out your best assets and work experience.

The first step is to take the abilities and tasks you have listed and put them into categories similar to the ones in the following list:

Planning and organization
Project coordination and management
Writing and editing
Supervision
Training
Purchasing
Record-keeping
Word processing

If you have a definite career objective, state it on your resume. However, if you state your job objective, such as executive secretary, you may be limiting yourself to a specific job market. There may be another job available that can combine all your skills with a title that does not even resemble that of executive secretary. On the other hand, you may have determined in your research that you definitely want the particular type of job atmosphere associated with the title *executive secretary.*

Preparing the Resume   It is possible to put identical information into different resumes and thereby present totally different images with each one. The choice of format will depend on the way you want to focus attention on your proficiencies.

The appearance of your resume is almost as important as its content, for it is a reflection of your professionalism. As such, it should project a businesslike image.

- Use 8½ - by 11-inch white or off-white paper in a 20-pound bond weight.

- Use a high-quality copying process such as offset printing or laser printings. Use a photocopier only if it produces copies of exceptional quality.

- Don't include personal information other than your name, address, and telephone number. Employers do not need to know your marital status, height, weight, or sex and cannot legally require you to provide extensive personal information. Certain facts, such as gender and physical appearance, will be determined at your interview.

- Include a heading (name, address, and home or work telephone number), your job objective (optional), work experience, and educational background.

- Use the active voice throughout and be careful not to change verb tenses in the body of the resume.

- Try to keep the format open, uncluttered, and easy to read. Avoid overuse of underlining and all capitals.

- Spell out names of organizations and titles.

- Proofread your resume carefully. In fact, have someone else proofread it for you a final time before you have it printed. There is nothing more embarrassing than finding a mistake on your resume after you've given it to a prospective employer.

Resume Format   Resumes are prepared in different formats, depending on the information you want to emphasize and the type of job you are seeking. Unless you are having your resume prepared by a writing service specializing in resume preparation, you should take time to read an up-to-date book on this subject. Most bookstores and libraries have copies available. Resume guides describe suitable formats for different positions and backgrounds, as well as provide numerous models to follow.

Chronological Format. The chronological format (see model on pages 60–61) is one of the most common resume formats. A reverse chronological resume lists your job experience beginning with your current or most recent job. It is easy to follow and focuses on your career development. Only the inclusive years should be used to designate employment dates; there is no need to specify months.

Functional Format. If you want to emphasize your skills as opposed to the individual tasks for each position that you have held, you may want to use a functional format for your resume (see model on pages 62–63). This format details your skills under the specific function areas that you choose to highlight. A disadvantage of this format is that your interviewer may want to relate your duties to each previously held job. However, this format will give you an opportunity to cover each position in more detail at your interview. If you have had more than three or four jobs or if your experience looks scattered, this is an excellent format to use. Because the functional resume focuses on your marketable skills rather than on your job history, it also can be used advantageously if you are worried that a prospective employer will be concerned with too many moves.

Cover Letter for Resume   When you write to a prospective employer, you should always send a cover letter with your resume. The letter should be brief and formal while sparking the interest of the prospective employer (see model on page 64). Try to give a reason why you should be interviewed for the advertised position. Never prepare a cover form letter for photocopying and submission to numerous firms. Such letters indicate that the sender is lazy and not interested in taking the time to write personally to a prospective employer. Study the models of winning cover letters provided in resume books, and consider having the letter prepared by a professional resume-writing service if you have any doubts about doing it yourself.

Job Information Sources

Newspapers   This is probably the first place people look when they are trying to get information on available jobs. The classified section often breaks down job opportunities by general categories of professional help, such as medical, business, and sales. Most secretarial jobs are advertised in the business section of the classifieds, but specialized positions like that of medical secretary might appear under a medical section. Look through all of the jobs.

Keep a file of ads you have answered so that you do not answer the same ad or apply for the same position twice. Do not call the company unless a telephone call is requested. If the ad requests a resume, send one with a cover letter.

Try to avoid blind ads using newspaper box numbers instead of company names. Companies placing blind ads usually want to avoid sending out reply letters to the applicants. If the ad sounds appealing, however, apply; but don't hope for a quick answer. If you answer an ad placed by an employment agency, be sure to call first to see whether or not the job is still available. Agencies often run tantalizing ads just to draw clients into the agency, or they run ads for jobs that have already been filled.

Trade and Specialty Publication Advertisements   If you are looking for a job in a specialized industry, check the classifieds in professional trade journals. If you are looking for a job in advertising, for example, you may want to look through publications devoted to the subject of advertising. Your local library will have trade journals and specialty publications available for you to browse through.

Employment Agencies   If you are going to use an employment agency to find a job, look for one specializing in secretarial jobs. You

Chronological Resume Format

LINDA LEE WEBB
19 Monroe Drive
Cambridge, MA 02140
617-555-0000

Objective

To secure an administrative/executive position offering responsibility, growth, and public contact.

Experience

1993–Present   DATRONICS, INC.
                 Burlington, MA

                 <u>Executive Secretary to Vice President/Personnel</u>

                 Scheduled Executive Committee Meetings and recorded minutes for distribution to Committee members.

                 Acted as liaison between employees filing grievance procedures and Executive Committee.

                 Maintained company activity calendar of social functions.

                 Composed reply letters to applicants for executive positions.

                 Typed and scheduled newspaper ads for corporate job openings.

                 Disseminated confidential personnel information to regional branch offices.

1991–1993   DUNN AND TAYLOR ADVERTISING, INC.
                 Medford, MA

                 <u>Account Secretary</u>

                 Organized and maintained client files for three account executives.

                 Scheduled layout and design meetings with freelance designers.

Chronological Resume Format, continued

LINDA LEE WEBB   page 2

Corresponded with clients relative to scheduled advertising activity.

Arranged travel and planned itineraries for account executives.

Recorded meetings with clients for files.

Scheduled launch meetings with staff writers and prepared account agendas.

**Education
and Training**

1989–1991   Secretarial Training Program
                   Katharine Gibbs School
                   Boston, MA

1989   B.A., History
                   University of Massachusetts
                   Amherst, MA

Functional Resume Format

GEORGE F. WARD
119 Oakley Boulevard
Chicago, IL 60606
312-753-1324

Objective

Position as administrative secretary with opportunity to use strong
communications skills.

Professional
Experience

Administration   Standardized contract filing systems for sales
                          department.

                          Prepared schedules and agendas for national sales
                          meetings.

                          Developed active lead follow-up system for sales
                          staff.

                          Maintained department personnel records.

                          Developed standardized sales call report format.

                          Formatted sales inquiries on word processor.

                          Planned exhibits and trade shows.

Communication   Corresponded with customers regarding product
                          information and shipment schedules.

                          Handled customer complaints.

                          Communicated operational procedures to field
                          sale managers in five regional offices.

Public relations   Coordinated and wrote sales department newsletter
                          detailing sales achievements and new product
                          information.

Functional Resume Format, continued

GEORGE F. WARD   page 2

	Acted as company representative at trade shows and exhibits.
	Acted as department liaison with all levels of personnel.
Technical skills	Operational knowledge of computer, fax, voice mail, copier, and other modern office equipment and systems.
	Familiar with word processing, desktop publishing, database, and financial software.
Employment History	
1991–Present	Administrative assistant to national sales manager Parker-Hill Chemical Company Chicago, IL
1989–1991	Sales support secretary Bona Pharmaceuticals Company Chicago, IL
Educational Background	
1991	Certified Professional Secretary Institute for Certifying Secretaries Kansas City, MO
1989	Bachelor of Arts — English University of Chicago Chicago, IL

Cover Letter for Resume

100 School Street
Framingham, MA 01701
508-555-0505

February 13, 1995

Ms. Valerie Kaishian
Personnel Manager
Trademark Publications
50 Broad Street
Boston, MA 02110

Dear Ms. Kaishian:

I would like to apply for the position of editorial secretary advertised on February 12 in the Boston Globe. I believe this position would give me an opportunity to apply my years of experience in publishing and to use my strong educational background in English and communication.

I greatly enjoyed my work in the acquisitions departments of two other publishing companies. In addition to handling the manuscript-review process, I communicated with outside authors extensively in relation to meeting deadlines and manuscript production schedules.

It would be a challenge to work with the writers and editors at Trademark Publications, a company well known for its excellent products, and I would like to discuss my qualifications and your needs in person. I look forward to hearing from you about the possibility of a personal interview and can be reached during business hours at 555-8326, extension 451.

Thank you very much, Ms. Kaishian.

Sincerely,

Elizabeth Simms

Enc.: Resume

will be able to tell from the newspaper ads and from the listings in the Yellow Pages which agencies are best suited to your needs and qualifications. Agencies screen and test job candidates before sending them on interviews. Hence an agency interview should be treated like an interview with a prospective employer.

Companies requiring confidentiality and desiring prescreened candidates usually use employment agencies. If the hiring company has experienced success with employee placements from a particular agency, the employment counselor at that agency may be able to lead you to a good job. Avoid high-pressure agencies, those whose walls are adorned with high-performance plaques for best placement records. Such agencies are more interested in the fee paid by the hiring company than in helping you find a job that fits your abilities.

Most agencies give skill tests, such as typing, to applicants for secretarial jobs. If you are unfamiliar with the equipment on which you will be tested, ask to practice for a while before taking the test. If you do poorly on the test, ask to take it again. Most employment counselors are understanding in testing situations since people are usually nervous.

When the agency sends you on an interview, it will do all the communication and negotiating with your prospective employer before and after the interview. Do not call the company where you have been interviewed until you hear from your employment counselor. If a job has been advertised as "fee paid," the hiring company may pay for the placement services. However, since some agencies charge placement fees to new hires, you should ask what the fees are before signing an employment contract.

School Placement Services   If you are a recent college or business school graduate, you should register with the school's placement office. Companies often list job openings with school registrars. Be prepared to give the placement office full information on your background and job interests, the same as you would do with an employment agency.

The Interview

Interviewing is stressful, and everyone who has been on a job interview recognizes that uncomfortable feeling of being put on the spot. You must prepare yourself psychologically for the interview so that you can take control. Think of the interview as an opportunity to emphasize all of your positive professional qualities. At the same time, you must be aware of your weaknesses and know how to defend them or put them in a more positive perspective. In any case, being positive and enthusiastic is crucial to a successful interview.

Image The first thing you should do is consider your image. Dress conservatively and professionally in a suit or other outfit that you are comfortable with. Both men and women with long hair should be certain it is clean and neatly combed. Women should also avoid using heavy makeup or too much jewelry or trying a new hairstyle for the interview. All interviewees should follow the same rule used by employed persons: Look as though you are going to a business meeting rather than attending a nightclub or going on a camping trip.

Preinterview Research Give yourself plenty of time to get to the interview. If you are unsure of the directions, call and confirm them with a receptionist. Find out as much about the company as you can before you go to the interview. If you are dealing with an employment agency, you should be able to glean some of this information from the employment counselor. If you are leaving your present job for a negative reason, do not discuss it with the interviewer. Do not discuss former jobs in any context other than your work experience. Speak confidently, and try not to appear nervous or jittery when answering questions.

Salary If the salary range was not stated by the employment agency or in the company's advertisement, wait for the interviewer to introduce the topic. If you use an employment agency, it will handle the salary negotiations. If you are asked for your salary requirements, ask what the salary range for the position is (if you don't know) *before* you answer the question. Keep in mind that you should aim for an increase in salary when you make a job change. Ask questions about benefits packages, overtime, and the salary and performance review process. If you are going to be reviewed within six months for a salary increase, you may be willing to start at a lower rate than if you will not be reviewed for a year from your starting date with the company.

Interview Questions Prepare yourself in advance for some of the more difficult questions an interviewer might ask.

> *Interviewer:* Why are you leaving your present job?
> *Applicant:* I've been at my present job for three years, and although I have had two promotions, I feel that I need to make a move for my professional growth.

Many interviewers have stopped asking about candidate's weaknesses because applicants expect the question and have an appropriate answer memorized. But if you are asked a question about your weaknesses, try to focus on a weakness that can also be a positive quality in your profession.

Interviewer: We have discussed your strengths, Ms. Clark. What about your weaknesses?

Applicant: I think my biggest weakness is being a perfectionist. Sometimes I take my work too seriously and strive too hard for perfection. I take pride in my work, and if I feel it isn't perfect, it really bothers me.

Open questions are always difficult, and most of the questions a good interviewer asks require answers that reveal a lot about the job candidate.

Interviewer: Why do you think you want this job?

Applicant: I think this job would give me the opportunity to use the skills I have to the best of my abilities. I also think I could learn a great deal from working in a successful, established company.

Another open question with a twist is shown in the next hypothetical example. You should answer this question assertively and truthfully, yet without sounding conceited.

Interviewer: Why should we hire you?

Applicant: From what you have told me about the job specifications, you require a person with (*specify the kind of*) educational background, state-of-the-art skills, such as (*specify the skills*), and dependability (*or whatever else*). I know that I can offer those attributes.

Try to anticipate as many difficult questions as you can and prepare yourself for them. The key to a good interview is being able to respond to questions with intelligent, confident, honest answers — answers that sound like a personal response, not a memorized cliche.

Interview Follow-up   Always send a thank-you letter to your interviewer. It may be the touch that gets you the job over another equally qualified applicant who neglects this basic courtesy.

Refer to the interview follow-up model on page 68 for an example of a brief but thoughtful thank-you message.

Follow-up Thank You Letter

100 School Street
Framingham, MA 01701
508-555-0505

February 17, 1995

Mr. Lee C. Costa
Sponsoring Editor
Trademark Publications
50 Broad Street
Boston, MA 02110

Dear Mr. Costa:

Thank you for the opportunity to discuss the editorial secretary position at Trademark Publications. I'm very excited about the job you described during my interview yesterday. It sounds stimulating, and I know that the activities involved in the position would challenge me.

I want to reiterate my strong interest in this position, and I also want to thank you for taking time to show me around the company and explain in detail the nature of its publications. I look forward to further discussions with you.

Thank you very much, Mr. Costa.

Sincerely,

Elizabeth Simms

HUMAN RELATIONS

PERSONAL INTERACTION

Getting along with other people is an essential part of your job. You don't have to like someone personally to foster a good working relationship. If you present an even-tempered, positive image to all your coworkers, they will probably respond to you in the same way. Your ability to get along with many different personalities will play a major role in your ultimate career development. It's a challenge to deal with a difficult person successfully — one that you will encounter many times.

To survive in a business environment, you must be objective and aware of the ways in which you interact with other people. Everyone has prejudices or predetermined ideas about others affecting their communication ability, but it is important to avoid stereotyping people. To deal with people effectively, you must be perceptive and understanding. Stereotyping builds an immediate barrier against open communication — a barrier that will hold you back from effective, sensitive interactions with others. Learn to evaluate your interaction with other people as well as their interaction with you. If you have an innate understanding of why people project certain images, it will be easier for you to interact positively with employers, coworkers, customers, and clients.

Personal contact with visitors, servicepersons, and customers should always be pleasant and businesslike. People associate a business with the person from that organization with whom they have had direct contact. You are "the company" to anyone from the outside, and the corporate image projected by you should be above reproach at all times.

Image

Your image is the portrait you present to the people with whom you interact. Numerous factors are involved in developing this portrait, ranging from attitude to physical appearance to competency and intelligence. The more professional and knowledgeable you appear to be, the more favorably others will respond to you.

Disposition   Certain characteristics are so important that they influence most of the other factors affecting your image. Disposition is such a factor. For example, it is necessary to be even-tempered and good-natured to maintain a pleasant working atmosphere. A moody or irritable employee can adversely affect the morale of the entire office. Also, a good sense of humor can help you through stressful situations. Many times you will be asked to do a rush job that will involve overtime, or you will be requested to perform a task in an unreasonably short time. If you allow the situation to upset you emotionally or make you lose your temper, you could be displaying an immaturity that will haunt you when you want to make a career move later. People remember unpleasant situations.

Stability   You could be well dressed and highly skilled in specific tasks, but if your responses to problems are emotional and ineffective, your image will suffer and your good qualities will be overshadowed. A well-integrated personality stands out in a crowd. If you are able to keep calm when an upsetting situation develops, you will become known as a stable employee.

Problem solving is part of a secretary's job. A clear and logical approach to a problem would be to identify it, break it down into components, and then determine a workable solution. Much valuable time and energy can be wasted by overreacting to a situation instead of trying to devise a sensible way to change the situation for the better. The more responsibility you assume, the more problems you will encounter. If you learn to deal with problematic situations as they occur in a step-by-step fashion, your self-confidence in assuming more responsibility will be enhanced.

Flexibility   Your image will be directly and significantly affected by your flexibility. Business environments change rapidly as a result of growth, changes in the management, a fluctuating economy, and many other factors. To maintain a position in a business that is going through such changes, you must be able to adapt easily to new situations and be flexible enough to accept changes in personnel, your job duties, and office practices and procedures.

Effective Listening

How well you listen can profoundly affect your business relations with others. It has been said that we hear only 20 percent of what is being said and listen to only 10 percent of what we hear. To follow instructions and handle many of the tasks a secretary must perform, your listening ability must be markedly above the norm.

The first step is learning how to listen actively. Try to clear your mind of all other thoughts and concentrate only on what is actually being said. Take notes and avoid interrupting the speaker until his or her thought has been completed. Try not to analyze what you are listening to until you have heard the complete message. If you don't take the time to listen carefully, you may end up having to do projects over. Sometimes a speaker does not convey a thought as clearly as you may need to follow directions. But if you have taken notes, you should be able to ask the right questions to clarify the instructions. It is very irritating to a busy executive when a secretary continually returns with numerous questions, the answers to which were already given in previous instructions.

Office Etiquette

A certain protocol must be followed in a business office. Even though some practices, such as the use of first names, may vary from one office to another, basic courtesy should be an integral part of your work habits. For example, if you share an open space with others, care should be taken not to disturb your coworkers. If your company allows smoking and you smoke, use only the areas designated for smoking by your company.

Some rules of etiquette are obvious to anyone qualified to assume an office position. You should not, for example, cough or sneeze without covering your mouth or nose; nor should you use crude language or attend to grooming at your desk. But other rules of etiquette may not be as obvious; for example, the rule concerning whose name you mention first in making an introduction.

This chapter describes some of the important rules of etiquette that affect a secretary's interaction with personnel and visitors in the office.

Chapter 8 describes the rules that apply in voice mail and other tele-communications contacts.

Interaction with Coworkers and Visitors Secretaries regularly have contacts with assistants, coworkers, executives, and visitors. The trend today is toward informality in the office among all personnel, particularly in a small company. Nevertheless, secretaries should follow the established pattern in the offices and companies where they work and wait to be asked before addressing supervisors and executives by their first names. Even when an executive asks a secretary to use his or her first name in the office, the executive should be referred to with a title, such as *Mr.*, *Ms.*, or *Dr.*, in the presence of visitors or on the telephone.

Maintaining the proper degree of formality and respect with visitors does not mean adopting a stiff, cold tone. Not only is it possible to show respect and be friendly at the same time, but secretaries should aim to do no less. Whether you are talking on the telephone or greeting a visitor entering your office, the voice-with-a-smile approach is mandatory.

Visitors should never be ignored. If they have questions, be as helpful as possible, referring them to another office if appropriate. When they must wait to see an executive, offer them a chair and reading material. If they need to make a telephone call, direct them to a telephone where they will have some privacy (if possible).

Making Introductions Inevitably, you will have to announce and introduce some visitors. Your office may have a specific procedure that you must follow. An executive may have an open-door policy, for example, and may want you to tell all visitors to go right in without asking for their names or the purpose of their visit. More likely, you will be expected to find out the person's name and reason for wanting to see an executive.

Before sending someone into an executive's office, you may be expected to announce the person over the intercom or to step into the executive's office, present the visitor's business card, and receive instructions from the executive. Even with such a policy, however, there likely will be certain people, such as the president of the company, who should be told to go right in without the usual inquiries about the purpose of the visit. In some offices you might be expected to make appointments for visitors before the executive will see them.

When you are in a position necessitating that a visitor be introduced, the rule is simple. Usually, mention the name of the higher ranking person first. But if you are introducing a client, mention the client's name first regardless of rank.

Dr. Samuels, this is Ms. Baker from the Word Processing Department.

Mr. Brewster [*client*], this is Dr. Samuels.

Mrs. Nielson, this is Joel Inman. He has a question about the new chemical formula we released last week.

To introduce yourself to an unannounced visitor, mention both your name and your boss's name, and ask if you can be of help.

Good morning. I'm Carla Foster, Mr. McDermitt's secretary. May I help you?

Good afternoon, Ms. Whitman, I'm David Eastman, Mr. Winslow's secretary. I'm afraid he just stepped out, but is there anything I could help you with?

If you and the visitor know each other, the introduction is obviously unnecessary, but it is always polite to ask if you can be of help.

Good morning, Mrs. Anderson. What can we do for you today?

Gift Giving   Executives often give holiday and birthday gifts to their secretaries, but secretaries are not required to give gifts to their employers. However, a secretary may be expected to keep an address list and a record of all employees and customers or clients to whom an executive sends cards or gifts. Many secretaries maintain this list by computer so that it can be quickly and easily revised. A gift list should state the gift and amount spent each year. This information can serve as a guide for future years and will help ensure that an executive doesn't unintentionally give someone the same gift the following year.

For gifts to foreign countries consult a guidebook on that region. Protocol for gift giving varies in different countries, and it is very important to determine the practices in the particular country to avoid offending someone. A clock, for example, has a morbid connotation in China, and handkerchiefs suggest the breaking of a relationship in the Middle East. White flowers in Japan are associated with death, and red roses in Germany signal a romantic interest.

Office Politics

The term *office politics* often has a negative connotation, though it shouldn't. It's true that getting involved in office politics in terms of gossip and deceitful behavior is negative. But to get your job done, you will find it necessary to understand the overall political structure of your office and your place within that structure. Whether the office is large or small, there always is a political structure based on power and decision-making. People striving for advancement in business regularly develop and apply new strategies to enhance their positions within the corporate political structure.

The secretary lacking keen political savvy can easily be caught in the middle of some very difficult, tricky situations. To avoid this, you must be observant and aware of other people's positions within the organization. Determine who gets certain jobs done and who makes the really important decisions. Treat those people accordingly. Read the company's organizational chart and determine the structure of your own office and that of the corporation in general. This kind of knowledge will help you when dealing with other departments and disseminating information outside your own office. Few things are more embarrassing than making political blunders because of your ignorance about someone else's position.

Beneficial Office Politics   Secretaries who accept the fact that office politics exists can use it as a beneficial tool rather than a hindrance. Instead of waiting and simply responding to situations and conditions, for example, you could actively develop your own program.

- Regularly demonstrate a commitment to your employer in terms of interest, appreciation, and loyalty.

- Absorb as much information as you can — every day — about your job and the company.

- Develop as many contacts as possible in your own office, in other offices, and outside the company.

- Show a willingness to take on additional responsibilities.

- Treat both company personnel and outsiders with consideration and respect at all times.

- Cultivate a reputation for being cooperative and helpful.

- Offer praise when due, and never criticize assistants or coworkers in the presence of others.

- Ignore gossip, and do not participate in the spread of rumors.

- Document your progress and achievements, and periodically provide a brief status report to your boss; this will help counteract the efforts of others to claim credit for your work.

- Always use honest, legitimate, and ethical strategies to advance your position.

- Refute unfair or inaccurate claims against you immediately with clean and accurate facts, but do not lose your temper or get involved in an emotional argument.

- Never reveal confidential information or give others reason to doubt your trustworthiness.

- Don't hesitate to accept honest offers of assistance that will advance your career, but beware of offers that have undesirable conditions placed on you.

Assertiveness   Often a fine line exists between being assertive and aggressive. Aggressive behavior is usually counterproductive, but assertiveness can be beneficial. You can stand up for your own rights at work without being hostile, and you should be able to deal with those who may be rude or try to take advantage of you without becoming emotionally upset, intimidated, or overaggressive in response. Assertiveness training teaches you to express your opinions and feelings candidly and freely without putting others down. You can do this by using the pronoun *we* when problems exist: *We* have a problem; what should *we* do about it?

Avoid continual emphasis on *I* (not "*I* think; *I* want; *I* need") to the extent that you sound demanding and self-centered. Giving the impression that "we're all in this together" and "we all want what's best for the company" will help ensure that your assertiveness is not mistaken for hostility or aggressiveness.

Your local bookstore or library may have books on assertiveness training. In the highly competitive business environment of today, a sensitivity to the well-documented profiles of the assertive personality, the nonassertive personality, and the aggressive/hostile personality is essential to job survival and enjoyment.

Personnel Problems

The types of personnel problems that develop in a company are as varied as the people who work there. The problems that a secretary must deal with may be different from those that an executive must handle. It is usually not the secretary's responsibility to deal with absenteeism, for example, unless the secretary's assistant is regularly late or absent. Then the secretary must discuss this problem with the assistant, monitor the situation, and report it to the executive in charge if dismissal appears necessary. Other problems, though, may require a response and decision on the secretary's own initiative. For example, a disruptive situation in the office may require deliberate but levelheaded action by the secretary.

Sexual Harassment   One of the most serious problems that a secretary may face is sexual harassment. Although specific guidelines are available from the Equal Employment Opportunity Commission (EEOC), the manner in which individuals define sexual harassment is not always the same.

According to the EEOC, sexual harassment includes any unwelcome attention that focuses on an employee's sex rather than his or her status as an employee. It can include leering, offensive remarks, unwanted touching, and demands for sexual favors. Therefore, using sexual references or gestures to create a hostile or intimidating environment is illegal, and receiving sexual favors may not be made a condition of employment or advancement in a company. Companies may be held legally responsible for any acts of sexual harassment by their employees and are required to take steps to prevent this occurrence.

If you feel intimidated, pressured, or uncomfortable, you may take the following action:

- Firmly state to the person doing the harassing that the behavior disturbs you and you want it to stop immediately. Hesitation or delay could cause the harasser to believe you are willing to tolerate the behavior.

- Document the behavior. Write down all dates, times, circumstances, and types of improper and unwanted behavior.

- If the actions persist, write to the harasser explaining that the behavior is disturbing and again state that you want it to stop. Be certain to keep a copy of your letter where it cannot be found and destroyed by the harasser.

- If the letter does not end the problem, reveal it to a trusted coworker. Collect written comments or other evidence that you are a skilled and successful employee whose good work and proper behavior will dispel any suggestions by the harasser to the contrary.

- If it is necessary to take more drastic steps, discuss the matter with your boss or the person specified in your company's complaint guidelines.

- If all else fails, file a formal complaint with a local EEOC office or with your state's department of labor or local human rights commission.

- Finally, consult a reliable attorney if you have questions concerning a possible lawsuit against the harasser.

Substance Abuse   Alcoholism and other forms of substance abuse cost companies millions of dollars in lost productivity, inferior-quality work, and absenteeism. If someone has such a problem and it affects your work, you have no choice but to respond to it. Although it would be unwise to play doctor or psychologist, if you are asked for help you may want to recommend that the person seek professional assistance and provide names and addresses where such help can be found.

Do not, however, agree to cover for a person who is jeopardizing his or her job, your job, and the welfare of the company. If such a threat is real and serious, report the problem to your supervisor or to the person designated by your company to handle such matters.

Injuries and Illnesses   Accidents and illnesses are a part of life and must be handled in the workplace as well as at home. Most companies have standard procedures for handling emergencies and minor problems. Usually, the proper steps are outlined in the employee handbook.

In large companies a doctor or nurse may be on the premises and should be contacted immediately in case of emergency. If a coworker is ill or injured but can report to a nursing station without help, offer to take the person's telephone calls and notify the person's supervisor of his or her absence. If in-house medical help does not exist, telephone the paramedics or hospital emergency room if an employee is severely ill or injured. If the problem is minor, offer to call a taxi or find someone to drive the person to a doctor. In general, be as helpful as possible, and make the person's health and well-being the major consideration.

Troublemakers   Some people thrive on disruptive behavior, but secretaries know that a cooperative, harmonious atmosphere is essential for them to perform effectively. Although it is often best to ignore disruptive behavior, unresolved conflicts divert energy from the job and may escalate into violence. If unpleasant behavior doesn't dissipate from lack of attention (what most troublemakers want), it is necessary to deal with it.

Hostile employees create stress and tension in the office for everyone. But sometimes it is possible to defuse a situation by agreeing without really agreeing. For example:

Hostile employee: I'm sick of this stupid company and all the stupid people in it. All I ever do is work, work, work.

Secretary's response: Now and then we all need to get away from everything and everyone. I can appreciate your frustration if you haven't had a break for a while. Why don't you ask Mr. Brown for a little time off?

If someone is angry at you, keep a comfortable distance between you and the irate individual. Either stand and face the person or invite the person to sit down. Make eye contact, use your listening skills, and show concern by nodding or asking questions. If you have made an error, admit it and express your strong interest in rectifying matters. If you haven't made an error, express appreciation for the person's concern and calmly explain the real facts. If the situation escalates, state that you don't want to disturb others in the office and suggest talking in another place or at another time. You could also suggest that the two of you meet with your supervisor to resolve the matter.

Above all, don't allow yourself to be goaded into a shouting match or violent argument. If you believe you are in danger, immediately call for personnel or your security department, step into your boss's office, or ask another person nearby for assistance.

Ethics in the Office

Ethical behavior is the only acceptable behavior. Some companies have a written code of conduct that describes proper procedures for safeguarding confidential information and protecting the privacy of sensitive company decisions and actions. Companies have a right to expect their employees to conduct themselves ethically and properly and to demonstrate their loyalty to the company when their behavior is put to the test. However, companies do not have a right to ask employees to break the law or commit some questionable, dishonest act on their behalf. Employees can and should refuse to commit a crime or behave improperly, unethically, or immorally.

In the absence of written rules or guidelines, employees should, on their own initiative, conduct themselves properly. The following rules of ethical conduct, therefore, should become a part of your daily behavior at work:

- Do not discuss with outsiders your employer's private business affairs or any dealings with clients or customers.

- Do not participate in conversations or actions designed to injure the reputation of or compete unfairly against another person.

- Do not take credit for another employee's accomplishments.

- Do not allow another employee to be blamed for your errors or failures.

- Do not take company supplies for personal use.

- Do not use company equipment (fax, computer, copier, telephone, etc.) for personal purposes.

- Do not leave private company files, diskettes, or other confidential material in an unprotected or unsecured area.

- Do not leave drawers, files, storage areas, and other rooms or containers unlocked overnight or at other times when you are away.

- Do not allow visitors to wait in your boss's office while he or she is away.

- Do not leave sensitive material on your desk uncovered and in full view for everyone to read.

- Do not discard sensitive documents without shredding them (follow state and federal laws and company policy regarding the disposition of documents).

- Do not copy paper or electronic documents illegally (observe the copyright statement on the material).

WORKING WITH YOUR BOSS

Successful secretaries know not only how to work *for* someone but *with* someone. They understand the goals of their bosses or supervisors and the overall objectives of their companies. By exercising initiative, using common sense, and accepting responsibility, they are able to work effectively as team players. As a secretary your ability to accept responsibility and be accountable for your tasks will be judged on a daily basis. If you are conscientious and well organized, you should be able to perform those tasks efficiently. Your willingness to assume additional responsibility will also be looked upon as an asset when your boss or superior evaluates your performance.

One way of increasing your worth is to assist your boss actively in managing the flow of projects in the office. To effect true executive-secretarial teamwork, you should meet with the executive at least once a day, preferably early in the day, to set priorities for the day's activities, including appointments, anticipated telephone calls, dictation, correspondence keyboarding, and incoming and outgoing mail.

Try to avoid crises by knowing your executive's daily plans in advance; then you can at least attempt to expedite the influx and outflow of people and paper. Be certain that the executive's appointment book and calendar entries match yours. Take the initiative to call expected visitors if you know that the executive is running behind schedule. Try to remember what took place the day before (consult your calendar or appointment book) so that you can, if possible, anticipate tomorrow's events. If your boss travels a lot, know where he or she can be reached at all times, and find out what is required of you in your boss's absence.

Getting along with your boss is essential. To a great extent, he or she will have a marked effect on your future. Many qualified secretaries have lost chances for advancement because of personality conflicts or other situations that resulted in poor recommendations. Learning to control your temper and emotions in business is therefore essential to your professional development. If you take criticism personally and harbor resentment about it, you probably will not be able to handle your job well. Learn to evaluate a situation before you take any oral or written action. Often the criticism is warranted and is meant to help you improve your work rather than to hurt your feelings. But sometimes you may have to work with an extremely difficult boss. Even though you may make every effort to get along with that person, it just won't work. In such a case, you should ask your personnel office for a transfer or look for another job.

Trust is another factor in a successful relationship with your boss. Many executives are under a great deal of pressure and will use you as a sounding board for confidential matters, particularly if you display good judgment. Absolute loyalty to your boss is essential and can mean the difference between working *with* instead of *for* someone. If you are able to look upon your working relationship as a team effort, you will be considered capable of assuming as much responsibility as your boss is willing to delegate.

Working for One Boss

Most secretaries work for just one boss or supervisor, but the job similarity may end there. A secretary's duties and relationship with an executive will depend on the type of activities handled by the executive and the type of person the executive is — an easygoing individual, a workaholic, someone who likes to delegate responsibility, someone who dislikes delegating work, and so on. Regardless of any difference in personalities and duties from one office to another, a few general guidelines apply in most cases.

- Use open and regular communication with your boss to contribute to a more successful and enjoyable relationship.

- Do everything possible to encourage a spirit of teamwork and cooperation.

- Respect your boss and show appreciation for the demands and pressures of the executive's position.

- Support the executive's policies and practices in and out of the office, whether or not you have other preferences or opinions.

- Learn how to accept criticism and use it as a learning experience to improve your skills and abilities.

- Use tact and diplomacy in pointing out serious errors made by the executive (correct minor errors yourself without mentioning them).

- Do not let annoying personal traits in your boss weaken the relationship; you may have annoying habits as well.

- Regularly demonstrate a willingness to learn and perform new and difficult tasks that will help your boss and increase your value to the executive.

Working for More Than One Boss

A secretary who works for more than one boss has to be especially adaptable. The personalities and types of work may vary, and a secretary will then need to make abrupt shifts during the day to adjust to each person's needs and work load. The same guidelines just listed for a secretary who works for only one boss apply here, too, with a few additional tips.

- Do not let any personal preferences for one executive or for one type of work over another show; rather, treat everyone as part of the team pursuing the same overall objectives for the benefit of the company.

- Do not criticize or find fault with a more demanding executive; adjust your own work habits to fit each situation and each person.

- If problems in scheduling occur, discuss them with *each* executive so that they can work out a priority schedule that is agreeable to everyone; keep all of them informed about your workload so that they do not develop unreasonable expectations.

- Study time-management guidelines (see Chapter 2) and implement those suggestions that will help you handle an unpredictable and, at times, complex schedule of work.

Working with a Satellite Office

A secretary whose boss travels or is stationed in a remote location, such as another business office or a home office, has to handle many functions in a different way. The executive is no longer immediately available to solve unexpected problems, meet visitors, sign letters, and do all of the other things an on-site executive normally does. Nevertheless, many of the guidelines described in the previous two sections not only apply but become more critical, and a few new requirements come into play when an executive works by telecommuting.

- Be prepared to work independently, without supervision, most of the time.

- Be prepared to assume greater responsibility since you will have to take over some duties usually handled by an on-site executive.

- Develop clear guidelines with your boss concerning the limits of your authority.

- Develop clear guidelines with your boss concerning the proper procedures for handling specific tasks, such as who signs a letter dictated over the telephone (make a list of such duties and ask your boss to comment on each one).

- Make full use of E-mail, fax machines, voice messaging, and other communication devices and processes to overcome the distance between you and the satellite office.

- Ask your boss whom you should contact in his or her absence in case an emergency arises that you can't handle.

WORKING WITH ASSISTANTS

At some time almost every secretary will have to work with an assistant. Whether the person is hired part-time or full-time, the task of training and supervising the assistant usually falls to the secretary.

Delegating Guidelines

The only way an assistant can help you cope with a work overload is if you delegate the extra work. Although you may be able to solicit help from other secretaries or persuade your boss that he or she must handle certain tasks when you are seriously behind schedule, the best solution is often a temporary assistant or a regular part-time or full-time assistant.

To delegate effectively, you need to know something about your assistant so that you don't have to redo work that really wasn't appropriate for the assistant. For example:

- What education level and skills does the assistant have?
- Is the assistant known to be accurate and capable?
- How much time must you spend in training the assistant?

Be certain that the assistant can do the work you want to delegate, and make your expectations fit the person and the situation. Give very clear, precise instructions; write them down if necessary, and ask questions to be certain the assistant understands. Especially, be willing to give up some of your duties, even if you would rather do the work yourself, and give the assistant a chance.

Training and Supervising an Assistant

Most assistants will need some training and ongoing supervision. Presumably, they will know how to use basic office machines and will have learned the fundamentals of filing and processing routine information. But they need to learn the specific practices and procedures used in your office, and they need to be briefed on the activities of your company. Certain traits and strategies will help both you and the assistant develop an effective working relationship.

- Welcome the newcomer and show the assistant around the office and the company. Invite the assistant to join you and other coworkers for lunch.

- Conduct an orientation session that covers the use of your office equipment and any standard practices and procedures used in your office. Give the assistant a copy of the employee handbook and assure him or her that it is not necessary to absorb everything at once, that your will answer questions and provide more detailed assistance later.

- Be patient and adjust your training to the learning rate of the assistant.

- Use your sense of humor to alleviate tension and help the newcomer relax.

- Set up a routine, such as a morning conference to introduce new work and review the previous day's work.

- Explain all new tasks slowly and carefully, including very basic information that you may take for granted.

- Regularly test the assistant's level of understanding by asking him or her to demonstrate some task.

- Regularly encourage questions and give the assistant time to ask them.

- If your initial instructions appear to fail, try a different approach. Do not show boredom or impatience.

- Discourage any tendency of the assistant to use office time discussing personal matters.

- Make all criticism positive ("only two errors this time; soon you'll be doing error-free work"). Build up rather than tear down the person's confidence and self-esteem.

- Compliment the assistant whenever praise is due and offer any other comments or suggestions that will motivate the person to work harder and better.

- Monitor the assistant's progress and discuss all problems and solutions with the assistant as soon as possible.

- If you believe the assistant is the wrong person for the job, discuss the problem with your boss and, if necessary, direct the assistant to a more suitable position and find a replacement.

A properly trained assistant can be very helpful to a busy secretary and the executive. Although the training task may seem time-consuming in the beginning, it should save time in the end if the assistant successfully adjusts to the work and becomes a useful member of the office team.

WORD PROCESSING

The processing of documents containing both text and graphics is one of the most important secretarial functions in the electronic office. Many people use the term *word processing* narrowly to refer only to the use of a computer and word processing software to create, format, edit, print, and store documents. But in its broadest sense, the term refers to the processing of documents regardless of the particular equipment used.

In some offices, for example, electronic typewriters are also used to prepare typewritten material. Dictation and transcription equipment may be needed, and in companies that produce sophisticated in-house documents, such as magazines, desktop publishing equipment may be used. The duplication of company documents may be handled in-house by a computer printer, copier, or small offset press.

The generation of documents is an important and highly visible means of communication and presentation for companies, executives, and secretaries. Without the refined skills of secretaries in receiving information, transcribing the spoken word to the written word, and producing effective, accurate documents, business would come to a debilitating and expensive halt. Word processing, in fact, is the application used most often by secretaries and other office personnel.

WORD PROCESSING SKILLS

The following basic steps in word processing point to the skills that are needed to create any type of document:

Format
Input
Edit
Save
Proofread (screen)
Print
Proofread (paper)
Correct
Save
Print
Store

Not everyone follows all these steps in precisely this order. Secretaries who transcribe machine dictation will include "transcription" in the input step. Highly skilled secretaries may find so few errors that all will be corrected during the on-screen machine proofreading (such as spell-check and grammar-check), eliminating the need for the final correction step (but not the final proofreading of hard copy). But the series of steps generally suggests the basic skills that a secretary should have.

Even though a word processing program has numerous features, secretaries must still be fast and accurate typists. In addition to having good keyboarding skills, they must know how to format correctly and attractively. Especially, they must have excellent language skills, with high competency in spelling, punctuation, grammar, word choice, and general composition, such as sentence and paragraph development (see Chapters 10 and 11).

One of the most important but sometimes neglected skills is proofreading. No person or machine automatically does perfect work. A spell-check program, for example, would accept the word *lose* as correct even if you really meant *loose*. But careful proofreading of printouts can compensate for such machine or keyboarding deficiencies and enable you to produce error-free documents.

COMPUTER PREPARATION OF DOCUMENTS

Document preparation by computer is the easiest and fastest procedure for processing text and graphics. (Different computer systems are described in Chapter 1.) With a computer, secretaries can print out as many originals as desired, make revisions without having to retype entire documents, combine two documents with only a few keystrokes, merge a letter with a list of varying address headings and thus create dozens of individual letters for distribution, and automatically and quickly search through hundreds of documents to locate the one needed. The list of capabilities is increasing every day as newer and faster technology becomes available.

Basic Computer Capabilities

When a computer is used for word processing, the secretary relies on the equipment capabilities to handle the required input, processing, output, storage, and communication. Refer to Chapter 1 for a description of the equipment used in these steps.

Input   In the electronic office the input function corresponds to traditional activities such as taking notes or dictation, typing, and listening — activities whereby information is recorded or taken in. In office-information systems the most common input devices are the computer keyboard and the mouse, although other input devices, such as the light pen, scanner, and voice, are also used. Once the information has passed through an input device to become digitized (made electronic in form), it can be automatically processed, moved, stored, and output as printed text, graphs, or drawings.

Processing   A processing unit, the brains of a computer, manipulates the information that is input according to instructions given to it through software. It may, for example, automatically combine numbers or shift paragraphs in a letter, store material in files locally or in remote office locations, hyphenate and justify text, and check for spelling errors before printing.

Output   The output in word processing is the usable and legible form in which the information is produced. It corresponds to all the end products of office work: final texts of speeches, reports, letters, and so on. The most common output devices in automated offices are the printer and the computer screen, although other output devices are used in certain offices, for example, plotters, which generate information such as graphs and drawings. Offices producing a lot of printed information might also have photocomposition units to transform text automatically from a word processing memory unit into printed copy.

Storage   A storage unit files information in the computer's memory or outside it on disks or computer tapes. Whereas in traditional offices the storage takes place in filing cabinets, libraries, ring binders, desk drawers, and so forth, in the automated office this array is replaced by electronic storage at different levels of accessibility and related cost. If the information is stored within the computer terminal, it is said to be stored *on-line*, one of the most accessible forms of storage. It can also be stored on removable floppy disks. Micrographic devices (see Chapter 1) that transfer information from computer memory onto microfilm for storage are usually found more often in libraries and offices with large volumes of fixed information, such as personnel files and general ledgers.

Communications The information generated through word processing must be communicated in some way. Traditionally, communications has been the action binding offices together, making the information flow from decision to outcome and back again. In the electronic office communication devices link computers and word processors to intelligent copiers, to other computer terminals around the company, and through them to databases or electronic files, as well as to the corporation's software.

The media used in communication can take many forms, from the familiar telephone to the two-way coaxial cable to fiber optics. Information can also be moved via satellite around the world and through switching mechanisms, such as the private branch exchange (PBX). Exchanges route voice and data messages through the maze of transmission lines and operating systems to a variety of destinations — executive and secretarial workstations, computers, printing presses, and so on.

Word Processing Software

To create a document by computer using word processing software, you need to understand how to select options and give commands. The specific steps differ from one program to another, so you should follow the instructions that accompany your own word processing program. Generally, you will be using menus, command languages, or icons.

Menus A *menu* in a word processing program is a list of the options that are available. A menu enables you to give the system commands and open and close the doors to avenues of travel within the various levels of the software. A menu might appear on the screen as a vertical list of items with a small check-off box next to each one, or it might appear as a bar across the top, bottom, or side of the screen with options printed on the bar.

With the list type of menu you select the desired item by moving the cursor or a little character called an *acceptance block* from one check-off box to the next. With the bar type you highlight the item on the command bar or indicate the desired item by placing the cursor on it. After indicating the desired menu selection, you can pick that item by pressing the *execute, select,* or *return* key, depending on your system.

Command Languages   A system using command language does not have to rely on a menu to receive instructions. Command language enables you to give the system direct instructions in the form of a system code. Each code invokes a specific action by the system. An example is *$Email;r.jones**.

- The *$* signals the system that a command is being given.

- The *Email;* signals that the user wants to access the system's electronic mail application.

- The *r.jones* signals that the system is to open the mail file of Robert Jones.

- The *** indicates that a wild card search of the file is wanted and that all items in the file should be displayed on the screen.

Command code language enables you to combine several steps at once, saving time and increasing your operating speed. However, it is not considered user friendly in a word processing environment. This type of user interface can be very complicated and requires the operator either to memorize dozens of commands and formulas or to refer to tables and charts listing the desired function and their associated commands. Modern programs are moving away from complicated procedures toward easy-to-learn and easy-to-use processing.

Icons   An icon-based interface uses pictures or images to represent system functions. Icon-based systems usually feature touch-sensitive screens or mouse selection of options. A system with an electronic mail application, for example, might have a small picture of a mailbox on the screen. By touching the on-screen mailbox or by positioning the cursor with a mouse and selecting it, you would be able to "look into the mailbox" and read the messages sent to that address. Manufacturers offer touch screens, icon-based menus, mice, and innovative menu designs that are being combined to produce fast and easy-to-use systems requiring minimal operational training.

Creating Documents

When you prepare a document by computer, you use the capabilities of the word processing software to manipulate the data on the screen. In addition to providing important features such as on-screen *Help* (see illustration) and special features such as *Merge* (for example, to combine an address list with a standard letter), most programs offer these basic word processing functions to help you create and edit your documents:

- *Vertical and horizontal scrolling: Vertical scrolling* is the ability of the workstation screen to move up the text automatically as additional text is entered. The text might scroll up one line at a time, or it might move up only when the screen becomes full. *Horizontal scrolling* allows you to have lines of text wider than the width of the screen itself. The workstation screen slides the text to the left as additional text is added to the line.

- *Wordwrap:* Wordwrap enables you to enter text without concern about placing a return at the end of each line. As text is being entered, the wordwrap feature determines whether or not a word can fit at the end of a line and will move it to the start of the next line if space is a problem.

- *Create:* The create capability refers to the actual creation of a new document or the opening of a new file. This function automatically

Help Screen

```
┌─────────────────────────────────────────────────────────────┐
│▣══════════════════════ HELP SCREEN ═══════════════════════   │
│                                                               │
│                      How to Use HELP                          │
│                                                               │
│             Press Enter or Click for Instructions             │
│                                                               │
│  On-line HELP provides information and step-by-step instructions for the │
│  program you are using.                                       │
│                                                               │
│  Choose any of these topics to learn more about using HELP.   │
│                                                               │
│         ☐ Using the HELP index                                │
│         ☐ Using commands, dialog boxes, and messages          │
│         ☐ Using HELP with your document                       │
│         ☐ Printing a HELP topic                               │
│         ☐ Moving around in HELP                               │
│                                                               │
└─────────────────────────────────────────────────────────────┘
```

places an entry in the system's document index file and lets you assign information to it, such as name, author, operator, date, and special instructions.

- *Insert:* The insert function lets you pick a particular place in the text and enter new words there. The system automatically adjusts the rest of the text to accommodate the new entry without requiring that the page be retyped.

- *Delete:* Delete works on the same principle as insert. Through the delete function you can select text to be removed from the document. Afterward, the remaining text is automatically adjusted to reflect the change.

- *Copy:* The copy function lets you select any text in a document and have that text copied to another part of the same document or to another document without having to retype the text.

- *Move:* Move lets you select text in a document and have this text moved automatically to another part of the same document or to another document without having to first delete and then retype the text. This capability combines the delete and copy functions described earlier in one step.

- *Indent:* The indent function lets you indent an entire block of text. It can be used to alter an existing document or during text input to create an indented block.

- *Center:* By using the center function, you can type text that will be placed on the center of the line. Like the indent capability, the center function also can be used to edit existing text.

- *Search:* The search capability lets you automatically search for words, punctuation, spaces, or some other aspect of your document. After locating what you specified, you can make the desired changes.

- *Replace:* The replace function lets you select text or something else for deletion in an existing document and gives you a chance to replace it with something new. This feature combines the delete and insert functions described earlier. A global replace function combines the regular replace capability with that of the search feature. Global replace will search through a document, find what you specify, and replace it with what you have specified at every occurrence.

- *Decimal alignment:* The decimal alignment capability lines up numbers on their decimal points to allow for creation of numeric columns. Each number in the column will have its decimal point positioned below the one above it.

For more about creating specific business documents and correspondence, refer to Chapters 5 and 6.

Formatting Documents

The more powerful your word processing program is, the more formatting options you will have. If you prepare a lot of tables or text with multiple columns, lists, and other special material, you will want a program that enables quick and easy setup of each item. Programs with such capability have provisions for creating style sheets where you can retain standard formats for future use. In addition, certain basic formatting options are available in all programs.

- *Document format:* Document format refers to the number of characters to the line, the number and position of tabs, the document's line spacing, and so on.

- *Format lines and rulers:* The information about the document's format is contained in the format line or ruler of the document. It specifies the positioning of tabs, line length, and line spacing. This information may be modified at any point so that changes in the format are possible within the same document.

- *Reformatting:* To reformat a document, you simply change the format line or ruler of an existing document to a new configuration of tab spaces, line length, and line spacing. The system then automatically modifies the text associated with it to the new desired format.

- *Justification:* Text justification is the system's ability to modify the arrangement of the characters on each line to make both left- and right-hand margins even. This capability makes some documents, such as a book or newsletter, look more professional.

- *Line spacing:* The system's line-spacing capabilities let you use a wide range of spacing possibilities: single, double, triple, and so on. You would specify the desired spacing in the format line or ruler.

- *Margins:* Document margins are usually specified in the format line or ruler. You can select any width line up to the width of paper used for printing out the document. Top and bottom margins can also be varied at your own discretion, and the space between columns on multiple-column pages can be adjusted as you prefer.

- *Font:* The font option lets you select any style of type that your printer provides. You can also specify the size of type you want, according to your printer's capability.

- *Type style:* You can specify text to be printed in an italic style, in a bold style, in small capitals, with underscoring, or as superscripts (raised characters) or subscripts (lowered characters). This may be done as the text is input.

Page Management   An important part of formatting is the management of pages. Versatility is important if you prepare a variety of documents. Many powerful word processing programs approach the capabilities of desktop publishing programs, described later in this chapter, in the ability to create multiple columns, headlines, footnotes, and so on. Even when routine material, such as a report, is prepared, certain basic features are needed to ensure that pages are set up properly and attractively. The particular keys you strike may differ from one program to another, but the results are similar.

- *Page creation:* Page creation is usually made possible through the use of a command code. You may be able to define the end of a page by positioning the cursor at the point where the page break is desired and by striking the appropriate keys. The system then creates the page break, marking the end of the page with a special indicator that appears only on the screen. See also "Pagination" below.

- *Page numbering:* To number the pages of a document, you must indicate the desired numbering sequence, the points at which this sequence is to begin and end, and the location of the numbers on the pages. This information may be required at the time of print-out, which would take the form of a print menu, or as part of a footer command (described below).

- *Pagination:* Pagination, the act of placing page breaks in an unpaginated document, can be manual or automatic. In the manual mode you scroll through the document, viewing screen after screen, and insert page breaks in appropriate locations. In the automatic mode you specify the length of a page and the system places page breaks according to designated page length. Automatic page numbering can be carried out on screen or at printout.

- *Repagination:* Often it is necessary to make major edits in the text that include page deletions and additions. Such changes throw off the original numbering sequence, resulting in a need to repaginate the whole document. Repagination can be either manual or automatic, with the automatic mode being viewed on screen or at printout. Numbering during repagination overrides the original numbering scheme, thereby creating a new sequence.

- *Headers and footers:* A *header*, or a *running head*, is a text entry to be repeated in the top margin of all pages in a document. This text entry could be anything from a single character or number to a more detailed document description with date and reading instructions. A *footer*, such as a page number, is similar to the page header except that it is positioned at the bottom of the page instead of the top. In most word processing programs the creation and attachment of footers are handled in the same way as the setup of page headers.

- *Columns:* You can set up pages in one or more columns and specify the width of each column and the space between columns.

Special Features In addition to providing basic editing and formatting capabilities, large word processing programs commonly have special features, such as sorting and index generating. The number of special features and the procedure in employing them vary from one program to another, and new capabilities are regularly being introduced. The following are examples of special features that are available in many programs.

- *List or record processing:* Many word processor programs provide a list or record-processing application. List processing provides a data processing type of capability and an easy way to set up lists or records of information such as names, dates, places, telephone numbers, and part numbers. The program also helps you maintain these lists, sort through and extract specific pieces of information from them, and generate reports based on them. List processing uses a database of records or lists, and specific types of data on a record constitute a *field*. For example, a record containing information used for billing purposes would have a field for the amount of payment requested and a separate field for the name of the person billed. The rest of the information on the record would also be broken up into data fields. A group of records all dealing with the same type of data kept together on the system is referred to as a *file*.

- *Sort:* A sort capability provides an easy way in which to order documents, records, or lists of information into a variety of hierarchical schemes. Sort capabilities can be applied to multiple fields at one time and can be ordered in an alphanumeric sequence if lists or columns contain letters and numerals in combination. Sorts can be alphabetical or numeric and can operate strictly on uppercase characters, strictly on lowercase characters, or on both uppercase and lowercase characters. All sorts can be organized in ascending or descending order.

- *Glossary or boilerplate: Glossary* and *boilerplate* are terms used to describe a document process in which you can create standard documents by providing only key pieces of information while the system is creating the document. For example, a contracts department may have a glossary designed to generate a document to be distributed to various manufacturers as a request for proposal. A glossary can generate all of the standard portions of the request and can stop and prompt you to fill in any portions wherein non-standard wording is required.

- *Math:* Some programs offer calculator capability ranging from simple math to complex equation handling. When you activate the calculator capability, the figures and numeric calculations appear in the form of an on-screen display. This electronic scratch pad — a temporary screen — is kept separate from any other document you may have been working on at the time that the calculator was activated. Once the calculations have been completed, the screen can be erased, and regular word processing can resume.

- *Security:* Many word processing systems have no security features, others have simple password capabilities, and still others have complex features that track a user and keep a record of that user's activities. For most purposes a simple password system is sufficient. This type of system enables you either to password-protect individual documents or to assign passwords to individual users for access into the system. The security systems for highly sensitive work are very complex and costly and require maintenance by special administrators. This type of security might be found in the banking, insurance, medical, and defense fields.

- *Spell-check and grammar-check:* Spelling verification applications enable you to have a document automatically checked for misspelled words (but not misused words, such as *to* in place of *too*). The simplest way to spell-check is to run the completed document through a batch process that marks the errors by highlighting the affected words. You can then make corrections to the text or to the error list, depending on the type of program being used. Some programs also will provide a list of suggested corrections for each error. Programs that have a grammar-checking feature operate in a similar way, searching for and alerting you to possible grammatical mistakes that do not fit the program's specified grammatical boundaries.

- *Dictionary:* The electronic dictionary is designed to function like a print dictionary. The electronic version lets you indicate the word requiring a definition by typing it in a fill-in field or by highlighting an existing word in the text. The program will then automatically search the dictionary database for the entry and will display the definition on screen. The database might be a traditional dictionary database, a specialized industry or trade-specific dictionary containing medical or legal terms, or a user-created dictionary composed of definitions relating to specific departments, jobs, or individuals.

- *Thesaurus:* The electronic thesaurus is very similar to the electronic dictionary in that it functions like a print version. Its approach is also similar. You specify the word to be checked by highlighting it or typing the word in a special field. The thesaurus application then finds the word in its database and displays the desired data on screen. A thesaurus provides not a definition but synonyms. There is usually a direct tie into the word processing editor enabling you to replace the indicated word in the text with one of the synonyms chosen from the thesaurus display.

- *Letter generation:* An electronic letter application enables you to select the type of letter you want from a menu of several different types. It asks you to supply the name and address of the recipient, the salutation, and the general tone desired. You then will receive a completed business letter ready for final review. The more advanced letter applications can produce many business letters, all treating the same subject but with no two being exactly alike. This capability is derived from the use of a thesaurus database in conjunction with the letter generation application. A letter generator adds a personal quality to what would otherwise be standard form letters.

- *Autohyphenation:* Programs that have hyphenation capability may simply flag the words requiring hyphens at the ends of lines or automatically flag the word requiring attention and then determine the correct position for the hyphen. This type of hyphenator uses either a lexical database, in which the hyphenation location for each word contained therein is shown, or a set of rules that determine the proper hyphenation locations.

- *Indexing:* Automatic index generation operates by taking a completed word processing document and running it through the generator process in a batch mode. The application provides an index of subjects cross-referenced to the page numbers of the document on which they were found. It looks at each word and, based on a set of rules, places words of certain categories into the index. The words are usually nouns, words beginning with capital letters and not starting sentences, words in parentheses, biographical names, geographic designations, and so forth. The completed index either can be generated into a separate document for you to edit or can be automatically attached to the end of the processed document.

Computer Care and Maintenance

Electronic computer equipment is sensitive and must be properly maintained to avoid damage or malfunction. Read your instruction manual for tips on cleaning and safeguarding the equipment. In general, keep the equipment free of dust, liquids, and other contaminants, and avoid extremes of heat and cold. Use a surge protector to prevent damage from power disruptions. Keep magnets away from equipment and diskettes, and store the diskettes in a clean, dry place. Do not use cloths or cleaning solutions that might damage the display screen or other parts of the system, and keep foods and beverages away from the computer. Follow the equipment instructions for protecting the data on your hard disk if you must move the machine. Avoid exchanging diskettes, which may be contaminated with a virus, and use an up-to-date antiviral program for further protection.

TYPEWRITER PREPARATION OF DOCUMENTS

Electronic typewriters exist alongside computers in many offices. Often they are used primarily to type special material, such as index cards and envelopes, but they are also suitable for preparing letters, memos, and brief reports. (See Chapters 5 and 6.) Although it is possible to buy electronic typewriters with a large storage capacity, separate display screen, and some ability to communicate over the telephone lines, computers are more common for sophisticated applications. Refer to Chapter 1 for a description of typewriter and computer equipment.

Electronic Typewriter Capabilities

Electronic typewriter capabilities vary according to the manufacturer and the particular model. Even small portables, however, house a computer that not only guides the print mechanism but also stores the document you type. The most elaborate models, known as *personal word processors* or *add-on word processors*, have features and capabilities that rival a personal computer. New technology being developed uses voice activation for text input rather than traditional keyboarding.

Standard Features Since models vary widely, it is important to study the instruction manual that accompanies your machine. The following features, however, are common on many machines, particularly the high-end models, and are used to format and edit documents:

- *Pitch selection:* Basic options include 10, 12, and 15 pitch (characters per inch) and proportional spacing (variable characters per line).

- *Margins and tab settings:* Electronic typewriters can store several optional margin and tab settings, in addition to the machine's default (preset) settings.

- *Carrier return:* A wordwrap feature, similar to that of a computer, means that the print carriage automatically returns when it is time to move to the next line. The return key is needed to start a new paragraph.

- *Centering:* A word or phrase will be centered on the line automatically if you depress the appropriate center key and type the characters to be centered. The light-emitting diode (LED) usually indicates that you are in the centering mode.

- *Underlining:* A word or phrase will be automatically underlined if you depress the appropriate key. The LED will indicate that the underscore has been turned on.

- *Bold print:* Most electronic typewriters can automatically provide darker characters either by using a bold key or a combination bold and underline key.

- *Expanded print:* Many electronic typewriters have the logic to add additional space between characters automatically as you type. This capability (a form of letter spacing) helps make titles and headings more pronounced.

- *Reverse print:* Some electronic typewriters offer the ability to print white characters within a solid black background. The machine creates the black background and then lifts off only the character outline, resulting in reversed printing.

- *Justification:* Most electronic typewriters offer automatic justification, a mode in which the machine automatically counts the total number of characters and spaces in a full line and then adds additional space in small increments to stretch out the line to fit exactly within the margin. Justified print will give an even right margin (unjustified print is referred to as having a ragged right margin).

- *Indention:* One or more lines may be automatically indented on the left or right, or both, by using the appropriate indent key.

- *Editing:* Electronic typewriters enable you to manipulate text; for example, they can copy and move it or delete it. You can also mark a certain portion of text and print only that selection.

- *Formatting:* A number of formatting features are available, such as multiple-column setup, pagination (dividing text into pages), page numbering, and decimal alignment of numbers.

- *Widow and orphan adjustment:* With this feature you can prevent the short last line of a paragraph from appearing at the top of the next page (widow) or the first line of a paragraph appearing alone at the bottom of a page (orphan).

- *Assembly and merge:* Previously prepared stored documents can be assembled and merged to create an entirely new document.

- *Search and replace:* With global search and replace you can instruct the machine to locate certain text and replace it with certain other text at every occurrence. With basic search and replace you have the option of substituting different text at each individual occurrence.

- *Relocation:* The relocation feature means that the machine will automatically return to the typing position after you have gone back in the text to correct an error.

- *Phrase and format memory:* Most typewriters have at least limited memory for recalling stock phrases and entering them into the text. Similarly, some models can store and recall format settings other than the default settings.

Special Features   Some special features, similar to those of a computer, are offered as options for the more sophisticated models of electronic typewriters.

- *Spell-check and grammar-check:* The spell- and grammar-check features are similar to those used in a computer's word processing program. The spell-checker searches for and points out misspelled words, and the grammar-checker identifies improper grammatical text, such as wordiness or misused phrases.

- *Thesaurus:* Like a computer thesaurus, the electronic typewriter's thesaurus suggests synonyms for words.

- *Expanded memory:* Electronic typewriters use both internal and external memory. Internal memory can be used to store standard text and format settings. External memory, often provided on a diskette, can be used to store completed documents. Additional memory can be purchased to increase the storage capacity of higher-end models.

- *Forms mode:* A forms mode will enable you to set up a form once and use the same template or form setup to type multiple revisions of that form.

- *Merge:* A merge feature will let you merge individual information, such as different addresses or different payment amounts, with a standard text.

Typewriter Care and Maintenance

Like computers, electronic typewriters are sensitive to extreme heat or cold, inadequate air flow, physical jarring, power surges, dust and other contamination, and diskette misuse. Read your instruction manual for further tips on the proper care of your equipment. Also, purchase ribbons that are authorized for your machine, and store the ribbons and correction tapes in a cool, dry place.

DESKTOP PUBLISHING

Desktop publishing (DTP) is a computerized application that allows you to prepare complex documents by computer using a broad range of typefaces and incorporating graphics, borders, and other special features. Brochures, newsletters, magazines, annual reports, letterheads, and other material can be produced in-house by computer using either DTP software or word processing programs that have some DTP and graphics capability. A major advantage of DTP is that you can view each finished page on your computer screen exactly as it will appear when printed out.

Although the quality of the output may be inferior to that of other methods of composition, such as phototypesetting, which uses a high-resolution photographic technology, the similarity to other word processing activities makes DTP a logical extension in many companies. Keyboard operators can apply the same skills to both DTP and basic word processing. The DTP operator, however, often must possess a better understanding of graphics, scanning processes, and publishing terminology. Refer to Chapter 1 for a description of computers, scanners, and DTP equipment.

DTP Terminology

In addition to understanding general computer and word processing terms, such as *format* and *input*, secretaries who are involved in DTP activities should be familiar with the following terms:

- *Font:* A particular size and style of type. A font includes all the capital, lowercase, and small capital letters, punctuation marks, and math or other symbols associated with the particular type family.

- *Graphics:* Any type of pictorial image, such as a chart or graph; also, a software program that lets you create, insert, or merge pictures, tables, maps, charts, graphs, and so on into other documents.

- *Justified type:* Type that is set with an even right margin; that is, the last words of each line of type are aligned. The type in this book is justified.

- *Leading:* The space between lines of type, usually measured in points (described below). Publishers commonly add one or two additional points space between lines (10/12 means that the type is 10 points and the leading is 12 points). This book has a leading of 13 points.

- *Lowercase:* A reference to small letters; often written in abbreviated form as *lc* by typesetters.

- *Page proof:* A copy of each full page of material prepared by DTP, presented to the secretary, author, or other appropriate person for proofreading.

- *Pica:* A unit of measure used to indicate the length of a line (6 picas = 1 inch, and 12 points = 1 pica); this line of type is 25 picas wide. In reference to type size, 10 spaces of pica type equal 1 inch, whereas 12 spaces of elite type equal 1 inch.

- *Point:* A unit of measure used to indicate the size of type (72 points = 1 inch). This book is set in 12-point type.

- *Ragged right:* A reference to an uneven right margin; that is, the last words of each line of type are not aligned, and each line may be a different length from the others. Business letters and memos are usually typed ragged right.

- *Roman type:* A style of type with upright characters and serifs (described below) and vertical lines thicker than horizontal lines, unlike *italic*, which has oblique letters. This book is set in a roman typeface.

- *Sans serif:* A style of type in which there are no serifs (described below) that finish off the main strokes of a letter; also called *gothic*. This sentence is set in sans serif type.

- *Serif:* A fine line that finishes off the main strokes of a letter. This book, for example, has a typeface with serifs.

- *Typeface:* The style of printed characters, identified by the name that is given to it. This book, for example, is set in Garamond type.

- *Uppercase:* A reference to all capital letters; often written in abbreviated form as *uc* by typesetters.

- *WYSIWYG:* An acronym for "what you see is what you get," pronounced *wiz-ee-wig*, in reference to being able to view pages on screen in DTP in the way that they will be printed out.

The Advantages and Disadvantages of DTP

Advantages   Organizations use DTP for various reasons. Without this capability, certain complex material would have to be sent to an outside compositor, usually at higher cost than using in-house DTP. If an organization already has large-capacity computers and word processing software, it may be cost-effective to purchase DTP software, train one or more of the word processing operators for DTP, and produce most, if not all, complex material in-house.

Disadvantages   DTP may be less desirable, however, if company personnel do not have the time or skills to handle DTP and if an organization is already overburdened with other work. Also, if exceptional quality material is required, other forms of composition, such as photocomposition, may be preferred. In addition, the cost savings using in-house DTP may be less significant if an organization must also purchase scanning equipment and graphics programs to supplement the DTP equipment and software. Each organization must conduct its own analysis and weigh the pros and cons in terms of its own situation.

Using DTP

When manuscripts presented to the DTP department are first prepared by computer using a word processing program, the diskette on which the material is filed must be prepared according to the instructions of the department. The precise instructions will vary depending on the type of DTP software that is used.

Usually the DTP operator will need a diskette(s) containing an unformatted document. Headlines, for example, should be in a regular typeface, without bold, italic, or other styling (this will be up to the designer). Everything should be positioned flush left (no paragraph indentions), with no extra space between lines or around heads and only one character space between sentences, after colons, and so on. Depending on the DTP program, you may also be expected to tag or code each special element (see illustration on page 106), such as lists, subheads, and footnotes, in a specific way, for example: *@CHAPTER TITLE = Word Processing.*

Even when the diskette you submit to the DTP department contains an unformatted document, your manuscript printout should be formatted and double-spaced. This is necessary for ease in editing and will make it clearer and easier for the proofreader to use after the copy is set in the DTP department.

Creating Documents

The specific steps to follow in creating a document with DTP will vary. A brochure with photographs or drawings will require additional design and graphics considerations compared to an announcement of a company picnic that consists of text only. Depending on the publication you

Tagged Document

TAGGED DOCUMENT

@CN:Chapter 4
@CT:Word Processing
@H1:Word Processing Skills
@NORMAL:The basic steps in word processing point to the skills that are
needed to create any type of document.
@UNL:Format
@UNL:Input
@UNL:Edit
@UNL:Print
@H2:Basic Computer Capabilities
@H3:Input
@NORMAL:In the electronic office, the input function corresponds to
traditional activities such as taking notes or dictation, typing, and listening —
activities whereby information is recorded or taken in.

---

are producing, you may be concerned with some or all of these steps:

- Using a standard word processing program to write and edit your manuscript

- Using a computer graphics program to create your illustrations or a scanner to input already prepared illustrations

- Developing a format using the master-page feature of your DTP program (selecting column width, boxes, headers, and so on)

- Bringing the text from your word processing diskette, graphics from your graphics program or from scanned input, and so on into the DTP program, where on-screen DTP prompts will help you position the material within the format you developed

- Viewing each completed page on-screen and making final adjustments as desired

- Printing out a master copy with your laser printer or, for higher quality output, sending your disk to a service bureau with compatible high-resolution equipment

Refer to Chapter 6 for more about the preparation of different kinds of business documents.

DICTATION AND TRANSCRIPTION

Dictation and transcription functions are handled differently according to the type of system (described in Chapter 1) that is used and the remote or on-site location of the person who is dictating. In an integrated office the computers, facsimiles, copiers, and dictation equipment are all tied to the firm's telecommunications system (see Chapter 8). Hence dictation might be provided from a remote location using voice mail, a computer network, specialized dictation units linked by a telecommunications channel, or all three.

The Workstation

When a dictation system is installed in executive offices and workstations throughout the company, the location of the units and the media should be chosen with concern for employee traffic and the work environment. A desktop transcription unit, for example, should be located in a place that is close enough to your typewriter or word processor so that both the manual buttons and foot pedal are operable from your chair. The unit should be far enough away from the edge of the desk so that it will not be accidentally knocked off the desk. If your work area is noisy or if there are frequent passers-by, you will want to have headphones readily accessible. Food or beverages should not be placed on or near the equipment.

The dictation media should be stored in a clean, low-traffic place. Normally, magnetic dictation media are almost indestructible and indefinitely reusable, but should the media become dust-covered or should you find fingerprints on them, wipe them with a clean, dry cloth. Fingerprints may cause malfunctioning in the record or playback functions of some media.

Dictation

Guidelines   Whether you yourself dictate material for an assistant to transcribe or whether you must transcribe the dictation of your boss or someone else, it is important to understand the process and the rules that apply.

- Dictate early in the day if you want a faster turnaround time for the transcription.

- Organize your material in the order of importance and collect any files or data that you may need.

- Review the correspondence or documentation being answered to be sure that your dictation will cover all aspects, and outline in your mind or on paper a logical sequence for presenting the material.

- If you are dictating for an unknown operator in a word processing center, identify yourself, your department or location number, and your telephone extension.

- Describe your material (letter, memo, report, and so on), and give the approximate length. If you use a machine with a counter, state the beginning and ending numbers.

- State how many copies of the final document you want to receive and indicate the type of stationery to be used, enclosures, and other such instructions.

- State personal preferences, such as how your name and title should be typed, the complimentary close you prefer, and whether the addressee should be addressed in the salutation by his or her first name or last name.

- Indicate any need for confidentiality when applicable, and give instructions for erasing the material from tape or for destroying or storing the written version of the dictation.

- Give complete addresses or state where they can be found, and spell out unfamiliar words or unusual spellings.

- Speak at a slow, intelligible rate, and state carefully and clearly any dates, names, and figures; dictate numbers one at a time (1995: one nine nine five).

- If you want to have certain forms of punctuation inserted, indicate them as they occur.

- Indicate the beginning of each new paragraph and the end of each document.

Dictation Simulation   The following is a step-by-step simulation of dictation. Although the instructions begin with directions for using a machine for recording, the instructions to a transcriber and the actual dictation are conducted in the same manner. The steps will depend on the requirements of your particular machine (check your instruction manual), but the following are common with many units.

- Make sure that the tone, speed, and volume controls are at the appropriate settings.

- Insert the cassette and close the holder. When you have done this, the tape will automatically rewind if necessary.

- Place a fresh index strip (see illustration), if used, into its compartment.

- Hold the separate or built-in microphone the required distance from your mouth.

- Depress the dictate switch, if any, and the light will come on. If required, slide the start/stop switch downward when you begin dictating.

- To give instructions to the transcriber, use the designated switch, and the index strip or electronic cuing system will be marked.

Index Strip

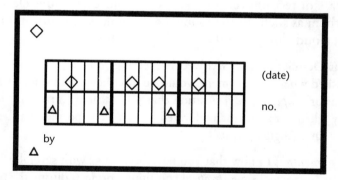

The index strip illustrated here has fifteen calibrations, each representing one minute of recorded dictation. The diamond symbol is used to indicate the end of a letter, and the triangle symbolizes the location of an instruction or correction. This index strip indicates that the first item is twenty-five lines long; the second, forty-five; the third, twenty; and the fourth, thirty. There are instructions for items one, two, and four.

- Write on each cassette or case the date and any other identification required in your office.

- Do not erase or record over the tapes until the dictation has been transcribed or until you are authorized to destroy the voice copy.

Your instructions to the transcriber should be as complete as is necessary, for example:

> This is Amanda Billings, Director of the Elementary Education Division. I will dictate a letter to Robert Desmond in our West Coast office. His address is in the personnel files. I would like a copy to go to Carl Edwards on the third floor and two copies to my office. Use single spacing with two lines between paragraphs and begin each new paragraph flush left, with no indentations.

In the above example the transcriber already knows the type of stationery to use, the dictator's preferences for the closing, and other such details. If the dictation was going to an unknown operator, the dictator would have to go into greater detail about these requirements.

The actual dictation should be as clear as possible. Don't hesitate to mention details, such as unfamiliar words that must be capitalized, even though this information may seem obvious to you. Stating punctuation is always helpful even to an assistant who is accustomed to your style of writing. If your machine does not permit or if it is difficult for you to erase or record over mistakes, state your corrections clearly and identify them as such. In the following example, the words in brackets are stated aloud along with the actual text of the letter.

> At our October 16 [*one six*] weekly meeting [*comma*] the question was asked when management would be interviewing candidates for the editor's [*apostrophe s*] position that was vacated [*correction*] left empty when Tom Westman relocated [*period*] The position has been vacant since August [*period*]
>
> [*new paragraph*] I know that you have been busy with several other projects [*correction*] time [*hyphen*] consuming projects during the past few months [*comma*] but I believe we should address the situation now [*period*] Therefore [*comma*] would you please fax by Thursday morning a brief job description to be used on the internal job postings [*period*]
>
> [*new paragraph*] Your description should include requirements such as previous experience [*comma*] educational background [*comma*]

and specific skills [*comma*] duties [*comma*] and responsibilities [*period*] [*correction: transpose educational background to precede previous experience*] You may want to retrieve a copy of Tom's [*apostrophe s*] job description to help you with this task [*period*]

[*new paragraph*] Thanks for your help [*comma*] Bob [*period*] [*end letter*]

Transcription

Transcribing the spoken words of another person is not as easy as it may seem. For example, accents, inflections, individual speech patterns or impediments, and specialized vocabularies all can and do affect what the transcriber hears. As a result, the hard copy may or may not accurately reflect the information that the dictator was trying to relay.

Because of the sophistication of modern business equipment, corporations have available many options from which to choose their dictation systems and thus satisfy their documentation and communication needs. It is important that you know how to use the designated equipment correctly. This is necessary not only for the purposes of dictation and transcription but also in terms of day-to-day maintenance and the ability to train assistants and other coworkers.

A flawless document is the just reward of transcribing dictation well. To aim toward perfection, you must develop the techniques that work for you, the ones that will help you get the job done accurately and swiftly. Use the following and add any others that apply to your particular equipment or company system:

- If you have not already done so, read your instruction manual; not all equipment is the same, and your machine's requirements may differ from the one you used previously.

- Collect all supplies and reference material that you will need — stationery, addresses, files, dictionary, and so forth; place them within reach of your transcription unit and computer or typewriter.

- Put the cassette or other recorded medium into your machine.

- Connect the headset or earpiece.

- Adjust the foot pedal or the thumb-control panel.

- Check the start button, tone, volume, and speed-control levers for correct positions.

- Insert the index strip, if used (see illustration on page 109).

- Move the scanner to or otherwise locate the first-priority item.

- Determine the length of the item by reading the index strip or by other means.

- Listen to any instructions concerning priority of material and other matters before beginning to type.

- Set margins, tabs, and other format options.

- Activate the machine and continually listen to enough material to be able to key without interruption.

- Upon completion, proofread the material carefully on screen and then in hard copy.

Refer to Chapter 5 for further information about the preparation of correspondence.

DUPLICATION PROCESSES

Documents that are created by typewriter, computer, or desktop publishing usually have to be duplicated, whether only one file copy is needed or whether hundreds or even thousands of copies are needed. Four common duplication processes are photocopying, computer printing, stencil and spirit duplicating, and offset printing.

Photocopying

Since the introduction of the copier at midcentury, photocopying has been a useful means of making paper copies and transparencies (for use with overhead projectors) directly from original letters, memos, and other documents. In most businesses and even small home offices, the copier is an essential reproduction machine. Although it is most often used for limited-volume copying, high-speed, high-volume copiers can handle thousands of copies a month. Refer to Chapter 1 for a description of copying equipment.

Centralized Reproduction Department   In a large organization with many departments and high copy volumes, you are likely to find a centralized reproduction department (CRD) and satellite reproduction centers for high-volume work and individual copying machines elsewhere in the building for mid- or low-volume use. The CRD may have both high-volume photocopying equipment and offset presses, as well as machines for various support and finishing operations such as offset platemaking, collating, binding, drilling, padding, and folding.

The high-speed copying machines in a CRD are likely to have many special features such as computer forms feeder, automatic document handler, collator, automatic two-sided copying, and variable enlargement and reduction. Follow the instructions for using the particular features of your machine. If your equipment has a wide range of reduction selections, refer to Table 4.1 for selected standard settings and Table 4.2 for selected variable settings.

The CRD will have a manager and trained staff to operate the equipment. Sometimes a word processing center is associated with the CRD for document preparation. Satellite centers are smaller than the CRD. They usually have mid- or high-volume copying equipment staffed by a trained operator. They are often located at a distance from the CRD for the greater convenience of users and are able to relieve the CRD of smaller and less complex jobs.

Decentralized Copiers Decentralized copying machines are individual units located in work areas for walk-up use. In a large company they may be mid-volume copiers used by departmental staffs for general administrative work or low-volume desktop units located in executive suites. To save secretarial time, heavily used decentralized equipment

Table 4.1 Standard Reduction Percentages

ORIGINAL SIZE	REPRODUCE ON 8½ × 11 INCH	REPRODUCE ON 8½ × 14 INCH
8½ × 11 inch	100%	100%
8½ × 14 inch	77%	100%
11 × 15 inch	74%	77%
11 × 17 inch	65%	77%
8½ × 11 inch with a narrow margin	98%	98%

Table 4.2 Determining Variable Reduction Percentages

% Reduction Chart

Original Dimension in Inches	5	5.5	6	6.5	7	7.5	8	8.5	9	9.5	10	10.5	11	11.5	12	12.5	13	13.5	14
17												62	65	68	71	74	76	79	82
16.5												64	67	70	73	76	79	82	85
16											62	65	69	72	75	78	81	84	87
15.5											65	68	71	74	77	81	84	87	90
15										63	67	70	73	77	80	83	87	90	93
14.5									62	65	69	72	76	79	83	86	90	93	96
14									64	68	71	75	79	82	86	89	93	96	100
13.5								63	67	70	74	78	81	85	89	93	96	100	
13							61	65	69	73	77	81	85	88	92	96	100		
12.5							64	68	72	76	80	84	88	92	96	100			
12						62	67	71	75	79	83	87	92	96	100				
11.5						65	69	74	78	83	87	91	96	100					
11					64	68	73	77	82	86	91	95	100						
10.5					67	71	76	81	85	90	95	100							
10				65	70	75	80	85	90	95	100								
9.5			63	68	74	79	84	90	95	100									
9			67	72	78	83	89	94	100										
8.5		65	71	76	82	88	94	100											
8	62	69	75	81	87	93	100												

Copy Paper Dimension in Inches

often has automatic document feeding, collating, and stapling capabilities, as well as other features depending on the special needs of the department. Although copiers vary widely in size, price, and capabilities, some manufacturers have adopted standard symbols (see illustration) to designate different operations.

Computer Printing

Electronic printers print images they receive in digital form from a nearby or remote computer or terminal. No conventional hard-copy original or master is needed, although an outside document can be scanned into a computer for editing and printout. Electronic typewriters also function as printers and can produce letter-quality output.

Chapter 1 describes the major types of computer printers and scanning equipment.

Since printer speed, number of fonts, and the quality of output varies, businesses may have more than one type of printer. For example, there might be high-speed, low-quality dot matrix printers for drafts and other work where type quality is unimportant and laser

Standard Symbols for Duplicators and Document Copying Machines

On (Power)	Off (Power)	Standby	Contrast	Start (Of Action)
Stop (Of Action)	Time Switch/Timer	Clear	Repeat	Ready
Single-sided Original	Double-sided Original	Single-sided Copy	Double-sided Copy	Lighter Copy
Darker Copy	Reduction	Enlargement	Primary Sheet Paper Supply	Additional Sheet Paper Supply
Sorter	Staple	Call for Maintenance	Add Sheet Paper	Add Toner
Interrupt	Single Feed	Remove Copies	Information	Paper Jam

printers for correspondence and other work requiring high-quality output and a variety of fonts. Some high-quality printers that have the features of both copiers and computer printers combine microprocessor, laser, and photocopier technology in one unit and can print up to a hundred pages a minute.

Printer Operations   Like copiers, computer printers may be located in a central department or in individual offices or workstations. The specific steps required to initiate printing depend on your software program and the type of printer. Dot matrix printers commonly use continuous-form paper and are loaded differently than sheet-fed laser printers, which typically house paper in trays similar to a copier tray. Secretaries should thoroughly study instruction manuals accompanying the printer and be prepared to train assistants on its use.

Program Control   Printers are controlled by the program used to create the document to be printed. Your word processing program, for example, has certain formatting commands, and the program sends those commands to your printer, translating them into other commands that your printer can understand. A printer driver (PRD) file in your word processing program contains information that tells your program what your printer can do and how to instruct it to do it.

Depending on your equipment and word processing program, the printed version of your document may look different from the on-screen version. The special characters you see on screen may not appear or may look different on the printed page. Use your printer's self-test feature, which displays all the characters your printer will print. If you have questions that aren't answered by your instruction manual, call the toll-free number of the software vendor.

Stencil and Spirit Duplicating

Stencil and spirit duplicating machines make duplicates from special masters that first must be prepared by typing or some other means. Both types of duplicating are older processes still used in schools and churches and occasionally in other organizations.

Stencil Duplicating   Stencil duplicating, or mimeographing, offers better quality copies and longer run lengths (several thousand copies) than the spirit process, but it is more costly and less convenient to use. The stencil master has three parts: the stencil itself, which is a fine mesh coated with a waxy material; a cushion sheet; and the backing sheet, which is light card stock. The stencils can be cut by typing or drawing on them with a stylus. Stencils also can be made with electronic stencil cutters and thermal stencil makers. Electronic stencils are more fragile.

Spirit Duplicating Spirit duplicating is one of the oldest of these reproduction processes. It is an inexpensive and fast way to make a relatively small number of prints (several hundred copies). The most common print color is purple, although red, green, blue, and black also can be printed. The spirit master set has three parts: a master sheet, a slip sheet, and a carbon sheet covered with a thin layer of aniline dye. The image can be created on the master sheet by typing or drawing with a stylus, ballpoint pen, or other hard smooth implement. Images can be transferred automatically with an infrared copying machine and special spirit master sets.

Offset Printing

Offset Process Offset printing is based on the principle that water and grease do not mix. It uses a grease-based ink that sticks to the dry image area on the offset master (also called the *plate*). The nonimage areas of the master are kept wet to repel the ink. Offset printing presses are high-speed machines that can create thousands of impressions of consistently excellent quality from an offset master. The process is used by commercial printers, publishers, and centralized corporate reproduction departments for long runs in which multiple colors or photographs are being printed, and in cases where very high quality is desired. It is less economical for short runs, however, because of the initial investment in equipment and the time and skill involved to create masters, set up the job, and clean up afterward.

Platemaking The offset master is a specially coated sheet. The image can be created directly on a paper master with typing, pen, pencil, rubber stamp, carbon paper, or xerographic copying. Special electrostatic platemaking equipment also can be used to make masters quickly and inexpensively. These masters must be handled with care because they can be smudged or marked. Direct-image masters can be created by several automatic processes as well. Some xerographic copiers will copy a typed or etched original image onto a direct-image master. Direct-image masters are economical, easy to create, and suitable for relatively short run jobs. More durable and precise offset masters are created photographically on sensitized metal plates. They may be photo-direct masters that create the master directly from camera-ready original copy, or they may be photo-indirect masters that require creation of an intermediate negative. Several manufacturers offer platemaking equipment.

CORRESPONDENCE

Secretaries spend substantial time every day preparing correspondence for conventional mail or electronic transmission. They may compose and sign their own letters and memos or create messages that someone else will sign. Often they are expected to edit and type messages drafted by their boss or another executive. In each case, the physical appearance of the letter (format, neatness, and overall visual impact) as well as the content (accuracy, tone, clarity, and general effectiveness) will determine how favorably or unfavorably the recipient will view the sender and his or her company. Correspondence, therefore, has a major impact on an organization's image and its dealings with customers, clients, and the public.

STATIONERY

Quality stationery indicates a company's concern about its public image. Since secretaries are usually responsible for ordering stationery and sometimes help select the paper, you need to know something about weight, texture, and color. A printer who handles a lot of stationery can be very helpful, and you should not hesitate to ask for detailed information before placing an order.

The paper you select for your stationery will probably be used in a dot matrix, laser, or ink-jet printer (see Chapter 1) as well as in a typewriter. It may also be used in your office copier. Most manufacturers recommend a 20- or 24-pound weight for these machines. (Paper weight refers to the weight in pounds of one ream, or about 500 sheets, cut to standard size.) If the paper is too light, it may not be strong enough to feed properly; if it is too heavy, the thickness may cause paper jams.

Since stationery is often folded to fit into a standard envelope, it should form a clean, even crease. Also, the ink from the printed letterhead must not bleed through to the back side. The color and texture must allow the typed characters and handwritten signatures to be clean and clear, without blotches.

Letterhead should be printed on the felt side of the paper — the side from which you can read the watermark (a marking or design in quality paper that is visible when held up to the light). Also, you should type on the felt side of a continuation sheet. All continuation sheets and envelopes should match the letterhead in color, texture, and weight.

LETTER FORMATS

Common Formats

Three common business letter formats are the full-block, modified-block, and simplified formats. A personal style, used on personal (non-company) stationery, is appropriate for certain personal or social business letters, such as a personal thank you or a congratulatory note to a business friend. A personal letter may be set up in either a full-block or modified-block format, according to preference. Some companies also use a variation of one of the standard formats or a combination of two or more formats.

The model formats on pages 121–124 illustrate their principal differences and indicate formatting specifications, such as proper spacing between elements, margins, and indentions. Once you have selected a format, store the specifications, described in the following sections, in your computer for future recall.

Major Parts of a Business Letter

The major parts of a business letter are the date, reference, confidential notation, inside address, attention line, salutation, subject, body, complimentary close, signature, identification line, enclosure notation, mailing notation, copy-distribution notation, postscript, and continuation-page heading. These elements must be properly and attractively centered on the page with ample margins (usually a minimum of 1¼ to 1½ inches on all sides).

Full-Block Format

COMPANY LETTERHEAD

January 4, 1995

Our file PCC-21

Mr. Peter C. Cross
ABC Chemicals Ltd.
321 Park Avenue East
City, ST 98765

Dear Mr. Cross:

FULL-BLOCK LETTER FORMAT

This is a full-block letter format, featuring all elements aligned with the left margin. The date is placed two to four line spaces below the letterhead and the reference two line spaces below the date. The inside address may be from two to twelve line spaces below the date or reference.

The salutation appears two line spaces below the inside address and the subject two line spaces below the salutation. The body begins two line spaces below the subject. If an attention line is used, it is placed two line spaces below the inside address, before the salutation.

The complimentary close is placed two line spaces below the last line of the message, and the typed signature is about four line spaces beneath it. Concluding notations may be single- or double-spaced, depending on available space.

Sincerely,

John M. Swanson
Executive Vice President

JMS:mdv

Encs.: 4

Modified-Block Format

COMPANY LETTERHEAD

1-Page Fax to 800-555-6543

February 14, 1995

Dr. David J. Peters
State Insurance Corporation
4556 Hightower Boulevard
City, ST 98765

Dear Dr. Peters:

MODIFIED-BLOCK LETTER FORMAT

This is the modified-block format, which is a more traditional style than the full-block format. The date, complimentary close, and signature block are all aligned just past the center of the page.

A fax notation may be placed above or below the letterhead data, centered or flush left. When this notation is used, the date begins two line spaces below the notation, and the reference (which is optional) two line spaces below the date. The inside address, salutation, and subject line are positioned as they would be in a full-block format.

Except for the fact that the complimentary close and signature block are aligned under the date, to the right of the page center, the spacing is the same as that used in the full-block format. Identification initials and enclosure notations may be single- or double-spaced.

Cordially,

Donna W. Reardon
Personnel Manager

mdv

Simplified Format

COMPANY LETTERHEAD

August 4, 1995

Ms. Barbara C. Mackie
HCI Corporation
One State Street
City, ST 98765

SIMPLIFIED LETTER FORMAT

Ms. Mackie, this is a model of the simplified format. It is a clean, modern format preferred by many companies.

The date is flush with the left margin two to four line spaces beneath the letterhead. The inside address, also flush left, is two to twelve line spaces below the date. There is no salutation in this format, but the addressee's name is mentioned in the first and last paragraphs.

The subject line is placed three line spaces below the inside address, and the message begins three line spaces after that. Since there is no complimentary close, Ms. Mackie, the signature is placed about five line spaces below the message; often it is typed in all capital letters, with a short title following it. The notations are handled the same as they are in other formats.

JANE M. WRIGHT — SENIOR EDITOR

mdv

cc: Marietta K. Lowe
      Roberta Y. Peterson

Encs. 3

Personal Format

PERSONAL LETTERHEAD

October 11, 1995

Mr. William Stowe
19 Forest Road
City, ST 98765

Dear Will,

This is the personal letter format I promised to send you. As you can see, it is typed on my personal letterhead, and it omits business parts such as a reference line and subject line. This format is suitable for personal and social letters.

The date is placed two to four line spaces beneath my personal address and the inside address two to twelve line spaces below that. The salutation appears two line spaces below the inside address. Notice that a comma follows the salutation in a personal letter, rather than a colon as used in business and social letters. The message begins two line spaces after the salutation.

The complimentary close and signature are aligned with the date, a little to the right of the center of the page. The spacing, however, is the same as that used in a business letter.

As you probably guessed, Will, since this is a personal letter, there aren't any identification initials or other business notations.

All the best,

Michael Robinson

Date   The date includes the month, day, and year: *September 15, 1995*. In military style the day is placed before the month and no comma is used: *15 September 1995*.

Place the date two to four line spaces below the last line of the letterhead, flush left in the full-block and simplified formats and slightly right of the page center in the modified-block format.

Reference   A file, policy, invoice, order, or other reference number may be included in your letter. If you are replying to someone who used such a number, include the same number in your reply.

Position the reference two line spaces under the date, aligned with the date either flush left or slightly right of the page center, depending on the letter format. If you include your own reference as well as the addressee's reference, place your reference directly under the addressee's reference.

September 15, 1995

Your reference 12345
Our reference 678910

If your letterhead has a reference line already printed on the page, fill in your number after that line, regardless of the position of the date. In that case, place the addressee's reference *after* the printed line.

In reply please refer to: 678910
Your reference 12345

Confidential Notation   A confidential or personal notation is used when only the addressee should open and read a letter. Therefore, you should place it on the envelope as well as on the letter. (See the section "Envelope Formats.")

Position the word *Confidential* or *Personal* on the letter two to three line spaces below the reference or date, flush left in all formats. The word may be in all capitals or have an initial capital letter only; it may be underlined for emphasis.

January 15, 1995

CONFIDENTIAL

Inside Address   Always place the inside address flush left, regardless of letter style. It may be two to twelve line spaces below the date or reference, depending on the length of the letter.

Table 5.1 Inside Addresses: Questions and Answers

QUESTION	ANSWER
How do I style the addressee's name and business title?	Check the letterhead or the signature block of previous correspondence for correct spelling, or check with the writer. If necessary, call the recipient's secretary for spelling verification. An incorrect title or a misspelled name creates a negative impression.
When may I use abbreviations in an inside address?	You may abbreviate titles such as *Mr., Ms., Dr.,* and *Esq.* But avoid the title *Ms.* in international correspondence, since it is not common outside the United States. Do not abbreviate company names, departmental designations, or corporate titles. You may, however, abbreviate *Co., Inc.,* or *Ltd.* if they have been abbreviated on the printed letterhead and form part of the official company name. Words such as *Street* should not be abbreviated on the letter but may be abbreviated on the envelope. For automated sorting use the capitalized, unpunctuated abbreviations recommended by the U.S. Postal Service. (See the section on addressing envelopes.) In all cases use the capitalized, two-letter state abbreviations of the Postal Service.
How do I handle overlong lines in an inside address?	When an addressee's title (such as *Vice President, Research and Development*) runs too long, carry over part of the title to another line and indent it.
How many lines should an inside address have?	Usually an inside address should not exceed five full lines (runovers excepted), unless the additional information is vital for proper delivery.
How do I style addresses?	Spell out all numerical street names through *twelve: Third Avenue; 46th Street.*
How do I style numbered houses and buildings?	Use figures for all numbered houses or buildings above *one: One Fifth Avenue; 2 Fifth Avenue.*

Table 5.1, continued

QUESTION	ANSWER
Where do I position suite numbers, mail stops, and so on?	Usually, put suite, room, and apartment numbers on the street address line, two spaces after the last word on the line: *500 Fifth Avenue, Suite 44V.* If a building name is given, put the number after the name: *Johnson Towers, Room 611.* Mail stop indicators often appear two spaces after the last word on the corporate name line: *CCC Corporation, MS 12Z 451.*
How do I style an inside address involving two or more recipients having different addresses?	Type two (or more) complete sets of names and addresses, one after the other in order of importance or in alphabetical order, with one line space separating the units one from another. Single-space each unit internally. If a letter is going to two or more people at the same address, also stack the names in order of rank or alphabetically within a single inside address block. Refer to the text for more about writing inside addresses.

Include all data necessary for correct identification and delivery of the letter. This may include the recipient's name; job title; company name; department; street address; suite or other number; and city, state, and ZIP code, as well as the country in the case of international mail.

If two names are given in the inside address, place the name of the person of the higher rank first; if both are equal, list the names alphabetically. The job title is sometimes omitted if the address is particularly long, although often it is helpful for delivery in a very large company. When information is too long to fit on one line, indent all carryover lines.

The examples following on page 128 contain acceptable arrangements of data. Also, refer to Table 5.1 for answers to commonly asked questions about the inside address, including proper forms of address in international correspondence. See "Forms of Address" later in this chapter for more about the use of personal and professional titles.

Ms. Joan Goodwin
Vice President, Sales
CCC Corporation
1234 Matthews Street, Suite 4
City, ST 98765

Dr. Beverly G. Ryan, President
CCC Corporation, Inc.
12 - 34 Street
City, ST 98765

Mr. J. H. Parsons, Manager
CCC Corporation Ltd.
Research and Development Division
One Boyleston Avenue, Room 10
Ottawa, ON K1A OB1
CANADA

Dr. Beverly G. Ryan, President
Mr. J. H. Parsons, Manager,
    Research and Development Division
CCC Corporation, Inc.
34 West 15 Street, N.W.
City, ST 98765

CCC Corporation, Inc.
Sales Department
2000 Second Avenue
City, ST 98765

Attention Line   Address your letter to the company and use an attention line on both the envelope and the letter when you want to be certain that someone will open and read the letter if the person named in the attention line is absent. You may also address a letter to one person and name another in the attention line. Then if the addressee is absent, the person named in the attention line will open the letter.

Position the attention line flush left, two line spaces below the inside address, in all formats. Use the person's full name without a title. When the letter is addressed to a company, make the salutation to the company, not to the person named in the attention line.

ABC Incorporated
567 Tower Court
City, ST 98765

Attention Roland B. Stiers Sr.

Ladies and Gentlemen:

Salutation   Place the salutation two line spaces below the attention line or inside address, flush left in all formats. However, it should be omitted in the simplified format.

The word *Dear* and the words of a title such as *Your Excellency* are capitalized, and a colon follows the salutation of a business letter. A salutation should not be given to a company or department (*not* Dear Sales Department *or* Dear XYZ Company), only to a person(s) (*Dear Staff Members*).

First names, although common in domestic correspondence, should be used only when it is clear that the recipient wants to be addressed that way. Use first names in international letters only when the recipient has specifically asked to be addressed that way. Also, avoid use of the title *Ms.* in international letters since it is seldom used in other countries.

Refer to Table 5.2 on page 130 for answers to commonly asked questions about the salutation, and refer to "Forms of Address" later in this chapter for information on the use of personal and professional titles.

Dear Ms. Smith:
Dear Ms. Smith and Mr. Thomas:
Dear Jan:
Dear A. B. Renfro:
Dear Professor Lee:
Ladies and Gentlemen:
Ladies: [*women only*]
Gentlemen: [*men only*]
Dear Sir: [*very formal*]
Dear Madam: [*very formal*]
Most Reverend Sir: [*very formal*]
To Whom It May Concern:
Dear Friends:

Subject Line   A subject summarizes the main topic of a letter and makes it unnecessary for the writer to announce the subject in the first paragraph.

Table 5.2 Salutations: Questions and Answers

QUESTION	ANSWER
When are *Dear Sir* and *Dear Madam* acceptable?	*Dear Sir* and *Dear Madam* are used mostly in letters to dignitaries such as an ambassador and, sometimes, when neither name or title are known or when neither name, title, or gender are known: *Dear Sir or Madam.*
What is the proper salutation when gender is unknown?	Omit the title *Mr., Ms., Mrs.,* or *Dr.* and use the person's first name instead: *Dear Lee Lawson.*
What is the proper way to address a mixed-gender group?	Style the salutation collectively: *Dear S & S Engineers; Dear Departmental Managers; Ladies and Gentlemen.*

Place the subject line two line spaces below the salutation, flush left in the full-block and simplified formats and indented the same as the paragraphs in the modified-block format.

Often the word *Subject* is omitted. If it is used, it may be typed with an initial capital or in all capitals, followed by a colon. (Law offices commonly use the words *In re* or *Re* rather than *Subject.*) The words used to summarize the letter topic are then typed after the colon. The full subject line may be typed in a variety of styles, according to preference.

NOVEMBER SALES MEETING

SUBJECT: NOVEMBER SALES MEETING

SUBJECT: November Sales Meeting

Subject: November Sales Meeting

Message   Single-space the message, or body, of a letter, and leave a blank line space between the paragraphs. Begin the body two line spaces below the subject line or salutation. Paragraphs should be flush left in the full-block and simplified formats and indented about ½ inch in the modified-block format.

Business reports prepared as letters may have subheads and other features, such as lists, that are common in a longer report. (See Chapter 6.) If headings are used, they may be positioned flush left, with one or more blank line spaces above and below each head, or they may be run in with the first line of a paragraph. Headings may be typed in all capitals, with important words capitalized, or with an initial capital only, and they may be underlined or printed out in a larger size or in a bold face. It is usually best, however, to avoid distracting design flairs and flourishes in correspondence.

Lists in a letter should be set off from the rest of the body, usually with one blank line space before and after the list and often a space between each list item. A list may also be indented from the left (or from both the left and right) as a block, using the same amount of indention as that of each paragraph, about ½ inch. Single-space a list the same as the rest of the message.

Quotations that exceed four to five lines should be set off from the rest of the body as a blocked quotation, or extract. (Chapter 11 explains the proper use of quotation marks.) An extract is usually indented the same amount as the paragraphs, or about ½ inch. Leave one blank line space before and after an extract.

If a letter runs over to a second page, follow the instructions for setting up a continuation-page heading at the end of this section.

Complimentary Close   A complimentary close is used in all formats except the simplified format. Place the close two line spaces below the message, flush left in the full-block format and slightly right of the page center in the modified-block format.

Capitalize the first word of the close, and place a comma after the last word. Table 5.3 on page 132 gives examples of suitable closes ranging from very informal to highly formal. A close should be selected based on the relationship between the writer and the recipient. Although friendly, familiar closes are common in domestic letters, more formality is preferred in international letters.

Signature   The signature block consists of the sender's typed name and, possibly, job title, as well as the handwritten signature. The information is positioned flush left in the full-block and simplified formats and slightly right of the page center in the modified-block format.

When the signature block consists of the sender's name and, possibly, job title, it should be typed about four line spaces below the complimentary close (or five line spaces after the message in the simplified

Table 5.3   Complimentary Close Wording

TONE	EXAMPLE
Most informal; indicates close personal relationship between writer and recipient	Regards, Best regards, Best ever, As ever, Kindest regards, Best wishes,
Informal and friendly; indicates personal relationship between writer and recipient who may or may not be on a first-name basis	Cordially, Most cordially, Cordially yours,
Friendly but neutral; appropriate to all but the most formal letters	Sincerely, Sincerely yours, Very sincerely, Most sincerely, Very sincerely yours, Most sincerely yours, Yours sincerely,
Suitable only for formal correspondence; highly formal; indicates that the recipient outranks the writer; often used in diplomatic, governmental, and ecclesiastical correspondence	Respectfully, Respectfully yours, Most respectfully, Yours respectfully, Very respectfully,

format). When a company name is included (not common in the simplified format), it is typed two line spaces below the complimentary close, and the person's name and job title are placed about four line spaces below the company name. (This form is used by accountants and others who want to make clear that the letter represents a company opinion or report.) If the sender's name is printed in the letterhead, however, it is not necessary to type it again at the bottom of the page.

The handwritten signature should be the same as the typed signature. If the typed signature is *Barry F. McCoy*, the letter should not be signed *B. F. McCoy*. A personal title, such as *Mrs.*, should be placed in parentheses before the typed name if the recipient otherwise would not know that you want to be addressed that way. If no title is given, recipients will assume that a man should be addressed as *Mr.* and a woman as *Ms.* The titles *Mr.* and *Ms.* are placed in parentheses before the signer's name only when gender would not otherwise be clear or when a woman who wants to be addressed as *Ms.* is writing to a recipient in another country where the title *Ms.* is unknown.

(Mr.) P. R. Thompson [*gender unclear*]

(Ms.) Jane Steele [*international*]

Academic initials (*Ph.D.*), initials designating a religious order (*SJ*), or evidence of certification (*CPA*) may be placed after a typed signature even if a job title is also included. *Esq.* (*Esquire*), although uncommon, may be placed after the name of a prominent professional man or woman; no title should precede a name when *Esq.* follows it.

Paul R. Thompson, Sc.D.
Professor of Molecular Physics
Paul R. Thompson, Esq.

The following examples are acceptable business forms of the typed signature following a complimentary close.

Sincerely,

Michael A. Roberts, M.D.

Sincerely,

(Mrs.) Sharon C. Warner
Vice President, Marketing

Sincerely,

THE ACCOUNTING COMPANY

Michael A. Roberts, CPA
General Manager

Sincerely,

Sharon C. Warner, President

A secretary or someone else may sign a letter for his or her boss. The following forms are acceptable.

Sincerely,

Amanda Wilson

For Arnold K. Steinberg

Sincerely,

Amanda Wilson

Secretary to Mr. Steinberg

Sincerely,

Arnold K. Steinberg
                aw

Arnold K. Steinberg

In the simplified format, the signer's name may be typed in all capitals, with a short job title on the same line. A dash or a comma may separate the name and job title, according to preference.

> Thank you for writing, Mr. Brisson. We hope you enjoy the program as much as we have.

WENDY A. MCPHERSON — EDITOR

Identification Line   The identification line indicates who signs, dictates, and types a letter. Although this information is useful only to the sender, companies often type it on all copies, including the recipient's copy, to avoid having to add it later only on the file copies.

Place the signer's initials first, then those of the person who dictated the letter, and last those of the typist.

> AV:mj [*signer and dictator the same*]
> AV:MT:mj [*signer and dictator different*]

Place the identification line two line spaces below the signature block. This line and notations that follow may all be single- or double-spaced, depending on the length of the letter and available room. In either case, the information is positioned flush left in all formats.

Enclosure Notation   When you are enclosing other material with a letter, add a notation to this effect flush left, one or two line spaces below the identification line. Space all notations consistently.

Especially important enclosures should be identified. *Enclosure* or *enclosures* may be abbreviated as *Enc.* or *Encs.* Generally, spell out abbreviations in international correspondence since the recipient may be unfamiliar with domestic abbreviations.

Enc.

Encs. 3

Encs.: P & L Statement
    Policy ABC-123

Mail Notation   If you send your letter by some means other than regular postal mail, add a notation below the enclosure notation. Single- or double-space the various notations as space permits. If the letter is to be faxed and no cover sheet will be used, you may prefer to type a special fax notation centered *above* the letterhead data (if space permits) or two line spaces below the letterhead data. In the latter case, it may be aligned with the date and typed in all capitals or with an initial capital only. Underlining may be used if desired. When a fax notation is placed beneath the letterhead, position the date two lines spaces below the notation.

By certified mail (*regular mail notation*)

By UPS Next-Day Air (*regular mail notation*)

Two-page fax to 800-555-6170 (*fax notation*)

Copy Notation   The copy notation is used to show who, other than the addressee, will receive a copy of the letter. Place the notation below the mail notation. Single- or double-space the same as the other notations.

Common designations are *Copy* or *c* for any "copy," *cc* for "computer copy," *pc* for "photocopy," and *fc* for "fax copy."

cc: Harold T. Martin

c: Lucille M. Baxter
   Benjamin R. Taylor
   Avery B. Wexler, Jr.

When you send a copy to someone and do not want the addressee to know about it, place a blind-copy notation (*bc*) only on your file copy and the blind-copy recipient's copy.

bc: Jean McGhee

Postscript   A *postscript*, introduced by the initials *P.S.*, is a brief, additional comment unrelated to the principal message; it should not be something you forgot to include in the main message.

Place the postscript two line spaces below the last notation, flush left in the full-block and simplified formats and with a paragraph indent in the modified-block format. Type the sender's initials at the end.

P.S. Have you heard when the next meeting of the Science Club is scheduled? DVC

Although more than one postscript should be avoided, if it is necessary to include two, use the abbreviation *P.P.S.* for the second one.

Continuation-Page Heading   If your message exceeds one page, use paper for additional pages that matches the letterhead stationery. If your company does not have printed continuation pages, use matching blank sheets. Always carry at least two lines of the letter body over to the continued page. Reformat the first page if necessary to allow for this. Begin the continuation-page heading four to six lines from the top edge of the paper or two to four line spaces below any printed line on the continuation sheet.

Three styles of heading are common in business: stacked, run on, or centered across the page. Use the addressee's full name, with or without a personal title. Figures or words may be used for the page numbers.

Mary Dennison
January 15, 1995
page two

Mary Dennison, January 15, 1995, page two

Mary Dennison   January 15, 1995   page 2

MEMO FORMATS

Common Formats

A memo format differs from a letter format in that it lacks an inside address, salutation, and complimentary close. Instead, headings such as *Date, To, From,* and *Subject* are printed or typed beneath the letterhead address, and the sender fills in the appropriate information after each word. Sometimes other headings, such as *Reference* or *Attention,* are also included.

Because of their informal appearance, memos are most common in interoffice communication and in exchanges among business associates who have developed a casual, friendly, informal relationship. This informality extends to matters of formatting too. Although memos are often prepared on regular business stationery (8½ by 11 inches), they may be written on half-size pages (8½ by 5½ inches) or any other size that a company wants to use. The memo format is also the preferred choice for electronic mail (see Chapters 1 and 9).

Commercial designs sometimes have ruled lines for the sender to hand-write rather than type a message. Certain styles have a carbonless attachment that the recipient can use for sending a reply on the same page as the sender's message. The model on page 138 uses regular business letterhead and resembles a business letter in its placement on the page and its margin settings. Consult a printer if you want to see samples of various sizes and designs.

Fax cover sheets are sometimes styled like memos. Although companies usually design their own cover sheets, standard commercial forms are also available. Like memos, most include headings (*Name, Date, Message,* and so on) followed by ruled lines where the sender can fill in the appropriate addressee data and write a brief message.

Major Parts of a Memo

The major parts of a memo are the confidential notation, headings, message, identification line, enclosure notation, copy-distribution notation, postscript, and continuation-page heading. Like business letters, memos should be properly positioned on the page, using adequate margins of at least 1¼ inches on all sides. Although memos may vary in size and arrangement of certain elements, particularly the headings, a standard memo begins with the headings and ends with any notation or postscript.

Confidential Notation   A confidential or personal notation may be used if a memo contains sensitive material. Depending on the design of the memo, place the notation close to the top of the page, preferably above the letterhead data and the headings. Follow the instructions for styling the notation given previously for a confidential notation in a letter.

Headings   The most common memo headings are *Date, To, From,* and *Subject.* But other data can be added as required. You may, for example, have headings for an *Attention* line and a *Reference* line. If the letterhead does not provide a fax or telex number, an office telephone extension, or an E-mail address, this information can be typed in beneath the last line of the letterhead data. One purpose of a memo is to provide essential information quickly and easily, so there is no restric-

Standard Memo

COMPANY LETTERHEAD

DATE: December 13, 1995   FROM: Arthur Lee

TO: Janice Wilcox   SUBJECT: Memo Format

This is an example of a reduced-size full-page company memo with typed-in headings. Margins and other specifications are similar to those used for a letter. The body also should be prepared like that of a letter.

Begin the message at least three line spaces below the last guide heading, and handle displayed lists like this:

- Leave one blank space between the text and the first item in the list.

- Block and, if desired, indent the list.

- Leave one line space between each item, and use single spacing within an item.

- Leave one blank line space between the last line of the list and the first line of regular text.

You may--but need not--add your initials at the end of the message two line spaces below the last line of text. Notations, such as *Enc.,* should begin two line spaces below your initials, if any, or the last line of the message.

mjk

cc: Mary Allen
    Sandra Kendall

tion, other than appearance or practicality, on the number and variety of headings you may choose to add.

The headings may be printed on special memo stationery or typed in on your regular letter stationery. If you type in the headings, begin two to four line spaces below the letterhead data. Headings may be capitalized (*SUBJECT*), abbreviated (*REF*), punctuated (*TO:*), or styled in some other way, according to preference. Each heading, however, should be styled the same as all the other headings.

To align the material that is filled in after each head, begin typing one or two character spaces to the right of the longest head.

DATE: January 15, 1995

TO: Martin T. Phillips

FROM: Ann C. Messenger

SUBJECT: Executive Bulletin--March

If you are printing out and sending an original copy of the memo to several people, type the word *Distribution* and an asterisk after the heading *To*, or write "See Distribution" after *To*.

TO: Distribution*

TO: See Distribution

Then, two line spaces after the last notation or postscript in the memo, repeat the word and list each intended recipient by rank or in alphabetical order.

Distribution: Martin Phillips, President
              Jennifer Abbott, Director of Research
              Steven Bartlett, Executive Assistant

Style the *From* name(s) the same as the *To* name(s). If you use initials only (*M. T. Phillips*) with the *To* name(s), also use initials only with the *From* name(s). (Although a memo has no signature, the sender may type or write his or her initials two line spaces below the body, slightly to the right of the page center.) Style the other heading information — *Subject, Reference, Attention* — as described previously for these parts in a letter.

Message   The message, or body, in a memo should be handled the same as that in a letter, as described earlier. Paragraphs in a memo also may be flush left or indented, and a memo, too, may contain subheads, lists, abstracts, and other display features. These elements are often more common in a memo, which is intended to distill and provide factual information in a clear, easy-to-read format. The memo format, in fact, is used for short reports more often than the letter format.

Identification Line   Place the identification line flush left, two line spaces below the message (or signature initials). Follow the instructions given previously for styling an identification line in a letter. This line and any notations that follow may be single- or double-spaced, depending on the length of the memo and available space.

Enclosure Notation   Place the enclosure notation flush left, one or two line spaces below the identification initials depending on whether you single- or double-space the various notations. Follow the instructions given previously for styling an enclosure notation in a letter.

Copy-Distribution Notation   Place the copy-distribution notation flush left, one or two line spaces below the enclosure notation depending on whether you single- or double-space all notations. Use the same abbreviations and follow the instructions given previously for styling a copy-distribution notation in a letter.

Postscript   Place the postscript flush left or with a paragraph indent, the same as the style used in the body of the memo. Begin two line spaces below the last notation, and follow the instructions given previously for styling a postscript in a letter.

Continuation-Page Heading   Use printed or blank stationery that matches the letterhead stationery for continued pages, and always carry at least two lines of the memo body over to the continued page. Follow the instructions given previously for styling a continuation-page heading in a letter. The three styles of continuation headings commonly used for letters are also appropriate for memos.

ENVELOPE FORMATS

Common Formats

A wide variety of sizes and styles are available in commercial envelopes. Office-supply stores and printers can provide most of the standard regular and window envelopes. Regular business letterhead (8½ by 11 inches) can be folded in thirds to fit a No. 9 or No. 10 commercial envelope. Smaller sizes, such as 3⅝ by 6½ inches, can be used for notes, invoices, and other material that will easily fold to a smaller size. The U.S. Postal Service requires that envelopes measure no less than 3½ by 5 inches.

Letters and external memos should be sent in envelopes that match the letterhead in color, texture, and weight. Internal memos, however, are generally routed in larger, unsealed, string-tied interoffice mailers. These envelopes have lines on which you write the recipient's name and office. After the recipient removes his or her enclosure, the person's name is crossed off and the envelope reused.

Major Parts of Envelopes

The principal parts of a standard envelope consist of the sender's return address; postage and mail instructions, such as *Special Delivery*; special notations or other instructions, such as *Address Correction Requested*; and the address block. The model below illustrates the placement of data on an envelope addressed for sorting by the U.S. Postal Service's optical character reader equipment.

Return Address   The sender's return address is usually printed in the upper left corner of the envelope. Businesspeople who use company envelopes may type their department or room number above or below the return address if the printed data omits this.

Postage and Mail Instructions   Mail instructions are placed about two line spaces below the postage that is applied in the upper right corner. Write the instructions in all capital letters: *SPECIAL DELIVERY*.

Notations   Letter writers may add special notations or instructions about two line spaces below the sender's return address. Write the information in all capital letters.

Envelope Format

Return Address ADDRESS CORRECTION REQUESTED	**Postage** SPECIAL DELIVERY

(top line no more than 2¾" from bottom of envelope)

ABC-123-S
HEATHERVILLE INDUSTRIES
ATTN MS MC ADAMSON
1891 WEST AVENUE
CITY, ST 98765

(½" minimum left margin)

(⅝" minimum bottom margin)

(½" minimum right margin)

[Return Address]
CONFIDENTIAL

[Return Address]
ADDRESS CORRECTION REQUESTED

Address Block   The traditional style is to write the person's name, job title, company and department, street, and city, state, and ZIP code centered on the envelope, capitalizing all important words.

Mr. J. G. Dougherty, Treasurer
RRR Corporation, Inc.
Business Department
13 Franklin Street
City, ST 98765

The U.S. Postal Service, however, prefers that addresses be typed in all capital letters and positioned within a designated rectangular address area. Envelopes so addressed can be more easily and quickly processed by equipment designed for automated handling.

The address block must be written at least ½ inch from the left and right edges and at least ⅝ inch from the bottom edge of the envelope. Unit numbers, such as a room number, must be placed after the street on the same line. A box number should be placed before a station name. Nonaddress data, such as a date or reference number, should be placed on the line immediately above the first line of the address. Type the address in all capital letters without punctuation. For further information, refer to a current edition of the U.S. Postal Service's *Domestic Mail Manual* and *International Mail Manual*.

Table 5.4 lists the authorized two-letter abbreviations for U.S. states and dependencies; Table 5.5 gives approved postal abbreviations for streets and words often appearing in place names; and Table 5.6 provides the accepted two-letter abbreviations for Canadian provinces.

ZIP Codes

The first three digits of a ZIP code identify the delivery area of the sectional center facility (SCF) or major city post office (unique three-digit ZIP code office) serving the area where the address is located. The next two (the fourth and fifth) digits identify the delivery area of an associate

Table 5.4   Two-Letter Abbreviations for U.S. States and Dependencies

STATE	ABBREVIATION	STATE	ABBREVIATION
Alabama	AL	Missouri	MO
Alaska	AK	Montana	MT
Arizona	AZ	Nebraska	NE
Arkansas	AR	Nevada	NV
California	CA	New Hampshire	NH
Canal Zone	CZ	New Jersey	NJ
Colorado	CO	New Mexico	NM
Connecticut	CT	New York	NY
Delaware	DE	North Carolina	NC
District		North Dakota	ND
of Columbia	DC	Ohio	OH
Florida	FL	Oklahoma	OK
Georgia	GA	Oregon	OR
Guam	GU	Pennsylvania	PA
Hawaii	HI	Puerto Rico	PR
Idaho	ID	Rhode Island	RI
Illinois	IL	South Carolina	SC
Indiana	IN	South Dakota	SD
Iowa	IA	Tennessee	TN
Kansas	KS	Texas	TX
Kentucky	KY	Utah	UT
Louisiana	LA	Vermont	VT
Maine	ME	Virginia	VA
Maryland	MD	Virgin Islands	VI
Massachusetts	MA	Washington	WA
Michigan	MI	West Virginia	WV
Minnesota	MN	Wisconsin	WI
Mississippi	MS	Wyoming	WY

Table 5.5 Abbreviations for Streets and Words Often
Appearing in Place Names

STREET/PLACE NAME	ABBREVIATION	STREET/PLACE NAME	ABBREVIATION
Academy	ACAD	Central	CTL
Agency	AGNCY	Church	CHR
Air Force Base	AFB	Churches	CHRS
Airport	ARPRT	Circle	CIR
Alley	ALY	City	CY
Annex	ANX	Clear	CLR
Arcade	ARC	Cliffs	CLFS
Arsenal	ARSL	Club	CLB
Avenue	AVE	College	CLG
Bayou	BYU	Common	CMM
Beach	BCH	Corner	COR
Bend	BND	Corners	CORS
Big	BG	Course	CRSE
Black	BLK	Court	CT
Bluff	BLF	Courts	CTS
Bottom	BTM	Cove	CV
Boulevard	BLVD	Creek	CRK
Branch	BR	Crescent	CRES
Bridge	BRG	Crossing	XING
Brook	BRK	Dale	DL
Burg	BG	Dam	DM
Bypass	BYP	Depot	DPO
Camp	CP	Divide	DV
Canyon	CYN	Drive	DR
Cape	CPE	East	E
Causeway	CSWY	Estates	EST
Center	CTR	Expressway	EXPY

Table 5.5, continued

STREET/PLACE NAME	ABBREVIATION	STREET/PLACE NAME	ABBREVIATION
Extended	EXT	Haven	HVN
Extension	EXT	Heights	HTS
Fall	FL	High	HI
Falls	FLS	Highlands	HGLDS
Farms	FRMS	Highway	HWY
Ferry	FRY	Hill	HL
Field	FLD	Hills	HLS
Fields	FLDS	Hollow	HOLW
Flats	FLT	Hospital	HOSP
Ford	FRD	Hot	H
Forest	FRST	House	HSE
Forge	FRG	Inlet	INLT
Fork	FRK	Institute	INST
Forks	FRKS	Island	IS
Fort	FT	Islands	IS
Fountain	FTN	Isle	IS
Freeway	FWY	Junction	JCT
Furnace	FURN	Key	KY
Gardens	GDNS	Knolls	KNLS
Gateway	GTWY	Lake	LK
Glen	GLN	Lakes	LKS
Grand	GRND	Landing	LNDG
Great	GR	Lane	LN
Green	GRN	Light	LGT
Ground	GRD	Little	LTL
Grove	GRV	Loaf	LF
Harbor	HBR	Locks	LCKS

Table 5.5, continued

STREET/PLACE NAME	ABBREVIATION	STREET/PLACE NAME	ABBREVIATION
Lodge	LDG	Pass	PASS
Loop	LOOP	Path	PATH
Lower	LWR	Pike	PIKE
Mall	MALL	Pillar	PLR
Manor	MNR	Pines	PNES
Meadows	MDWS	Place	PL
Meeting	MTG	Plain	PLN
Memorial	MEM	Plains	PLNS
Middle	MDL	Plaza	PLZ
Mile	MLE	Point	PT
Mill	ML	Port	PRT
Mills	MLS	Prairie	PR
Mines	MNS	Radial	RADL
Mission	MSN	Ranch	RNCH
Mound	MND	Ranches	RNCHS
Mount	MT	Rapids	RPDS
Mountain	MTN	Resort	RESRT
National	NAT	Rest	RST
Naval Air Station	NAS	Ridge	RDG
Neck	NCK	River	RIV
New	NW	Road	RD
North	N	Rock	RK
Orchard	ORCH	Row	ROW
Oval	OVAL	Run	RUN
Palms	PLMS	Rural	R
Park	PARK	Saint	ST
Parkway	PKY	Sainte	ST

Table 5.5, continued

STREET/PLACE NAME	ABBREVIATION	STREET/PLACE NAME	ABBREVIATION
San	SN	Terminal	TERM
Santa	SN	Terrace	TER
Santo	SN	Ton	TN
School	SCH	Tower	TWR
Seminary	SMNRY	Town	TWN
Shoal	SHL	Trace	TRCE
Shoals	SHLS	Track	TRAK
Shore	SHR	Trail	TRL
Shores	SHRS	Trailer	TRLR
Siding	SDG	Tunnel	TUNL
South	S	Turnpike	TPKE
Space Flight Center	SFC	Union	UN
		University	UNIV
Speedway	SPDWY	Valley	VLY
Spring	SPG	Viaduct	VIA
Springs	SPGS	View	VW
Spur	SPUR	Village	VLG
Square	SQ	Ville	VL
State	ST	Vista	VIS
Station	STA	Walk	WALK
Stream	STRM	Water	WTR
Street	ST	Way	WAY
Sulphur	SLPHR	Wells	WLS
Summit	SMT	West	W
Switch	SWCH	White	WHT
Tannery	TNRY	Works	WKS
Tavern	TVRN	Yards	YDS

Table 5.6 Abbreviations for Canadian Provinces

PROVINCE	ABBREVIATION	PROVINCE	ABBREVIATION
Alberta	AB	Nova Scotia	NS
British Columbia	BC	Ontario	ON
Manitoba	MB	Prince Edward	
New Brunswick	NB	Island	PE
Newfoundland	NF	Quebec	PQ
Northwest		Saskatchewan	SK
Territories	NT	Yukon Territory	YT

post office or a branch or station of a major city post office. All post offices are assigned at least one unique five-digit ZIP code. Larger post offices may be assigned two or more five-digit ZIP codes (multi-five-digit ZIP code offices). Separate five-digit ZIP codes are assigned to each delivery unit at these offices. Unique three-digit and multi-five-digit ZIP code post offices have street listings in the *National Five-Digit ZIP Code and Post Office Directory*, available for public use in most post offices.

The most complete ZIP code is a nine-digit number consisting of five numbers, a hyphen, and four numbers, which the United States Postal Service describes by its trademark "ZIP + 4." The correct format for a numeric ZIP + 4 code is five numbers, a hyphen, and four numbers. The first five digits represent the five-digit ZIP code; the sixth and seventh digits (the first two after the hyphen) identify an area known as a "sector"; the eighth and ninth digits identify a smaller area known as a "segment." Together, the final four digits identify geographic units such as a side of a street between intersections, both sides of a street between intersections, a building, a floor or group of floors in a building, a firm within a building, a span of boxes on a rural route, or a group of post office boxes to which a single U.S. Postal Service employee makes delivery.

Military Mail

Overseas military addresses must conform to domestic addressing standards. The delivery line (the second line from the bottom in the address) must show the ship name; the unit number, Consolidated Mail Room (CMR) number, or Postal Service Center (PSC) number; and the box number (if assigned). The last line must contain the designation APO (army/air force post office) or FPO (navy post office) and the appropriate two-letter "state" abbreviation, followed by the ZIP + 4 or five-digit ZIP code. The abbreviations AA (area Americas), AE (area Europe), and AP (area Pacific) must precede the three-digit ZIP code prefixes 340, 090–098, and 962–966, respectively. In addition:

- Mail addressed to army personnel must show grade; full name, including first name and middle name or initial; and unit number.

- Mail addressed to air force personnel must show grade; full name, including first name and middle name or initial; and PSC or unit number.

- Mail addressed to navy and Marine Corps personnel must show rank or rating; full name, including first name and middle name or initial; and ship number or PSC number for shore-based units.

Mail addressed to military personnel within the United States must show the name of the military installation, state, and either the correct ZIP code or ZIP + 4 code. In addition:

- Mail addressed to army personnel must show grade; full name, including first name and middle name or initial; and organization.

- Mail addressed to air force personnel must show grade; full name, including first name and middle name or initial; organization; and box number (if served by a PSC).

- Mail addressed to navy and Marine Corps personnel must show full name, including first name and middle name or initial; rank or rating; and organization.

International Mail

The U.S. Postal Service offers the following guidelines for addressing international mail.

- At least the entire right half of the address side of the envelope, package, or card should be reserved for the destination address, postage, labels, and postal notations.

- Addresses in Russian, Greek, Arabic, Hebrew, Cyrillic, Japanese, or Chinese characters must bear an interline translation of the names of the post office, and country of destination in English. If the English translation is not known, the foreign language words must be spelled in Roman characters (print or script).

- Mail may *not* be addressed to a person in one country "in care of" a person in another country.

- The name of the sender and/or addressee may *not* be in initials except where they are an adopted trade name.

- Mail may *not* be addressed to *Boxholder* or *Householder*.

- The house number and street address or box number must be included when mail is addressed to towns or cities.

- The bottom line of the address must show only the country name, written in full (no abbreviations) and in capital letters.

MR THOMAS CLARK
117 RUSSELL DRIVE
LONDON WIP 6HQ
ENGLAND

For mail to Canada, either of the following address formats may be used when the postal delivery zone number is included in the address:

MS HELEN SAUNDERS
CANADIAN ENTERPRISES
1010 CLEAR STREET
OTTAWA ON K1A OB1
CANADA

MS HELEN SAUNDERS
CANADIAN ENTERPRISES
1010 CLEAR STREET
OTTAWA ON CANADA
K1A OB1

FORMS OF ADDRESS

The correct forms of address must be used in the inside address, salutation, and envelope address. The following sections describe the proper forms of personal, scholastic, official, and honorary titles.

Women

In domestic business correspondence, the most common title for single, married, widowed, and divorced women is *Ms.* The title *Mrs.,* however, may be used if you know that the woman prefers it. The title *Ms.* should not be used for addressees in other countries where it is uncommon or unknown.

Ms. Angela McCarthy
Mrs. Angela McCarthy

The plural of *Ms.* is *Mses.* or *Mss.*

Mss. Angela McCarthy and Laura Phelps
[Address]

Dear Mss. McCarthy and Phelps:

The plural of *Mrs.* and *Madam* is *Mesdames* (*Mesdames Angela McCarthy and Laura Phelps*). In informal business correspondence, however, it is more common to repeat *Mrs.* with each name in the address and salutation.

Mrs. Angela McCarthy
Mrs. Laura Phelps
[Address]

Dear Mrs. McCarthy and Mrs. Phelps:

Madam is used primarily in formal salutations to government officials and diplomats.

Dear Madam:

Dear Madam Justice:

If a woman holds another title, such as a religious, military, or scholastic title, use it rather than *Ms.* or *Mrs.* unless you know that the woman prefers a personal title.

The Reverend Angela McCarthy
Captain Angela McCarthy
Dr. Angela McCarthy

If you can't determine whether the addressee is a man or woman, omit the title.

A. R. McCarthy
[Address]

Dear A. R. McCarthy:

Men

The title *Mr.* should be used unless a man has earned another title.

Mr. Leonard Eastman

Senator Leonard Eastman

The plural of *Mr.* is *Messrs.* (*Messrs. Leonard Eastman and Walter Grey*). In informal correspondence, however, it is more common to repeat *Mr.* with each name in the address and salutation.

Mr. Leonard Eastman
Mr. Walter Grey
[Address]

Dear Mr. Grey and Mr. Eastman:

Spouses

When addressing a business letter to spouses, use the same title for each spouse that you would use if you were writing to each person alone.

Mr. Leonard Eastman
Ms. Angela McCarthy-Eastman
[Address]

Dear Mr. Eastman and Ms. McCarthy-Eastman:

Dr. Leonard Eastman
Dr. Angela McCarthy-Eastman
[Address]

Dear Dr. Eastman and Dr. McCarthy-Eastman:

Mr. Leonard Eastman
Dr. Angela McCarthy-Eastman
[Address]

Dear Mr. Eastman and Dr. McCarthy-Eastman:

Officials and Dignitaries

Esq. (*Esquire*) is not common in the United States but is occasionally used for attorneys and people in the consular corps. Omit the personal or other title when *Esq.* follows the name.

Angela McCarthy, Esq.
[Address]

Dear Ms. McCarthy:

The Honorable is used before the names of certain prominent officials. Refer to Table 7 on page 154 for further examples.

The Honorable Leonard Eastman
[Address]

Dear Governor Eastman:

Use of the title *Reverend* depends on the person's religious affiliation. Some religious groups have abandoned use of *The* before *Reverend,* although others have retained it. The examples in Table 7 are shown with the use of *The.*

The Reverend Leonard Eastman
[Address]

Dear Dr. Eastman:

Reverend Leonard Eastman
[Address]

Dear Dr. Eastman:

Use *Reverend* alone with a surname (no first name) only if a personal or scholastic title intervenes.

The Reverend Dr. Eastman

The Reverend Ms. McCarthy

MODEL LETTERS

Writing Effective Business Letters

An effective message, whether prepared for conventional or electronic transmission, should follow the correct style and format described in this chapter and in Chapter 11. Each message should be consistent with the rules of grammar and composition described in Chapters 10 and 11. It should also have an appropriate tone for the intended reader

Table 5.7 Forms of Address

Note: Use the official's business address for business and business-related social correspondence, and use the official's home address (when known) for social or personal letters and invitations. The salutations given in this table are (1.) formal and (2.) informal.

GOVERNMENT OFFICIALS

President	The President The White House [Address] 1. Mr. President: 2. Dear Mr. President:
President-elect	The Honorable Marcus Shipley The President-elect [Address] 1. Dear Mr. Shipley: 2. Dear Mr. Shipley:
Former president	The Honorable Marcus Shipley [Address] 1. Sir: 2. Dear Mr. Shipley:
Vice president	The Vice President United States Senate [Address] 1. Mr. Vice President: 2. Dear Mr. Vice President:
Speaker of the House of Representatives	The Honorable Jean Shipley Speaker of the House of Representatives [Address] 1. Madam: 2. Dear Madam Speaker: Dear Ms. Shipley:

Table 5.7, continued

GOVERNMENT OFFICIALS	
Former speaker	The Honorable Marcus Shipley [Address] 1. Sir: 2. Dear Mr. Shipley:
Cabinet officer	The Honorable Jean Shipley Secretary of _____ [Address] 1. Madam: 2. Dear Madam Secretary:
Former cabinet officer	The Honorable Marcus Shipley [Address] 1. Dear Sir: 2. Dear Mr. Shipley:
Undersecretary, department	The Honorable Jean Shipley Undersecretary of _____ [Address] 1. Madam: 2. Dear Ms. Shipley: Dear Madam Undersecretary:
Attorney general	The Honorable Marcus Shipley Attorney General of the United States [Address] 1. Sir: 2. Dear Mr. Attorney General:
U.S. senator	The Honorable Jean Shipley United States Senate [Address] 1. Madam: 2. Dear Senator Shipley:

Table 5.7, continued

GOVERNMENT OFFICIALS

Senator-elect	The Honorable Marcus Shipley Senator-elect United States Senate [Address] 1. Dear Sir: 2. Dear Mr. Shipley:
Former U.S. senator	The Honorable Jean Shipley [Address] 1. Dear Madam: 2. Dear Ms. Shipley:
U.S. Senate committee, subcommittee chair	The Honorable Marcus Shipley Chairman _____ Committee United States Senate [Address] 1. Dear Mr. Chairman: 2. Dear Mr. Chairman: Dear Senator Shipley:
U.S. representative	The Honorable Jean Shipley House of Representatives [Address] 1. Madam: 2. Dear Ms. Shipley:
Former U.S. representative	The Honorable Marcus Shipley [Address] 1. Dear Sir: Dear Mr. Shipley: 2. Dear Mr. Shipley:

Table 5.7, continued

GOVERNMENT OFFICIALS

Territorial delegate	The Honorable Marcus Shipley Delegate of _____ House of Representatives [Address] 1. Dear Sir: Dear Mr. Shipley: 2. Dear Mr. Shipley:
Heads of independent U.S. organizations	The Honorable Jean Shipley Postmaster General [Address] 1. Madam: 2. Dear Madam Postmaster General:
State governor	The Honorable Marcus Shipley Governor of _____ [Address] 1. Sir: 2. Dear Governor Shipley:
State lieutenant governor	The Honorable Jean Shipley Lieutenant Governor of _____ [Address] 1. Madam: 2. Dear Ms. Shipley:
State secretary of state	The Honorable Marcus Shipley Secretary of State of _____ [Address] 1. Sir: 2. Dear Mr. Secretary:
State attorney general	The Honorable Jean Shipley Attorney General State of _____ [Address]

Table 5.7, continued

GOVERNMENT OFFICIALS

	1. Madam:
	2. Dear Madam Attorney General:
State senate president	The Honorable Marcus Shipley
	President of the Senate
	of the State of _____
	[Address]
	1. Sir:
	2. Dear Mr. Shipley:
State speaker	The Honorable Jean Shipley
of assembly, house	Speaker of the Assembly/House
	of Representatives of the
	State of _____
	[Address]
	1. Madam:
	2. Dear Ms. Shipley:
State treasurer,	The Honorable Marcus Shipley
auditor, comptroller	Treasurer of _____
	[Address]
	1. Dear Sir:
	2. Dear Mr. Shipley:
State senator	The Honorable Jean Shipley
	Senate of _____
	[Address]
	1. Madam:
	2. Dear Senator Shipley:
State representative,	The Honorable Marcus Shipley
assemblyman, delegate	House of Delegates of _____
	[Address]
	1. Dear Sir:
	2. Dear Mr. Shipley:

Table 5.7, continued

GOVERNMENT OFFICIALS	
State district attorney	The Honorable Jean Shipley District Attorney State of _____ [Address] 1. Dear Madam: 2. Dear Ms. Shipley:
City mayor	The Honorable Marcus Shipley Mayor of _____ [Address] 1. Sir: 2. Dear Mr. Mayor/Dear Mayor Shipley:
City board of commissioners president	The Honorable Jean Shipley President Board of Commissioners of the City of _____ [Address] 1. Dear Madam: 2. Dear Ms. Shipley:
City attorney, counsel, corporation counsel	The Honorable Marcus Shipley City Attorney [Address] 1. Dear Sir: 2. Dear Mr. Shipley:
Alderman, alderwoman	Alderwoman Jean Shipley City Hall [Address] 1. Dear Madam: 2. Dear Ms. Shipley:

Table 5.7, continued

COURT OFFICIALS

Chief justice of U.S.
    Supreme Court
	The Chief Justice
	The Supreme Court
	[Address]
	
	1. Sir:
	2. Dear Chief Justice:
	    Dear Chief Justice Shipley:

Associate justice
    of U.S. Supreme Court
	Madam Justice Shipley
	The Supreme Court
	[Address]
	
	1. Madam:
	2. Dear Madam Justice:
	    Dear Justice Shipley:

Retired associate justice of U.S. Supreme Court	The Honorable Marcus Shipley [Address] 1. Sir: 2. Dear Mr. Justice Shipley:

Chief justice, judge,
    of state supreme court
	The Honorable Jean Shipley
	Chief Justice of the Supreme Court
	    of _____
	[Address]
	
	1. Madam:
	2. Dear Madam Chief Justice:

Associate justice
    of state's highest court
	The Honorable Marcus Shipley
	Associate Justice of the Supreme Court
	    of _____
	[Address]
	
	1. Sir:
	2. Dear Justice:
	    Dear Justice Shipley:

Table 5.7, continued

COURT OFFICIALS

State presiding justice	The Honorable Jean Shipley Presiding Justice, Appellate Division Supreme Court of _____ [Address] 1. Madam: 2. Dear Justice: Dear Justice Shipley:
Judge of court	The Honorable Marcus Shipley Judge of the United States District Court for the _____ District of _____ [Address] 1. Sir: 2. Dear Judge Shipley:
Clerk of court	Jean Shipley, Esq. Clerk of the Superior Court of _____ [Address] 1. Dear Madam: 2. Dear Ms. Shipley:

DIPLOMATIC AND FOREIGN OFFICIALS

Note: When officials are not at their posts, add the name of the country where they are based (*American Ambassador to Great Britain*). For officials who hold military rank, use that title instead of *The Honorable.* The words *United States* should be used instead of the word *American* when a U.S. official is assigned to a country in South or Central America (*The Ambassador of the United States*). In other countries the phrase *American Ambassador* may be used. When foreign officials have personal titles such as *Dom* or *Dr.,* that title may be combined with the diplomatic title (*His Excellency Dr. Marcus Shipley*).

Table 5.7, continued

DIPLOMATIC AND FOREIGN OFFICIALS

American ambassador	The Honorable Jean Shipley Ambassador of the United States of America [Address] 1. Madam: 2. Dear Madam Ambassador: 　 Dear Ambassador Shipley:
American minister	The Honorable Marcus Shipley Minister of the United States of America [Address] 1. Sir: 2. Dear Mr. Minister: 　 Dear Minister Shipley:
American chargé d'affaires, 　consul general, consul, 　vice consul	Jean Shipley, Esq. Chargé d'Affaires ad interim 　of the United States of America [Address] 1. Madam: 2. Dear Ms. Shipley:
U.S. high commissioner	The Honorable Marcus Shipley United States High Commissioner 　for _____ [Address] 1. Sir: 2. Dear Mr. Shipley:
Foreign ambassador 　in the United States	Her Excellency Jean Shipley Ambassador of _____ [Address] 1. Excellency: 2. Dear Madam Ambassador:

Table 5.7, continued

DIPLOMATIC AND FOREIGN OFFICIALS

Foreign minister in the United States	The Honorable Dr. Marcus Shipley Minister Embassy of _____ [Address] 1. Sir: 2. Dear Dr. Shipley:
Prime minister	Her Excellency Jean Shipley Prime Minister of _____ [Address] 1. Excellency: 2. Dear Madam Prime Minister:
British prime minister	The Right Honorable Marcus Shipley, K.G., M.P. Prime Minister [Address] 1. Sir: 2. Dear Mr. Prime Minister: Dear Mr. Shipley:
Canadian prime minister	The Right Honorable Jean Shipley, C.M.G. Prime Minister of Canada [Address] 1. Madam: 2. Dear Madam Prime Minister: Dear Ms. Shipley:
President, premier, of a nation	His Excellency Marcus Shipley President of _____ [Address] 1. Excellency: 2. Dear Mr. President:

Table 5.7, continued

DIPLOMATIC AND FOREIGN OFFICIALS

Foreign chargé d'affaires ad interim in the United States	Ms. Jean Shipley Chargé d'Affaires ad interim of _____ [Address] 1. Madam: 2. Dear Ms. Shipley:

UNITED NATIONS OFFICIALS

Note: American citizens are addressed as *The Honorable* rather than *His* or *Her Excellency*.

Secretary-general	His Excellency Marcus Shipley Secretary-General of the United Nations [Address] 1. Excellency: 2. Dear Mr. Secretary-General: Dear Mr. Shipley:
Undersecretary	The Honorable Jean Shipley Undersecretary of the United Nations The Secretariat United Nations [Address] 1. Madam: 2. Dear Ms. Undersecretary: Dear Ms. Shipley:
U.S. representative to the United Nations, ambassadorial rank	The Honorable Marcus Shipley United States Representative to the United Nations [Address] 1. Sir: 2. Dear Mr. Ambassador:

Table 5.7, continued

UNITED NATIONS OFFICIALS

Foreign representative to the United Nations, ambassadorial rank	Her Excellency Jean Shipley Representative of _____ to the United Nations [Address]
	1. Excellency:
	2. Dear Madam Ambassador:

MILITARY SERVICES: ARMY, AIR FORCE, MARINE CORPS

Note: The same titles are used in the army, air force, and Marine Corps, although the designation for each branch of service differs: *USA* (U.S. Army), *USAF* (U.S. Air Force), *USMC* (U.S. Marine Corps). The reserve is indicated by adding *R* to the service designation: *USAFR*.

General, lieutenant general, major general, brigadier general	General Marcus Shipley, USA [Address]
	1. Sir:
	2. Dear General Shipley:
Colonel, lieutenant colonel, major, captain	Colonel Jean Shipley, USMC [Address]
	1. Dear Colonel Shipley:
	2. Dear Colonel Shipley:
First lieutenant, second lieutenant	First Lieutenant Marcus Shipley, USAF [Address]
	1. Dear Lieutenant Shipley:
	2. Dear Lieutenant Shipley:
Warrant officer	Chief Warrant Officer Jean Shipley, USA [Address]
	1. Dear Ms. Shipley:
	2. Dear Ms. Shipley:

Table 5.7, continued

MILITARY SERVICES: ARMY, AIR FORCE, MARINE CORPS

Retired officer | Colonel Marcus Shipley, USMC, Retired
[Address]

1. Dear Colonel Shipley:
2. Dear Colonel Shipley:

MILITARY SERVICES: NAVY, COAST GUARD

Note: The same titles are used in the navy and Coast Guard, although the designation for each branch of service differs: *USN* (U.S. Navy), *USCG* (U.S. Coast Guard). The reserve is indicated by adding *R* to the service designation: *USNR*.

Admiral, vice admiral,
    rear admiral | Admiral Marcus Shipley, USN
[Address]

1. Dear Admiral Shipley:
2. Dear Admiral Shipley:

Captain, commander | Captain Jean Shipley, USCG
[Address]

1. Dear Captain Shipley:
2. Dear Captain Shipley:

Lieutenant commander,
    lieutenant, lieutenant
    (jg), ensign | Lieutenant Commander Marcus Shipley, USN
[Address]

1. Dear Commander Shipley:
2. Dear Commander Shipley:

Warrant officer | Chief Warrant Officer Jean Shipley, USCG
[Address]

1. Dear Ms. Shipley:
2. Dear Ms. Shipley:

Retired officer | Commander Marcus Shipley, USN, Retired
[Address]

1. Dear Commander Shipley:
2. Dear Commander Shipley:

Table 5.7, continued

RELIGIOUS OFFICIALS

Note: Churches follow different practices in the use of *The* preceding *Reverend*. Some organizations have abandoned the use of *The,* whereas others have retained it. Follow the organization's preference. (*The* is used in the examples that follow.) Many men and women religious now also prefer to be addressed by their last names (*Dear Sister Shipley*) rather than their first names (*Dear Sister Jean*). Some heads of congregations have adopted a title such as *President* or *Director,* rather than the traditional *Father* or *Mother Superior.* Follow the person's usage and preference in individual cases.

The pope	His Holiness, The Pope [*or* His Holiness, John Paul] Vatican City, Italy 1. Your Holiness: Most Holy Father: 2. *never informal*
Apostolic pro-nuncio	His Excellency The Most Reverend Marcus Shipley Titular Archbishop of _____ The Apostolic Pro-Nuncio [Address] 1. Your Excellency: 2. Dear Archbishop Shipley:
Roman Catholic cardinal in the United States	His Eminence Marcus Cardinal Shipley Archbishop of _____ [Address] 1. Your Eminence: 2. Dear Cardinal Shipley:

Roman Catholic archbishop
  in the United States
	His Excellency The Most Reverend
	  Marcus Shipley, D.D.
	Archbishop of _____
	[Address]

Table 5.7, continued

RELIGIOUS OFFICIALS

	1. Your Excellency: 2. Dear Archbishop:
Anglican archbishop	The Most Reverend Marcus Shipley Archbishop of _____ [Address]
	1. Your Grace: 2. Dear Archbishop Shipley:
Roman Catholic bishop in the United States	The Most Reverend Marcus Shipley Bishop of _____ [Address]
	1. Most Reverend Sir: 2. Dear Bishop Shipley:
Protestant Episcopal bishop	The Right Reverend Marcus Shipley, D.D., LL.D. Bishop of _____ [Address]
	1. Right Reverend Sir: 2. Dear Bishop Shipley:
Protestant Episcopal presiding bishop	The Most Reverend Marcus Shipley, D.D., LL.D. Presiding Bishop of the Protestant Episcopal Church in America [Address]
	1. Most Reverend Sir: 2. Dear Bishop Shipley:
Anglican bishop	The Right Reverend Marcus Shipley The Lord Bishop of _____ [Address]
	1. Right Reverend Sir: 2. Dear Bishop Shipley:

Table 5.7, continued

RELIGIOUS OFFICIALS	
Methodist bishop	The Reverend Marcus Shipley, D.D. Methodist Bishop [Address] 1. Reverend Sir: Dear Bishop Shipley: 2. Dear Dr. Shipley:
Protestant Episcopal archdeacon	The Venerable Marcus Shipley Archdeacon of _____ [Address] 1. Venerable Sir: 2. Dear Archdeacon Shipley:
Protestant Episcopal dean	The Very Reverend Marcus Shipley, D.D. Dean of _____ [Address] 1. Very Reverend Sir: 2. Dear Dean Shipley:
Protestant Episcopal canon	The Reverend Marcus Shipley, D.D., LL.D. Canon of _____ [Address] 1. Reverend Sir: 2. Dear Canon Shipley:
Roman Catholic monsignor (higher rank)	The Right Reverend Marcus Shipley [Address] 1. Right Reverend Monsignor: 2. Dear Monsignor Shipley:
Roman Catholic monsignor (lower rank)	The Very Reverend Monsignor Marcus Shipley [Address] 1. Very Reverend Monsignor: 2. Dear Monsignor Shipley:

Table 5.7, continued

Roman Catholic father superior	The Very Reverend Marcus Shipley, M.M. Director [Address]
	1. Dear Father Shipley: 2. Dear Father Shipley:
Roman Catholic mother superior	Mother Jean Shipley, I.B.V.M. President [Address]
	1. Dear Mother Shipley: 2. Dear Mother Shipley:
Roman Catholic priest	The Reverend Marcus Shipley, Th.D. [Address]
	1. Dear Dr. Shipley: 2. Dear Dr. Shipley:
Episcopal priest, high church	The Reverend Marcus Shipley, D.D., Litt.D. [Address]
	1. Dear Dr. Shipley: 2. Dear Dr. Shipley:
Protestant minister	The Reverend Jean Shipley, D.D., Litt.D. [Address]
	1. Dear Dr. Shipley: 2. Dear Dr. Shipley:
Jewish rabbi	Rabbi Marcus Shipley [Address]
	1. Sir: 2. Dear Rabbi Shipley:
Military chaplain	Chaplain Marcus Shipley, Captain, USAF [Address]
	1. Dear Chaplain Shipley: 2. Dear Chaplain Shipley:
Roman Catholic brother	Brother Marcus Shipley [Address]

Table 5.7, continued

	1. Dear Brother:
	2. Dear Brother Marcus:
	Dear Brother Shipley:
Roman Catholic sister	Sister Jean Shipley
	[Address]
	1. Dear Sister:
	2. Dear Sister Jean:
	Dear Sister Shipley:

COLLEGE AND UNIVERSITY OFFICIALS

President, chancellor	Dr. Jean Shipley, President
	[Address]
	1. Madam:
	2. Dear Dr. Shipley:
Dean, assistant dean	Dr. Marcus Shipley, Dean
	[Address]
	1. Dear Sir:
	Dear Dr. Shipley:
	2. Dear Dean Shipley:
Professor, assistant professor, associate professor	Dr. Jean Shipley
	[Address]
	1. Dear Madam:
	Dear Dr. Shipley:
	Dear Professor Shipley:
	2. Dear Dr. Shipley:
	Dear Professor Shipley:
Instructor	Mr. Marcus Shipley
	[Address]
	1. Dear Sir:
	Dear Mr. Shipley:
	2. Dear Mr. Shipley:

and comment on an intellectual level that is suitable for the reader. Although a letter or memo may differ depending on how well you know the recipient and what your objective is, following these strategies will make it more effective.

- Get right to the point; the recipient may have many more letters to read.

- Use short sentences and paragraphs whenever possible, particularly in international correspondence.

- Use the active voice ("We are excited about your proposal") instead of the passive voice ("Your proposal has been met with excitement on our part") unless you have a special reason to be indirect.

- Precede bad news with good news whenever possible; this makes the recipient feel better: "Thank you, Bob, for your proposal about the product marketing survey. It would be wonderful if we could use the FRT sampling techniques as you suggest. Unfortunately, we don't have enough money in this year's budget to adopt that plan."

- Avoid bureaucratic jargon ("Operational life-cycle statistics re the configuration of this system belie the system's estimated utility vis-a-vis strategic plans"); however, don't be too folksy (*not* "Gosh, we'd love to talk to you guys about your proposal"). A straightforward businesslike approach is always preferred.

- Order your thoughts and the paragraphs containing them in a logical, coherent manner. See Chapter 11.

- Use a very short, to-the-point concluding paragraph to state any action you want the reader to take, to thank the reader, or to summarize the main point of your letter.

Models

The following model letters are examples of common types of business correspondence.

Adjustment

Dear Ms. Schorsch:

We were very sorry to learn about the condition of the electronic typewriters delivered to you on September 1. The damage was apparently caused by the shipper, but I have asked that replacement models be sent to you immediately at no additional cost.

We realize the inconvenience you have experienced and therefore are sending the replacement typewriters by Express Freight. We are also enclosing in the shipment a small gift to thank you for your patience.

Please let me know, Ms. Schorsch, if there are any problems with this next shipment. We value your business and look forward to working with you again.

Sincerely,

Application

Dear Mr. Broughton:

It was a pleasure meeting with you and Leslie Maguire during lunch Tuesday. It's always nice to find other Brooklyn Medical School graduates in our city.

I was particularly impressed with what you had to say about the Society of Medical Practitioners, and I am accepting your offer to become a member. Please consider this my application. I'm also enclosing a copy of my resume, as well as several letters of recommendation.

Thank you so much for offering to sponsor me, Mr. Broughton. I appreciate your interest and am eagerly looking forward to becoming a member of your organization.

Sincerely yours,

Appointment

Dear Ms. Stedham:

Mr. Walsh would like to know if you could meet him in his office (Room 1421) on Friday, August 7, at 4 o'clock.

He has reviewed your proposal to enlarge our company library and wants to discuss possible cost and staff requirements for such an expansion. I know that he is eager to learn more about your idea.

Please let me know whether this time is convenient, Ms. Stedham; my extension is 7600. Thank you.

Sincerely,

Appreciation

Dear Dr. Nelson:

Thank you for your recent order, Dr. Nelson, which we have shipped by Walton Express Services, according to your request. It's always a pleasure to welcome a new customer to Legg & Greene.

We know the extent to which joint medical practices such as yours are expanding, and we are ready to fill whatever equipment needs you may have in the months and years ahead. I'm enclosing a copy of our spring/summer catalog.

Please let us know if you have any questions about your order. We look forward to hearing from you again.

Sincerely,

Collection

Dear Mr. Lewitt:

We are sorry that, effective today, your credit line is closed to further purchases. We have written to you several times, Mr. Lewitt, and have also telephoned to remind you of the importance of keeping your account current. Unfortunately, the amount of $639.98 is now four months past due.

We urge you to protect your credit rating and avoid the additional costs you will incur if legal action is required. Please call or write today, Mr. Lewitt, to discuss your past-due account and how you can meet your obligations.

Sincerely,

Complaint

Ladies and Gentlemen:

I am returning for a refund one self-inking stamp and stamp pad. The stamp and pad were ordered from your catalog on April 24 and were paid for by my check No. 6161 for $16.98.

The enclosed stamp pad was advertised as self-reinking. But the ink is too faint to produce an effective imprint. Although it is described in your catalog as black ink, the faint imprint appears light gray instead.

Please send your refund check of $16.98 to Ms. Cynthia Edison at the return address given at the top of this letter. Thank you.

Sincerely,

Congratulations

Dear Mr. Rome:

We at Stevens & Stevens are delighted to send you our sincerest congratulations on the tenth anniversary of Ergonomics Designers!

Your collection of ergonomic products has been a much-needed solution to cumulative trauma disorders in the workplace. Our own employees once suffered from this serious problem before discovering your back supports and other ergonomic aids.

We have enjoyed preparing your Ergonomic Series catalogs and new product advertisements each year, Mr. Rome, and are very pleased to wish you and everyone else at Ergonomic Designers many more years of progress and prosperity.

Cordially,

Follow-up

Dear Will:

Have you had a chance to think about addressing my data processing class at our June seminar? Since we expect to send the program to our desktop publishing group on May 1, I'd appreciate receiving your decision on this by Tuesday, April 22 (hope it'll be yes).

Thanks, Will.

Best regards,

Inquiry

Ladies and Gentlemen:

Do you have any booklets or other literature about health care financing? If so, please send an order form, as well as any free material you have on this subject. If you have nothing available, could you direct me to another source?

Thank you.

Sincerely,

Introduction

Dear Mr. Bentley:

I'm happy to introduce James Newton, who has worked for this firm during the past two years. I understand he is interested in joining the Council of City Trial Attorneys, and I wholeheartedly endorse his application.

Mr. Newton is a capable, hard-working attorney who has taken on several difficult cases for us and has performed superbly. His credentials and law school record are impeccable, and he is well versed in your state law since he served as a judicial assistant to criminal court Judge John M. Mahoney before being employed in our firm.

If you need any further information about Mr. Newton, please call me at 123-555-5000. I'll appreciate any consideration you can give to his application.

Sincerely,

Invitation

Dear Roy:

I'd like to invite you to be my guest for lunch along with Cindy Medline on Thursday, August 7. I've made reservations at the Bar and Grill, and we could meet in the lobby about noon on Thursday.

I'd appreciate it, Roy, if you could let me know by Tuesday whether you can come--both Cindy and I hope you can. We're eager to hear about your tour of Europe last month and want to catch up on other news too.

Best regards,

Order

Dear Mr. DiDominici:

Please send the following item to my attention at Shipley Associates, 12 State Street, City, ST 98765:

One (1) #133-6466-01 balance beam $250
scale (to 400 pounds)

Since we need to receive this item by March 6, 1995, could it be shipped by Second Day Air Express?

Thank you.

Sincerely,

Sales

Dear Powermate Customer:

Thank you for participating in our cartridge recycling program. We're happy to enclose your refund check for $5. To receive your refund, follow these two simple steps:

1. Go to any authorized Powermate store where your refund check can be applied toward the purchase of your next Powermate dry-ink cartridge.

2. Present the refund check when you purchase your next cartridge, and $5 will be deducted from the purchase price.

Thanks to environmentally conscious customers like you, our cartridge recycling program is a huge success. So as long as you keep recycling cartridges, we'll keep sending you refund checks!

If you have any questions about our program, call 800-555-1201. We're always happy to hear from you.

Sincerely,

Transmittal

Dear Mrs. Dennison:

Thank you, Mrs. Dennison, for asking about our easel pads. Here is the brochure you requested.

Presentations for Business offers a complete line of easel products, including the unique static image pad described in the enclosed brochure. This pad can be used with dry erase or permanent markers, so it's perfect for meetings, presentations, brainstorming sessions, signs, and messages.

If we can answer any questions, Mrs. Dennison, or help you select the right products for your meetings, please call our customer representative at 800-555-7707. We appreciate your interest in Presentations for Business products.

Cordially,

BUSINESS DOCUMENTS

Secretaries prepare a variety of documents in addition to letters and memos (see Chapter 5). In addition to typing the material, some secretaries assist in the research, writing, and editing phases. Companies may have their own preferred format and style for reports and other documents, and secretaries should follow company practices. In the absence of company guidelines, the information in this chapter can be applied to most situations.

PRESS RELEASES

The press release is an example of a short document that secretaries commonly process. Companies issue press releases to help maintain a high public profile and thereby increase sales. A press release might be issued to promote the launch of a new product or announce the appointment of a new chief executive officer. The press release is a highly visible indicator of corporate style and substance, and it must be devoid of all errors. Since secretaries are often called upon to type and proofread press releases, your role in maintaining your company's public image is very important.

Arrangement of Data

A press release is really a news story, and the writer should follow journalistic style by putting the most important data in the first paragraph.

- *Who* did *what*?
- *Where* and *when* was it done?
- *Why* was it done?

Supporting data are included in subsequent paragraphs and arranged in order from the most to the least important. The news or broadcast editor can then prune the story from the bottom up without inadvertent deletion of crucial facts.

Format

Letterhead   A press release may be prepared on special 8½- by 11-inch stationery headed *Press Release, News Release,* or *News from [Company],* or it may be typed on your regular business stationery.

Margins should be 1¼ or 1½ inches, and there should be 2 to 3 inches of blank space between the printed letterhead data and the first line of text. The receiving editor will use this space to write a headline and note other production instructions.

Source   In addition to the printed letterhead data providing the company's name, address, and telephone, fax, and other numbers, there may be the name of the writer and the person to contact for further information. Memo-style subheads are used for this:

> **From:**   Samuel Martin
> **Contact:** Laura Mason

This information is usually typed immediately under the letterhead data against the right margin.

Release Date   Center the date and time that the material may be published or broadcast 2 to 3 inches below the source.

> FOR IMMEDIATE RELEASE
>
> FOR RELEASE MONDAY, MAY 2, 8 A.M.

Headline   If you want to supply your own headline, center it in the 2 to 3 inches of space that you leave after the source data. Receiving editors, however, usually delete such headlines and write their own.

Body   Type the body double spaced, with paragraph indentions of ½ to 1 inch. Double spacing is required to give the receiving editor room to edit the document for publication. Begin the first line with the place and date (dateline).

> Boston, June 3:

Put a colon after the date, or insert a dash between the date and the first word of the story.

If the story exceeds one page, center *-more-* in uppercase or lower-case letters at the bottom of the first page, and continue the story on continuation sheets (see Chapter 5) that match the letterhead stationery. Use key words from the headline or first paragraph along with the page number at the top of the continued page, three to six line spaces below any printed heading or below the top edge of the sheet.

ABC Sales Increase--2

Signal the end of the story by typing *-30-* or *-END-* two to three line spaces below the last typed line of the body.

Refer to the model release on page 182 for general style and format.

Proofreading   After using your spell-checker, manually proofread the entire document line-for-line against the original. Check for typographical, grammatical, and factual errors. Query the writer if a fact appears to be inconsistent with other data or if you think it might be wrong. After making any necessary corrections, read the document again from beginning to end.

REPORTS

Several kinds of reports are generated in business: short, informal memo and letter reports and long, complex formal reports. These documents serve many needs and are directed to various readership levels inside and outside the company. A report might introduce and then analyze in detail a given market; discuss a particular business problem in depth and then offer a solution; lay out an annual or multiyear strategic plan; delve into a highly complicated legal or financial question; provide impetus for the research, development, and launch of a new product; or offer a stock or investment prospectus. Reports may be destined for staff, line management, top management, or outside clients. Reports may be general or highly technical.

Secretaries usually organize and keyboard the draft materials in a logically ordered, consistently and neatly typed final product devoid of typographical and factual errors. Some secretaries also help produce tabular and graphic exhibits and help with the research. In addition, secretaries often are responsible for proofreading, fact checking, duplication or printing, collation, binding, and distribution.

Press Release

COMPANY LETTERHEAD

For further information:
Jane Arnold, 202-555-1611

FOR IMMEDIATE RELEASE

Boston, June 3--ABC Company reported today that it has achieved the strong growth in sales and earnings projected for 1995. The company attributes this growth to its entry into the notebook computer market.

Net sales for the year reached a record high of $219.2 million, exceeding by 15.5 percent the previous year's $189.7 million. Net income for 1995 increased 23.5 percent to $13.2 million from $10.7 million in 1994. Primary earnings per share were $2.16 in 1995 compared with $1.79 in 1994.

At its October meeting the Board of Directors voted a quarterly dividend of $0.22 per share. This dividend will be payable February 22, 1996, to shareholders of record on October 22, 1995.

- 30 -

Research

If you are asked to handle some of the research, be prepared to go outside your own office and internal library. Although company files and personnel represent a useful source of information, it is often necessary to visit the reference room in an outside library, call schools and other organizations listed in the Yellow Pages or another directory, or access an on-line database through your company's system or through a subscriber service.

If you are using an outside database that must be accessed by computer and modem over telephone lines, it is important to be very clear and specific in providing key words for the computer search. If you are vague, the computer either will be unable to provide what you want or will provide massive amounts of nonessential information that will involve lengthy and expensive telephone usage. Before you begin, read the relevant section in your instruction manual. Most services provide suggestions for choosing key words and controlling your searches.

Style and Format

Although shorter reports are often dictated as memos, the longer ones may be handwritten or drafted by computer. In many cases a long report represents the work of more than one executive. The summary in a new product report may be written by your boss, and the sales forecast may be prepared by the sales director. The manufacturing cost estimates and production schedule may be worked out by a manufacturing manager, and the other financial data may be prepared by a business manager or an accountant, with the advertising or promotion strategy developed by an advertising manager or an outside agency.

All reports are subject to errors and inconsistencies, and multiauthor reports often have a large number of stylistic, spelling, and factual inconsistencies. Before starting to type a report, read the entire document from beginning to end and note all inconsistencies, errors, and unclear points. Flag them with self-sticking notes, and query the writer(s) responsible for the problematic points or sections. Check all major and subsidiary headings in the text to ensure consistency of style. Find out where the displayed tables and graphics are to appear. Will they be scattered throughout the text (if so, room must be left for them), or will they be clustered together at the end or in a separate appendix? If possible, key the report into a computer program, and store it for final editing and correction. Also store the format you use for future documents.

Corrections

Documents in word processing memory are easily edited and corrected with no visible sign of the changes in the final printout. Depending on the machine's capabilities, corrections can also be edited in and fresh copy printed out with an electronic typewriter. When typewriter corrections must be made on paper by another method, the options include self-correcting typewriter ribbons, chalk-coated papers, and correction fluids.

Informal Memo and Letter Reports

For a short, two- to three-page report intended for in-house distribution, executives often prefer to use memo or letter stationery. These reports should be formatted the same as any letter or memo, with the possible addition of subheads, lists, and other elements that will make the body of the report easier to read. Letter reports are usually set up in a full-block or modified-block format. If a report is intended for numerous recipients, it is often more convenient to use the memo format with a distribution list at the end of the report. Refer to Chapter 5 for guidelines on formatting letters and memos.

Instead of a report title, as would be used in a long, formal report, a subject line is used in both a letter and memo report. A variety of styles should be developed for headings to distinguish one level from another. Two or three levels are adequate for most small reports. More than this could be difficult to follow. For examples, refer to the discussion of the subject line in Chapter 5 and to the model letter report in this chapter.

Table 6.1 on page 187 suggests approximate settings for various format elements. Adjust the spacing to fit the length of your report and the type of binding (if any) that will be used.

Proposal Report

Proposals may be either long or short. Although brief informal proposals are prepared as memo or letter reports, formal proposals should be styled and formatted the same as a long formal report (see the next section). Some proposals, however, must be prepared on fill-in forms provided by the requesting organization.

A typical company proposal is the technical job proposal prepared for an outside client in which an organization or person proposes to do certain work for a specified fee or price. Office-supply stores have standard forms for bids or brief quotations and cost estimates. But if additional detail is required, a more complex format may be developed.

Letter-Report Format

COMPANY LETTERHEAD

December 13, 1995

Mr. Arthur R. Lacey
Lacey, Middleton & White
123 Beacon Street
City, ST 98765

Dear Mr. Lacey:

REPORT HEADINGS

This is a model letter-report format in which the title is written as a subject line in all capitals.

FIRST-LEVEL HEAD

The first-level head is often centered and written in all capitals. It is usually not underscored.

Second-Level Head

The second-level head may be centered or flush left. It is commonly written in uppercase and lowercase letters, usually without underscoring.

Third-Level Head

The third-level head is frequently positioned flush left. It is often written in uppercase and lowercase letters, usually without underscoring.

<u>Fourth-Level Head</u>. The fourth-level head is most often run in with the paragraph text to which it relates. It is usually written in uppercase and

Letter-Report Format, continued

Continuation-Page Letterhead

Arthur R. Lacey
December 13, 1995
page two

lowercase letters and is often underscored or written in an italic or bold
face.

Notice that additional space is placed before and after freestanding heads.
Typically, two blank line spaces precede the head and one blank line space
follows it.

The four levels of heads illustrated in this letter are sufficient for most
memo and letter reports. If additional levels are needed, some variation of
these styles could be devised, such as a run-in head written with an initial
capital only. Or if the letter text has indented paragraphs, a lower-level
head could also be indented like the paragraphs.

Sincerely,

Robin N. Brown
Word Processing Department

RNB:mdv

Table 6.1   Report Formatting

Margins

Unbound or top-bound

Top — page 1	12 lines minimum
Top — page 2 and following	6 lines minimum
Bottom — all pages	6 lines minimum
Left & right — all pages	1¼ to 1½ inches

Side-bound

Left — all pages	1½ to 2 inches

Spacing

Body of report	Single- or double-space, depending on length
Between paragraphs	If single-spaced paragraphs, double-space between to separate them; if double-spaced paragraphs, no space between regular paragraphs
Quoted matter, displayed	Single- or double-space, the same as the report body
Lists, tables, etc.	Single-space within units; double-space between units
Footnotes	Single-space or, if text is double-spaced, double-space if desired
Bibliography	Space the same as footnotes

Indention

Paragraphs	Modified-block format: ½ to 1 inch; full block format: no indention
Quoted matter, lists, tables, etc.	Indent the same as the text paragraphs, or ½ to 1 inch
Footnotes	Indent the same as the text paragraphs, or ½ to 1 inch

Table 6.1, continued

Bibliography	No indent on first line; $\frac{1}{2}$-inch indent on runover lines
Pagination	
Unbound or top-bound	Numerals 3–6 lines from bottom center, each page
Side-bound	Numerals 3–6 lines from top of page or 3–6 lines from bottom; centered on remaining page after binding
Title page	Number not typed
Front matter (table of contents contents, lists of tables and graphics, preface, foreword, executive summary)	Include number beginning with table of contents; small roman numerals
First text page	Begin arabic numeral 1
Subsequent text pages (body of report, appendix, index, etc.)	Continue with arabic numeral 2, 3, etc.

A detailed proposal, for example, may begin with an *introductory section* in which the problem to be solved is defined, the objectives of the study are set forth, the proposed solution to the problem is described in steps or work phases, the resultant benefits to the client are given, and the capabilities of the contracting company are delineated. The introduction is followed by a *technical operations plan* — a detailed section explaining how the goals and objectives will be met and how the total program will be implemented step-by-step. Next comes the *management plan* detailing the project's organization — the number of personnel required, the ongoing documentation to be generated (e.g., progress reports), and the quality-control procedures to be maintained throughout the program. The report often concludes with a *financial section* outlining the forecast costs and fees. This basic format is augmented as needed by other sections and subsections.

Formal Report

A formal report may be distributed to an outside client or internally to other members of the writer's company. Table 6.1 describes general formatting specifications suitable for a formal report: margins, spacing, indentions, and pagination. The following sections describe the principal parts of a formal report, although not all formal reports include all of these parts. Some, for example, may have no cover or flyleaves; others may omit the letter of authorization or the acknowledgments page. But a long, complex formal report should always have a title page and a table of contents in addition to the body and any material associated with the text, such as a list or table.

Cover   If you use a cover, select one that will protect the report over the long term and one that is appropriate for the overall length of it. A ring binder, for example, is appropriate for a five-year plan consisting of hundreds of pages. The cover should contain a gummed label bearing the title and perhaps the writer's name or the name of the company. The label should be neatly and clearly typed.

Flyleaf   Formal reports often have a flyleaf — a blank page appearing after the cover at the very beginning. Sometimes a report may have two of them, one at the beginning and another at the end. Flyleaves protect the rest of the document and allow space for the reader to write comments.

Title Page   If a report does not have a separate cover, the title page must serve that purpose. Usually, information on the title page is centered on the available space after calculating any room required for a side binding (if any).

A title page should state the report title, to whom it is submitted, by whom it is submitted, and the date it is submitted. The submission information may include the writer's and receiver's departmental affiliation or job title.

Job numbers, purchase orders, or contract numbers may be included if required. If the report is a revision of an older work, that fact should be noted too. Sometimes key words reflecting the main topics discussed in the body of the report are appended to the title page for use in subject-coded computerized information-retrieval systems. Type and spell the key words exactly as the author has written them.

Position the report title about a third of the way down the page, typed in uppercase and lowercase or in all capital letters. Place the "submitted to" information in approximately the center of the page, midway between the title and the "submitted by" information.

Submitted to
Jason Van Vleet
Manager, Sales Department
A-Z Data Processing, Inc.
1111 West Avenue
City, ST 98765

Place the "submitted by" information and the date at the bottom of the page, leaving a blank space between the address and the date.

Submitted by
Lynda C. Colwell
Director, Market Research
The Research Company
2132 Parkway North
City, ST 98765

February 6, 1995

Letter of Authorization or Transmittal   If official written authorization was given to do a study, the writer may include a copy of the letter in the front matter of the report. A letter of transmittal summarizing the purpose, scope, and content of the study may also be included if the report has been commissioned by an outside source. The letter of transmittal replies to the letter of authorization and says, "Here is what you asked for." This letter should be typed on company letterhead and signed by the writer or the person having overall responsibility for the project. Ensure that the left margin of the letter is wide enough to accommodate any side binding, and format the letter according to the guidelines for correspondence given in Chapter 5.

Acknowledgments Page   When other people or organizations have contributed to the report, a brief notation acknowledging their help, support, and work may be included. Acknowledgments of this type are included on a separate page, usually styled in one or two short, single-spaced paragraphs. The word *Acknowledgments* is typed in uppercase and lowercase or in all capital letters the same as other chapter or division titles. Begin all titles the same distance from the top of the page (see Table 6.1). The text paragraphs, if single-spaced, should be separated by double spacing. All of this material should be centered and balanced attractively on the page.

Table of Contents The table of contents is important in a long, complex report because it presents at a glance an outline of the major and subsidiary topics covered in the report and the appropriate page numbers. To compile the table of contents, use the major and subsidiary headings found in the body of the report. If the writer has used roman numerals and letters to introduce the headings, include them in the table of contents. If the writer has used an all-numeric system of signaling heads in the text, use these numbers in the table of contents. Word the headings in the table of contents *exactly* as they are worded in the text.

Center the table of contents on the page, leaving ample margins all around. Double-space between headings and subheads; single-space runover lines within these headings. Align heading and page numbers horizontally and vertically. Also align numbers, letters, or other devices introducing heads.

Use a continuation sheet for a table of contents exceeding one page, and head the continuation sheet *"Contents--Continued"* or a variation thereof. This heading should be centered and typed in uppercase and lowercase letters near the top of the page. (Refer to the suggested spacing in Table 6.1.) The heading on the first page — *Contents* — should be styled the same as other chapter or division titles and should begin on the same line as the titles of chapters and divisions.

The use of leaders (horizontally typed periods) to link headings with their page numbers is optional. Leaders may be set tight (typed consecutively in a line with no intervening spaces) or spaced (typed consecutively in a line with one space between each period). Leaders must align vertically as illustrated in the model table of contents on page 192.

Wait until the report is finished to prepare the table of contents since last-minute changes may affect the wording of subheads and the page numbers. After the table of contents has been drafted, check all items and page numbers against the text subheads and page numbers.

Lists of Figures and Tables If the report has more than a few illustrations, prepare either a combined list of illustrations or separate lists of figures (drawings, graphs, and so on) and tables (tabular matter). Common titles are "List of Illustrations," "List of Figures," "List of Graphics," and "List of Tables."

Table of Contents

vi

These lists should be formatted the same as the table of contents. If tables and graphics are combined in one list, use heads such as "Figures" and "Tables" and group the appropriate illustrations in proper order under these headings.

Foreword and Preface   Although uncommon in a business report, a foreword or preface or both may be included. The *foreword* — written by someone other than the writer of the report — comments on the work, usually with words of praise or a statement about the importance of the work. The preface — written by the author of the report — is a short statement regarding the purpose, scope, and content of the study, often including a summary of the research and methodology that was used. These sections should be single- or double-spaced, the same as the body of the report. Style and position the title the same as all other titles in the report.

Abstract or Summary   An abstract or summary is more common than a preface in a business report. Styled and formatted the same as a preface, it also states the purpose, scope, and content of the report; summarizes the research and methodology; and briefly states the author's conclusions. Sometimes the information is provided as a list of up to a dozen points. Although an abstract might consist of dozens or even hundreds of pages, it is more commonly presented in two hundred words or less.

Body   The body, or text, of a business report typically includes an introduction, a methodology or background section, the main discussion or data analysis, and the final statement of conclusions and recommendations. The body may be single- or double-spaced, but it is usually single-spaced when the report is very long. Follow the style and format suggestions in Table 6.1, and refer to the models of the first text page and the first main section of a long report on pages 194 and 195.

Complex business reports use different levels of headings in the body to present the information in a clear and orderly arrangement and assist readers in following it. Four levels of headings are usually all that is needed, but if a report is very complex, one or two additional levels may be used. The author also may use arabic numbers (1, 2, 3, 4, and so on) or roman numerals (I, II, III, IV, and so on) or an alphabetical system (A, B, C, D, and so on). Some business reports, especially technical reports, are written using an outline system for headings. For example:

First Text Page of Long Report

AVAILABLE INFORMATION

The corporation is subject to the informational requirements of the Securities Exchange Act of 1934 and in accordance files reports, proxy statements, and other information with the Securities and Exchange Commission. Such reports, proxy statements, and other information filed by the company can be inspected and copied at the public reference facilities maintained by the commission at Room 1024, 450 Fifth Street, N.W., Washington, DC 20549, and at the commission's regional offices at Room 1028, Everett McKinley Dirkson Building, 219 South Dearborn Street, Chicago, IL 60604.

INCORPORATION OF DOCUMENTS BY REFERENCE

Each of the following documents is incorporated by reference into this prospectus:

1. The corporation's Annual Report on Form 10-K for the year ended December 31, 1994, filed pursuant to Section 13 or 15(d) of the Securities Exchange Act

2. The plan's Annual Report on Form 11-K for the year ended December 31, 1994, filed pursuant to Section 13 or 15(d) of the Securities Exchange Act

3. All other reports filed pursuant to Section 13 or 15(d) of the Securities Exchange Act with respect to the corporation and the plan since the end of the fiscal year covered by the reports referred to in items 1 and 2

4. The corporation's definitive Proxy Statement filed pursuant to Section 14 of the Securities Exchange Act in connection with the latest

1

First Main Section of Long Report

SECTION I

SUMMARY OF THE PLAN

1.   General

The XYZ Corporation Employees' Savings and Thrift Plan has been established to encourage retirement savings by participating employees of the corporation and of designated subsidiaries and affiliates of the corporation. Beginning January 1, 1995, such savings shall be effected by means of pretax salary-adjustment arrangements. The corporation will also make matching contributions to the plan in an amount based on certain savings by members.

All of the corporation's contributions will be invested in common stock of the corporation, and all or part of the members' savings may be so invested. All contributions and savings will be held in trust and invested by Bank of New England, N.A., trustee of the plan. An Employees' Savings and Thrift Plan Committee, appointed by the Board of Directors of the corporation, will supervise and administer the plan.

The plan will form part of the corporation's program for providing competitive benefits for its employees. The operation of the plan is expected to encourage employees to make added provision, through savings on a pretax basis, for their retirement income. It will also encourage them to participate in ownership of the corporation's common stock.

On June 6, 1994, the corporation released the following statement:

The Board of Directors believes that the plan will provide an additional incentive to employees to contribute to the continued success of the corporation and will be in the best interests of the corporation and its stockholders.

3

1.0   FIRST MAIN SECTION
    1.1   First Main Subsection
    1.2   Second Main Subsection
    1.3   Third Main Subsection
        1.3.1   First subunit
        1.3.2   Second subunit
        1.3.3   Third subunit
    1.4   Fourth Main Subsection
2.0   SECOND MAIN SECTION

Such an outline system uses decimals to signal the level of headings. (Notice that the decimals are aligned vertically in each level of headings.) Another type of outline system consists of a combination numerical-alphabetical outline.

  I.   MAIN HEADING
    A.   Subheading
        1.   <u>Sub-subheading</u>
        2.   <u>Sub-subheading</u>
    B.   Subheading
        1.   <u>Sub-subheading</u>
            (a)   Most limited subcategory
            (b)   Most limited subcategory
        2.   <u>Sub-subheading</u>
 II.   MAIN HEADING

Follow carefully the writer's directions when using this format. Remember that if you have a heading labeled A, 1, or (a), you must have at least one other heading in the same set, such as B, 2, or (b). A heading in one set should never stand alone.

Appendix   An appendix contains supporting material, such as forms, tables, and charts, that are not inserted in the text. Usually, if more than one appendix is used, each is given a number or letter: *Appendix A: Trade Division Forecast, 1995.*

The appendix(es) are placed in the back matter immediately after the last text page and before the notes, glossary, bibliography, and index. Style and format the opening page the same as the first page of a chapter or other division. Refer to the model appendix format.

Notes   Although footnotes may be typed at the bottom of pages where they are referenced in the text, some writers prefer to collect them in a

Appendix Format

APPENDIX A

EMPLOYEES' SAVINGS AND THRIFT PLAN STRUCTURE

1. Current Administrative Information

The present members of the Employees' Savings and Thrift Plan Committee are John M. Roe, Jane T. Smith, Martin I. Miller, Joseph L. Edge, Sally A. Harris, Leila B. Summers, and John T. Williams.

Harry B. Selkirk and Lewis K. Callahan, directors of the corporation, are also directors of Bank of New England Corporation, the parent company of Bank of New England, N.A., trustee of the plan.

2. Members of the Plan

As of December 31, 1995, there were 999 employees participating in the plan, from a total number of approximately 1,600 employees eligible to participate. As of July 1, 1995, there were 981 employees participating out of 1,500 eligible.

3. Investment Performance

The following table indicates values for shares of the corporation's common stock in Fund B as of the indicated dates, which are based on the quoted New York Stock Exchange closing prices.

Valuation Date	*Fund B Price per Share of Common Stock of the Corporation**
December 31, 1994	$11.75
August 31, 1995	19.37
December 31, 1995	22.50

*Adjusted for 2-for-1 split on July 3, 1995.

55

notes section after the appendix. Sometimes, the notes that represent sources of quoted material are collected in a notes section, and those that represent additional comments (expository or substantive footnotes) are placed at the bottom of the appropriate pages. Often, then, the source notes are numbered and the expository notes lettered. In either case the numbering or lettering should be consecutive within chapters (if any) or throughout the entire report. The text letters or numbers that correspond to the footnote letters or numbers should be typed as superscripts just after the pertinent text passage: ". . . in a static market." [1]

Style and format the title of the notes section the same as the titles of other chapters or divisions in the report. Type each note in paragraph style, indented or flush left the same as a text paragraph, and type the letter or number preceding each note on line, as illustrated in the forthcoming examples. Single- or double-space the notes the same as the body of the report. See also Table 6.1 for further suggestions.

The following notes are examples of an acceptable style for a business report. *Ibid.* is used in reference to the immediately preceding note, and a short reference (author's last name and shortened title) is used to refer to a previous note other than the one immediately preceding. Both city and state are listed when the location may be unfamiliar to some readers; the city alone is sufficient for a well-known location such as Chicago. When the state is given, the traditional form of abbreviation (*Ill.*) should be used unless your employer requires the two-letter postal form (*IL*). For additional examples, consult a comprehensive style book such as *The Chicago Manual of Style.*

Book (one author or editor):
1. Samuel T. Brownstein, ed., *How to Reduce Your Taxes* (Chicago: ABC Press, 1994), 78.

Journal (two or three authors or editors):
2. James A. Schultz and Harriet Whitney Schultz, "How You Can Profit from Gold," *Business Journal* 101, no. 2 (1993): 16–21.

Magazine (more than three authors or editors):
3. Adam A. Kline et al., "Investing in the Future: Key Growth Companies," *Industry Today,* 10 May 1994, 5.

Newspaper (regular department or feature):
4. Securities and You, *Holbrook Daily News,* 17 March 1994, 2.

Translated book:
5. Jennifer M. Flagg, *The Stenmark Files,* trans. Thomas P. Jones (New York: Jones & Associates, 1993), 100–101.

Later edition:
6. Jennifer M. Flagg, rev., *Labor Relations,* 5th ed. (Concord, N.H.: McCain-Lewis, 1989), 364.

Report (corporate author):
7. *Report of the Commission on Arbitration* (New York: American Council on Arbitration, 1994), 3.

Short reference to a prior note:
8. Kline et al., "Investing in the Future," 5–6.

Interview:
9. Nancy C. Redstone, interview by author, Peoria, Ill., 3 November 1994.

Public document:
10. U.S. Senate Committee on Banking, *Report of Activities,* 99th Cong., 1st sess., 12 October 1985.

Unpublished paper:
11. Andrew M. Ardmore, "The True Cost of Inflation" (paper presented at the annual meeting of the Business Society, Chicago, Ill., June 1994), 21–23.

Reference to previous note:
12. *Ibid.,* 24.

Glossary   A glossary is placed after the notes section, before the bibliography or name-date reference list. It is an alphabetical list of special terms used in the document along with the definitions.

A glossary should be formatted the same as other main divisions, with consistent spacing and margins. The style adopted for the entries may vary, although terms are usually typed in italics or a bold face.

diode A device that permits electric current to pass in one direction but not the other.

Bibliography   A bibliography, which follows the glossary (if any), is an alphabetical list of books and other material consulted by the writer of the work in which the bibliography appears. If it includes only works referred to in the text or appearing in the notes section, it may be called "Works Cited" or "References." If it includes other works, it is usually called "Bibliography" or "Selected Bibliography."

The list is placed at the end of the book, report, or other document after the glossary or, if there is no glossary, after the notes section. A hanging indent format is used, with the first line flush left and runover lines indented about ½ to 1 inch, the same as the text paragraphs. A long dash is used for repeated authors' names in succeeding entries. Author entries precede edited, revised, and other entries. For example, *"John Doe, XYZ Book,"* precedes *"John Doe, ed., ABC Book."*

The following entries are based on the notes illustrated in the previous section. For additional examples, consult a comprehensive style book.

Ardmore, Andrew M. "The True Cost of Inflation." Paper presented at the annual meeting of the Business Society, Chicago, Ill., June 1994.

Brownstein, Samuel T., ed. *How to Reduce Your Taxes.* Chicago: ABC Press, 1994.

Flagg, Jennifer M. *The Stenmark Files.* Translated by Thomas P. Jones. New York: Jones & Associates, 1993.

_____, rev. *Labor Relations,* 5th ed. Concord, N.H.: McCain-Lewis, 1989.

Kline, Adam A., et al. "Investing in the Future: Key Growth Companies." *Industry Today,* 10 May 1994, 5–11.

Redstone, Nancy C. Interview by the author. Peoria, Ill., 3 November 1994.

Report of the Commission on Arbitration. New York: American Council on Arbitration, 1994.

Schultz, James A., and Harriet Whitney Schultz. "How You Can Profit from Gold." *Business Journal* 101, no. 2 (1993): 16–34.

Securities and You. *Holbrook Daily News,* 17 March 1994.

U.S. Senate Committee on Banking. *Report of Activities.* 99th Cong., 1st sess., 12 October 1985.

Reference List   Instead of using numbered notes for documentation, a writer may use author-date text citations and an accompanying reference list in place of a bibliography. This is a practical, easy-to-use system. Instead of placing a superscript number in the text corresponding to the note number, a writer places the author's last name and the year of the publication in parentheses after the quoted passage. No source footnotes or notes section for source notes is needed since a reader can locate the full data in the reference list.

If the same author has several works, all published in the same year, they can be differentiated by placing *a, b, c,* and so on after the appropriate year.

(Brown 1987a)
(Brown 1987b)

If two authors have the same last name, initials designating first names can be added.

(J. Brown 1987a)
(M. Brown 1994)

The abbreviation *et al.* is used for four or more authors.

(Davis, Hendricks, and Meirs 1994)
(Davis et al. 1991)

Since no notes section for source notes is needed, the list of references to which the text citations refer is placed after the glossary or, if there is no glossary, after the appendix or last text page. The list resembles a bibliography except that the date is placed immediately after the author's name. The following reference list entries are based on those developed in the preceding section to illustrate bibliography style and format.

Ardmore, Andrew M. 1994. "The True Cost of Inflation." Paper presented at the annual meeting of the Business Society, Chicago, Ill., June.

Brownstein, Samuel T., ed. 1994. *How to Reduce Your Taxes.* Chicago: ABC Press.

Flagg, Jennifer M. 1993. *The Stenmark Files.* Translated by Thomas P. Jones. New York: Jones & Associates.

_____, rev. 1989. *Labor Relations,* 5th ed. Concord, N.H.: McCain-Lewis.

Kline, Adam A., et al. 1994. "Investing in the Future: Key Growth Companies." *Industry Today,* 10 May, 5–11.

Redstone, Nancy C. 1994. Interview by the author. Peoria, Ill., 3 November.

Report of the Commission on Arbitration. 1994. New York: American Council on Arbitration.

Schultz, James A., and Harriet Whitney Schultz. 1993. "How You Can Profit from Gold." *Business Journal* 101, no. 2: 16–34.

Securities and You. 1994. *Holbrook Daily News,* 17 March.

U.S. Senate Committee on Banking. 1985. *Report of Activities.* 99th Cong., 1st sess., 12 October.

Index An index is often needed for a long, detailed report. Like the index at the back of this book, it will list alphabetically all major and subsidiary topics along with the applicable page numbers.

Indexes can be developed manually or with computer assistance. Even with computer assistance, you must still select the items to go in the index and keyboard the entries. However, with the appropriate indexing and sorting software, the computer will alphabetize entries, check cross-references, and format the entries.

If you prepare the index without the assistance of an indexing program, you will need a 3- by 5-inch index card file with alphabetical dividers. The entries can be handwritten or typed on the index cards; typing will take longer but will provide a clearer record and thus reduce the chances of introducing errors.

The first step is to take a copy of the document and on each page underline words and phrases that will become main entries or subentries. Most indexes to business documents have a combination of main entries and one level of subentries.

Input systems
    for computers, 22, 53–63
    optical character recognition for, 16
Input/output units, 53–63

In this example, *Input systems* and *Input/output units* are main entries. The first word of the main entry is initially capitalized, while the other words are lowercased unless they are proper nouns, trademarks, or other important words that are always capitalized. Main entries are arranged alphabetically by the first key word.

A subentry represents a topic of secondary importance. It appears under the main entry with which it is associated. Subentries, ordered alphabetically by the first key word, are indented an additional amount. Like main entries, subentries are composed of headings and page numbers. Subentries are lowercased throughout unless they contain proper nouns or other important words that should be capitalized. In the previous example, *for computers* and *optical character recognition for* are subentries.

Some indexers devise a system to distinguish entries and subentries while underlining key words during the initial step. They may, for example, put a checkmark by any underlined item that they believe should become a main entry. Whether you prefer to make such decisions while underlining key words or later, it is important to write only one item on a 3- by 5-inch card.

After you have underlined all appropriate items on the pages of the document, transfer each underlined word to a separate index card and after the word write the page number where it appears. Eventually you may have several cards for a single item or word, each with a different page number. After all underlined items have been transferred to cards, page numbers for succeeding cards with the *same* item can be transferred to the first card.

Arrange the cards by subject before you alphabetize them. For example, collect all cards pertaining to "input systems" together. If the decision about which item is a main entry was not made during the underlining step, make that decision now, and group the items that will become subentries *behind* the card for the main entry.

Arrange all main entry cards in alphabetical order, and arrange all subentry cards in alphabetical order behind each main entry. Once you have the cards organized alphabetically, you can begin editing and polishing. For example, the subentry card behind the main entry "Input systems" may say only "computers." You may decide to add the word *for* in front of *computers.*

Input systems
    for computers, 22, 53–63

If you have not already combined the various cards with pages numbered 22 and 53 to 63, do so now.

Add any cross-references that are needed, for example:

Input, 35, 61. *See also* Input systems.

Edit all main entries and subentries for consistency in capitalization and punctuation. When you are satisfied that the index is complete and accurate, type it on paper that matches the rest of the document, with the same spacing, margins, and so on.

Illustrations Tables and figures may be numbered consecutively from beginning to end (1, 2, 3, and so on) or consecutively within a chapter (1.1, 1.2, 2.1, 2.2, and so on). The number is preceded by the word the writer has chosen for the document, such as *Table, Figure, Exhibit,* or *Illustration.*

Reference should always be made to each illustration in the text: *See Table 7 and Figure 14.* Ideally, the appropriate table or figure is placed in the text at or near the text reference to it. In some business documents, though, illustrations are collected at the ends of chapters or at the end of the document after the appendix. In all cases, the numbers and titles that are used should be consistent with the numbers and titles appearing on the list(s) of illustrations in the front matter.

Table titles and figure captions should be as short as possible. Additional description can be added as a table subtitle or a figure legend or as a general note immediately after the body of the table or figure.

Table 12
Policy Claims by Age Group, 18–65

Figure 9
Basic Accounting Record-Keeping System

A table subtitle may be placed on a separate line below the table title or on the same line, separated from the title by a colon. A figure legend also may be on a separate line or on the same line separated from the caption by a period.

Table 2
Career Paths: Occupational Titles and Work Functions from Secretary to Information Worker

Figure 3
Chronological Resume. The chronological format starts with your latest job experience and works backward. Only inclusive years should be used, without months.

Footnotes to a table or figure should be formatted like text notes, described earlier, and placed immediately after the table or figure body. A source note, stating the source of the illustration (if any) is listed first, followed by any general note that applies to the table or figure as a whole. A source note is usually preceded by the word *Source* and followed by a colon (*Source:*); a general note is usually preceded by the word *Note* and followed by a colon (*Note:*). The word *Source,* however, does not precede a brief credit line for an illustration, for example, *Courtesy J. R. Miller Co.* Numbered or lettered notes are listed after any general note, and corresponding superscripts are placed at appropriate places in the body of the table or figure.

Column headings in tables should be brief and descriptive. If necessary, subheads may be included, or a two-tier "decked" head may be used.

1995	
Country	No. of Delegates

Important words should be capitalized, and column heads may be singular or plural, except for the head above the stub (left-hand column), which should be singular. The body of a table or figure may be either single- or double-spaced. If illustrations are prepared by computer, follow the instructions of your graphics, word processing, or desktop publishing program (see Chapter 4).

Transparencies Depending on your equipment capabilities, you may be expected to make transparencies to accompany a conference paper or other similar document. Check that the brand you plan to use is appropriate for your copier, and follow the instructions given with the transparency package and your equipment. Also check that the illustration to be displayed has been typed or drawn to fit the screen size of the overhead projector to be used.

RECORDS MANAGEMENT

Records management is a form of information management that involves the systematic analysis and control of all types of records, including paper records, magnetic media, microimage media, and optical media. Although the use of magnetic and optical media for document creation and storage is increasing, the use of paper has not diminished and, in fact, is also increasing.

The management of paper records is the primary focus in many offices, but the problems of finding adequate storage space are forcing organizations to develop procedures for handling nonpaper records. These records may include machine-readable media such as microforms, videotapes, and diskettes created by word processors, microcomputers, microfilm equipment, and various automated office systems. Large quantities of machine-readable magnetic disks and tapes are maintained by centralized computing facilities, and such records account for a rapidly growing percentage of most organizations' information resources. Like their paper counterparts, photographic and machine-readable records require appropriate storage facilities, must be carefully organized for effective retrieval, and must be protected from inadvertent damage or destruction.

THE SECRETARY'S ROLE

Secretaries are actively involved in the creation and maintenance of records. Whether or not an organization has a formal records-management program, it must have certain basic procedures to follow, or the accumulation of information will rapidly become unwieldy and chaotic.

The Secretary as Liaison

The size of an organization often determines what type of records-management program exists. Some mid- to large-size corporations, government agencies, or other organizations have formal centralized programs staffed by one or more full-time professionals. In such organizations departmental secretaries typically serve as liaisons who provide the records-management staff with essential information about departmental files and record-keeping requirements. They help prepare records inventories, implement records-retention schedules, prepare records for transmittal to off-site storage, identify potential microfilming applications, help select filing equipment, and help develop filing systems. In most departments the secretary is the person most familiar with record-keeping practices, and the liaison role is critical to the success of a records-management program.

The Secretary as Records Manager

In many smaller organizations — and some larger ones — there is no formal records-management program. Consequently, individual secretaries must assume full responsibility for records-management activities in their offices or departments. Although some aspects of records management require technical expertise, many records-management concepts are based on common sense and an orderly approach to problem solving characteristic of much of the professional secretary's work.

MANAGING ACTIVE RECORDS

Organization

Organizing files for easy retrieval of material later is a primary concern in records management. Often, though, the need to improve a filing system isn't apparent until it becomes increasingly difficult to find material. Also, filing is considered low-priority work, and secretaries tend to put it behind other work. This lack of attention and interest is a serious obstacle to designing and maintaining an effective and efficient system.

Official versus Personal Files

Where Official Files Are Used   Records managers often insist that an "official" file be established. The official-file concept emphasizes that an official file will be the sole, complete, and authoritative accumulation of an organization's records.

Official files are common in insurance claims processing, accounts receivable, purchasing, and other *transaction-oriented* activities, where work is performed in readily identifiable stages by office employees, each of whom contributes information to the file. Official files are found less frequently in scientific research, engineering, architecture, law, and other *project-oriented* activities, where the work is performed in a discretionary manner by professional employees.

Where Personal Files Are Used   In project-oriented settings individual employees usually maintain "personal" files. These files, stored in individual offices or in adjacent secretarial work areas, offer the convenience of close proximity, but they can vary greatly in scope and content.

Often, personal files are incomplete, and they may be arranged so that only their creator can comprehend them and, consequently, are inaccessible to other workers who may need to retrieve information when the creator is out of the office. If the creator leaves the organization before completing a project or other activity, it can be very difficult for others to reconstruct what was done.

When Both Personal and Official Files Are Needed   One way to solve the problem of only the creator knowing how to use his or her personal file is to establish this clear guideline: All participants in project-related activities *must* route all documents associated with the project to a single official file, even if *copies* are retained in the participant's personal file. Having one official file will eliminate time-consuming searches in multiple personal files, and having one complete file will increase the likelihood of retrieving accurate information.

Adopting an official file does not mean that personal files are unnecessary. Employees may still keep in their own offices certain *personal* or *sensitive* material, and they may want to keep *copies* of documents sent to the official files for use in their own offices. However, a personal file would not have any unrestricted business document that isn't in the official files as well. To control the growth of personal files, some organizations limit the amount of personal filing space to one cabinet or less per person.

Centralization   An official file may be centralized or decentralized. *Centralization* typically occurs at the department or division level, rarely at the organization level. A common pattern is a centralized repository for the official files of *all* projects undertaken by a given department or division.

Centralization encourages the development of filing systems and the standardization of filing practices. Staff training is simplified and work performance is enhanced, largely because personnel can give their full attention to filing work rather than dividing their time among a variety of clerical tasks. Compared to having a number of scattered files, centralization usually requires fewer file maintenance personnel. In addition, file control and security are usually improved. However, the distance between workers and the central file area often causes some delay in retrieval, and document-routing procedures must be strictly enforced if the central file is truly to be complete.

FILING SYSTEMS

A variety of filing systems are available, and different offices may use one or more systems. For example, an office may have an alphabetical personal file and also use the numerical official file of a particular department or division in which the office is located. Most offices or departments devise a system that is best suited for their specific type of activity. It may be a combination of standard alphabetical or numerical systems or some other adaptation of a standard system.

General Guidelines

Determining Location by Size   The room, section, bin, shelf, drawer, or other destination of file containers is usually determined first by size, before any consideration of informational content. Letter-size material, for example, is routed to a location with space suitable for letter-size documents, such as the lateral files illustrated on page 210. Similarly, reel-to-reel tapes are sent to a location with space suitable for reel-to-reel containers, and large rolled blueprints are sent to a location with space suitable for large tubes. When a variety of material of different sizes is segregated in this way, codes must be developed to identify the room, shelf, or other location of the material.

Designing an Appropriate System   Regardless of the general location of containers, and regardless whether the files are paper, magnetic, microform, or optical, a manageable system must be developed not only to accommodate current records but also to allow for future expansion.

Lateral Files

If more than one type of file includes the same material, for example both a paper and an electronic copy of a certain document, either the same naming system, alphabetical or numerical, must be used for both, or a cross-index must be developed for one of them. Secretaries who file documents on disk or other media should follow the file-naming instructions of the word processing or other program that they use.

The principal authority consulted by many systems designers is the Association of Records Managers and Administrators (ARMA International) in Prairie Village, Kansas. The ARMA publishes numerous books, reports, guidelines, standards, audiovisual aids, and home-study material. Secretaries who are helping devise an effective filing system should request a free *Technical Publications Catalog* from the ARMA.

Alphabetical Files

Some form of alphabetical filing can be applied to names, places, and other subjects. Although the same words may be used in both paper and computer filing, they would likely be abbreviated on a disk file. *Property Management,* for example, could be typed in full on the label of a paper file folder or the tab of a paper file division but would likely be abbreviated as *PtyMgt* or something else in a computer file name.

Alphabetizing Rules Although general A to Z alphabetizing rules are familiar, special rules apply in certain situations.

- Personal names are typically inverted for filing, with the last name first, then the first name, and last the middle initial (*Jones, John W.*).

- Last names beginning with *De, Des, La, Les, Van, Von,* or similar prefixes are treated as single filing units.

- Some systems, following widely accepted library practice, equate *Mc* with *Mac* for filing purposes. Others retain the conventional filing sequence.

- Acronyms and initialed names are often filed at the beginning of the appropriate alphabetical section, before any filing units consisting of complete words.

- Abbreviations are spelled out, as space allows, for filing as a full word.

- Cross-reference cards or sheets in the paper files, placed in the alphabetical location of an abbreviation, direct users to the spelled-out name. Similar cross-references are used in a computer index.

Sorting System As secretaries who have used computer file names are aware, there may be considerable variation in the sorting of spaces, hyphens, numeric digits, and other nonalphabetical characters found in names and subject headings. Some alphabetical filing systems use letter-by-letter sorting in which embedded spaces are disregarded and names or other filing units are treated as a continuous string of characters. Thus *diskette* precedes *disk file,* which is read as one word (*diskfile*). More commonly, the word-by-word sorting method is used. Here, *disk file* (two words) precedes *diskette*. In this method articles, such as *the,* and nonessential words, such as *for,* may be disregarded.

Tabs and Guides In paper files alphabetical filing is compatible with both the drawer- and shelf-type filing equipment mentioned later in this chapter. The name or other filing unit to be alphabetized commonly appears on the tab of a file folder or, in the case of card files, at the top of an index card. Guides or other dividers, marked with single- or double-letter alphabetical designations, separate groups of individual folders and draw your eye to the desired alphabetical section of the file. Although guides can be typed, several companies sell printed alphabetical guides. Alphabetical filing systems also use color coding for misfile detection, and a number of companies offer special folders for this purpose.

Subject Files

A–Z Filing. A simple A to Z filing system is often the easiest type of system to use for organizing material by subject. Little training is needed for setup or maintenance. When this system causes both general and specific headings to be mixed, however, a more complex variation may be needed.

For example, consider a hypothetical subject filing system used by the marketing department of an electronics company. This subject file contains product literature and published articles pertaining to various microcomputer products and components. A typical section of such a file might include these headings:

Anadex Printers
Application Software
BASIC Interpreters
Central Processing Units
Compilers and Interpreters
Diablo Printers
Display Terminals
Dot Matrix Printers
Hard-Disk Drives
Hazeltine Display Terminals
Magnetic-Tape Cassette Drives
Microprocessors
Microsoft BASIC Interpreter
Minifloppy Disk Drives
Operating Systems
Read-Only Memories
Typewriter-Quality Printers
Winchester Disk Drives

This list contains a mixture of general and specific headings. Material on related subjects — the various types of printers, for example — is scattered throughout the list. None of the general headings is subdivided to reflect specialized facets of a given topic, and there is no broad framework for establishing new headings. In actual practice, some subjects will likely contain many documents while others will contain only a few pages.

Hierarchical Filing. A more complex subject system — sometimes called a hierarchical subject system or a classification system — is designed to address these problems. Rather than have topical headings in conventional alphabetical sequence, the documents are arranged in a network of logically interrelated subdivisions representing general and specific facets of a given subject or activity.

The first step in designing this type of customized subject file is to subdivide all records into very broad groups called *series*. In the microcomputer information file example described previously, the subject file might include the following series:

Central Processing Units
Input Peripherals
Output Peripherals
Auxiliary Storage Devices
System Software
Application Software

Each of these series might be subdivided into two or more primary categories. For example:

Output Peripherals
    Paper Printers
    Display Terminals

A primary category may be further subdivided into secondary categories as follows:

Output Peripherals
    Paper Printers
        Dot Matrix Printers
        Typewriter-Quality Printers
        Line Printers
        Display Terminals
        CRT Displays
        Flat-Panel Displays

A secondary category may be further subdivided as required. For example:

    Output Peripherals
      Paper Printers
        Dot Matrix Printers
          Impact
          Thermal
          High Speed

Additional subdivision is possible within secondary categories. For example:

    Output Peripherals
      Paper Printers
        Dot Matrix Printers
          Impact
            Single Pass
            Multipass

Advantages of Hierarchical Filing. The subject system just described is truly systematic, because it reflects the structure of the activity through which the documents themselves were created. These systems are well suited to browsing since related documents are grouped together in the file. For the same reason they allow you to retrieve documents at varying levels. In the previous example all information about microcomputer output devices can be obtained in one location.

Disadvantages of Hierarchical Filing. This type of system is time-consuming to construct and typically requires a thorough understanding of the activity by which the documents were created. Thus to design a subject file for a marketing department that maintains information about microcomputers, you need to know quite a bit about the microcomputer industry. A secretary may lack the time and background required to design such a system, although it might be initially designed by a records manager or other trained specialist with the departmental secretary's assistance. Once such a system has been designed, you should be able to maintain and, if necessary, modify it.

As a further limitation, this type of subject system provides only one place to file a given document, even though the document's contents may reflect several different subjects or several facets of the same subject. This limitation can be overcome by duplicating documents for filing in multiple locations or by creating a cross-index. Neither method is entirely satisfactory, however. The obvious shortcoming of filing duplicate copies is that they substantially increase the load of filing labor and the size of the files. An index can provide a means of accessing documents by subjects other than the one under which the document if filed, but such indexes can also prove time-consuming to maintain.

Geographic Files   A geographic arrangement — a variant form of alphabetical filing — is widely used in sales offices, distribution outlets, and similar organizations. The typical geographic file is initially subdivided by state or other territorial grouping and is arranged alphabetically. Each state then may be subdivided into cities or regions, again arranged alphabetically. Within each of these subdivisions, names of correspondents or customers are arranged alphabetically. The purpose of geographic files is to cluster together the records pertaining to particular sales or distribution territories.

Numeric Files

As the name suggests, numeric systems are widely used for case files, transaction files, financial records, and similar applications in which documents are numbered and requested by an identifying number. In some cases, name files or other alphabetical files are converted to numeric codes to ensure privacy or to decrease filing labor. Compared with alphabetical systems, numeric systems require fewer rules to cover special situations, although a name-to-file number index must be maintained.

Sequential Numeric Files   Sequential numeric filing is the simplest and most widely encountered type of numeric system. It features the consecutive arrangement of files (1, 2, 3, and so on), with the highest numbers being added to the end of the file. Like alphabetical systems, sequential numeric systems are compatible with drawer- and shelf-type filing equipment. Printed or customized guides can be used to subdivide the file into readily identifiable segments, and color-coded guides are available to simplify misfile detection. Sequential numeric filing systems are easily learned and implemented, but several significant disadvantages limit their utility in certain situations.

In situations in which numbers are sequentially assigned to newly created folders, the most active records will be clustered at the end of the file. In large centralized filing situations, therefore, personnel often must wait to file or retrieve documents. A related limitation is the inequitable distribution of file-maintenance work. Also, sequential numeric systems typically require time-consuming "backshifting" of folders to make room at the end of the file for newly created records as older records are purged.

Terminal-Digit Files Terminal-digit systems are well suited to large centralized records-management applications where reference activity must be distributed throughout a file and responsibility for particular file segments will be assigned to specific people. Terminal-digit techniques are especially useful in accounts payable, accounts receivable, insurance claims adjustment, and similar transaction-processing applications. They are also widely used in medical records management.

The terminal-digit system requires an identifier of six or more digits. When shorter record numbers are involved, the number sequences can be padded with zeros to increase the length. For filing purposes a number is rewritten as three pairs of two digits each, with the resulting pairs being separated by hyphens. For example:

- The number *365461* is subdivided as *36–54–61* where *61* is described as the primary pair of digits, *54* as the secondary pair, and *36* as the tertiary pair.

- The digit pairs are rearranged accordingly, and the resulting number is filed as if it were *615436.* It will be physically adjacent to *355461* and *375461.*

- Number *365462,* which would normally follow *365461* in a conventional sequential numeric system, will be filed as *625436* and will be located in a different part of the file between folders numbered *355462* and *375462.*

The scattering of sequentially numbered files allows for a more equitable distribution of filing, reference, purging, and other file-maintenance activity. Furthermore, the backshifting of folders following purging is eliminated.

Generally, the original transaction number, case number, or other identifier is not changed on a file folder. The required transpositions are made at the time the folders are to be filed or retrieved. As with sequential numeric systems, terminal-digit systems commonly have printed or customized numeric guides in the paper files to divide a file into easily recognizable segments. Color-coded folders also can be used.

Middle-Digit Files Middle-digit systems, a variant form of nonsequential numeric filing, also require a six-digit record identifier divided into three pairs of two digits each. But unlike the case with the terminal-digit system, in this system the middle pair of digits is considered the primary pair, the first pair of digits is considered the secondary pair, and the third pair of digits is considered the tertiary pair. For example, number *365461* would be filed as *543661.*

As with terminal-digit filing, printed or customized guides and color-coded folders can be used in the paper files. In large centralized applications where the even distribution of filing activity is desired, a middle-digit arrangement results in a scattering effect similar to, but somewhat less radical than, that of terminal-digit filing. In certain situations, however, conversion from sequential numeric to middle-digit filing can prove simpler than conversion to terminal-digit filing, since groups of one hundred consecutively numbered folders can be moved at one time.

Chronological Files   Chronological filing — a variation of numeric filing — is widely used in small personal files. In chronological filing, records are arranged by date, with the most recent date at the beginning. It is commonly used for correspondence and transaction files.

Alphanumeric Files

Alphanumeric systems, in which the file identifier contains a mixture of alphabetical characters and numeric digits, combine alphabetical and sequential numeric filing techniques. Depending on the procedure used, numerals may be sorted before or after alphabetical characters.

Series Designations   In some filing systems, individual series are assigned a numeric or alphanumeric designation. For example:

100	Central Processing Units
200	Input Peripherals
300	Output Peripherals
400	Auxiliary Storage Devices
500	System Software
600	Application Software

The hierarchical nature of such systems can be reflected in decimal subdivisions indicating the logical subordination of categories to one another and primary categories to series. Using decimal subdivisions, for example, the series "Output Peripherals" might be subdivided as follows:

```
300   Output Peripherals
      301   Paper Printers
            301.01   Dot Matrix Printers
                     301.0101   Impact
                                301.010101   Single Pass
                                301.010102   Multipass
                     301.0102   Thermal
            301.02   Typewriter-Quality Printers
                     301.0201   Selectric
                     301.0202   Daisy Wheel
                     301.0203   Print Thimble
            301.03   Line Printers
                     301.0301   Low Speed
                     301.0302   Medium Speed
                     301.0303   High Speed
      302   Display Terminals
            302.01   CRT Displays
            302.02   Flat Panel Displays
                     302.0201   LCD Displays
                     302.0202   Electroluminescent Displays
```

Phonetic Filing   Phonetic filing is designed for large name files in which surnames may sound alike (*Smith, Smythe*) but have variant spellings or frequent misspellings. In a primitive form of phonetic filing, one of the spellings of a given surname is selected for use, and all its variant spellings are filed under that form. Cross-references are placed in the file to direct the user to the right spelling.

The Soundex method, a more sophisticated approach to phonetic filing, was developed by Remington Rand. It converts surnames to a four-character alphanumeric code that generally results in the identical filing of similar sounding names of different spellings. The following table is used to create the code:

LETTERS	CODE NUMBER
B, F, P, V	1
C, J, K, Q, S, X, Z	2
D, T	3
L	4
M, N	5
R	6

In Soundex coding, the first letter of the surname becomes the first alphanumeric code character. All vowels and the consonants *h, w,* and *y* are then dropped, and the first three remaining characters are converted to numeric digits using the table. Thus the surname *Johnson* would be coded as *J525,* as would *Jahnsen.* If a name lacks a sufficient number of consonants, the code is completed with zeros. Double letters are treated as a single character as are those adjacent characters with an equivalent numeric value in the Soundex table. Soundex codes are filed according to rules for alphanumeric arrangements.

Electronic Files

Electronic Storage and Retrieval With computer-assisted document indexing, index data are stored and processed electronically, but the documents themselves remain in paper or microform. True electronic filing systems store entire documents in machine-readable, computer-processable form on magnetic disks or other media.

On-Line Storage. After creating a document, the operator can enter a file name or other indexing term. Rather than print out a copy for storage in paper files or by microfilming, the document is retained on a disk for later retrieval. This technique is particularly effective in multi-terminal installations where documents can be accessed from remote workstations. Storing documents in computer-processable form saves space compared to paper-filing space requirements, and retrieval occurs at high speeds.

Although the concept of electronic filing is attractive, data stored on computer-processable magnetic media are not stable and must be recopied periodically to prevent loss from deterioration. Also, data generated by one word processing system are often incompatible with other systems or with newer versions of the same system, thereby prohibiting the electronic transfer of documents from one system to another.

Off-Line Storage. For extensive records and large databases, the storage space provided by most word processors is too limited. As available disk space becomes full, older records must be transferred elsewhere for off-line storage, for example magnetic tape or microfilm. The use of CD-ROMs and other recording media provides additional disk-storage opportunities, thereby enhancing the potential of electronic filing systems by allowing more documents to remain on-line for a longer period.

Refer to Chapter 1, "The Parts of a Computer," for a description of available storage devices, including the diskette, hard disk, CD-ROM, WORM disk, magneto optical disk, and videodisk.

Document Retrieval. Compared to computer-assisted indexing of paper or microform documents, electronic filing offers a single-step retrieval procedure at the keyboard. Index data and entire documents can be displayed at the same workstation, and the retrieved documents can be re-filed or routed to printers for paper output. Storage and retrieval systems usually include sophisticated software that can search the entire text of documents for specified key words or phrases, thereby significantly expanding the retrieval capabilities.

In large, centralized filing facilities, retrieval is handled by authorized file personnel who follow established company procedures for retrieval and release to interested personnel. Passwords, antiviral programs, and other safeguards are part of any centralized electronic filing system.

Computer Indexing Indexes are often needed in filing systems. A numeric system, for example, may need an index to names or other subjects. A hierarchical system may need an index to individual topics that are grouped under more general headings. Virtually any type of index that is desired can be maintained by computer. Since a computer can move or adjust copy automatically, new entries can be added and an up-to-the-minute index printed out as needed.

In computer-assisted document indexing of paper files, you first search a computer-maintained index — usually via an on-line terminal, although some systems use computer-printed indexes. In the on-line mode the search is interactive. Computer software guides you in the selection and narrowing of appropriate index terms. If the search is successful, you are instructed to remove specific numbered documents from a paper file.

Required Hardware and Software. The required computer hardware usually includes a large-scale mini- or microcomputer, one or more video terminals or equivalent input devices for the entry of index data, one or more video displays or printers used in retrieval operations, and magnetic disks or other media for storing index data. Either a commercial or custom-developed program may be used. Regardless, the indexing software must permit the entry of index data about specific documents; the addition, deletion, or other modification of previously entered index data; and the identification of documents to be retrieved.

Systems Design. The design of computer-assisted document indexing systems begins with the identification of indexing parameters. An *indexing parameter* is a category of information by which a document will be retrieved. Although specific parameters will vary with the application, the following list is suitable for a broad range of document indexing requirements:

- *Document accession number:* A sequentially assigned identifier. In applications in which the indexing system supports several departments or activities, alphabetical or alphanumeric prefixes may be used to identify documents by originating department, project name, or other broad grouping. In any case, multipage documents are assigned a single identifier.

- *Document type:* Letter, memorandum, report, fax, and so on. In many applications, document types are abbreviated by a simple two-character identifier.

- *Document originator:* The name of the person who created or signed the document.

- *Originator affiliation:* The name of the internal department or outside organization with which the document originator is associated.

- *Document recipient:* The name of the addressee or other recipient of the document.

- *Recipient affiliation:* The name of the internal department or outside organization to which the document is addressed.

- *Document date:* Month, day, and year, as appropriate.

- *Subject(s):* Single-term key words or multiterm key phrases indicating the document's subject content. Most systems permit the assignment of three to six subjects to a single document.

- *An abstract:* A brief summary of document content. Although it is not provided in every application, an abstract, when retrieved on-line, provides information that might satisfy you in place of the entire document and enables you to determine that particular documents are not relevant and need not be removed from the document file.

Indexing Procedure. Typically, documents are routed to a central file area or other indexing point where numbers are assigned. Index parameters are then entered at a computer terminal or other input device for on-line storage. Often, the indexing software displays a formatted screen with labeled areas and adjacent blank spaces corresponding to index parameters. The terminal operator fills in the blank spaces with the index terms relevant to a given document.

Storage of Indexed Documents. Following indexing, paper documents are placed in file cabinets in appropriate sequence. This constitutes the major physical difference between computer-assisted document indexing and conventional filing systems where logically related documents are physically grouped within a file. In computer-assisted indexing systems, documents stored in the same portion of a file are seldom related to one another. Logical relationships among documents are maintained in the *index;* related documents can be retrieved through index searches.

Retrieval of Indexed Documents. To retrieve documents, you would enter a combination of index terms and search commands at an on-line terminal. Computer-assisted document indexing systems are much more effective than conventional systems in complicated retrieval operations involving multiple indexing parameters, such as all of the correspondence received by a particular person on a given subject between specified dates. Because the index is searched electronically, the total transaction time will prove shorter than that associated with conventional filing systems.

If a search is successful, one or more numbers will be displayed. Multiple documents will usually be scattered throughout the paper files, but the computer-assisted indexing produces lists of documents that were preselected for relevance. If that isn't adequate, abstracts can be included to make the selection process even more precise.

In a variant approach, computer-assisted retrieval (CAR), documents are recorded on microfilm or microfiche and their microform addresses are indexed as just described for paper storage. At retrieval time you select a particular film and frame location.

Electronic versus Conventional Systems   Once a computer-assisted document indexing system has been established, many secretaries find it easier to use than a conventional system. Computer-assisted systems are compatible with both centralized and decentralized file configurations. Both index and document storage can be centralized, or the storage of documents can be decentralized within individual departments while an on-line index resides in a centralized computer system. In a decentralized approach both documents and index data can be maintained at the department level, with the index data residing in a microcomputer located in the file area.

FILING EQUIPMENT AND SUPPLIES

Paper Files

Containers   Paper files represent the oldest form of storage, and the associated equipment and supplies are familiar in most offices. The most common equipment or container is the standard metal office file cabinet, usually with two or more drawers. But other styles include open-shelf units, portable files, rotary files, tray files, motorized files, printout files, and miscellaneous cartons and containers for storing both standard and odd-size paper documents. Most office cabinets have locks, and the keys are available only to certain personnel. Often the secretary and his or her employer are the only personnel authorized to remove material from the office files.

Supplies   Most containers for paper storage have labels containing large letters to identify the contents. File folders, guides, and tabs also contain labels with printed or typed words, letters, numbers, or other designations to identify the associated material. Standard labels, folders, guides, cross-reference sheets, and *Out* cards are sold in office-supply stores. All of these items are available in different colors so that offices can use a color-coding system to distinguish categories and easily spot misfiles.

Out cards, placed in the files when a folder or document is removed, provide pertinent data such as who has the material, when it was removed, and when it is due back. *Cross-reference sheets* similarly provide a place to record pertinent data. For example, if a document could logically be filed under both *Western Manufacturing* and *Suppliers,* a cross-reference sheet could be placed in the *W* section of the files: *Western Manufacturing. See Suppliers.* Stores that sell filing equipment and supplies usually provide free catalogs and brochures for individuals and businesses that purchase this type of material.

Nonpaper Files

Containers   Containers and labels are also needed for nonpaper files, such as magnetic disks and tapes, optical disks, CD-ROMs, and microforms. Since this type of storage media is usually very small, the containers also may be relatively small. Diskettes, for example, may be filed in small plastic boxes that in turn are stored in a dust-free, locked cabinet. Tapes, too, may be kept in round metal or plastic containers.

Supplies   Such storage containers and the cabinets in which they are stored must be labeled the same as the containers used for paper files. Office-supply stores and computer dealers provide free catalogs displaying a variety of containers and labels.

REMINDER AND FOLLOW-UP SYSTEMS

All businesses need some type of records for handling reminders and follow-ups. Usually, this involves calendars and tickler or follow-up files.

Executive-Secretary Communication

Communication between the executive and secretary concerning calendar scheduling is imperative. Imagine the embarrassment that might ensue if the executive would schedule an appointment with one guest or client while you would schedule another appointment for the same hour. One way to avoid double bookings is to have an understanding with the executive whereby you schedule *tentative* appointments. You would notify the visitor that the meeting or appointment is tentative and that confirmation will follow. After checking the date and time with the executive, you would then confirm the appointment and note it on both calendars. In addition, you should routinely check the executive's calendar early each morning — and throughout the day, if warranted — to be certain that the items on your calendar correspond to the items on the executive's calendar.

Calendar Management

Effective calendar management not only means having the right calendars and keeping notations consistent on both your calendar and the executive's calendar; it means making the best possible use of the calendar as a reminder system, scheduling both short-term and long-term events.

Calendar Entries Many activities should be entered more than once. If a client's anniversary is August 9, you must make a notation on the page for August 9 and also note on August 1 or 2 that the executive should be reminded to write the letter. Then make a notation on your calendar to type and mail the letter by August 4 or 5, depending on the client's location.

From previous calendars you can compile a list of annual events — holidays, tax dates, family birthdays, insurance-premium due dates, and so on. Add those that pertain only to *your* duties to *your* calendar, but put those that concern the executive on *both* calendars. Don't worry if the dates change later. You can always change them on the calendar at that time. Until then, having them on the calendar will at least remind you and the executive that an activity is approaching.

Types of Calendars Most secretaries like a desk calendar that opens flat on the desk to the current day. For scheduling numerous appointments or activities, a calendar with 15-minute time slots is helpful. Executives also like a desk calendar and, in addition, may carry a small pocket calendar while traveling or attending meetings. If your boss has two calendars, desk and pocket, you will need to keep both consistent with your calendar. Depending on the type of work in your office, you may also be required to maintain an oversize wall or desk calendar showing special dates, such as meeting dates, for a week, a month, or even a year.

Electronic reminder systems are also used in automated offices (described in the next section), but they supplement rather than replace desk or pocket calendars. Often it is faster and easier to jot down something on a paper calendar than it is to go to the computer, call up the electronic calendar, key in the entry, and print out a revised copy.

Tickler Files

Advantage of Tickler Files Sometimes a tickler file is more appropriate than a calendar reminder. For example, if you have written a letter and need a reply by a certain date, you will have to follow-up before that date to be certain that you receive a reply on time. It might be easier to put a copy of your letter in a tickler file. If your boss needs someone's report before leaving town, you also could put a memo about it in the tickler files.

Types of Follow-Up Files The two standard types of conventional follow-up files are letter-size and card-size files. The card-size files are often kept on top of the secretary's desk, and the letter-size files may be kept in a desk file drawer or other nearby file. A variety of electronic follow-up and reminder systems are also available.

Letter Follow-up Files. The letter-size follow-up file needs twelve monthly folders and thirty-one daily folders, as well as one folder for future years. Copies of correspondence or memo reminders that need follow-up on a certain day are dropped into the folder for that day. Usually, the current month's daily folders are placed first in the file, followed by the twelve monthly folders and, last, the one folder for future years. As each day arrives, you should check the folder for that day and send out follow-up notices as needed. Place the new follow-up copy and the previous copy in the folder for another day to be followed up again if no reply is received. As soon as a reply is received, remove all initial and follow-up copies.

Card Tickler Files. A card tickler file is arranged the same way except that copies of full-size letters cannot be dropped in folders. Instead, notations are written or typed on cards, and the cards are then filed behind numbered guides (one through thirty-one), monthly guides, or the one guide for future years.

Electronic Follow-up Files. With an electronic follow-up system you key in the appropriate reminder instead of typing or writing it on a card. The computer organizes your entries by day and time of day so that each morning you can print out a list of items that need follow-up on that date. Most reminder software programs can display or print out daily, weekly, monthly, or annual schedules. As something is taken care of, it is deleted from the program.

MANAGING INACTIVE RECORDS

Some records, although they are no longer referred to daily, must be kept to meet legal requirements, because of their historical significance, or simply in case they need to be consulted some time in the future. Often, inactive paper records accumulate in office work areas and occupy valuable space in the active filing cabinets. This creates overcrowding, an increase in the potential for misfiles, and wasted time in handling filing duties.

Records Inventory

Taking inventory of existing records is a necessary first step before plans to store or dispose of the records can be put into effect.

In organizations with formal, centralized records-management programs, individual departmental secretaries are often asked to complete inventory worksheets specifically designed to gather essential data about the department's records. In some cases the records-management staff will also interview secretaries and other department members. In the absence of a centralized records-management program, individual secretaries must prepare their own survey instruments and conduct their own inventories. In either case records are commonly inventoried at the series level. A *record series* is a group of related documents supporting a common activity and usually having a common name.

Examples of widely encountered record series include general correspondence, budget reports, purchase orders, and personnel files, but every department will have some series that are unique to it and reflect its work. For each series, the following information is commonly collected:

- The name by which the series is known to department members and other users

- The form name and number if the series consists of standardized forms

- A brief description and statement of purpose, indicating the functions that the series supports

- Physical location — that is, the address of the office or other facility where the records are stored

- Inclusive dates

- Physical format: paper, microfilm, videotape, floppy disks, and so forth

- The arrangement of documents or other records within the series — for example, alphabetical by patient name for a medical record series or numeric by claim number for a series of insurance files

- Series volume, expressed in terms of the number, type, and condition of the file cabinets or storage containers occupied by the records

- Annual growth rate, typically estimated by comparing file segments for different years or, if necessary, by counting documents from a representative sample of the series

- Physical attributes, such as the size of documents or other media condition, color, and texture

- Frequency of reference and names of user departments

In most cases, this information can be determined by carefully examining the records or by interviewing appropriate personnel. If desired, inventory results can be summarized on a tabular worksheet by listing the individual series in rows and the categories of information in columns.

Records Scheduling

Records should never be discarded without authorization, and a properly developed schedule will help to prevent such mistakes.

Retention Schedule   A schedule should list all record series and state the retention period for each type of record and where it is to be stored. If something is to be discarded, the schedule will also state the date and method of destruction. Confidential records, for example, might have to be shredded, whereas surplus conference programs, which provide public information, might be delivered intact to a recycling site.

Most schedules indicate whether a record series or type of document should be held for a short, medium, or long term.

Short-term retention: Many records are needed for a brief period but have little continuing utility and will be discarded a short time — perhaps several months to two years — after their creation or receipt. Such records are typically retained in office locations until discarded.

Medium-term retention: Other records must be retained for a specified period — perhaps for one to ten years — but eventually will be discarded. Such records are often retained in office locations during a relatively brief initial period of active reference and, when reference activity subsides, are transferred to lower-cost, off-site storage facilities from which they are eventually discarded.

Long-term retention: A final, often large, group of records must be retained indefinitely. In many cases, such records are put on magnetic tape, optical disk, or microfilm to save space, and the original paper documents are discarded. Some may be stored in office locations or off-site, depending on the possibility that they may be consulted from time to time.

Legal requirements for retaining records may relate to tax records, pension funds, waste disposal, and other activities subject to government regulation. Often, government contracts have clauses that specify what has to be retained and for how long. State statutes, which vary from state to state, also specify minimum or maximum retention periods for certain records. Because of the legal requirements for some records, retention and disposal schedules are usually developed by or at least reviewed by an attorney. Also, because secretaries work with files and other records almost daily, the information they can provide is very valuable in any records-management program. In addition, records-management textbooks and publications provided by the ARMA and other professional groups are available to help those who need guidance in developing a retention and disposal schedule.

Periodic Reviews Developing a retention and disposal schedule is only the first step, albeit an important step. Once a schedule has been prepared, it should be open to periodic review and modification as needed.

Retention and disposal schedules must be revised periodically as new records series are created and as experience reveals the need for modification of previously established retention periods. An annual review of retention schedules is strongly recommended.

The actual *implementation* of retention schedules is typically the secretary's responsibility. Some secretaries prefer to allot a specific period during the summer or other slack periods for this purpose. In some organizations the records-management unit performs compliance audits to determine that retention schedules are being appropriately implemented.

Records Centers

A *records center* is a warehouse designed specifically to store inactive records until they are destroyed. This type of storage facility differs from one providing permanent storage. Some records centers won't accept records that don't have a destruction date; others, however, will additionally house permanent records if they have been placed on disks, tapes, or microform media.

Inactive Records Storage   Whether the records are in hard copy, magnetic or optical media, or film, they must be placed in suitable boxes or other containers. Each container must then be labeled, and the records must be described on a special inventory form. This form should indicate not only the contents but the location of the storage container in the warehouse. Secretaries and other personnel who are involved in transferring inactive records should follow the organization's instructions for packing, labeling, and inventorying.

Precautions must be taken to protect the documents from theft or from damage or destruction caused by fire, humidity, water, or other peril. Protection, therefore, is a principal consideration in selecting a storage site.

Inactive Records Retrieval   Some inactive items will occasionally be needed by the transmitting department. Specific reference arrangements vary considerably. In the absence of a formal records-management program, for example, a records center may be shared by several departments, each of which services its own records. When a formal records-management program exists, the records center is usually operated by a small staff. In such organizations the records center functions as a custodial agency rather than a generally accessible reference library.

Records center storage is usually considered an extension of the transmitting department's own filing space, and the department controls access to the transmitted records just as if they had never left its own offices. Reference requests generally require departmental approval. Before contacting the records center, the department will consult its copies of the records inventory sheets to determine the shipment number and container location of the desired records. The records center typically responds to reference requests by returning the requested containers or file folders to the transmitting office. If only a few items are involved, some records centers will provide photocopies.

Microstorage

If an organization is storing massive amounts of paper documents, the space requirements and the cost will eventually become overwhelming. Many organizations, therefore, must copy paper records onto a reduced-size media. The most popular media for reduced-size storage are described in Chapter 1 (diskettes, WORM disks, CD-ROMs, magnetic tape, optical disks, videodisks, and microforms). Some of these media are more suitable than others. Diskettes, for example, hold relatively little information and must be recopied periodically because of deterioration. Microforms, on the other hand, are relatively more permanent, although a secure and protected environment is needed for all types of permanent records.

Microrecords Production   Material stored on computer diskettes and tapes can be easily copied from hard-disk files or scanned from hard-copy sources. Microforms can be produced from paper documents (*source-document microfilming*) or from computer-processed data (*computer-output microfilm*). Microfilm cameras and other equipment are needed for source-document microfilming. The processed film is then duplicated to provide an extra security (or working) copy. The process of computer-output microfilming (COM) transfers computer-processed, machine-readable data directly onto microfilm or microfiche. Organizations may have their own COM recorders or retain a service bureau specializing in COM production.

Display and Printing   Although microforms are intended for permanent storage, certain records must be recalled from time to time. Special display and printing equipment is then needed to enlarge and read the microimages. Microform readers are a type of projection device used for this purpose. If the equipment is both a reader and a printer, you can either view a document on a screen, similar to a computer display, or print out a hard copy of it.

Unlike microforms, magnetic tapes and disks do not require additional equipment. They can be viewed on the computer monitor and printed out on the computer printer the same as any freshly created computer document. Equipment needs — and the cost — are, therefore, an important consideration in developing an appropriate records-management program.

TELECOMMUNICATIONS

CHAPTER

8

Telecommunication is communication between two or more people at different locations using equipment to overcome the distance between them. This may involve traditional telephone communication, electronic mail, voice mail, or any other conventional or electronic exchange, usually over the telephone lines or by satellite. This chapter focuses on voice communication, and Chapter 9 describes the *written* forms of communication that are transmitted by way of the telephone lines.

As offices become more integrated, telecommunications assumes a prominent place among the new technologies. Computers, fax machines, and copiers in particular are all linked to modern telecommunications systems. Industry experts predict that the workstation will soon be completely integrated, with the distinction between voice and data systems fading and voice technology becoming the predominant form of communication.

THE TELEPHONE INDUSTRY

With the court-ordered divestiture of AT&T, twenty-two local operating companies of the Bell System were combined into seven independent regional operating companies. The new companies and their antecedents are listed in Table 8.1. Under the new arrangement the Bell Operating Companies provide the actual telephone network, your connection to it, and all the customer services involved, much like a utility company supplies electricity. You can get your telephone instruments from any vendor you choose and should contact that vendor for any equipment problems. But you should go to the telephone company to get line problems fixed.

Table 8.1   Bell Operating Companies

COMPANY	BELL ANTECEDENTS
Nynex Corporation	New York Telephone New England Telephone
Bell Atlantic Corporation	Bell of Pennsylvania Diamond State (Delaware) Telephone Chesapeake & Potomac Telephone of Washington, DC Chesapeake & Potomac Telephone of Maryland Chesapeake & Potomac Telephone of Virginia Chesapeake & Potomac Telephone of West Virginia New Jersey Bell
Ameritech	Illinois Bell Indiana Bell Michigan Bell Ohio Bell Wisconsin Telephone
BellSouth Corporation	Southern Bell SouthCentral Bell
Southwestern Bell Corporation	Southwestern Bell Telephone Co.
U.S. West Inc.	Northwestern Bell Mountain Bell Pacific Northwest Bell
Pacific Telesis Group	Pacific Telephone Nevada Telephone

Other Common Carriers

Other Common Carriers (OCCs), also called *Specialized Common Carriers* (SCCs), are non-Bell long-distance telephone companies to which you can subscribe. Some have their own intercity microwave and cable networks, while others, called *resellers,* lease circuits or WATS lines from telephone companies. To use an OCC, follow the particular company's instructions.

Transmission Facilities

A ten-digit telephone number (such as 311-555-6611) is standard in the United States and Canada. In this example the first three digits (311) designate the Area Code, the next three (555) designate the central office or exchange to which the line is attached, and the last four (6611) designate the line. In many areas long-distance numbers must be preceded by the digit *1*.

All telephones are connected to a central office where the switching takes place. Calls between numbers of the same prefix are handled within the central office. Calls to numbers with a different prefix must be routed over interoffice trunk lines. In large cities with many central offices, interoffice calls are routed through tandem offices. Calls to another Area Code are routed through your central office's associated toll center. The call may be routed through various other switching centers, depending on destination and line traffic, until the connection has been completed. Even if you call the same long-distance number many times, the routing could be different each time.

TELEPHONE TECHNOLOGY

An enormous proportion of any modern organization's business is conducted over the telephone. Effective use of the telephone depends on an understanding of the functioning and capabilities of the hardware and an awareness of proper telephone techniques. The first part of this chapter describes the hardware, and the second part deals with the correct ways to use the telephone.

Most telephones use pushbutton dial mechanisms. If you have an older rotary telephone subscription with the telephone company, however, you can only use a rotary telephone; if you have a pushbutton subscription, you may be able to use either.

Rotary telephones trigger the telephone company switching mechanisms by sending pulses of electricity. Pushbutton telephones send musical tones to the switching mechanisms. You must push each button for at least two tenths of a second to be sure of producing the right tone. A pulse-dialing telephone has pushbuttons but produces the same dial pulses as those of a rotary telephone. A pushbutton mechanism is required to use most of the telephone features described in this chapter.

Telephone Systems

Telephone systems are designed for different size offices. Traditionally, small and medium-size offices used key, or pushbutton, systems, and larger offices had private branch exchanges (PBXs). As the technology evolves, however, the distinction is disappearing, and new systems may borrow features from both types of systems. The five principal types of systems are the following:

- *Two-line telephone.* Very small offices may use only two outside lines, with two to three telephones plugged into wall jacks. When making or answering a call, you press a key to select line one or line two.

- *KSU-less system.* This system, suitable for up to five people, refers to a system that has no central apparatus. Since all the gadgetry to run the system is inside the telephones, they can be wired together without the need for a key service unit (KSU), or central apparatus. These systems offer itercoms and standard features of a regular telephone, such as speed dialing.

- *Key system.* The most popular system for small- to medium-size offices, the key system can service as few as five or as many as fifty people. With a key system, anyone — not just a central operator — can answer incoming calls at his or her extension, place a call on hold, or call another extension. This system is often used when it doesn't matter who answers the telephone.

- *PBX.* Traditionally, exchanges have been used for organizations with more than fifty people; current PBXs, in fact, can serve more than a hundred people. With this type of system all calls go to a central mechanism that generally requires one or more attendants to route each call to the right extension.

- *Hybrid.* Large key systems and small PBXs may have hybrid features that appeal to medium-size organizations. These systems may have a PBX-type attendant console but will also allow each user to have a desk telephone that functions like a key system. Fax and modem telephone lines are often more easily integrated with a hybrid type of system.

Telephone Features

As new telephone systems are developed, the traditional features may change, and new ones may be added. The fact that features once applied only to a key system or a PBX system may now apply to both is particularly evident in the case of a hybrid system or a PBX system that includes *piggybacking*. In the latter case an organization would have a general PBX system but would also have key systems in certain offices or departments.

The following telephone features, or some variation of them, are widely available:

- *Answering machines:* These devices answer the telephone with a recording and then record whatever message the caller leaves. Advanced features include a remote key allowing you to call in from another telephone and listen to the recorded messages. Units with a speaker can be used for call screening. You leave the machine on, and if you hear someone to whom you want to talk leaving a message, you can break in and speak to that caller.

  Combination answering machines and pagers can both take messages and broadcast messages to hundreds of pagers in virtually any location. Some digital units will receive voice and fax mail messages and forward them to you wherever you are.

- *Automatic attendant:* With this feature a digitally recorded message greets callers and allows them to route themselves to the desired extension or voice mailbox by pressing certain numbers. Both PBX and key systems may offer this feature as an option.

- *Automatic call distribution:* Organizations such as airline reservation offices that experience a lot of incoming calls will usually set up a department of call takers served by an automatic call distributor (ACD). The ACD distributes incoming calls to the call takers, and calls that cannot be answered are put on hold with music and a reassuring message. Sophisticated ACDs can gather statistics on how many calls were abandoned, break down the traffic by time of day, and monitor the productivity of the individual call takers such as airline ticket agents.

- *Automatic dialing:* Also called *speed dialing, memory dialing,* or *abbreviated dialing,* this feature allows you to program a list of telephone numbers (intercom or outside) into your desk telephone.

Depending on the system, a programmed number can be reached either by pushing a button or by dialing code numbers.

- *Call accounting:* Through a feature sometimes called *station message detail recording* (SMDR), you receive a printout of every call made from each extension. Some SMDRs provide detailed management reports that analyze telephone traffic.

- *Call forwarding:* With call forwarding you can program your system so that calls will be routed to another extension if no one answers after a certain number of rings or if the line is busy.

- *Call transferring:* This feature allows you to transfer a call to another telephone number either by dialing a special code or by momentarily depressing the switch hook and then dialing the new number.

- *Call waiting:* This feature gives you a visual or audible signal while you are on the line if someone else is trying to reach you. You then have the option of putting the present call on hold while you answer the other call.

- *Caller ID:* Through a small device attached to your telephone or built into it, you can see the telephone number of an incoming call on a small display before you answer the call. In areas where it is available, Caller ID Service must be arranged through your local telephone company. Callers, however, can make arrangements to block the display of their numbers as well as any other information the device may provide about them.

- *Camp on:* If your line is busy, the attendant can use camp on to attach a call to your line, and the call will go through as soon as you have hung up.

- *Conferencing:* With call conferencing you can be connected to several outside lines at once. All the parties can talk and hear each other. Although conferencing is often limited to three lines, it can be expanded further to as many as six or perhaps more. For information on teleconferencing, refer to Chapter 12.

- *Cordless telephones:* The receivers of portable telephones can be picked up and used as portable units within a specified distance from the source.

- *Dial restrictions:* A dial-restrictions device prevents unauthorized people from dialing restricted outside numbers, exchanges, area codes, long-distance numbers, or any other numbers. Such systems are usually not as sophisticated as PBX long-distance control systems.

- *Digital transmission:* Some modern PBX systems use not only computerized switching mechanisms but also computerized telephone instruments. The telephone encodes your voice as a high-speed digital bit stream. Since computers also use digital transmission techniques, it may be possible to connect computer equipment directly to the office telephone network and transmit at very high speeds. This advantage does not extend to outside (nondigital) lines.

   Some digital telephones include a one-line alphanumeric readout that can give the number of the calling party, show the cost of your call while still in progress, and provide other information, while also doubling as a digital clock.

- *Direct inward dialing:* Direct inward dialing (DID) systems allow telephone numbers within a company to be reached by dialing them directly from the outside. However, outgoing calls are subject to the office's PBX or key system. Calls between numbers within the DID system can be placed as conference calls by dialing the last four digits.

   The DID system may be installed in addition to the PBX, it may be a feature of the PBX, or it may be embodied in special wiring at the telephone company's facilities. This last variant is often called a Centrex system, described later in the section about telephone services.

- *Direct inward system access:* With direct inward system access (DISA) you can call into a system as though you were in the building that houses the system. A person at home could therefore access the company system and place a long-distance call through it.

- *Distinctive ringing:* This feature enables users to determine by sound whether a call is coming from inside or outside the company.

- *Exclusive hold:* To prevent anyone on a key system from picking up a call placed on hold, the exclusive hold feature can be activated. Only the person who put the call on hold can then pick it up.

- *Flexible line assignment:* This feature allows you to program a key system so that groups of outside lines are assigned to specific individuals or departments for their use only.

- *Flexible ringing assignment:* Key systems can be programmed so that only certain extensions ring with incoming outside calls. The PBX equivalent, *night service,* enables you to route incoming calls to certain extensions when the attendant has gone home for the night.

- *Hold:* Any key system will allow you to put a call on hold. Options include a periodic tone (so that the caller will not think the line has gone dead), music, or a taped message. *Recall from hold* means that after a set period on hold the telephone will start buzzing. See also "Exclusive hold," described earlier.

- *Intercom calls:* On small systems, such as one linking a secretary and an executive, a button is pushed to alert the person being called, who then pushes the intercom button, lifts the handset, and speaks. With a *dial-selective intercom,* you usually push the intercom button and then dial one, two, or three digits to reach another person. To make a call, you press the button assigned to the person you want to reach. In large systems the only person with a direct station selector will be the receptionist.

  A *call-announcing system* allows you to alert the called party via a speakerphone and usually permits you to hear the other person's response. Paging through the system's speakerphones to the whole office or to groups of numbers also may be allowed.

- *LCD displays:* Key systems often have LCD displays that show which features you activated, which number you dialed, and other information.

- *Last-number redial:* Last-number redial is like automatic dialing, except that the number in the memory unit is the last number you dialed, which in most systems can be redialed by pressing the # (pound) button. This feature is useful when making attempts to get through to a busy number.

- *Least-cost routing:* With this feature, when you make a long-distance call, the system tries to find the least expensive way of placing your call. This usually means waiting a preset period for a

WATS line or other discount transmission facility to become available. If none becomes available, your call is placed via direct-distance dialing (DDD). How long you have to wait usually depends on the priority assigned to your telephone; executives might get through immediately, for example. Least-cost routing is also known as *automatic route selection.* See also "long-distance control system."

- *Line status indicators:* Key systems may have buttons that light up to show whether a line is busy, on hold, or free.

- *Long-distance control system:* Often offered with least-cost routing, a long-distance control system (LDCS) requires that you dial in special access codes before you are allowed to make a long-distance call. For instance, you may be required to dial "88" to reach the controller, followed by your personal code number and the number you want to reach; then you wait for the least-cost router to find an unused WATS line. Depending on the limitations put on your code number, you may be prohibited from making international calls, calls to certain areas, or any outside calls at all.

- *Message-waiting:* With message-waiting a special light or tone on your telephone is activated to show that the receptionist has a message for you. Some companies have message centers to which all calls are routed if not answered after three rings. Most modern systems can be programmed to route an unanswered call back to the receptionist.

- *Messaging:* This feature enables you to call another extension and leave a short message that is converted into words on the person's small telephone display. You can also input a message that people calling you will read on their display if they call while you are away; for example, you might leave the message "Back at 1:00 P.M."

- *Music on hold:* A tape or radio station can be connected to your system so that callers will hear music or comments when they are placed on hold.

- *Paging:* With this built-in feature, announcements can be broadcast through all speakerphones connected to a key system. PBX systems can provide the same thing if they are connected to separate paging systems.

- *Pocket beepers:* A *beeper* (or *pager*) is a pocket-sized paging device that alerts the bearer that a telephone message has been received. Beepers are worn by people such as physicians or news photographers who must always remain accessible to their offices. To alert a beeper user, you call the telephone number associated with that person's beeper and leave a message. The pager company then sends out a radio signal triggering the beeper's alarm mechanism. Some systems also will broadcast your recorded message, and some other beepers with digital readouts will display the telephone number the user is supposed to call.

- *Priority override:* With this feature you can break in on other conversations.

- *Privacy:* This feature prevents other people from accessing a line already in use. The priority override feature, though, usually enables you to break in regardless of the privacy feature.

- *Remote station answering:* With this feature you can answer someone else's telephone from your own telephone by dialing a special code or pushing a specific button. See also "Flexible ringing assignment," described earlier.

- *Security:* Scrambler telephones, such as those used by the military, range from inexpensive devices, whose encoded output may still be understood by the practiced ear, to sophisticated devices intended to thwart professional cryptanalysts. But an unused telephone also can be a security threat. A device called an *infinity transmitter* can be installed in your telephone allowing someone to call it, keep it from ringing, and then listen to everything being said in your office. If you're in a sensitive business, you should always greet unexpected telephone repair people with skepticism.

- *Speakerphones:* This feature enables you to talk into as well as listen to the speaker, without picking up the telephone receiver. This should not be confused with *on-hook dialing*, which only allows you to dial — not speak — without lifting the receiver. The better speakerphones suppress or avoid the annoying hollow sound and echo that are often common. High-quality devices are often called *teleconferencers.* These units operate in a full-duplex mode, which means that both parties can talk at the same time without one clipping off the other's voice.

- *Speed dialing:* Most systems enable you to store frequently called numbers and dial them by pressing only one or two buttons.

- *T1 lines:* High-speed digital lines can be leased to connect two locations that have telephone traffic. A digital telephone with a T1 interface must be used with T1 lines.

- *Toll restriction:* This feature allows you to restrict the type of calls that can be made from certain extensions. Hence it may not be possible to make 900 calls or international calls from those extensions.

- *Trunk line:* Also called an *exchange line* or a *central office line,* this is the telephone line that carries calls from inside a building to the local telephone exchange.

- *Voice mail:* Voice mail involves the automated delivery of telephone messages through computerized processing of the speaker's voice. A voice mail system is usually attached to an office telephone system as a peripheral device, but it also may be a telephone company service.

  By using the buttons of a key telephone, a user can invoke the voice mail system, input the telephone number of the recipient and any special commands (such as delivery at a designated hour), and speak the message. The message is digitalized and stored within the computer. The computer then calls the recipient — either immediately or at a designated time — and plays the message. If the recipient's telephone is busy or no one answers, the computer can keep trying until it gets through.

  Voice mail is usually used for short messages, with the advantage being that you do not have to waste time trying to reach your recipient. Possible options include access to and from outside telephones, the ability to edit messages, audio message headers stating who sent the message and when, delivery verification, message filing, and delivery to multiple recipients.

- *WATS extender:* A WATS extender attached to a PBX allows you to call the PBX from another telephone and use the system's

WATS line. The procedure is often the same as making a call through an OCC. For more about WATS, refer to the upcoming section on telephone services.

TELEPHONE COST CONTROL

Call Abuse

In firms in which no effort is made to control telephone costs, a substantial portion of the telephone bill may result from call abuse, that is, employees using the office telephones to make personal long-distance calls. The best tool in combating call abuse may be simple psychology — reminding everyone that long-distance calls are not a salary perk and announcing that a campaign has been launched against telephone abusers, who can expect to be caught.

Pressure also can be brought to bear by circulating a copy of the telephone bill and requiring each person to read and sign it or by simply posting the bill on the bulletin board. You may see the bill drop even if no further action is taken. Call accounting also could help identify the call abusers, but nothing will be of much help unless management demonstrates its continuing resolve to take action against telephone abusers.

Cost-Control Measures

Proper training is important in cost control, especially when you realize that one way of making a call can be much more expensive than another. Employees should be warned against making person-to-person calls and repeatedly reminded that WATS calls are not free. You also may wish to check inventory and ensure that all the lines and equipment you are being billed for have in fact been installed. In large organizations undergoing constant change there is a good chance that an expensive mistake has been made.

Telephone system management is a broad subject requiring specialized knowledge, especially now that the market is open to broader competition. Any information supplied by an account representative or equipment salesperson should be taken with the realization that he or she has a financial interest in your decisions. Organizations intending to change or upgrade their equipment should contact several vendors for recommendations and estimates. In addition, the cost of purchasing versus leasing should be considered.

TELEPHONE COMPANY SERVICES

Depending on the telephone company you are using, some or all of these services may be available.

- *Cellular telephone service:* This service enables you to use a telephone in a moving vehicle the same as a stationary office telephone. Cellular technology divides a city into cells, each of which has transmitting and receiving equipment. As a vehicle moves from one cell to another (roaming), the telephone is switched to the next cell. The telephone can be portable or hard-wired into the vehicle's electrical system. Numbers are called from a cellular telephone the same as from an office telephone. Cellular telephone features also resemble the features of an office system, for example, memory dialing and data interfaces.

- *Centrex:* Local telephone companies provide a service similar to an in-house PBX system. The telephone company assigns a number of lines to your company and provides the necessary central switching mechanism that you would otherwise have to purchase. Centrex-compatible key systems and KSU-less systems are also available.

- *Credit card calling:* Telephone companies provide calling cards to enable you to call from other telephones and have the cost of the call charged to your telephone.

- *Custom calling:* For an extra fee your local telephone company may be able to provide ordinary telephones with features similar to some of those built into office telephone systems. These features include speed dialing, call waiting, call forwarding, automated answering services, and three-way calling (a form of conferencing).

- *Direct-distance dialing:* Direct-distance dialing (DDD) involves ordinary long-distance calls that you dial yourself. International direct-distance dialing (IDDD) is available from certain cities in the United States to many other countries. Table 8.2 provides a list of international dialing codes and time differences.

- *Foreign exchanges and tie lines:* If your office makes a lot of calls to a specific city, you can get a foreign exchange (FX) line to that city. An FX is essentially a direct line. When you lift the handset of an FX telephone, you are getting a dial tone from the city to which it is connected. There is usually no usage fee, only the monthly lease for the line. A *tie line* is a similar leased line between two PBXs in distant cities.

- *Integrated Services Digital Network (ISDN):* The ISDN is an international standard for the high-speed transfer of voice, data, and video communications. Although existing telephone lines can be used, the ISDN provides a new type of exchange by sending a different type of signal. The network will be mainly digital, but the older analog telephone equipment will also work on the network, although without many of the benefits of a digital telephone system. (*Note:* Analog transmissions are in the form of a continually varying electrical current. Digital transmissions are in the form of discrete units.)

- *Inward WATS:* Inward WATS lines use the 800 Area Code and are toll-free to the caller. The calls are automatically paid for by the receiver. Recent enhancements include *customized call routing,* whereby calls from different areas of the country are routed to different offices, and *variable call routing,* whereby after-hours calls are routed to a separate office. The information operator for toll-free numbers can be reached at 800-555-1212. WATS numbers are listed in a WATS directory rather than in the regular telephone directory. See also the description of outgoing WATS at the end of this list.

- *Marine radiotelephone:* Ships in port or near a coastal city can be reached through the marine operator in that city, obtainable through your local operator. Your call is patched through a shortwave radio link to the ship's radio room. Appropriately equipped ships at sea can be reached through the maritime satellite network (INMARSAT) with the same procedure used for international calls. For more about placing calls, refer to the discussion of outgoing calls later in this chapter.

- *Time and charges:* You may tell the operator that you want time and charges and then stay on the line after the call is completed. The operator or a recording will come on and tell you the length of the call and its cost. If you forget and hang up at the end of the call, the operator should call you back immediately and give you the time and charges.

- *WATS:* For outbound wide-area telephone service (WATS), a special telephone line can be installed at your office. This service allows for outgoing long-distance calls under a billing arrangement that *may* result in lower telephone costs. Depending on your telephone system, you may have to dial a code before dialing the number you want to call using the WATS line. See also "Inward WATS," described earlier.

Table 8.2   Dialing Codes and Time Differences

Dialing codes: To call a number in another country, dial *011 + country code + city code + local fax or other number.* Follow any additional instructions of your system or subscriber service.

Time differences: To find out the time in another country, check the time change, calculated from Eastern Standard Time. (Ask your contacts whether standard time or a form of daylight savings time applies in their countries.) For example, if you want to know when a fax being sent to London will arrive and it is 9 A.M. Eastern Standard Time where you work, add five hours (+5) to determine the time in London: 2 P.M.

COUNTRY CODE	CITY CODE	TIME CHANGE
Albania 355	Durres 52, Elbassan 545, Gjirocastra 726, Korce 824, Tirana 42	+7
Algeria 213	None required	+6
Andorra 33	All points 628	+6
Angola 244	All points area code 2 plus 6 digits	+6
Argentina 54	Buenos Aires 1, Córdoba 51, La Plata 21, Rosario 41	+2

Table 8.2, continued

COUNTRY CODE	CITY CODE	TIME CHANGE
Armenia 7	All points 885	+8
Australia 61	Adelaide 8, Brisbane 7, Melbourne 3, Sydney 2	+15
Austria 43	Graz 316, Linz Donau 732, Vienna 1 or 222	+6
Azerbaijan 7	Bakic 8922, Sumgait 89264	+8
Bahrain 973	None required	+8
Bangladesh 880	Barisal 431, Chittagong 31, Dhaka 2, Khulna 41	+11
Belarus 7	Minsk 0172, Mogilev 0222	+8
Belgium 32	Antwerp 3, Brussels 2, Ghent 91, Liège 41	+6
Belize 501	Belize City 2, Corozal Town 4, Punta Gorda 7	−1
Benin 229	None required	+6
Bhutan 975	None required	+10½
Bolivia 591	Cochabamba 42, La Paz 2, Santa Cruz 3	+1
Bosnia-Herzegovina 38	Sarajevo 71, Zenica 72	+6
Botswana 267	Francistown 21, Jwaneng 38, Kanye 34, Lobatse 33, Gaborone 31	+7
Brazil 55	Belo Horizonte 31, Rio de Janeiro 21, São Paulo 11	+2
Brunei 673	Bandar Seri Begawan 2, Kuala Belait 3, Tutong 4	+13

Table 8.2, continued

COUNTRY CODE	CITY CODE	TIME CHANGE
Bulgaria 359	Plovdiv 32, Rousse (Ruse) 82, Sofia 2, Varna 52	+7
Burkina Faso 226	None required	+5
Burundi 257	Bubanza 42, Bujumbura 22, Bururi 50, Cibitoke 41, Gitega 40, Muramuya 43, Muvaro 44, Ngarara 23, Ngozi 30	+7
Cambodia 855	Phnom Penh 23	+12
Cameroon 237	None required	+6
Canada	Dial 1 + area code + local number	0 (Ottawa)
Cape Verde 238	None required	+4
Central African Republic	All points area code 61 plus 4 digits	+6
Chad 235	Abeche, Faya, and Mondou 69, N'djamena 51 plus 4 digits, Sarh — none required	+6
Chile 56	Concepción 41, Santiago 2, Valparaiso 32	+1
China 86	Beijing (Peking) 1, Fuzhou 591, Ghuangzhou (Canton) 20, Shanghai 21	+13
Colombia 57	Barranquilla 58, Bogotá 1, Cali 23, Medellin 4	0
Comoros 269	Anjouan 71, Moheli 72, Moroni 73	+9
Congo 242	None required	+6
Costa Rica 506	None required	−1

Table 8.2, continued

COUNTRY CODE	CITY CODE	TIME CHANGE
Croatia 38	Rijeka 51, Zagreb 41	+6
Cyprus	Limassol 51, Nicosia 2, Paphos 61	+7
Czech Republic 42	Brno 5, Havirov 6994, Ostrava 69, Prague (Praha) 2	+6
Denmark 45	Aalborg 8, Aarhus 6, Copenhagen 3 plus 7 digits (suburbs 4 plus 7 digits), Oddense 7	+6
Djibouti 253	None required	+8
Ecuador 593	Ambato 2, Cuenca 7, Guayaquil 4, Quito 2	0
Egypt 20	Alexandria 3, Aswan 97, Asyut 88, Benha 13, Cairo 2	+7
El Salvador 503	None required	–1
Equatorial Guinea 240	Bata 8 plus 4 digits, Malabo 9 plus 4 digits	+6
Estonia 372	Tallinn 2	+8
Ethiopia 251	Addis Ababa 1, Akaki 1, Asmara 4, Assab 3, Awassa 6	+8
Fiji 679	None required	+17
Finland 358	Espoo (Esbo) 0, Helsinki 0, Tampere (Tammerfors) 31, Turku (Abo) 21	+7
France 33	Lyon 7, Marseille 91, Nice 93, Paris 1 plus 8 digits beginning with 3, 4, or 6	+6
Gabon 241	None required	+6
The Gambia 220	None required	+5

Table 8.2, continued

COUNTRY CODE	CITY CODE	TIME CHANGE
Georgia 7	Sukhumi 88122, Tblisi 8832	+8
Germany 49	Berlin 30, Dresden 351, Leipzig 341, Bonn 228, Frankfurt 69, Munich 89, Rostock 381	+6
Ghana 233	Accra 21, Koforidua 81, Kumasi 51, Takoradi 31	+5
Greece 30	Athens (Athinai) 1, Iraklion (Kritis) 81, Larissa 41, Piraceus Pireefs 1	+7
Guatemala 502	Guatemala City 2, all others 9	−1
Guinea 224	Conakry 4, Kindia 61, Labe 51 Mamou 68	+5
Guinea-Bissau 245	None required; all numbers 6 digits beginning with 20, 21, 22, or 25	+5
Guyana 592	Bartica 5, Georgetown 2, New Amsterdam 3	+2
Haiti 509	None required — all numbers 6 digits	0
Honduras 504	None required	−1
Hungary 36	Budapest 1, Derbrecen 52, Gyor 96, Miskolc 46	+6
Iceland 354	Akureyri 6, Keflavik Naval Base 2, Reykjavík 1	+5
India 91	Bombay 22, Calcutta 33, Madras 44, New Delhi 11	+10½
Indonesia 62	Jakarta 21, Medan 61, Semarang 24	+12
Iran 98	Esfahan 31, Mashad 51, Tabriz 41, Tehran 21	+8½
Iraq 964	Baghdad 1, Basra 40, Kerbela 32, Kirkuk 50, Mousil 60, Najaf 33	+8

Table 8.2, continued

COUNTRY CODE	CITY CODE	TIME CHANGE
Ireland 353	Cork 21, Dublin 1, Galway 91, Limerick 6 or 61	+5
Israel 972	Haifa 4, Jerusalem 2, Ramat Gan, Tel Aviv 3	+7
Italy 39	Florence 55, Genoa 10, Milan 2, Naples 81, Rome 6	+6
Ivory Coast 225	None required	+5
Japan 81	Kyoto 75, Osaka 6, Sapporo 11, Tokyo 3, Yokohama 45	+14
Jordan 962	Amman 6, Irbid 2, Jerash 4, Karak 3, Ma'an 3	+7
Kazakhstan 7	Alma-Ata 3272, Chimkent 3252, Guryev 31222	+11
Kenya 254	Kisumu 35, Mombasa 11, Nairobi 2, Nakuru 37	+8
Kirghizia (Kyrgyzstan) 7	Osh 33222, Pishpek 3312	+11
Kiribati 686	None required	+17
Korea, South 82	Inchon 32, Pusan (Busan) 51, Seoul 2, Taegu (Daegu) 53	+14
Kuwait 965	None required	+8
Laos 856	Vientiane 21	+10
Latvia 371	Riga 2	+8
Lebanon 961	Beirut 1, Sidon 7, Tripoli 6	+7
Lesotho 266	None required	+7
Liberia 231	None required	+5

Table 8.2, continued

COUNTRY CODE	CITY CODE	TIME CHANGE
Libya	Benghazi 61, Misuratha 51, Tripoli 21, Zawai 23	+7
Liechtenstein 41	All points 75	+6
Lithuania 370	Vilnius 2	+8
Luxembourg 352	None required	+6
Macedonia 38	Bitola 97, Skopje 91	+6
Madagascar 261	Antananarivo 2, Diego Suarez 8, Fianarantsoa 7, Moramanja 4, Tatatave 5	+8
Malawi 265	Domasi 531, Makwasa 474, Zomba 50	+7
Malaysia 60	Ipoh 5, Johor Bahru 7, Kajang 3, Kuala Lumpur 3	+13
Maldives 960	None required	+10
Mali 223	None required	+5
Malta 356	None required	+6
Marshall Islands 692	Ebeye 871, Majuro 9	+17
Mauritania 222	None required	+5
Mauritius 230	None required	+9
Mexico	Acapulco 748, Cancún 988, Celaya 461, Cordoba 271, Culiacan 671, Guadalajara 36, Hermosillo 621, Jalapa 281, Leon 471, Mérida 99, Mexico City 5, Monterrey 83, Tampico 121, Tijuana 66, Toluca 721, Torreon 17, Veracruz 29	−1 (Mexico City)

Table 8.2, continued

COUNTRY CODE	CITY CODE	TIME CHANGE
Micronesia 691	Kosrae 370, Ponape 320, Truk 330, Yap 350	+16
Moldova 373	Kishinev 2	+8
Monaco 33	All points 93	+6
Mongolia 976	Ulan Bator 1	+13
Morocco 212	Agadir 8, Beni-Mellal 48, El Jadida 34, Casablanca — none required	+5
Mozambique 258	Beira 3, Chokwe 21, Maputo 1, Nampula 6	+7
Namibia 264	Grootfontein 673, Keetmanshoop 631, Mariental 661	+7
Nauru 674	None required	+17
Nepal 977	None required	+10½
Netherlands 31	Amsterdam 20, Rotterdam 10, The Hague 70	+6
New Zealand 64	Auckland 9, Christchurch 3, Dunedin 24, Hamilton 71	+17
Nicaragua 505	Chinandega 341, Diriamba 42, Leon 311, Managua 2	−1
Niger 227	None required	+6
Nigeria 234	Lagos 1	+6
Norway 47	Bergen 5, Oslo — city codes 22, 66, or 67, Stavanger 4, Trondheim 7	+6
Oman 968	None required	+9
Pakistan 92	Islamabad 51, Karachi 21, Lahore 42	+10
Panama 507	None required	0

Table 8.2, continued

COUNTRY CODE	CITY CODE	TIME CHANGE
Papua New Guinea 675	None required	+15
Paraguay 595	Asunción 21, Concepción 31	+2
Peru 51	Arequipa 54, Callao 14, Lima 14, Trujillo 44	0
Philippines 63	Cebu City 32, Davao 82, Iloilo City 33, Manila 2	+13
Poland 48	Crakow (Krakow) 12, Gdansk 58, Warsaw 22	+6
Portugal 351	Coimbra 39, Lisbon 1, Porto 2, Setubal 65	+5
Qatar 974	None required	+8
Romania 40	Arad 966, Bucharest 1, Cluj-Napoca 951, Constanta 916	+7
Russia 7	Moscow 095, Nizhny Novgorod 8312, St. Petersburg 812	+8
Rwanda 250	None required	+7
San Marino 39	All points 549	+6
São Tomé 239	All points area code 12 plus 5 digits	+5
Saudi Arabia 966	Hofuf 3, Jeddah 2, Makkah (Mecca) 2, Riyadh 1	+8
Senegal 221	None required	+5
Serbia 38	Belgrade (Beograd) 11, Novi Sad 21	+6
Seychelles 248	None required	+9
Sierra Leone 232	Freetown 22, all other points 232	+5
Singapore 65	None required	+13

Table 8.2, continued

COUNTRY CODE	CITY CODE	TIME CHANGE
Slovakia 42	Bratislava 7, Presov 91	+6
Slovenia 38	Ljubljana 61, Maribor 62	+6
Solomon Islands 677	None required	+16
South Africa 27	Cape Town 21, Durban 31, Johannesburg 11	+7
Spain 34	Barcelona 3, Madrid 1, Seville 54, Valencia 6	+6
Sri Lanka 94	Colombo Central 1, Kandy 8, Kotte 1	$+10\frac{1}{2}$
Suriname 597	None required	+2
Swaziland 268	None required	+7
Sweden 46	Goteborg 31, Malmo 40, Stockholm 8, Vasteras 21	+6
Switzerland 41	Basel 61, Bern 31, Geneva 22, Zurich 1	+6
Syria 963	Aleppo 21, Damascus 11, Halab 21, Hama 331, Homs 31	+8
Taiwan 886	Kaohsiung 7, Tainan 6, Taipei 2	+13
Tajikistan 7	Dushanbe 3772	+11
Tanzania 255	Dar es Salaam 51, Dodoma 61, Mwanza 68, Tanga 53	+8
Thailand 66	Bangkok 2, Burirum 44, Chanthaburi 39	+12
Togo 228	None required	+5
Tonga 676	None required	+18
Tunisia 216	Bizerte 2, Kairouan 7, Msel Bourguiba 2, Tunis 1	+6

Table 8.2, continued

COUNTRY CODE	CITY CODE	TIME CHANGE
Turkey 90	Ankara 4, Istanbul 1, Izmir 51	+7
Turkmenistan 7	Ashkhabad 3632, Chardzhou 37822	+10
Tuvalu 688	None required	+17
Uganda 256	Entebbe 42, Jinja 43, Kampala 41, Kyambogo 41	+8
Ukraine 7	Donetsk 0622, Kharkiv 0572, Kyiv 044, Lviv 0322	+8
United Arab Emirates 971	Abu Dhabi 2, Ajman 6, Al Ain 3, Dubai 4, Sharjah 6	+9
United Kingdom 44	Belfast 232, Birmingham 21, Glasgow 41, London (inner) 71, London (outer) 81	+5
Uruguay 598	Canelones 332, Mercedes 532, Montevideo 2	+2
Uzbekistan 7	Karish 37522, Samarkand 3662, Tashkent 3712	+11
Vanuatu 678	None required	+16
Venezuela 58	Barquisimeto 51, Caracas 2, Maracaibo 61, Valencia 41	+1
Vietnam 84	Hanoi 4, Ho Chi Minh City 8	+12
Western Samoa 685	None required	–6
Yemen 967	Amran 2, Sana'a 1, Taiz 4, Yarim 4	+8
Zaïre 243	Kinshasa 12, Lubumbashi 222	+6
Zambia 260	Chingola 2, Kitwe 2, Luanshya 2, Lusaka 1, Ndola 2	+7
Zimbabwe 263	Bulawayo 9, Harare 4, Mutare 20	+7

TELEPHONE TECHNIQUES

Projecting a positive company image is an important goal in every office. The secretary's role is especially significant because his or her voice is often the first one that a caller hears.

Telephone Etiquette

Answering Calls   The secretary can help create a positive image for the company by observing proper telephone etiquette. For example, any incoming call should be answered on the second ring, if possible. How the telephone is answered might depend on the preference of the executive.

If you work with just one person, you might answer by using his or her name:

Good morning, Mr. London's office.

If your work is more general — for a department rather than for a particular person — you might answer by identifying the department:

Good afternoon, Personnel Benefits.

The way in which you answer indicates your attitude toward the caller and toward your job. A friendly and helpful attitude will help project goodwill for you and your company.

Placing Calls   If you are calling someone, immediately identify yourself:

Good afternoon. This is Carol Stevens, Mr. Shandler's secretary.

Use the least-cost method, such as a WATS line, as indicated in the employee handbook or according to office policy.

It is always thoughtful to ask someone if it is convenient to talk when you call. Even if it is, this is not an invitation to launch a lengthy conversation that takes people away from their work. It is also important to avoid calling people at home about business matters, unless it is an emergency or unless you have been told to do so.

Try to have all material you need for reference in front of you. But if you must put someone on hold, first ask permission and then check in about every 40 seconds. If a delay is going to be extensive, ask if you can call the person back. For more about hold procedures, see the next section.

If you regularly call listings in other cities, consider ordering directories for those cities from your telephone company. In-state directories may or may not be free; out-of-state directories are usually sold.

Language   Language will tell the caller a lot about you and your company. A courteous secretary avoids crude expressions and replies distinctly with "Yes," rather than "Yeah" or "Uh-huh": "Yes, Ms. Baker." Signs of respect are readily conveyed with appropriate comments and responses such as "I beg your pardon," "Thank you," "I appreciate your help," and "Please."

The art of conversation should be practiced on the telephone as well as in face-to-face conversations. One should never speak with a mouth full of food or while chewing on an eraser. It is amazing how much you can detect over the telephone. Listening is a key ingredient in communication, and it is considered rude to interrupt or rush a caller.

Voice messages deserve the same attention as regular calls. Use a pleasant tone of voice, and be certain to include sufficient information for the other person. One of the most common mistakes is speaking too fast and not enunciating clearly.

Techniques for Incoming Calls

Placing a Call on Hold   Always ask the caller's preference before placing the call on hold. When you periodically return on the line, ask if the caller wants to continue to hold and indicate how long the delay will be:

> I'm sorry, but it appears that Ms. Slocum may be on the other line for another 5 minutes. Would you like to wait, or may I have her call you back?

You might also offer to transfer the call to someone else who could help the caller. If you must immediately place a caller on hold, you might say:

> Mr. Rukeyser's office. Will you please hold a moment?

Then return to the call as quickly as possible.

Answering Another Telephone   A ringing telephone should never go unanswered. Whether you are assigned to answer someone else's telephone or just happen to walk by another telephone that is ringing, you should be as helpful as possible. It might be necessary to explain to the caller that it's not your office. Rather than saying, "I don't know" or "I can't help you," there's nothing wrong with saying something such as this:

> I'm afraid there's no one in the office right now. May I have Mr. London or his secretary get back to you?

When taking a message, get all of the pertinent data — time, name of caller, title and company, telephone number including extension, and any message the caller might want to leave. In many offices arrangements have to be made to have telephones answered in the secretary's absence. Sometimes the secretaries have each other's extensions on their telephones.

If you must ask a coworker to answer your telephone, keep a pad and pencil on your desk and indicate where you can be reached and how long you will be gone. It is your responsibility to explain how the telephone should be answered, what calls might be expected by the executive, where the executive can be reached if necessary, and any other pertinent information.

Be sure to alert your coworker if the executive is expecting a particular call or if the executive does not want to accept certain calls. Explain how the executive prefers to have the telephone answered. You might call the executive by a nickname in the office or after hours, but it doesn't necessarily mean that he or she wants the telephone answered that way. *Charles* London might be preferable to *Chuck* London.

Transferring Calls If it's necessary to transfer a call, explain to the caller what you are doing. Don't just say "Hold on." Follow the correct procedure with your system. You may, for example, have to depress the switch hook or cradle once and release it immediately. When you hear a steady dial tone, you would then dial the desired extension and, when answered, announce the call and hang up.

If a call comes in on the wrong line, you might say:

> I'm sorry, Ms. Slocum is not on this extension. Her extension is 5551. If you'll hold a moment, I'll transfer your call.

It's a good idea to give the correct extension to the caller in case he or she gets cut off or wants to call back later.

If the executive wants to take the call on another extension, you might say:

Mr. London is in another office right now but would like to speak with you. Please hold on and I'll transfer you.

Stay on the line, and when someone answers the second extension, explain that you're transferring a call and give the name of the person to whom the call is being transferred.

Screening Calls   Executives differ about the way incoming calls should be handled. Some executives prefer to answer their own extensions. Others want their secretaries to answer and put through calls without asking who is calling. Some higher-level executives, however, believe their schedules won't permit them to take every call, and they expect their secretaries to find out who is calling. The secretaries then put through only certain calls, handling the others themselves or transferring them to a junior executive.

If you are required to ask who is calling, avoid giving the impression that you're screening the call. If you ask who is calling *before* stating that the executive is in, it sounds as though you'll decide whether to say the executive is in only after learning who is calling. Instead, you should say something such as this:

Secretary:	Ms. Peterson's office.
Caller:	Hello, may I speak to Ms. Peterson?
Secretary:	Yes, may I tell her who's calling?

If there's a chance Ms. Peterson might not want to speak with the caller, you could handle the situation this way.

Secretary:	Ms. Peterson's office.
Caller:	Hello, is Ms. Peterson in?
Secretary:	I believe she's on another line now. May I ask who's calling?
Caller:	Joe Ferguson in the mail room.
Secretary:	Oh, yes, Mr. Ferguson. I'm not sure when Ms. Peterson will be free. Could I help in the meantime?
Caller:	I don't know. I wanted to talk about a problem with the new indicia.
Secretary:	I think Sally Beloit was working on that. Why don't I transfer your call to her. She's at extension 5557.
Caller:	Okay. That'll be fine.

Handling Annoying Calls   Not everyone is pleasant and considerate on the telephone. Although it may be tempting to respond with a similar tone, secretaries need to resist this temptation and maintain a pleasant, cooperative attitude. Sometimes a concerned, calm, understanding tone will defuse a loud, angry caller. If not, do the same thing you would do for anyone else — offer to help if you can or, if you can't, offer to transfer the call to someone who can.

If a caller continues to be abusive, apologize for being unable to provide a solution, thank the caller for taking time to call, say good-bye, and hang up. If you believe the caller will persist, you might suggest that he or she write a letter to the company; follow company policy in regard to giving out names of executives to abusive callers.

Terminating a Call   Some callers ramble on as though you and your boss have nothing better to do than spend time visiting with them. These calls can be time-consuming and difficult to terminate. Your boss may ask you to interrupt an overlong conversation he or she is having with a caller. Perhaps the executive will buzz you on the intercom, which will be a signal to you to interrupt on some pretext, such as telling the executive that there is an incoming international call or reminding him or her of a meeting about to begin.

If you are also bothered by someone who likes to use your office hours for personal visits, do the same thing — interrupt when you can and pretend that another visitor has just walked up to your desk or say that you have a call coming in on another line. If possible, use an excuse that not only will end the call but also will remind the caller that you are a working person and have work to do during office hours. However, your excuse should not insult the caller; it is also important to leave a caller feeling good in spite of the need to end the conversation.

Message-Taking Procedures   A variety of message forms are available in office-supply stores and catalogs. A short form and a long form are illustrated on pages 262 and 263. It may be up to you to select a useful form, or your office may have a standard form that is used by everyone. Most forms have room to write certain key facts.

Date
Time of the call
Caller's name
Caller's title and company
Caller's telephone number
Reason for the call

Telephone Message Slip

Telephone Message

1/2/95   3:15 p.m.
Date   Time

Janet Mason
For

Jim Williams
From

1 (123) 456-7000   8910
Phone number   Extension

☑ Telephoned   ☐ Returned your call   ☐ Called to see you
☑ Please return call   ☐ Will phone again   ☐ Waiting to see you

Message
Wants to discuss presentation at Affiliates meeting

Mark Jones
Received by

GE 25-17 80

When taking a message, repeat the person's telephone number, and after finding out the reason for the call, consider whether someone else might be able to help the caller. In that case, offer to transfer the call to another extension.

Techniques for Outgoing Calls

Placing a Call for an Executive When placing a telephone call for an executive, ensure that you have the right number at hand (check the other party's company letterhead, the telephone book, or your own telephone list first). Be sure that you know the name of the person being called and that you can pronounce the name correctly. Check a time zone map, such as the one illustrated on page 264, before placing long-distance calls.

Be sure that the executive is still in the office when you place a call. Sometimes an executive will ask that a call be placed but then will step out for a minute or will become involved in an impromptu meeting. It is rude to keep the person being called on the line while you try to find the executive. If an unavoidable delay occurs and you cannot connect the parties right away, stay on the line with the person being called and ex-

Telephone Message Register

**Telephone
Message Register**

Date: *March 1, 1995*

Time	Name	Telephone	Subject and Action	
9:30 am	John O'Reilly	(123) 444-5555	Affiliates Meeting	returned
10:30 am	Loretta Davis	(231) 555-4444	Luncheon Friday	to call back
10:45 am	Martin Green	(222) 666-1111	Talk Show-writers	to call back
10:50 am	Nancy Nazinnee	(765) 432-1234	News Broadcast subject	returned
11:00 am	Tobias Quinn	ext. 2310	PR/Election Coverage	
11:15 am	Joe Montague	ext 6870	Contract for John Doe	
11:00 am	Lilly De Garve	(711) 987-6543	TV News Publicity	
1:00 pm	Barbara Gorham	ext. 0123	Mary Roberts contract	returned
1:30 pm	Bill Battrom	(803) 222-3434	Sales Meeting Presentation	ret'd
1:45 pm	Sidney Diamond	(345) 678-9101	a.m. news query	
2:00 pm	Carole Smith	(987) 655-1238	news analysis query	
2:15 pm	Lee Lohman	ext. 4444	News Dept. meeting	returned
3:00 pm	Naomi Walters	ext. 6789	Election '95 meeting	returned
3:15 pm	Peter Grayson	ext. 7654	Dinner 3/10/95 – reminder	
3:30 pm	Allen Camp	ext. 4988	Meeting re: Primaries	returned
4:00 pm	William Smith	ext. 6654	No message – please call back ASAP	
4:30 pm	Rachel Lee	(832) 223-3434	query – election news	
5:00 pm	Sally Benson	(983) 456-8348	query – election coverage	
5:15 pm	Peter Martins	684-3232	reminder – golf date 3/11/95	

GE – 1065 (5/83)

95-157 8.2

plain the situation. Never just put the other party on hold and hang up.

Give the person being called at least ten rings or about forty-five seconds in which to answer. Be prepared to speak as soon as the person does answer; you ought not to be talking with someone else or shuffling papers while attempting to introduce yourself. Use a pleasant tone of voice, and follow the rules of telephone etiquette given above.

Domestic Time Zone Map, United States and Canada

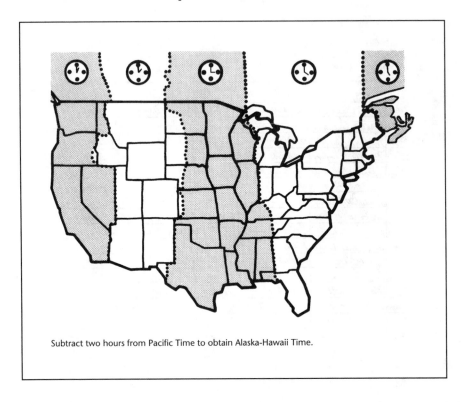

Subtract two hours from Pacific Time to obtain Alaska-Hawaii Time.

When the secretary to the person being called answers, you might say:

Hello. Mr. London from ZBC is calling. He would like to speak with Ms. Slocum, please.

As soon as Ms. Slocum comes on the line, buzz Mr. London and say:

Ms. Slocum is on the line.

If Ms. Slocum answers herself, you might say:

Hello, Ms. Slocum. This is Ann Beale from ZBC calling. Mr. London would like to speak with you. Shall I put him on?

If she says yes, then buzz the executive and simply say:

Here he is.

When placing calls in this way, try to avoid keeping either person waiting for more than a second or two.

If the person being called is not in, find out when he or she will be back. You can have the person return the executive's call, or you can have the executive call back, depending on each person's schedule. If the executive wants to call later, find out what time would be best for both parties in order to avoid "telephone tag" in which one of the parties is always unavailable.

Placing Long-Distance Calls   When you dial direct to call long distance, you simply dial the full number of the person you are calling, including the Area Code or international dialing code in the case of international calls. Refer to Table 8.2 beginning on page 246 for a list of international codes.

If you need to speak to a particular person, dial the operator and give the name of the person as well as the number. Person-to-person calls are more expensive and usually are used only if someone is seldom available and you need to avoid the cost of making numerous station-to-station calls while trying to reach the person.

If you accidentally call a wrong number or if there is a poor connection, immediately dial the operator. Report the error, and ask to have the charge removed from your monthly bill.

To place a long-distance call to a ship, plane, or train, you need to know the telephone number and, in the case of ships at sea, the international access code and the ocean code. Major airlines may offer in-flight telephone service, and certain Amtrak routes provide a similar service for rail passengers. Check with the particular airline, Amtrak, or a travel agent.

To reach someone on a ship, dial the operator and ask for the marine or high seas operator. The operator needs to know the ocean the ship is in and its telephone number. The maritime satellite service IN-MARSAT is used to send messages to ships, offshore barges, and oil platforms equipped with radioteletypes or radiotelephones. The international access code is 011. Ocean codes are 871 for the Atlantic, 872 for the Pacific, and 873 for the Indian Ocean.

Placing Credit Card Calls   Telephone companies issue calling cards for placing long-distance calls from another telephone away from the office. Some credit card issuers, such as MasterCard and Visa, may also allow their cards to be used for this purpose.

Follow the instructions provided by the issuer of the calling card or credit card, as well as any instructions posted by a pay telephone. You may, for example, have to dial 0 plus the Area Code plus the telephone number, wait for the tone, and then dial your calling card or credit card number. In other cases you may have to dial a four-digit personal identification number rather than the full card number. Telephone directories usually have instructions on the use of calling cards in the front of the book, along with information about many of the other aspects of telephone usage discussed in this chapter.

Criminals have found various ways to obtain calling card numbers, sometimes by using binoculars from a distance to read the card or the number that you dial in. As a security precaution, always shield from view your card and the number being dialed when you use a public telephone.

CONVENTIONAL AND ELECTRONIC MAIL

Processing incoming and outgoing mail is an important secretarial responsibility. In most offices the mail consists of both conventional paper mail and some form of electronic communication, such as fax or E-mail. Regardless of the type of mail, messages must be handled carefully and expeditiously. When they are not handled properly, the image of the company is affected adversely, and clients or customers may be lost as a result.

INCOMING MAIL

Although postal mail may arrive about the same time each day, private courier mail, E-mail, fax mail, telex mail, and other forms of communication may arrive throughout the day or night. Therefore, you should check computer mailboxes, fax machines, and other equipment or facilities the first thing each morning.

Practices for presenting incoming mail to an executive may differ. In some offices the secretary is expected to deliver incoming mail or electronic transmissions as they arrive throughout the day. In other offices the secretary is expected to make hard-copy printouts of electronic transmissions, add them to the incoming postal mail, and deliver all mail at one time to the executive each day. Only urgent messages would be presented individually as they arrive.

Sorting and Opening Procedures

Some office functions still cannot be relegated completely to automation. Opening the paper mail and sorting messages, as well as reading, annotating, and evaluating the contents are examples of routine manual procedures.

Initial Sorting of the Mail   Separate letters from periodicals and packages. With the envelopes still *unopened,* sort the letters into piles containing personal correspondence and business correspondence including first-class mail, bills and statements, and mass mailings (also known as *direct mail*). The categories in the initial sort will vary, depending on the nature of your business. If you organize the mail on a daily basis, you will soon discover an emerging pattern. Define your own groupings and sort accordingly. Eventually, you may become proficient enough to omit this step and sort and open at the same time.

An initial sort, however, should help you in the next stages: opening and reading. Out of respect to the writer and your employer, never open mail marked "personal" or "confidential." If you open something like this inadvertently, simply say so (an initialed notation on the envelope should suffice), and take measures to prevent it from happening again; that is, look at all envelopes carefully before opening them.

Opening the Mail   A hand-held, knifelike manual opener or an automatic device may be used to open the mail. Usually, however, you must receive a high volume of mail to justify the expense of buying an automatic opener. Whatever method is used, care should be taken not to slice through the contents of an envelope.

As you empty the contents of the envelopes, attach large enclosures in back of the letters and small enclosures in front of the letters. If enclosures are missing, promptly call or write to the sender and explain what is missing. If the letters do not have sufficient return addresses, also attach the envelopes or mailing labels to the appropriate letters. If a letter has a sufficient return address, discard the envelope unless the postmark date is required for an undated letter or for another reason. If it is standard procedure in your office to date the mail, stamp each piece of incoming mail with the date and time received. If a letter is sent to your office in error, write "Not at This Address" on the envelope and add it to your outgoing mail.

Final Sorting of the Mail   After all pieces of incoming mail have been opened and all printouts of electronic transmissions collected, divide the opened mail into final categories suitable for your type of business. General categories should include the following:

Correspondence
Bills and statements
Newspapers and periodicals

Direct-mail advertising
Other material

Unless the mail is voluminous, set up a file folder for each category, and keep the items in the respective folders until they are presented to the executive or otherwise disposed of. If all pieces are taken care of promptly, the same folders can be emptied and reused the following day.

Follow the practice in your office for disposing of direct-mail pieces (so-called junk mail). Executives often like to read about new products, seminars, and other material that is advertised or sold by mail. But if your boss does not want to receive mail from certain organizations, ask if the executive would like to have his or her name removed from their mailing lists and then write to the senders with this request.

Forward any items that your office does not handle to the appropriate person or department. Bills and statements, for example, may go to a bookkeeper or accounting department. Certain periodicals or other incoming material may have been ordered for someone other than your boss. If your office has mailroom pickup, put the item in an interoffice envelope or attach a routing slip with the appropriate person's name and department and put it in your out-basket. Otherwise, deliver the item yourself as soon as you are able to leave your desk.

Correspondence often requires additional sorting into at least three subcategories.

• Letters and memos for the executive
• Letters and memos for other personnel
• Letters and memos for you

As you become familiar with the activities in your office, you will learn who should handle the various items. For mail to be presented to your boss, separate personal and business letters, and place priority items requiring immediate attention on top or in a separate color-coded priority folder. In addition to putting priority letters on top of other letters, arrange all of the mail by category for presentation, with the most important category (usually priority correspondence) on top of other categories, such as newspapers.

If it will be helpful to the executive in replying to a letter to know more about a situation, attach the pertinent material, such as a report or file folder. Try to anticipate what will be needed and include it when you present the mail rather than wait for your boss to request additional information.

Handling Hate Mail

Hate mail, or poison-pen letters, often have the same effect on their readers as pathological or obscene telephone calls have on their listeners. If you feel endangered by the contents of a particular letter or parcel, do not hesitate to call your company's security guard, the police, or the Postal Inspection Service. Laws proscribe such abuse of the mail system just as other statutes forbid obscene and obnoxious telephone calls. Simple letters of disagreement, however, should be treated the same as any other correspondence.

Reading and Annotating the Mail

Occasionally, executives want their secretaries to read letters and memos and add pertinent comments on paper copies that will help them answer the correspondence. Some may want to have the gist of the letter summarized in the margin, to have questions answered, or to have key points underlined or highlighted with a yellow marking pen. Often, though, it is against policy to write anything on a letter except the time and date of receipt. In that case, the key points can be noted on removable self-sticking notes or, if comments are lengthy, typed on a memo that is attached to the letter. The same procedure should be followed in reading and annotating articles, reports, and other incoming material.

Maintaining a Mail Record

Some offices require that the secretary keep a daily record of all important pieces of mail received. Other offices have a record only of mail routed to others outside the office for action. You can maintain such a record by computer or manually using a columnar accounting sheet. In either case, you might have ten columns with these headings.

- Date received
- Time received
- Date on item
- Name and affiliation of sender
- Name and department of recipient
- Description of mail (such as an invitation to speak at a banquet)
- Type of mail (such as a fax message)
- To whom forwarded for action
- Type of action required
- Follow-up date (if any)

This type of record is very useful to traveling executives who like to have a summary of activity in the office when they aren't there to observe the work themselves.

Submitting the Mail

Follow the executive's preference in submitting the mail. The practice in your office may include some or all of the following:

- Collecting incoming conventional and electronic mail and submitting it to your boss one or more times a day, according to preference

- Organizing the mail according to category and priority, as described above, before submission

- Using colored folders or labels to separate categories or designate priority

- Attaching routing slips or using interoffice envelopes for items to be circulated among persons outside the office

- Photocopying important material when appropriate and routing the photocopy, keeping the original in the files

- Forwarding mail to absent employers and employees by fax, express mail, or other means, as preferred by the absent person

- Using action-requested slips for mail forwarded to others on which you can check off action requested, such as:
  - ❏ For your information
  - ❏ For your action
  - ❏ For your approval
  - ❏ For your comments
  - ❏ Please forward
  - ❏ Please return
  - ❏ Please review with me
  - ❏ Please file
  - ❏ _____

- Making printouts of waiting E-mail messages for submission (if hard copies are preferred by the executive)

- Annotating and highlighting the mail, as described earlier, before submission

- Attaching files and other pertinent material that will help the executive compose a reply

OUTGOING MAIL

After you have prepared a conventional or electronic message, as described in Chapters 4 and 5, you will need to follow the proper procedure in preparing each piece for mailing. Certain practices may differ from one office to another, but other steps are standard in all offices. Some small offices, for example, don't have enough mail volume to warrant the use of a postage meter and hence manually apply stamps to all postal envelopes. Other offices may have sophisticated electronic mailing equipment or send primarily faxes and E-mail. Although such matters may differ, other practices, such as carefully proofreading a message, should be mandatory in all offices.

Proofreading Outgoing Mail

A truly professional secretary scrutinizes all outgoing correspondence for everything from format to style to spelling to syntax. (For guidelines, see Chapters 4–6 and 10–11.) Whether the material is prepared by typewriter or computer or typed from a dictation belt or a handwritten draft, accuracy is essential.

Spell-checkers can relieve secretaries of part of the burden of proofreading but cannot find a missing sentence or a "correct" word such as *it's* that was inadvertently substituted for *its.* Some errors are likely to be found only if the typed material is read or checked against the original handwritten or dictated material. Since sloppy work, inaccuracies, and other errors can cause senders to lose clients and customers, and thus future or present income, the proofreading function should be handled with extreme care, and nothing less than 100 percent accuracy should be considered acceptable.

Getting Signatures

How to Present Mail for Signing   Letters, contracts, checks, or forms in need of signing may be submitted to the executive in several ways. You might place all such paperwork in a file folder labeled "To Be Signed," indicate on each piece where the signature and date are to appear (use a self-sticking note if it will be helpful), and submit the folder with items for signing at the executive's convenience. It is preferable to submit a stack of documents all at one time rather than seeking signatures several times throughout the day. However, a letter, contract, or form sometimes must get out quickly, and you will not be able to wait until you've accumulated numerous documents. That's when a clipboard comes in handy. It enables someone to sign a letter in the absence of desk space, such as while sitting at a computer terminal or in a reading chair.

Ask your boss if he or she prefers receiving the letters to be signed with or without envelopes attached. If envelopes aren't required, you can be typing them while your boss is signing the letters. If you sign letters on an executive's behalf, follow the instructions given in Chapter 5.

Before folding and inserting letters in their envelopes, check them one more time to be certain the executive did not forget to sign something. Sending out an unsigned letter indicates carelessness on your part, and certain material, such as an agreement, would be invalid without a signature.

E-Mail Confirmation Copies If you are sending E-mail or another type of electronic transmission, follow the practice in your office regarding confirmation copies. It is common in some offices to send a hard-copy printout of an electronically transmitted message by regular mail as a confirmation copy. Although E-mail messages are generally typed in a memo format (see Chapter 5), which requires no signature, some executives want to initial any printouts that are sent as confirmation copies.

Handling Enclosures

Before sealing each outgoing piece of mail, double-check that all required enclosures have been included. During the typing phase, an enclosure notation should have been added at the bottom of the letter. (See Chapter 5.) The advantage of specifying *what* is enclosed, such as *Enc.: Schedule,* is that you can glance at the enclosure notation before sealing the letter to be certain that nothing was omitted. If you did not specify *what* is enclosed, check the enclosures against your original instructions.

Small enclosures are usually attached in front of a letter and large enclosures behind it. Loose items, such as coins, should first be inserted in a small envelope or taped to a card. Because paper clips can damage mailing equipment, however, many secretaries prefer to fold enclosures and tuck them inside the fold of the letter rather than clip them to the letter. Enclosures too large to fold are placed flat and unattached *behind* the cover letter.

Handling File Copies

Before the letter is mailed, the required number of file copies should be made. In the case of electronic filing, the document should be saved in the appropriate file name and copied into different files as required. In the case of conventional filing, copies of the document should be filed in the appropriate alphabetical, numeric, or alphanumerical system. Refer to Chapter 7 for a description of the various filing systems.

Maintaining a Follow-up Record

Outgoing mail records are less common than incoming mail records that show the disposition of letters received and routed to others for action. If an outgoing record is required in your office as a follow-up guide, use a columnar format and include the following headings:

Date sent
Name and address of recipient
Description of material sent
Method of mail or transmission
Follow-up date

More common than a follow-up record, however, is the follow-up file or reminder system described in Chapter 7.

Preparing Envelopes

Envelopes prepared for postal delivery should be addressed according to the format and style requirements given in Chapter 5. Labels may be provided for private courier packages, although some courier services provide their own envelopes and prepare the labels themselves or attach a form that you have completed. If you do type a label, however, follow the same style of addressing used for postal mail. Check that the degree of color contrast between the envelope or mailing label and the typed address is sharp enough to be detected by optical character scanners.

Folding and Inserting Material

Standard Procedure. Letters should be folded and inserted according to the kind of envelope selected. Standard sizes are given in Chapter 5, and the illustration in this chapter indicates the traditional way of folding and inserting material in No. 6¾ and No. 10 envelopes.

If you're mailing multiple sheets, arrange them so that when the envelope is opened and the letter unfolded, the text will be right side up.

If you use clips to attach the pages, position the clip and insert the pages in the envelope so that the clip falls at the *bottom* of the envelope where it is less likely to damage the postal equipment.

Window Envelopes. Offices sending a lot of conventional international mail may use overseas airmail envelopes that are lighter than standard office envelopes. Window envelopes, often used in mass mailings, require careful insertion of letters. If the recipient's name and address do not appear through the window, the time you have saved by not addressing the envelope separately will have been wasted. Some letterhead stationery has a line indicating where to fold the page so that the recipient's name and address will show through the window. Generally, the procedure is to fold the sheet in thirds with the inside address outside

Folding and Inserting Stationery into Envelopes

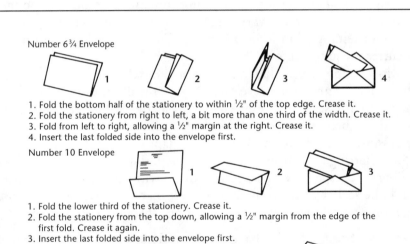

Number 6¾ Envelope

1. Fold the bottom half of the stationery to within ½" of the top edge. Crease it.
2. Fold the stationery from right to left, a bit more than one third of the width. Crease it.
3. Fold from left to right, allowing a ½" margin at the right. Crease it.
4. Insert the last folded side into the envelope first.

Number 10 Envelope

1. Fold the lower third of the stationery. Crease it.
2. Fold the stationery from the top down, allowing a ½" margin from the edge of the first fold. Crease it again.
3. Insert the last folded side into the envelope first.

Window Envelope

1. Fold the bottom third of the letter. Crease it.
2. Fan-fold the upper section of the letter back to the edge of the first fold so that the inside address will be on the outside and not on the inside. Crease it.
3. Insert the stationery so that the inside address is clearly visible through the window (¼" margins needed).

Note: Some printed letterhead intended exclusively for window applications is marked to indicate placement of the inside address. Printed fold lines are often included.

on the *top*. Allow about ¼ to ⅛ inch between the edge of the window and the address to prevent blocking any part of the address.

Enclosures. When including a letter with a larger item, you can fold and insert the letter into its matching envelope and pack it with the enclosure in a larger mailer. Or you can put both letter and enclosure into a single large envelope. If you choose not to fold them, add a piece of cardboard to prevent damage in transit. Use padded mailers for books, small manuscripts, press kits, files, or similar materials, and use diskette mailers for floppy disks. Other special mailers are available for photographs, rolled material such as blueprints, and other fragile or sensitive material.

Sealing Envelopes   Some small offices do not have electronic equipment that seals as well as meters the mail, and all offices occasionally mail odd-sized material that requires manual attention. There are several ways to seal an envelope or mailing container: by mouth, sponge, mailing tape, or staples. Very large, heavy packages may have to be banded or reinforced in some other way. Consult your local post office for current requirements.

Most people simply lick an occasional envelope to seal it or use a wet sponge for numerous envelopes. Notice the illustration of envelope placement for sealing several envelopes at once. The envelopes are stacked one behind the other with flaps open and the glue side up. After passing a wet sponge over them, the flaps can be folded down one by one, starting at the top. For mailing bags, staples work well, as does mailing tape, especially the kind reinforced with strands of fiber; boxes should be sealed with strong tape. Check that you have not left loose edges on a parcel that will jam postal or private courier equipment.

Stamping the Mail   You have several options for stamping outgoing mail, including postage meters, imprints, and manual methods. If you do not have a mailroom, you should have an accurate postage scale and lists of the current postage rates applicable to the classes of mail service that your office uses.

In some offices secretaries code the mail so that the mailroom can charge the appropriate office account. You may, for example, be required to pencil the code in a corner of the envelope or on the top envelope in a bundle. Before metering the mail or applying stamps, a mailroom clerk will record the code or key it into a meter designed to track expenditures by account.

Sponge-Sealing of Many Envelopes

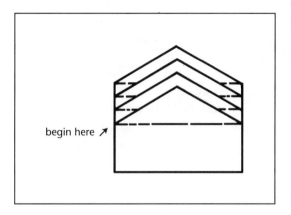

begin here ↗

Postage Meters. Postage meter bases are sold or leased by vendors licensed by the Postal Service. The part of a meter system that keeps track of how much money you've paid and how much of the postage you've used can only be rented from the Postal Service.

The amount of postage for which the meter is set must be purchased at a post office, and when the supply is depleted, the meter must be replenished and reset. In some cases, you can replenish the supply by telephone.

The meter portion of the system can be either a mechanical or electronic (pushbutton) device. Meters differ in speed and in other features. Some, for example, have a manual feed; others have an automatic feed. Most bases have tape dispensers for use with packages too large to feed through, but not all have envelope sealers. Some meters have cost-accounting features that enable you to keep track of expenditures by client or account. Contact equipment vendors and your local post office for details about metering your mail.

Permit Imprints. With a permit imprint an organization can have postage printed directly onto envelopes or postcards. Postage for presorted mail must be paid by meter, permit imprint, or precanceled stamps. A mailer must obtain a permit to use imprints and pay postage in cash before or at the time of mailing. Imprints may be used on labels, wrappers, envelopes, and other containers. Contact your local post office for further information about permit imprints and the regulations concerning *indicia* (the postal markings imprinted on envelopes and labels).

Postage Stamps. Postage stamps can be applied by hand to any type of envelope or package. Stamps are available in rolls or sheets, and the rolls can be inserted in small stamp dispensers sold in office-supply stores. Care must be taken to ensure that the moistened stamps adhere to the envelope or package surface. Envelopes and mailers made of glossy paper may shed their stamps before reaching the intended recipients. The letters then may be returned to you for postage, thus delaying delivery, or they may be delivered to the addressee with postage due. If you have a large mailing with this problem, notify your post office. Mail handlers will look for the problematic pieces and will help you to rectify the difficulty.

TYPES OF MAIL

Postal Mail

U.S. Postal Service mail accounts for a substantial portion of all conventional mail. Because such a significant portion of all mail is postal mail, secretaries need to be aware of the principal domestic and international classes of mail and the associated postal services.

Subscriptions to the *Domestic Mail Manual* and the *International Mail Manual* are available from the Superintendent of Documents in Washington, D.C. Also, miscellaneous brochures and pamphlets are available at no charge from local post offices, and the *National Five-Digit ZIP Code and Post Office Directory* can be purchased from The National Information Data Center, P.O. Box 96523, Washington, D.C. 20090-6523. All of these publications are helpful to secretaries who regularly handle outgoing mail.

Domestic Mail   Domestic mail consists of five major classifications. Each category within a particular classification must meet the requirements of the U.S. Postal Service. Since extensive rules and regulations apply, secretaries should consult their local post offices for full details. For a description of ZIP codes and ZIP + 4 codes, see Chapter 5.

> *Express Mail:* An expedited service for any mailable matter that is not excluded by the Department of Transportation, with next-day delivery to most destinations. Categories include *Express Mail next-day/second-day services, same-day airport service, custom-designed service,* and *military service.*

First-class mail: Any mailable matter that is not excluded by the Department of Transportation. *Priority mail* is first-class mail over 11 ounces. *Postal cards and postcards* (commercial) may be sent first class at a lower rate. *Presorted first-class mail, first-class carrier route, first-class barcoded flats,* and *first-class presorted barcoded letters and cards* all refer to various types of mailings of five hundred pieces or more.

Second-class mail: Generally used for newspapers and magazines issued regularly at least four times a year. Second-class mail includes *second-class — nonprofit, classroom, science-or-agriculture; second-class presort; second-class barcoded letters;* and *second-class barcoded flats.* These categories of mail may be eligible for a discount if properly coded and sorted.

Third-class mail: Generally, mail not required to be sent first class and not entered as second-class mail. The categories include *third-class eligible for nonprofit status, third-class barcoded flats, third-class basic and ⅗ presort, third-class carrier-route presort, third-class walk-sequence presort, third-class barcoded letters, machinable parcels,* and *third-class destination entry discount mailings.* Single-piece third-class rates are lower than first-class rates, and certain bulk third-class mailings of two hundred pieces or more may be eligible for a discount if prepared and sorted according to specific standards.

Fourth-class mail: Printed material and merchandise not sent as first-, second-, or third-class mail. The categories include *fourth-class bound printed matter, special fourth class, fourth-class library rate,* and *fourth-class parcel post.* Fourth-class mail is a slower, less expensive method of sending certain material. To qualify as fourth-class mail, the mailings must meet eligibility standards for single-piece and presort rates.

The Postal Service also offers a variety of services.

Business-reply mail: Allows permit holders to pay postage for mail received.

Certificate of mailing: Evidence of mailing.

Certified mail: Proof of delivery, with record of delivery kept at the recipient's post office.

Collect on delivery (C.O.D.): Allows the Postal Service to collect the price and cost of postage for an article at the time it is delivered.

Forwarding: Provides for the forwarding of all classes of mail provided the mail is properly prepared and addressed. Generally, there is no charge for Express Mail, first-class mail, and some fourth-class mail and single-piece third-class mail.

Insured mail: Indemnity coverage for merchandise.

Merchandise return service: Allows permit holders to pay postage for parcels received from customers.

Money orders: Provides for the transfer of funds to recipients.

Parcel airlift (PAL): Provides for air transport of parcels on a space-available basis to or from military post offices outside the forty-eight contiguous states for dispatch to other overseas military post offices or offices within the forty-eight contiguous states.

Registered mail: Provides the most secure service for domestic mail.

Restricted delivery: Directs delivery only to the addressee or an authorized agent.

Return receipt: Proof of delivery provided to the sender.

Return receipt for merchandise: Provides sender with a mailing receipt and a return receipt.

Special delivery: Preferential handling of mail if practical and expedited delivery at the destination.

Special handling: Preferential handling of third- and fourth-class mail if practical.

To improve address quality, the Postal Service offers to do the following for a designated fee:

- To correct name and address lists
- To correct occupant lists
- To sort mailing lists on cards by five-digit zip code

Corrections are marked directly on the list you submit to the Postal Service.

The Postal Service also provides the following ZIP + 4 information for a designated charge:

- *ZIP + 4 Database Tape and Quarterly Cumulative Updates,* which contain a master copy of the ZIP + 4 databases and quarterly updates since the last release date.

- *ZIP + 4 Database Tape and Monthly Transactions,* which contain a master copy of the ZIP + 4 database and monthly updates since the last release date.

- *Technical Guide,* which contains data formats and field definitions of the records in ZIP + 4 products. Although included with the updates just described, it can also be ordered separately.

International Mail   International mail consists of three major classifications. Each type of mail must meet the specific requirements of the U.S. Postal Service. As is the case with domestic mail, extensive rules and regulations apply to international mail, with country by country variations. Secretaries should therefore consult their local post offices for complete details.

Postal Union mail: Mail governed by the regulations of the Convention of the Universal Postal Union. Categories include *letters and cards* (LC mail), including aerogrammes, and *other articles* (AO mail), such as printed matter, books and sheet music, periodicals, matter for the blind, and small packets. Priority airmail is available for bulk mailers of LC and AO items.

Parcel post: Sometimes referred to as CP mail (colis postaux, referring to postal parcels), it includes only one category that is equivalent to domestic fourth-class, zone-rated parcel post.

Express Mail international service: An expedited service exchanged with other countries under agreements and memoranda of understanding with the postal administrations of those countries. The two categories are custom-designed service and on-demand service.

A variety of services are available to international mailers similar to the services offered by the Postal Service for domestic mail.

Certificate of mailing: Evidence of mailing.

Insured mail: Indemnity coverage for merchandise.

International business-reply mail: Allows permit holders to pay postage for envelopes and cards received from other countries.

International postal money orders: Provides for the transfer of funds to individuals or firms in countries that have this agreement with the United States.

International reply coupons: Allows a sender to prepay a reply by sending coupons that the recipient can exchange for stamps in countries that allow this.

Recall/change of address: Allows a sender to recall an item or change its address subject to certain conditions and the regulations in the destination country.

Registered mail: Provides additional protection and security for items but less indemnity than insured mail.

Restricted delivery: Generally, directs delivery only to the addressee or an authorized agent, but conditions vary from country to country.

Return receipt: Proof of delivery.

Special delivery: Preferential handling of mail and, depending on the regulations at the destination post office, more expeditious delivery of Postal Union mail.

Special handling: Preferential handling, if practical, of surface parcel post, printed matter, matter for the blind, and small packets.

The *International Mail Manual* describes the prohibitions, restrictions, required Customs forms, size limits, and other information that applies to each country of the world.

Private Delivery Services

Private shipping, delivery, and courier companies offer services that rival those of the Postal Service. In some instances these operations feature services that a post office does not provide. Most private companies will establish an account providing for regular billing and will supply you with preprinted mailing forms. The urgency of your mailings and your own budgetary concerns should always be considered in your choice of mailing methods.

Since each company has its own regulations, rates, and delivery schedule, it is necessary to contact each one for comparison. Check the yellow pages of your local telephone directory for names and telephone numbers (often toll-free), commonly listed under "Air Freight and Package Express Services," "Delivery Services," "Courier Services," or "Messenger Services." Some bus lines and other companies also offer package delivery as a secondary service.

National and International Services   Major delivery services offer both national and international service, including express service for overnight or other expedited transport. Secretaries need to consider whether the extra cost for overnight service is warranted. For example, it serves no useful purpose to send a package by overnight service on Friday if no one will be available at the destination on Saturday.

Delivery services will usually provide pickup as well as delivery, particularly if you maintain an account with the company. In other cases, you can visit an office of the company or take your material to a local mail service that serves as an agent for the delivery company. Such mail services add their own handling charge to the transport charge of the delivery company.

Local Services   In some cities local messenger services and taxis offer same-day delivery service within your city. They will collect a parcel from your office and deliver it across town, often within the same hour. The cost, however, can be high compared with the cost of sending the same parcel by postal mail. But the impact of a hand-delivered letter may offset the expense. Many lobbyists and politicians distribute their "media advisories" (press releases) by messenger because hand-delivered items are usually treated with higher priority in the recipients' offices. Check the messenger's references carefully.

Electronic Mail

Electronic mail refers to written messages that are transmitted and received electronically between terminals. For the transfer of material to take place, the terminals are usually connected by direct wiring of machines in a local area network (LAN) or by telephone lines or satellites. As explained in Chapter 1, businesses may have a stand-alone system that does nothing but handle E-mail or an integrated system that handles not only E-mail but word processing and other information/data handling. The illustration of E-mail systems in Chapter 1 depicts a system based on a central computer and one based on a computer network.

E-Mail Transmissions   A flexible E-mail system permits and expedites fast, accurate communication among individuals, groups, departments, and corporations. With E-mail software you can create ("write"), edit, transmit, read, and print out your own mail. Conversely, you can answer your incoming mail, forward messages to other people using the system, request that return receipts be sent to your terminal, and file the mail. After you have keyed in your message, it is transmitted at once — there is no delay involving mail pickup and delivery — and the recipient of the message can read that message right away or at a later, more convenient time (an additional advantage from the standpoint of workflow and time management).

E-mail software differs from word processing software, which enables you to produce a variety of complex documents and perform other tasks, such as mathematical calculations. E-mail software usually has less sophisticated editing capabilities and is designed not just to create a message but to program it for transmission.

To send something by E-mail, you keyboard the message on your computer according to the instructions of your software and enter the series of commands needed to tell your computer where the message is going. The particular codes to use and the required message format also depend on the software program you are using. If you belong to a subscriber network, you must follow the appropriate instructions for accessing the network and transmitting to other users on the network. After you press the required keys for transmission, your message will be sent to the recipient's receiving computer, where it is stored in memory referred to as an electronic mailbox.

E-Mail Capabilities   E-mail software usually deals with mail preparation, reception, filing, distribution, and utilities, such as indexing. Although programs differ in features and range of capabilities, a system might include the following mail functions:

> *Preparation:* Create, edit, send
> *Reception:* Read, answer, forward, print, delete
> *Filing:* File, search file, read list, print list
> *Distribution:* Send to, copies, mailing lists
> *Utilities:* Indexing

Many systems offer other capabilities either as standard or as options, for example:

Append: The system will allow you to attach prepared documents to the bottom of a message.

Directory: The system can supply a list of its users. (On public systems the directory may be intentionally restrictive.)

Distribution: The system can send the same message to a prestored list of recipients.

Editing: Text can be edited off-line before transmission.

Gateway services: You can send other messages, such as telexes, through the system.

Message status: The system can list the headers of incoming messages and the status of outgoing messages, for example, whether or not they have been transmitted.

Registered mail: The system sends you a confirmation when the recipient reads the message.

Reply requested: After you read a message, the system requires that you type a response, which immediately goes to the sender's mailbox.

Security provisions: Access can be restricted by passwords, by the encryption of messages, or by both.

Store and forward: The system can store a message for delivery at a later date.

Many of these capabilities can reduce or eliminate routine, time-consuming secretarial tasks. For instance, *Edit* disposes of drafts and redrafts. *Send* bypasses the fold-insert-into-envelope-affix-stamp operation. *Answer* enables the executive to respond to a letter or memo directly without intervention of the dictation-transcription-read-correct-edit operations. *File* and *search file* virtually eliminate one of the tasks most disliked by secretaries. Once you eliminate mundane chores such as filing, you will have more time to devote to other, more enjoyable and challenging responsibilities.

Advantages of E-Mail   E-mail combines the speed of a telephone call with the permanency and impact of a letter and at the same time liberates the secretary from the drudgery of the past. Other advantages stem from the ability of most equipment to operate unattended, thus eliminating "telephone tag" (people leaving telephone messages in response to previous messages but never reaching one another) and allowing overnight operation when transmission charges are lower. Another advantage to overnight transmission and unattended reception of messages is the fact that an executive returning late from a trip need not go into the office on the way home to obtain accumulated messages or call you for an update on the messages. The executive can, with proper equipment, dial into the mail system from any location at any time and receive the messages.

Public Systems Private organizations offer E-mail services on a subscription basis. You can exchange messages with any other subscriber, transmitting outgoing messages to the recipient's mailbox and downloading any messages you find in your own mailbox. Services like these are offered as an extra option by several packet-switching networks, data service companies, communications carriers, and specialized electronic-mail companies. The gateway services offered by some telex carriers are similar. Prices vary widely, as do service options.

Data Networks Computer-based message systems often employ LANs, described earlier, or packet-switching networks. Although some of them use other switching techniques, *packet-switching network* has become a generic term for them. Subscribers attach their computers directly to the network, and anyone can reach that computer as long as he or she has access to the network.

You can usually access a network through a local telephone number. After the connection has been established, the network may ask for a terminal identifier so that it can add special features (such as filler characters after a carriage return) to the data stream required by some terminals. Then you usually type in the code identifier of the computer you want to reach. If that computer accepts your call, thereafter you will be able to act as though you were attached directly to the computer, and the packet-switching network will become "invisible."

Mailgrams Mailgrams are electronic messages handled jointly by Western Union and the Postal Service. Senders may transmit their messages to Western Union by telephone, computer, fax, or teletypewriter. Western Union then transmits the message electronically to the post office nearest the recipient. There, it is delivered in the next regular mail.

The cost, which is based on the number of words, is lower than that of a telegram, described at the end of this chapter.

Fax Mail

Transmission Procedure   Using a fax machine or a computer equipped to send faxes, as described in Chapter 1, you can transmit text and graphics in seconds or minutes over the telephone lines to a receiving machine. Since the standards established by the Consultative Committee on International Telegraph and Telephone allow for compatibility between brands, the sender and receiver need not have machines manufactured by the same company.

With most fax machines you can transmit messages simply by inserting a document and pressing a "Start" button. Users of computer faxes should follow the instructions of their software. In addition to automatic sending and receiving, fax machines may have a variety of other features, either standard or as options, such as the following:

Polling: You can insert a document in the document feeder for automatic transmission to a fax when that fax calls; or you can call a remote fax and retrieve someone else's document programmed for polling.

Automatic receiving: You can set a fax machine in a similar manner to receive any incoming documents automatically.

Activity reports: The machine can print out a list of the transmissions and receptions that it performed on a given day.

Sender ID: As a sort of postmark the machine will print the telephone number or code name of the message sender, as well as the date, time, and page count across the top or bottom of the page.

Local copy: The machine can be used as if it were an office photocopier.

Computer printer: Although the coding used by Group III machines is not the same as ASCII (American Standard Code for Information Interchange) or any other data communications code, some machines have the ability to receive ASCII and function as if they were computer printers. The transmission can also be stored in a computer just as any other digital data can be.

Small portable fax machines can be used from any location where there are standard telephone jacks, hotel data jacks, or pay telephones with input jacks. Some of the machines can only send messages; others can also receive fax and E-mail messages. Some additionally provide electronic appointment calendars, calculators, currency converters, security codes, and other features.

Fax Services   Many businesses — from local mail services to drugstores — offer fax service where you can take your document to be sent for a fee. Also, the U.S. Postal Service and certain foreign postal services offer INTELPOST. This service enables you to transmit documents to or from some domestic post offices to a post office in a foreign city. At the destination it can be picked up or delivered through the regular mail system.

Telex Mail

A forerunner to the fax machine, the teletypewriter is still used in some U.S. businesses. (See Chapter 1.) It is more heavily used in Europe, however, than in the United States, where fax mail and E-mail are more popular. Using a keyboard-printer and a telephone dial-up system, a subscriber to a telex network can send a message that will be printed out on a recipient's teletypewriter. Unlike a fax machine, a teletypewriter will transmit only alphanumeric information. However, users can modify their computers to provide higher-quality and faster transmission than is possible with a teletypewriter.

Telex Networks   Private companies may have their own teletypewriter network, or they may use a network of Western Union or one of the international carriers. The principal networks are Telex I, Telex II (formerly TWX), and Teletex. The Teletex standard has surpassed the older telex technologies in both speed and quality of output. Unlike Telex I and Telex II, Teletex messages can be typed in uppercase and lowercase letters and formatted to look like a regular business letter.

All three networks are connected, and a subscriber on one can send a message to a subscriber on another. The vast telex network can also be used to send messages by satellite to ships and offshore oil platforms. Called INMARSAT, this service is offered by Western Union and the international carriers. Numbers of telex subscribers are listed in a telex directory.

Telegrams   Telegrams are a form of telex message sent to receivers who don't have a teletypewriter or teleprinter. Messages are given to Western Union, which transmits them by the fastest means and, at the destination, calls the recipient or delivers the message printed out. International telegrams (cablegrams) are handled at the destination according to procedures that are standard in the particular country. Cablegrams can also be sent through any international carrier offering this service. Costs, which are based on the number of words and are usually higher than other forms of transmission, may be charged to the sender's telephone number or billed to a customer account.

BUSINESS ENGLISH

Secretaries spend most of each day using some form of communication. Whether the communication is oral or written and whether it is being initiated by the secretary or being prepared for someone else, it must contain correct grammar and appropriate word choice. Secretaries therefore must have an above-average command of the English language so that their oral and written messages are accurate and effective. Errors in grammar and word usage will not only decrease the effectiveness of a message but will cast secretaries, their bosses, and their companies in an unfavorable light.

RULES OF ENGLISH

Grammatical Terms

To understand the basis of English grammar, it is first necessary to understand the grammatical terms that are used to describe the function of parts of speech and other words in a sentence. This chapter describes the eight parts of speech and the phrases, clauses, sentences, and paragraphs in which they are used. For definitions of the following terms, refer to the appropriate section.

TERM	SECTION
Abstract noun	Noun
Active voice	Verb
Adjective	Adjective
Adverb	Adverb
Affirmative adverb	Adverb

TERM	SECTION
Auxiliary verb	Verb
Case	Pronoun
Clause	Phrases, Clauses, Sentences, and Paragraphs
Collective noun	Noun
Common noun	Noun
Comparative degree	Adjective, Adverb
Complex sentence	Phrases, Clauses, Sentences, and Paragraphs
Compound sentence	Phrases, Clauses, Sentences, and Paragraphs
Compound and complex sentence	Phrases, Clauses, Sentences, and Paragraphs
Concrete noun	Noun
Conjunction	Conjunction
Conjunctive adverb	Adverb
Coordinate conjunction	Conjunction
Correlative conjunction	Conjunction
Declarative sentence	Phrases, Clauses, Sentences, and Paragraphs
Definite pronoun	Pronoun
Demonstrative pronoun	Pronoun
Dependent (subordinate) clause	Phrases, Clauses, Sentences, and Paragraphs
Exclamatory sentence	Phrases, Clauses, Sentences, and Paragraphs
Gerund	Verb
Imperative mood	Verb
Imperative sentence	Phrases, Clauses, Sentences, and Paragraphs
Inactive voice	Verb
Indefinite pronoun	Pronoun
Independent clause	Phrases, Clauses, Sentences, and Paragraphs
Indicative mood	Verb
Infinitive	Verb
Interjection	Interjection
Interrogative adverb	Adverb

TERM	SECTION
Interrogative pronoun	Pronoun
Interrogative sentence	Phrases, Clauses, Sentences, and Paragraphs
Intransitive verb	Verb
Irregular verb	Verb
Modifier	Adjective, Adverb
Mood	Verb
Negative adverb	Adverb
Nominative case	Pronoun
Nonrestrictive clause	Phrases, Clauses, Sentences, and Paragraphs
Noun	Noun
Objective case	Pronoun
Participle	Verb
Passive voice	Verb
Person	Verb
Personal pronoun	Pronoun
Phrase	Phrases, Clauses, Sentences, and Paragraphs
Positive degree	Adjective, Adverb
Possessive case	Pronoun
Predicate adjective	Adjective
Preposition	Preposition
Prepositional phrase	Preposition
Principal verb	Verb
Pronoun	Pronoun
Proper adjective	Adjective
Proper noun	Noun
Reciprocal pronoun	Pronoun
Reflexive pronoun	Pronoun
Regular verb	Verb
Relative adjective	Adjective
Relative pronoun	Pronoun
Restrictive clause	Phrases, Clauses, Sentences, and Paragraphs
Sentence	Phrases, Clauses, Sentences, and Paragraphs
Sentence adverb	Adverb

TERM	SECTION
Simple sentence	Phrases, Clauses, Sentences, and Paragraphs
Subjunctive mood	Verb
Subordinate conjunction	Conjunction
Superlative degree	Adjective, Adverb
Tense	Verb
Transitive verb	Verb
Verb	Verb
Verbal	Verb
Voice	Verb

Several other terms will also help you review the basics of grammar.

Antecedent: The word, phrase, or clause to which a pronoun refers: *Mr. Parsons* [noun] entered *his* [pronoun] office.

Appositive: A noun or noun phrase that explains another word(s): Phyllis Rogers, *president,* will retire this month.

Article: An adjective such as the indefinite articles *a* and *an* or the definite article *the:* She received *a* promotion.

Complement: A word(s) used after a verb to complete its meaning: The overactive economy caused the *inflation.*

Compound predicate: Two or more connected verbs or verb phrases: He *studied* and *analyzed* the problem.

Compound subject: Two or more words in the subject that are connected by conjunctions such as *and, or,* or *nor:* The *secretary* and the *executive* have adjoining offices.

Dangling modifier: A word(s) that does not modify or logically refer to any other word: *Having completed the letter* [dangling], the fax was transmitted. *Better: Having completed the letter, she* transmitted the fax.

Direct object: A word or phrase referring to the person or thing receiving the action of a verb; frequently, it answers the question "what" or "whom": She opened [what?] the *letter.*

Expletive: A word such as *there* that is placed where the subject normally would be positioned: *It* was caused by a computer malfunction. *Better:* A *computer malfunction* caused it.

Idiom: An expression peculiar to a particular language that is peculiar to itself grammatically or cannot be understood from the individual meanings of the elements: The company was prepared to *see it through.* (Idioms are often confusing to people in other countries and should be avoided in international correspondence.)

Indirect object: An object *indirectly* affected by the action of a verb: Mr. Schwartz gave his *secretary* [indirect object] a new computer [direct object].

Misplaced modifier: A word positioned so that it modifies the wrong word or changes the meaning of the sentence: He *only* writes [doesn't do anything else] technical reports. He writes *only* technical [not nontechnical] reports.

Predicate: The part of a sentence, including the verb, objects, or phrases governed by the verb, that modifies the subject: He *joined the committee.*

Split infinitive: An infinitive verb form that has an element, such as an adverb, interposed between *to* and the verb form: *to* firmly *unite.* Although this position is avoided by some writers, it is more desirable than creating an awkward construction by trying to avoid it: They want *to unite firmly* [awkward] the party.

Subject: The part of a sentence, including the noun, noun phrase, or pronoun, that denotes the doer of the action, the receiver of the action, or what is described by the predicate: *He* joined the committee.

Parts of Speech

The parts of speech that are described here are the noun, pronoun, verb, adjective, adverb, preposition, conjunction, and interjection. Knowing how these parts should be used in a sentence will help you avoid the mistakes that detract from both your message and your image as an office professional.

Noun   A *noun* is a word that names a person (*Joe*), place (*New York*), thing (*book*), or abstraction (*theory*). *Proper nouns* name specific persons, places, or things (*Silicon Valley; Internet*); *common nouns* are sometimes classified as *abstract nouns* that name ideas, beliefs, or qualities (*capitalism*) and *concrete nouns* that name tangible things (*computer*).

The forms of a noun can show possession (the *treasurer's report*) and number, singular or plural (*company, companies*), as explained next.

Number. Some nouns are singular (*telephone*) or plural (*telephones*); others may be used as both singular and plural nouns (*politics, mathematics*). Chapter 11 has more to say about spelling plurals and the use of variant forms. Some irregular nouns, for example, indicate the plural by a change in the base form (*child, children*) or vowel (*mouse, mice*), others have more than one acceptable plural form (*phenomena, phenomenons*), and still others undergo no change (*sheep, sheep*).

Collective Nouns. A *collective noun* denotes a collection of persons or things regarded as a unit. It takes a singular verb when it refers to the collection as a whole and a plural verb when it refers to the members of the collection as separate persons or things: The *committee was* in executive session. The *committee have* all left for the day. (In British usage, collective nouns are most often construed as plural: The *government are* committed to a liberal policy.) A collective noun should not be treated as both singular and plural in the *same* construction: The *company is* determined to press *its* [not *their*] claim. Examples of collective nouns are *clergy, committee, company, enemy, family, flock, group, public,* and *team.*

Use of Nouns. A noun can be the *subject* of a sentence: The *housing industry* is in trouble; the *direct object of a verb*: Spiraling interest rates and inflation have softened the *housing industry*; the *object of a preposition*: This is one of the hottest *issues* in the *housing industry*; or the *indirect object of a verb*: Give the *housing industry* a chance and it may recover.

Pronoun   A *pronoun* is a word substituted for a noun. It refers to a person or thing that has been named or understood in a particular context. Pronouns have grammatical case (nominative, possessive, or objective), number (singular or plural), person (first, second, or third), and gender (masculine, feminine, or neuter).

Case. The case of a pronoun is determined by its function in the sentence. The following pronouns are used in each case:

Nominative: I, we, you, he, she, it, they, who

Possessive: my, mine, our, ours, your, yours, his, her, hers, its, their, theirs, whose

Objective: me, us, you, him, her, it, them, whom

The *nominative case* is used in these instances:

- When the pronoun is used as the subject: *We* are ready.

- After a form of the verb *be* (in formal writing): It is *I.*

- After the conjunctions *as* and *than* (in formal writing): She is a faster typist than *I* [am].

- When the pronoun is used in apposition to the subject noun or a predicate noun: The two employees [subject noun] — Brad and *he* — were transferred.

The *possessive case* is used in these instances:

- To show relationships such as possession, source, or authorship: *Their* work is outstanding.

- Before a gerund (in formal writing): The article was complimentary to Mr. Lewis concerning *his* working hard on the project.

The *objective case* is used in these instances:

- When the pronoun is the object of a verb: The high absenteeism disturbed *him.*

- When the pronoun *whom* is the object of a verb (in formal writing): Mrs. Priestly is the speaker *whom* we most admired.

- When the pronoun is the object of a verbal, such as a participle or gerund: Meeting *her* was interesting.

- When the pronoun is the object of a preposition: Between you and *me,* the office is in chaos.

- After the conjunctions *as* and *than* when the pronoun is the object of a verb omitted from the sentence: Her boss praised her as much as [he praised] *him.*

- When the pronoun is used in apposition to a noun that is an object: The company promoted two sales representatives — Jennifer Black and *me* — last week.

Number. Pronouns can be singular or plural and should agree with their verbs accordingly: *He has* a good job. *They have* good jobs.
Person. Pronouns can be classified by person (first, second, third) and must agree with their verbs accordingly:

First person: *I* am, *we* are
Second person: *You* are
Third person: *He/she* is, *they* are, *it* is

Gender. Pronouns can be classified by gender, with *he* being masculine; *she,* feminine; and *it,* neuter. Contemporary writing favors a nonsexist application of these personal pronouns, using *he and she* or *they* when appropriate, rather than *he* alone. In any case, the property of gender must be consistent between a pronoun and its antecedent: The company [antecedent] has benefited from *its* [possessive pronoun] new location.

Classes of Pronouns.

Personal pronoun: A pronoun that stands for the names of persons, places, or things (*I, you, he, she, it, we,* and *they*): *We* will produce the program, and *they* will distribute it. *See also* the definition of a reflexive pronoun.

Relative pronoun: A pronoun such as *who, what, that,* and *which* that refers to an antecedent and introduces a dependent clause. *Who* is used with persons; *that* with either persons, animals, or inanimate objects; *what* with things; and *which* with animals or inanimate objects: She [antecedent] is a leader *who is destined for greatness* [dependent clause].

Interrogative pronoun: A pronoun such as *who, which,* and *what* that is used in a direct question: *What* do you want us to do?

Demonstrative (definite) pronoun: A pronoun such as *this, that, these,* and *those* that points definitely to persons or things to which the pronoun refers: *That* is the latest policy directive.

Indefinite pronoun: A pronoun that, like a demonstrative pronoun, also points out persons and things but does so less definitely. Examples are *all, any, anybody, anyone, anything, each, either, everybody, everything, few, neither, nobody, none, one, several,* and *some*: *Some* will no doubt drop out at the last minute.

Reflexive pronoun: A pronoun used as the direct or indirect object of a verb or as the object of a preposition: He bought *himself* a new computer. Reflexive pronouns can also be used for emphasis (I *myself* prefer a traditional office), although this construction should be avoided in business writing, and particularly in international correspondence.

Reciprocal pronoun: A pronoun such as *each other* that expresses mutual action or relationship: They helped *one another* during the power failure.

Verb   A *verb* expresses action (*open*) or state of being (*is*). It may make a statement, ask a question, or give a command.

> The office *is* open from 9 A.M to 5 P.M.
> *Do* you *have* the new catalog?
> *Take* the requisition to the purchasing department.

Classification of Verbs. Verbs may be classified as transitive or intransitive, as principal or auxiliary, and as regular or irregular.

Transitive: A verb is *transitive* when it has an object: She *worked* the keyboard [object] with nimble fingers.

Intransitive: A verb is *intransitive* when it has no object: She *worked* hard.

Principal: A *principal verb* is complete in itself: The executive *uses* a formal writing style.

Auxiliary: An *auxiliary verb* accompanies the main verb and helps express its meaning: The executive *will write* the report in a formal style. Examples of auxiliary verbs are *be, can, do, have, may, must, ought, should, shall, will, would.*

Regular: A *regular verb* usually forms the past tense and the past participle by adding *-d* or *-ed* to the present tense: He *called* this morning. Verb tenses are discussed later in this section.

Irregular: An *irregular verb* forms the past tense and the past participle in different ways: *begin, began, begun; draw, drew, drawn; meet, met, met; spread, spread, spread*: He *did* [past] the work. He *has done* [past participle] the work.

Voice. When the *active voice* is used, the verb is performing the action: He *signed* the contract. Writers use the active voice to give strength and directness to their messages.

When the *passive* (or *inactive*) *voice* is used, the subject is acted upon: The contract *was signed* by him. Since the passive voice is weaker than the active voice, writers generally avoid it unless they *don't* want to be direct: An error *was made* on page 5. *Avoid*: *You made* an error on page 5.

Mood. Verbs are used in an indicative, a subjunctive, or an imperative mood.

> *Indicative:* States a fact or asks a question: You *know* the procedure.

> *Subjunctive:* Expresses wishes, commands, or conditions contrary to fact; often, the verb is preceded by a conjunction such as *if, though, lest, that, till,* or *unless*: If I *were* you [but I'm not], I would recommend a change in that policy.

> *Imperative:* Expresses a request or command, often with the subject omitted: *Hand* me the new manual, please.

Tense. The tense of a verb specifies the time or nature of the action that occurs. When present, past, or future action is described as completed, or *perfected,* it is in the present *perfect,* past *perfect,* or future *perfect* tense.

> *Present (action occurring now):* I *am* in the conference room.

> *Past (action that occurred in the past):* I *was* in the conference room.

> *Future (action that is expected to take place in the future):* I *will be* in the conference room.

> *Present perfect:* I *have been* on my vacation.

> *Past perfect:* I *had been* on my vacation when you called last week.

> *Future perfect:* I already *will have been* on my vacation by the time we next meet.

The following table shows the various forms of the verb *write* in the past, present, and future tenses. It includes the present and past *progressive* tenses in which the action is expressed as being in progress.

TENSE	I	HE/SHE/IT	WE/YOU/THEY
present	write	writes	write
present progressive	am writing	is writing	are writing
past	wrote	wrote	wrote

TENSE	I	HE/SHE/IT	WE/YOU/THEY
past progressive	was writing	was writing	were writing
present perfect	have written	has written	have written
past perfect	had written	had written	had written
future	will write, am going to write	will write, is going to write	will write, are going to write
future perfect	will have written	will have written	will have written

Person and Number. A verb must agree with its subject in person (first, second, third) and number (singular, plural).

	SINGULAR	PLURAL
First person	I send	We send
Second person	You send	You send
Third person	He/She sends	They send

The verb *be* has various forms such as *am, are,* and *is.*

Certain words and expressions sometimes pose problems in connection with subject-verb agreement. For example, a verb must agree with the subject even when a singular or plural prepositional phrase intervenes: The manager is *one* of those people who *has* always maintained a positive attitude.

A verb must agree with a singular subject and not a plural phrase that follows the verb: The *topic* of my memo *is* fiscal irresponsibility and managerial incompetence.

The word *there* sometimes precedes a linking verb such as *be, seem,* or *appear.* In such cases, the subject or predicate nominative follows the verb: There *is* a *storage facility.* There *are* many *options.*

Extraneous expressions that intervene between a verb and its subject should be ignored in deciding upon subject-verb agreement: The *executive,* with a receptionist and two secretaries, *is* in charge of registrations.

A singular subject preceded by *each, every, many a, such a,* or *no* takes a singular verb even when two or more of such subjects are linked by *and: Each* manager and *each* division chief *has urged* the employees to invest in the thrift plan.

When *either-or* and *neither-nor* are used, the verb should agree with the subject closest to it: Neither the supervisor nor the union *members are* willing to negotiate.

Verbals. *Verbals* are forms derived from verbs that are used as nouns or adjectives. They are called "verbals" rather than "verbs" because they have the properties of both noun and verb and adjective and verb.

Both *infinitives* and *gerunds* are *verbal nouns*. The word *to,* originally a preposition but now treated as part of the infinitive, may be included or omitted: *To decide* is the first step. Please [*to*] *decide.* Infinitives may also be used as adjectives and adverbs.

Gerunds, formed by adding *-ing* to the root or stem of the verb, are used like nouns: He teaches *programming.*

Participles are *verbal adjectives.* Although the present participle of a regular verb is also formed by adding *-ing* to the stem, it is used as an adjective modifying a noun rather than as a noun: *Racing* machines droned on endlessly.

Adjective *Adjectives* modify words, phrases, and clauses that serve as nouns and pronouns. An adjective describes, qualifies, limits, or makes a word distinct and separate from something else: a *tall* building, a *reasonable* offer, a *two-story* house.

Kinds of Adjectives. Proper adjectives are derived from proper nouns: *German* industry. A *relative adjective* is a relative pronoun used as an adjective: She is the one *whose* telephone is out of order. A *predicate adjective* usually follows a linking verb but always modifies a noun or pronoun: The director is [linking verb] *happy* [describes the noun *director*].

Comparison of Adjectives. Adjectives may occur in the *positive, comparative,* or *superlative degree.* The regular forms of comparison are made by adding *-er* (comparative) or *-est* (superlative) to the positive form of the adjective.

> *Positive:* The *easy* method
> *Comparative:* The *easier* method
> *Superlative:* The *easiest* method

If a word has more than one syllable, comparison is usually made by adding *more* or *most* rather than *-er* or *-est.*

> *Positive:* The *reliable* source
> *Comparative:* The *more reliable* source
> *Superlative:* The *most reliable* source

Irregular adjectives have different forms than regular adjectives, and comparison must be made by using the correct form rather than by adding *-er* or *-est* or *more* or *most:*

Positive: A *good* suggestion
Comparative: A *better* suggestion
Superlative: The *best* suggestion

Adverb   An *adverb* may modify a verb (read *fast*), an adjective (a *very* fast reader), or another adverb (read *very* fast). A *sentence adverb* modifies an entire clause or sentence: *Unfortunately,* the stock split did not have the desired effect. An *interrogative adverb* is used in asking or stating a direct or indirect question: *How* are you feeling? *Yes* is an *affirmative adverb,* and *no* and *not* are *negative adverbs. Conjunctive adverbs* connect sentences: The conference is over; *therefore* work can return to normal.

Some adverbs can be identified by determining if they express time (when), place (where), manner (how), degree (to what extent), cause or purpose (why), or number (first, firstly, and so on). The following are examples of adverbs that fit these categories:

Time: already, finally, lately, never, now, then
Place: above, far, here, there, upstairs, where
Manner: easily, otherwise, surely, well
Degree: equally, fully, less, much, too
Cause or purpose: consequently, therefore, wherefore, why
Number: first/firstly, second/secondly, third/thirdly

Comparison of Adverbs. Like adjectives, regular and irregular adverbs can be compared by using the comparative or superlative form of the positive adverb. Regular adverbs commonly add the words *more* and *most* or *less* and *least* to make the comparison, although a few can add the word endings *-er (sooner)* and *-est (soonest).*

Positive: He is *often* available on Fridays.
Comparative: He is *more often* available on Fridays.
Superlative: He is *most often* available on Fridays.

Also like adjectives, some adverbs use different forms to indicate comparison, rather than add a word ending such as *-er* or a word such as *more.*

Positive: He did *badly* on the test.
Comparative: He did *worse* on the test than she did.
Superlative: He did *worst* on the test.

Adverbs Ending in -ly. Some adverbs are formed by adding *-ly* to an adjective, and some adjectives are formed by adding *-ly* to a noun. Often you can decide if a word is an adverb or an adjective by determining whether the root word, without the *-ly* added, is a noun or an adjective. For example, the root word in these cases is clearly an adjective. The result is therefore an adverb.

sang *beautifully*
sighed *calmly*
beamed *eagerly*
laughed *happily*
spoke *harshly*
walked *rapidly*
replied *tensely*

The word to which *-ly* has been added in the following cases is clearly a noun. The result is therefore an adjective.

brotherly concern
earthly vision
friendly employee
lovely decor
neighborly attitude
saintly demeanor
womanly appearance

A common mistake is the use of an adverb when an adjective is intended. See **bad, badly** in "A CONCISE GUIDE TO USAGE" beginning on page 307.

Preposition A preposition connects and shows the relationship between a noun or pronoun and other words or expressions in a sentence. The noun or pronoun is the *object* of the preposition. The preposition together with the noun or pronoun is a *prepositional phrase*: *in the office.* Prepositional phrases can indicate a variety of situations or conditions such as the following.

Accompaniment: Joe attended the meeting *with several* colleagues.
Cause: The trip was canceled *because of bad weather.*
Support: Those who are not *for us* are *against us.*
Destination: We drove *to the city.*
Exception: I have everything *but a private office.*
Possession: The arrogance *of that official* defies description.
Composition or makeup: I want a desk *of polished mahogany.*

Means or instrument: I worked out the problem *with my personal computer.*

Manner: Treat all visitors *with courtesy.*

Direction: I ran *across the hall* to find you.

Location: John is *in the office.*

Purpose or intention: They'll do anything *for a quick profit.*

Origin: The new manager is *from Chicago.*

Time: Call me *at noon.*

In addition to having easily recognized prepositions such as *in, to,* and *with,* the English language includes a variety of other prepositions, some of which also function as other parts of speech. *Above,* for example, is used as a noun, adjective, and adverb as well as a preposition. The following are examples of single-word prepositions:

across	during	regarding
along	except	since
before	inside	till
between	near	toward
but	out	under
concerning	over	without

The following phrasal, or compound, prepositions consist of more than one word but are treated as single prepositions.

according to	in addition to	on behalf of
along with	in case of	out of
aside from	in lieu of	regardless of
as well as	in place of	with reference to
contrary to	in regard to	
from between	in spite of	

When two or more phrases used together share the *same* preposition, without intervening words, it isn't necessary to repeat the preposition: The testimony is *equal* [*to*] and *tantamount to* perjury. If two different prepositions are required, however, retain both of them: Our *interest in* and *concern for* the welfare of our employees has led us to take steps to improve their working conditions.

Conjunction   A *conjunction* links words, phrases, clauses, or sentences and is used to show how one sentence is related to another. The three principal types of conjunctions are coordinate, subordinate, and correlative conjunctions. Conjunctive adverbs, such as *besides, however,* and *nevertheless,* described earlier in the discussion of adverbs, also connect sentences and words.

Coordinate Conjunction. Coordinate conjunctions, such as *and, or, but, yet, for, nor,* and *so,* connect elements of equal value.

> He is the president of the company, *and* he is her boss.
> She is successful *but* modest.

Subordinate Conjunction. Subordinate conjunctions, such as *as if, because, in case, inasmuch as, provided that, since, when,* and *where,* connect a subordinate element to another element in a sentence.

> *Because* the report is late [subordinate element], the meeting will have to be postponed.

> Andrew is a skilled writer, *although* he has difficulty researching complex subjects [subordinate element].

Correlative Conjunction. Correlative conjunctions, such as *neither-nor,* are used in pairs or a series. Correlatives are intended to connect elements of equal value and must be positioned correctly in the sentence to avoid confusion.

> *Either* the executive *or* the assistant is coming.
> Overpopulation has been a problem *both* in India *and* in China.

The following are common correlative conjunctions.

although . . . yet	not only . . . but also
as . . . as	now . . . now
as . . . so	now . . . then
both . . . and	so . . . as
either . . . or	though . . . yet
if . . . then	whereas . . . therefore
neither . . . nor	whether . . . or

Other Parts of Speech Used as Conjunctions. Pronouns and adverbs are also used as conjunctions to show the relation of one clause to another in a sentence. Refer to the description of relative pronouns and conjunctive adverbs in the sections about pronouns and adverbs.

Interjection An *interjection* is a word or words usually used to express emotion. It may be used alone (*Oh!*) or as part of a sentence: *Oh, come on!*

Phrases, Clauses, Sentences, and Paragraphs

Phrases A *phrase* is a group of words that does not have both a subject and verb and cannot stand alone:

> *Having addressed the sales force,* we then took questions from the floor.

> *Approaching that issue* was tricky.

> We will be delighted *to attend the meeting.*

Clauses A *clause* is a group of words that has both a subject and a predicate but cannot stand alone:

> *If you have performed unsatisfactorily,* it will be reflected in your performance review.

A *restrictive clause* is essential to the meaning of the sentence and should not be set off with commas:

> The employees *who have signed their performance reviews* will receive salary adjustments on schedule.

A *nonrestrictive clause* is not essential to the meaning of the sentence and should be set off with commas:

> Seven employees, *who have known each other for many years,* are participating in the review program.

A *dependent clause* occupies a subordinate position in a sentence and cannot stand alone:

> *When the meeting adjourns,* we will listen to the recording of the proceedings.

An *independent clause* is a complete sentence in itself and can stand alone. This example has two independent clauses joined by the conjunction *and:*

> *The supply of stationery is running low,* and *it is time for me to place a new order.*

Sentences A *sentence* is a group of words that has a subject and a verb and can stand alone. In writing, the sentence begins with a capital letter and ends with a period, question mark, or exclamation point: The Board of Directors has unanimously voted a dividend increase. When it does not have a complete subject or predicate but is punctuated as if it were complete, it is known as a *sentence fragment:* The Board of Directors having unanimously voted.

A sentence may be declarative (makes a statement), interrogative (asks a question), imperative (requests or commands), or exclamatory (expresses strong feeling):

Declarative: The applicants signed the forms.
Interrogative: Did you sign the form?
Imperative: Sign the form here.
Exclamatory: I wish they'd sign the forms and shut up!

A sentence may also be classified as simple, compound (two or more connected sentences), complex (containing a clause), or a combination of compound and complex.

Simple: Some people complain a lot.

Compound: Some people complain, some brood, and others don't care at all.

Complex: When people become dissatisfied with their jobs, they often complain.

Compound-complex: When people become dissatisfied with their jobs, they often complain, and management then has a problem that it must address.

A CONCISE GUIDE TO USAGE

Secretaries and employers both know that correct word choice is an important ingredient in business communication. Using the wrong word in conversation or written messages could cause someone to reach the wrong conclusion, or it could make the user appear unprofessional. To avoid this, be alert to the following commonly misused words. Although some words, such as *ability* and *capacity,* may be used interchangeably in casual domestic conversation or writing, it is important to consider even subtle differences in international messages and in formal domestic writing. Foreign readers often know English only as a second language and take even slight differences in meaning into account in their translations.

a, an. *A* is used before a word beginning with a consonant (*a building*) or a consonant sound (*a university*); *an* is used before a word beginning with a vowel (*an employee*) or a vowel sound (*an hour*). *A* rather than *an* should be used before words like *historical (a hysterical)* unless the *h* is not pronounced (*an herb*).

about. The construction *not about to* is sometimes used informally to express determination: We are *not about to* negotiate with strikebreakers. This usage should be avoided in business writing and, particularly, in international communication.

above. The use of *above* as an adjective or noun in referring to preceding text is common in some business and legal writing. In general writing, its use as an adjective (the *above* figures) is acceptable, but its use as a noun (read the *above*) should be avoided.

acquiesce. When *acquiesce* takes a preposition, it is usually used with *in* (*acquiesced in* the ruling) but sometimes with *to* (*acquiesced to* management's wishes).

admission, admittance. *Admission,* "achieving entry to a group or institution," has a more general meaning than *admittance,* "obtaining physical access to a place": To gain *admission* to the board is to become a member; to gain *admittance* to the board is to enter its chambers. One pays *admission* to a theater (a price paid to become a member of the audience) to be allowed *admittance* (physical entry to the theater itself).

adopted, adoptive. One refers to an *adopted* child but to *adoptive* parents.

advance, advancement. *Advance,* as a noun, is used for forward movement (the *advance* of our salespeople into the new market) or for progress or improvement in a figurative sense (a sales *advance* of 35 percent this year). *Advancement* is often used in the figurative sense: career *advancement.* In that sense there is a distinction between the two terms deriving from the transitive and intransitive forms of the verb *advance.* The noun *advancement* (unlike *advance*) often implies the existence of an agent or outside force. Thus the *advance* of research and development means simply the progress of the company's R & D efforts, whereas the *advancement* of research and development implies progress resulting from the action of an agent or force: The addition of $1.5 million to last year's budget has resulted in the *advancement* of our research efforts.

adverse. See **averse, adverse.**

advise. *Advise* in the sense "to counsel or give advice" is always acceptable in business contexts: The president *advised* employees to observe the new regulations. Avoid the pretentious use of *advise* for *say, tell,* or *let you know* in business correspondence.

affect, effect. *Affect* and *effect* have no sense in common. As a verb, *affect* is most commonly used in the sense "to influence": How will bad weather *affect* deliveries? *Effect* as a verb means "to bring about or execute": layoffs designed to *effect* savings. As a noun it means "a result": *effect* of the new policy.

affinity. *Affinity* may be followed by *of, between,* or *with*: *affinity of* persons, *between* two persons, or *with* another person. In technical writing *affinity,* meaning "a chemical or physical attraction," is followed by *for*: a dye with an *affinity for* synthetic fabrics. In general usage *affinity* should not be used as a simple synonym for *liking*: *affinity for living in California.*

affirmative. The expressions *in the affirmative* and *in the negative* (The client answered *in the affirmative*) are generally regarded as pompous. *Better*: The client answered *yes.*

agenda. *Agenda,* meaning "list" or "program," is well established as a singular noun. Its plural form is *agendas.*

ago. *Ago* may be followed by *that* or *when*: It was a week ago that [or when] I saw the invoice. It should *not* be followed by *since*: It was a week ago *since* the order arrived. *Since* is properly used without *ago*: It has been a week *since* the order arrived.

alibi. *Alibi* (noun) in its nonlegal sense "an excuse" is generally acceptable in written usage, but as an intransitive verb (They never *alibi*), it is generally unacceptable.

all, all of, all that. Constructions like *all us employees* should be avoided in formal writing; use *all of us employees*. The construction *all that* is used informally in questions and negative sentences to mean "to the degree expected": The annual meeting was not all that exciting this year. This usage is generally unacceptable in business writing and, particularly, in international correspondence.

alleged. An *alleged burglar* is someone who is said to be a burglar but against whom no charges have yet been proved. An *alleged incident* is an event that is said to have taken place but which has not yet been verified. In their zeal to protect the rights of the accused, newspapers and law enforcement officials sometimes misuse *alleged.* A man arrested for murder may be only an *alleged murderer,* for example, but he is a real, not an *alleged, suspect* in that his status as a suspect is not in doubt. Similarly, if a murder is known to have taken place, there is nothing *alleged* about the crime.

all of. See **all, all of, all that.**

all right, alright. It is not acceptable to write *all right* as the single word, *alright,* despite the parallel to words like *already* and *altogether* and despite the fact that in casual speech the expression is often pronounced as if it were one word.

all that. See **all, all of, all that.**

all together. See **altogether, all together.**

allude/allusion, refer/reference. *Allude* and *allusion* are often used where the more general terms *refer* and *reference* would be preferable. *Allude* and *allusion* apply to indirect reference that does not identify specifically: He *alluded to* her drug habit when he described the problems of dangerous outside forces. *Refer* and *reference,* unless qualified, usually imply direct, specific mention: She made *reference* to the book *ABCs of Teleconferencing* in her speech.

alternative. *Alternative* is widely used to denote simply "one of a set of possible courses of action," but many traditionalists insist that its use be restricted to situations in which only two possible choices present themselves: The *alternatives* are to attend a traditional college or to enter a vocational school. In this stricter sense, *alternative* is incompatible with all numerals (there are *three alternatives*), and the use of *two,* in particular, is redundant (the *two alternatives* are life and death). Similarly, *other* is unnecessary with *alternative*: There is no [*other*] *alternative.*

altogether, all together. *Altogether* should be distinguished from *all together.* *All together* is used with a group to indicate that its members performed or underwent an action collectively: The new computers were stored *all together* in an empty office. *All together* can be used only if it is possible to rephrase the sentence so that *all* and *together* may be separated by other words: The new computers were *all* stored *together*. *Altogether* is used to mean "entirely" or "completely": It is *altogether* possible that we will lose the contract.

alumni. *Alumni* is generally used to refer to both the alumni (masculine plural) and *alumnae* (feminine plural) of a coeducational institution.

A.M. See **ante meridian.**

among. See **between, among.**

and. Although *and* has been used throughout history to begin sentences, businesspeople should avoid this practice in all but very casual writing. See also **but.**

and/or. Although *and/or* is widely known to mean "one or the other or both," business writers should avoid this usage, particularly in international correspondence, where it may not be understood. Usually, it is sufficient to use either the word *and* or the word *or.*

ante meridian. In general, 12 A.M. denotes midnight and 12 P.M. denotes noon. However, sufficient confusion exists to make it advisable to use *12 noon* and *12 midnight* when absolute clarity is required.

anticipate, expect. Some traditionalists hold that *anticipate* should not be used simply as a synonym for *expect.* They restrict its use to senses in which it suggests some advance action, either to fulfill (*anticipate* my desires) or to forestall (*anticipate* the competition's next move). Others accept the word's use in the senses "to feel or realize beforehand" and "to look forward to" (often with the implication of foretasting pleasure): They are *anticipating* [*expecting*] a sizable dividend increase.

any. The phrase *of any* is sometimes used in informal contexts to mean "of all": That scientist is the best *of any* living authority on the subject. However, many find this construction unacceptable. *Any* is used to mean "at all" before a comparative adjective: Are the field office reports *any* better this month? The related use of *any* by itself to mean "at all" should be avoided: It didn't matter *at all* [not *any*] to the supervisor.

anyone, any one. The one-word form *anyone* is used to mean "whatsoever person or persons." The two-word form *any one* is used to mean "whatever one (person or thing) of a group." *Anyone* may join means admission is open to everybody. *Any one* may join means admission is open to any individual person of the people who are applying for admissions. When followed by *of,* only *any one* (two words) can be used: *Any one of them could do the job. Anyone* is often used in place of *everyone*: Dale is the most thrifty person *of anyone* I know. But the words *of anyone* are unnecessary in this context: Dale is the most thrifty person I know.

apparent. Used before a noun, *apparent* means "seeming": For all its *apparent* wealth, the company was leveraged to the hilt. Used after a form of the verb *to be,* however, *apparent* can mean either "seeming" (The virtues of the deal were only *apparent*) or "obvious" (The effects of the drought are *apparent* to anyone seeing the parched fields). Writers should take care that the intended meaning is clear from the context.

as . . . as, so . . . as. Comparisons with *as . . . as* may be used in any context, positive or negative: Their marketing is *as* good *as* ours. The *so . . . as* construction, when used, is restricted to negative comparisons, especially when the word *not* is involved: Their marketing is not *so* good *as* ours.

as, since. Both *as* and *since* are used informally to mean "because" or "inasmuch as." When used in this sense, *since* is preferred, and *as* should be avoided: *Since* [*because*] you're not interested, I'll remove your name from the mailing list. *As* has numerous other uses as a conjunction, adverb, pronoun, and preposition.

assure, ensure, insure. *Assure, ensure,* and *insure* all mean "to make sure or certain." Only *assure* is used with references to a person in the sense "to set the mind at rest": They *assured* the leader of their loyalty. Although *ensure* and *insure* are generally interchangeable, only *insure* is used in the commercial sense "to guarantee persons or property against risk." In the sense "to make certain," the British preference is *ensure*; American usage includes both *ensure* and *insure*: To ensure [*insure*] success, the company did a thorough market study.

as well as. *As well as* in the sense "in addition to" does not have the conjunctive force of *and.* Consequently, the singular subjects remain singular and govern singular verbs: The *parent company, as well as its affiliate,* was named in the indictment. *As well as* is redundant in combination with *both*: *Both* in theory *as well as* in practice, the idea is unsound.

averse, adverse. *Averse* and *adverse* are often confused. *Averse* indicates opposition or strong disinclination on the subject's part: The graduate was *averse* to joining the company. *Adverse* refers to something that opposes or hinders progress: an *adverse* economy, *adverse* circumstances.

aweigh. See **way, under way, aweigh.**

awhile, a while. *Awhile,* an adverb, is never preceded by a preposition such as *for,* but the two-word form *a while* may be preceded by a preposition. In writing, each of the following is acceptable: *stay awhile; stay for a while; stay a while* (but not stay *for awhile*).

back. The expression *back of* is an informal variant of *in back of* and should be avoided in writing: There was a small loading dock *in back of* [not *back of*] the factory.

backward. The adverb may be spelled *backward* or *backwards,* and the forms are interchangeable: *stepped backward;* a mirror facing *backwards.* Only *backward* is an adjective: a *backward* view.

bad, badly. One should avoid using the adverb *badly* as an adjective: I felt *bad* [not *badly*] about the ruined press run. Also avoid the use of *bad* and *good* as adverbs. Formal usage requires an adverb in these sentences: My tooth hurts *badly* (not *bad*); He drives *well* (not *good*). But when the subject is modified, an adjective is required: She feels *bad* [or *good*].

baleful, baneful. *Baleful* and *baneful* overlap in meaning, but *baleful* usually applies to that which menaces or foreshadows evil: a *baleful* look. *Baneful* is used most often for that which is actually harmful or destructive: the *baneful* effects of government regulations.

because, due to, owing to. *Because* is used with nonlinking verbs: He was exhausted *because* of lack of sleep. *Due to* means "caused by" and may follow a linking verb: His exhaustion was *due to* lack of sleep. *Owing to* is used as a compound preposition: His policies were successful *owing to* his firm commitment to progress.

behalf. *In behalf of* and *on behalf of* have distinct senses and should not be used interchangeably. *In behalf of* means "in the interest of" or "for the benefit of": We raised money *in behalf of* the United Way. *On behalf of* means "as the agent of" or "on the part of": The lawyer signed the papers *on behalf of* the client.

beside, besides. In modern usage the senses "in addition to" and "except for" are conveyed more often by *besides* than *beside*: We had few options *besides* the course we ultimately took. *Beside,* as a preposition, means "next to": His computer is positioned *beside* the scanner.

better, best. *Better* is used in a comparison of two: Which of the two accounting firms does the *better* job? *Best* is used to compare three or more: Which of these four methods works *best*? *Best* is also used idiomatically with reference to two in certain expressions: May the *best* man or woman win!

between, among. *Between* is used when just two entities are involved: the rivalry *between* Ford and General Motors. When more than two entities are involved, the choice of *between* or *among* depends on the intended meaning. *Among* is used to indicate that an entity has been chosen from the members of a group: *Among* the three executives, Pat seems most likely to become the next president. *Among* is also used to indicate a relation of inclusion in a group: He is *among* the best engineers of our time. *Between* is used to indicate the area bounded by several points: We have narrowed the search to the area *between* Philadelphia, New York, and Scranton. In other cases either *between* or *among* may be used. One may say either that a telephone pole is lost *among* the trees (in the area of the trees) or lost *between* the trees (in which case we infer that the trees had hidden the pole from sight).

bias. *Bias* defined as "a preference or inclination" may operate either for or against someone or something. But *bias* is now often used to refer to an unfair preference: Congress included a provision in the Civil Rights Act of 1964 banning racial *bias* in employment.

bimonthly, semimonthly. *Bimonthly* and *biweekly* mean "once every two months" and "once every two weeks." For "twice a month" and "twice a week," the words *semimonthly* and *semiweekly* should be used. But there is a great deal of confusion over the distinction, and a writer is well advised to substitute expressions like "every two months" or "twice a month" whenever possible. However, the word *bimonthly* is unavoidable when used as a noun to mean "a publication that appears every two months."

black. When used to refer to an *African-American*, the noun and the adjective *black* are often capitalized. Writing authorities recommend that you avoid color labels and instead refer to a person's heritage, such as *Asian-American*.

blatant, flagrant. *Blatant* and *flagrant* are often confused. In the sense that causes the confusion, *blatant* has the meaning "totally or offensively conspicuous or obtrusive." *Flagrant* emphasizes wrong or evil that is glaring or notorious. Therefore, one who blunders may be guilty of a *blatant* (but not a *flagrant*) error; one who intentionally and ostentatiously violates a pledge commits a *flagrant* act.

born, borne. In its literal sense the past participle *born* is used only of mammals and only in constructions with *to be*: The baby was *born*. It may also be used figuratively: A great project was *born*. *Borne*, said of the act of birth, refers only to the mother's role, but it can be used actively or passively: She has *borne* three children; Three children were *borne* by her [but not *born* to her]. In all other senses of *bear*, the past participle is *borne*: The soil has *borne* abundant crops; Such a burden cannot be *borne* by anyone.

borrow. In many American English dialects the expression *borrow off* is used in place of *borrow from*. This usage should be avoided, however. One writes: Gale *borrowed* $500 *from* (not *off*) the bank.

both. *Both* underscores that the activity or state denoted by a verb applies equally to two entities. Saying that *both* the employees have exasperated me emphasizes that neither escapes my impatience. As such, *both* is improperly used with a verb that can apply only to two or more entities. It is illogical to say they are *both alike,* since neither could be "alike" if the other were not. Similarly, *both* is unnecessary in a sentence saying that they *both* appeared together, since neither one can "appear together" by him- or herself. The expression *the both* (the office manager gave it to *the both* of them) should be avoided. In possessive constructions, *of both* is usually preferred: the shareholders *of both* companies (rather than *both their* shareholders).

bring, take. In most American English dialects *bring* is used to denote movement *toward* the place of speaking or the point from which the action is regarded: *Bring* the letter to me now; The Wall Street Journal *brought* good news about the economy. *Take* denotes movement *away* from such a place. Thus one normally *takes* checks to the bank and *brings* home cash, though from the banker's point of view, one has *brought* checks in order to *take* away cash.

burgeon. The verb *burgeon* and its participle *burgeoning,* used as an adjective, are traditionally restricted to the actual or figurative sense "to bud or sprout" or "to newly emerge": the *burgeoning* talent of the young attorney. They are not considered mere substitutes for the more general *expand, grow,* or *thrive,* although such use of the participle has become more acceptable.

but. *But* is used to mean "except" in some sentences: No one *but* a company officer can read it. In the sentence "No one *but me* can read it," *but* is treated as a preposition, and the pronoun is in the objective case. *But* is redundant when combined with *however:* But the division, *however,* went on with its own plans. Using *but* with a negative is unnecessary and should be avoided in sentences such as It won't take *but* an hour. *But what* should also be avoided: I don't know *but what* [*whether*] we'll arrive first. Do *not* substitute *but* for *than* in this type of sentence: It no sooner started *but* [*than*] it stopped. Beginning a sentence with *but* is now widely accepted. See also **and.**

callous, callus. The noun is spelled *callus* (a *callus* on my foot), but the adjective is spelled *callous*: a *callous* disregard for human rights.

can, may. Traditionally, *can* has been used only to express the capacity to do something and *may* to indicate permission: The supervisor said that anyone who wants an extra day off *may* have one; *May* I have that pencil? In informal speech, however, *can* is often used to express permission, and the "permission" use of *can* is even more frequent in British English. The negative contraction *can't* is frequently used in coaxing and wheedling questions: *Can't* I have the car tonight?

cannot. In the phrase *cannot but,* which is criticized as a double negative, *but* is used in the sense of "except": One *cannot but* admire the takeover strategy [one cannot do otherwise than admire the strategy]. Alternative phrasings are *can but admire, can only admire, cannot help admiring.*

capital, capitol. The term for a town or city that serves as a seat of government is spelled *capital.* The term for the building in which a legislative assembly meets is spelled *capitol.* It is capitalized (*Capitol*) in reference to the seat of the U.S. Congress.

celebrant, celebrator. *Celebrant* should be reserved for an official participant in a religious ceremony or rite (the *celebrant* of a Mass). It is also considered acceptable in the general sense of "participant in a celebration": New Year's Eve *celebrants. Celebrator* is an undisputed alternative.

center. *Center* as an intransitive verb may be used with *on, upon, in,* or *at.* Logically, it should not be used with *around,* since the word *center* refers to a point of focus: The discussion *centered on* [not *around*] the meaning of the law (with a possible alternative being *revolved around*). Some business authorities object to both *centered on* and *revolved around* in this context and prefer *focused on, concerned,* or *involved:* The discussion *focused on* the meaning of the law.

ceremonial, ceremonious. *Ceremonial* (adjective) is applicable chiefly to things; *ceremonious* (also an adjective), to persons and things. *Ceremonial* means simply "having to do with ceremony": *ceremonial* occasions; *ceremonial* garb. *Ceremonious,* when applied to a person, means "devoted to forms and ritual" or "standing on ceremony": a *ceremonious* chief of protocol.

certain. Although *certain* appears to be an absolute term (Nothing is more *certain* than death and taxes), it is frequently qualified by adverbs: *fairly* certain.

cite. See **quote, cite.**

commentate. The verb *commentate* has long been in use in the sense "to give a commentary." But in the sense "to provide a running commentary on," it is usually unacceptable: The announcer *commentated* [*gave a commentary*] on the Super Bowl.

common. See **mutual, common.**

compare, contrast. *Compare* means " to examine something for similarity or difference" and is followed by *with* or *to.* Use *with* when you examine two things for similarities or differences: We *compared* our program *with* theirs. Use *to* when you compare dissimilar things: They *compared* the mimeograph *to* a turtle. The verb *contrast* means "to show only differences." It is often followed by *with*: His views *contrast* sharply *with* his predecessor's views. The noun form is often followed by *to*: The Group IV fax machines, in *contrast to* the Group III machines, will operate at exceptionally high speeds.

complement, compliment. *Complement* and *compliment,* though distinct in meaning, are sometimes confused. *Complement* means "something that completes or brings to perfection": The thick carpet was a perfect *complement* to the executive suite. *Compliment* means "an expression of courtesy or praise": We paid them a supreme *compliment* at the testimonial banquet.

complete. *Complete* is generally held to be an absolute term like *perfect* or *chief,* which is not subject to comparison. It is sometimes qualified by *more* or *less,* however: A *more complete* failure I could not imagine; That book is the *most complete* treatment of the subject available today.

comprise, compose. The traditional rule states that the whole *comprises* the parts; the parts *compose* the whole: The Union *comprises* fifty states; Fifty states *compose* [or *constitute or make up*] the Union. However, *comprise* is used informally, especially in the passive, in place of *compose*: The Union is *comprised* of fifty states. Businesspeople are advised to retain the traditional distinction.

continuance, continuation, continuity. *Continuance* is sometimes interchangeable with *continuation. Continuance,* however, is used to refer to the duration of a state or condition: the president's *continuance* in office. *Continuation* applies especially to prolongation or resumption of action (a *continuation* of the board meeting) or to physical extension (the *continuation* of the railroad spur beyond our plant). *Continuity* is used to refer to consistency over time: the *continuity* of foreign policy. The *continuity* of a story is its internal coherence from one episode to the next; the *continuation* of a story is that part of the story that takes up after a break in its recitation.

contrast. See **compare, contrast.**

convince, persuade. Traditionally, one *persuades* someone to act but *convinces* someone of the truth of a statement or proposition: By *convincing* me that no good could come of continuing the project, the director *persuaded* me to shelve it altogether. If the distinction is accepted, then *convince* should not be used with an infinitive: They *persuaded* [not *convinced*] me to go.

council, counsel, consul. *Council, counsel,* and *consul* are never interchangeable, although their meanings are related. *Council* and *councilor* refer principally to a deliberative assembly (a *city council* or *student council*) and one of its members. *Counsel* and *counselor* pertain chiefly to advice and guidance and to a person who provides it: *counsel* of an attorney. *Consul* denotes an officer in the foreign service of a country: the *consul* in Bogota.

couple. *Couple*, when used to refer to two people who function socially as a unit, may take either a singular or a plural verb. Whatever the choice, usage should be consistent: The *couple are* now finishing *their* joint research [or The *couple is* now finishing *its* joint research].

criteria, criterion. *Criteria* is a plural form only (*criteria* for making a decision *are*) and should not be substituted for the singular *criterion*: his sole *criterion is*.

critique. *Critique* is widely used as a verb (*critiqued* the survey) but is regarded as pretentious jargon. The use of it as a noun in phrases like *give a critique* or *offer a critique* is acceptable.

data. *Data* is the plural of the Latin word *datum* and may be used with either a singular or plural verb: The *data are* [*is*] nonconclusive.

debut. *Debut* is widely used as a verb, both intransitively in the sense "to make a first appearance" (The play *debuts* at our new downtown theater tonight) and transitively in the sense "to present for the first time": We will *debut* a new product line next week. However, both of these uses are widely objected to because traditionalists do not like the shift of *debut* from a noun to a verb.

depend. *Depend*, indicating condition or contingency, is always followed by *on* or *upon*: It depends *on* who is in charge. In casual speech the preposition is sometimes omitted: It *depends* [*on*] who is in charge.

deprecate, depreciate. The fully accepted meaning of *deprecate* is "to express disapproval of." But the word has steadily encroached upon the meaning of *depreciate*. It is now used, almost to the exclusion of *depreciate*, in the sense "to belittle or mildly disparage": The cynical employee *deprecated* all of the good things the company had to offer. This newer sense is acceptable. *Depreciate* is primarily used to mean "lessening the price or value of something": A car *depreciates* immediately after you purchase it.

dilemma. *Dilemma* applies to a choice between evenly balanced alternatives, often unattractive ones: He faced the *dilemma* of choosing between a higher salary in another state or a lower salary close to home. It is not properly used as a synonym for *problem* or *predicament*: Hijacking has become a big *problem* [not *dilemma*] for our trucking subsidiary.

disinterested, uninterested. Traditionally, a *disinterested* party is one who has no stake in a dispute and is therefore presumed to be impartial. One is *uninterested* in something when one is indifferent to it. These two terms should not be used interchangeably, particularly in international correspondence.

distinct, distinctive. A thing is *distinct* if it is sharply distinguished from other things: a *distinct* honor. A property or attribute is *distinctive* if it enables us to distinguish one thing from another: This carpeting has a *distinctive* feel to it, meaning that the feel of the carpet enables us to distinguish it from other carpets. By contrast, thick-pile carpeting is a *distinct* type of floor covering, meaning that the thick-pile carpeting falls into a clearly defined category of floor coverings.

done. *Done* means "completely accomplished" or "finished": The entire project will not be *done* until next year. In some contexts, however, this use of *done* can be unclear: The work will be *done* next week. Does that mean that it will be finished next week or that someone will do the work next week? Alternatives, dependent on the meaning, would be: The work will *get done* next week; The work will *be done by* next week.

doubt, doubtful. *Doubt* and *doubtful* are often followed by clauses introduced by *that, whether,* or *if.* Often *that* is used when the intention is to express more or less complete rejection of a statement: I *doubt that* they will even try. In the negative it is used to express more or less complete acceptance: I don't *doubt that* you are right. When the intention is to express real uncertainty, the choice is usually *whether:* We doubt *whether* they can succeed. In fact, *whether* is the traditional choice in such examples, although some experts would accept *if* (which is more informal) or *that. Doubt* is frequently used in informal speech, both as a verb and as a noun, together with *but*: I don't *doubt but* [or *but what*] they will come. However, *doubt but* should be avoided in business writing.

drunk, drunken. *Drunk* (adjective) is used predicatively: The guard was *drunk.* For attributive use before a noun, the choice is usually *drunken*: a *drunken* guest. The attributive use of *drunk* is generally unacceptable. But in its use in the phrase *drunk driver,* it is supported by usage and statute to the extent that the two expressions *drunk driver* (one who has exceeded the legal limit of alcohol consumption while driving) and *drunken driver* (one who is inebriated) are not synonymous.

due, due to. The phrase *due to* is always acceptable when *due* functions as a predicate adjective following a linking verb: Our hesitancy was *due to* fear. But when *due to* is used as a prepositional phrase (We hesitated *due to* fear), the construction is unacceptable. Generally accepted alternatives are *because of* or *on account of.* See also **because, owing to.**

each. When the subject of a sentence begins with *each,* it is grammatically singular, and the verb and following pronouns must be singular as well: *Each* of the designers *has his* or *her* distinctive style. When *each* follows a plural subject, however, the verb and following pronouns generally remain plural: The *secretaries each have their* jobs to do. The redundant expression *each and every* should be avoided.

each other, one another. Traditionally, *each other* refers to two, and *one another* refers to more than two: Bob and Jane wrote to *each other*; The secretaries help *one another.* When speaking of an ordered series of events or stages, only *one another* can be used: The Caesars exceeded *one another* in cruelty, meaning that each Caesar was crueler than the previous one. *Each other* should not be used as the subject of a clause: We know what *each other* are thinking. *Better: Each* of us knows what the *other* is thinking. The possessive forms of *each other* and *one another* are written *each other's* and *one another's*: The machinists wore *each other's* hardhats.

effect. See **affect, effect.**

either. *Either* is primarily used to mean "one of two," although it is sometimes used for three or more: *either* corner of the triangle. When referring to more than two, *any* or *any one* is preferred. *Either* takes a singular verb: *Either* plant *grows* in the shade; I doubt whether *either of* them *is* available.

elder, eldest. *Elder* and *eldest* apply only to persons, unlike *older* and *oldest,* which also apply to things. *Elder* and *eldest* are used principally with reference to seniority: *elder* statesman; Pat the *Elder.* Unlike *older, elder* is also a noun: the town *elders*; Listen to your *elders.*

else. *Else* is often used redundantly in combination with prepositions such as *but, except,* and *besides*: *No one* [not *no one else*] *but* that witness saw the accident. When a pronoun is followed by *else,* the possessive form is generally written *someone else's* [not *someone's else*]. Both *who else's* and *whose else* are in use, but not *whose else's*: *Who else's* appointment book could it have been? *Whose else* could it have been?

emigrate. See **migrate, emigrate, immigrate.**

ensure. See **assure, ensure, insure.**

errata. The plural *errata* is sometimes employed in the collective sense of a list of errors. Nevertheless, *errata* always takes a plural verb: The *errata are* noted in an attached memo.

everyplace, every place. *Everyplace* and *every place* used adverbially for *everywhere* are found principally in informal writing or speech: *Everyplace* [or *every place*] I go, I hear raves about our product. *Better: everywhere* I go. *Every place* as a combination of adjective and noun is standard English: I searched in *every place* possible.

everywhere. The only acceptable word is *everywhere,* not *everywheres.* The use of *that* with *everywhere* (*everywhere that* I go) is superfluous.

except. *Except* in the sense "with the exclusion of" or "other than" is generally construed as a preposition, not a conjunction. A personal pronoun that follows *except* is therefore in the objective case: No one *except them* knew it; Every member of the committee was called *except me.*

excuse. The expression *excuse* away has no meaning beyond that of *excuse* (unlike *explain away,* which has a different meaning from *explain*). *Excuse away* is unacceptable: The general manager's behavior cannot be *excused* [not *excused away*].

expect. See **anticipate, expect.**

explicit, express. *Explicit* and *express* both apply to something that is clearly stated rather than implied. *Explicit* applies more particularly to that which is carefully spelled out: the *explicit* terms of ownership contained in the licensing agreement. *Express* applies particularly to a clear expression of intention or will: The corporation made an *express* prohibition against dealers' selling cars below list prices.

farther, further. Traditionally, *farther* is used for physical distance: The freight train went *farther* down the line. *Further* is used for nonphysical distance, as when referring to degree or time: *further* in debt; *further* steps to advertise our product. In some cases, however, especially in contemporary writing, either word is acceptable. One may say *further* from the truth or *farther* from the truth.

fatal, fateful. Although the senses of *fatal* and *fateful* have tended to merge, each has a different core meaning. The contrast between *fatal,* in the sense "leading to death or destruction," and *fateful,* in the sense "affecting one's destiny or future," is illustrated by the following sentence: The *fateful* decision to relax safety standards led directly to the *fatal* car crash.

fault. *Fault* used as a transitive verb meaning "to criticize or find fault with" is now widely acceptable: One cannot *fault* management's performance; To *fault* them is grossly unfair.

fewer, less. *Fewer, referring* to a smaller number, is correctly used in writing only before a plural noun: *fewer* reasons, *fewer* gains on the stock market. *Less,* referring to not as great an amount or quantity, is used before a mass noun: *less* music; *less* sugar; *less* material gain. *Less than* is also used before a plural noun that denotes a measure of time, amount, or distance: *less than* three weeks; *less than* sixty years old; *less than* $400.

finalize. *Finalize* is business jargon that is avoided by many careful writers: We will *finalize* plans to remodel twelve stores this year. *Better:* We will *complete* [*finish, make final*] plans to remodel twelve stores this year.

firstly. *Firstly, secondly, thirdly,* and so on are less desirable substitutes for *first, second, third,* and so on.

flagrant. See **blatant, flagrant.**

flammable, inflammable. *Flammable* and *inflammable* are identical in meaning. *Flammable* has been adopted by safety authorities for the labeling of combustible materials because the *in-* of *inflammable* was incorrectly believed by some people to mean "not": The liquid is *flammable.*

flaunt, flout. *Flaunt* and *flout* are often confused. *Flaunt* as a transitive verb means "to exhibit ostentatiously": The manager *flaunted* a corporate credit card and expense account. To *flout* is "to defy openly": They *flouted* all social proprieties.

flounder. See **founder, flounder.**

forbid. *Forbid* may be used with an infinitive: I *forbid* you *to smoke* in the elevators; or a gerund: I *forbid* your *smoking*; but avoid using it with *from*: I *forbid* you *from* smoking.

forceful, forcible, forced. *Forceful, forcible,* and *forced* have distinct, if related meanings. *Forceful* is used to describe something that suggests strength or force: a *forceful* marketing campaign; *Forceful* measures may or may not involve the use of actual physical force. *Forcible* is most often used concerning actions accomplished by the application of physical force: There had clearly been a *forcible* entry into the storeroom; The suspect had to be *forcibly* restrained. *Forced* is used to describe a condition brought about by control or by an outside influence: *forced* labor; a *forced* landing; a *forced* smile.

former. The *former* is used when referring to the first of two persons or things mentioned. It is best not to use *former* when referring to the first of three or more. For that purpose one may use *the first* or *the first-named* or, preferably, repeat the name itself: Computers, scanners, and copiers are integrated in many offices, with *computers* representing the dominant technology.

fortuitous, fortunate. *Fortuitous* is often confused with *fortunate. Fortuitous* means "happening by chance." *Fortunate* means "having unexpected good fortune." A *fortuitous* meeting may have either fortunate or unfortunate consequences. In common usage some of the meaning of *fortunate* has rubbed off on *fortuitous* so that even when it is properly used, *fortuitous* often carries an implication of lucky chance rather than unlucky chance. But the word is not synonymous with *fortunate* and is best used when it refers to something that came about by chance or accident: The meeting proved *fortuitous;* I came away with a much better idea of my responsibilities.

forward, forwards. *Forwards* should not be used in place of *forward* except in the adverbial sense of "toward the front": move *forward* or *forwards.* In specific phrases the choice of one or the other is often idiomatic: Look *forward*; from that day *forward*; backward(s) and *forward(s).*

founder, flounder. The verbs *founder* and *flounder* are often confused. *Founder* comes from a Latin word meaning "bottom" (*foundation*) and originally referred to knocking enemies down; it is now used to mean "to sink below the water" and "to fail utterly, collapse." *Flounder* means "to move clumsily; thrash about," and hence "to proceed in confusion." If the railroad's business between Chicago and Peoria is *foundering,* expect the line to be shut down; If the run is *floundering,* improved operating procedures and pricing policies may still save the service.

fulsome. *Fulsome* is often used, especially in the phrase *fulsome praise,* as the equivalent of *full and abundant.* This could lead to possible confusion because of the sense "offensively flattering or insincere"; hence *fulsome praise* could be taken to mean insincere, unctuous compliments.

further. See **farther, further.**

get. *Get* has a great number of uses, some of which are acceptable at all levels and others of which are generally felt to be informal. Avoid the use of *get* in place of *be* or *become*: The executives *get* promoted. Avoid the use of *get* or *get to* in place of *start* or *begin*: Let's *get* [or *get to*] working now. Also, avoid the use of *have got* in place of *must*: I *have got to* go now.

gift. *Gift* (verb) traditionally was used in the sense "to present as a gift; to endow": We *gifted* the charity with a $1,000 donation. In current use, however, *gift* in this sense is considered affected and should be avoided. *Gift* as a noun meaning "a present" is standard: We received your *gift.*

good, well. *Good* is used as an adjective with linking verbs such as *be, seem,* or *appear*: The future looks *good. Well* should be used as an adverb: The plant runs *well.*

government. In American usage *government* always takes a singular verb: The *government is* too bureaucratic. In British usage *government,* in the sense of a governing group of officials, is usually construed as a plural collective and therefore takes a plural verb: The *government are* determined to maintain strict reins on industry.

group. *Group* as a collective noun can be followed by a singular or plural verb. It takes a singular verb when the persons or things that make up the group are considered collectively: The planning *group is* ready to present its report. *Group* takes a plural verb when the persons or things that make it up are considered individually: The *group were* divided in their sympathies.

half. The phrases *a half, half of,* and *half a* are all correct, though they may differ slightly in meaning. For example, *a half day* is used when *day* has the special sense "a working day," and the phrase then means "four hours." *Half of a day* and *half a day* are not restricted in this way and can mean either four or twelve hours. When the accompanying word is a pronoun, however, the phrase with *of* must be used: *half of them.* The phrase *a half a* is unacceptable.

hanged. *Hanged,* as the past tense and past participle of *hang,* is used in the sense "put to death by hanging": Frontier courts *hanged* [not *hung*] many a prisoner after a summary trial. In all other senses of the word, *hung* is the preferred form as past tense and past participle: He *hung* the calendar by his desk.

hardly. *Hardly* has the force of a negative; therefore, it is not used with another negative: I *could hardly* see [not *couldn't hardly* see]. A clause following *hardly* is introduced by *when* or, less often, by *before*: We had *hardly* merged with one restaurant chain *when* [or *before*] a second chain made us an attractive offer. Such a clause is not introduced by *than* in formal style: *Hardly* had I walked inside *when* [not *than*] the downpour started.

head, headed up. The phrase *headed up* is sometimes used in place of the verb *head*: The committee is *headed up* by the city's most esteemed business leader. Use *head,* however, in business writing: The city's most esteemed business leader will *head* the committee.

headquarter, headquarters. The verb *headquarter* is used informally in both transitive and intransitive senses: Our European sales team will *headquarter* in Paris; The management consulting firm has *headquartered* its people in the New York Hyatt. Both of these examples should be avoided in business writing. As a noun *headquarters* is properly used with either a singular or a plural verb. The plural is more common: Corporate *headquarters* are in Boston. But the singular is sometimes preferred when reference is to authority rather than to physical location: *Headquarters* has approved the purchase of desktop computers for our engineers.

help. *Help* in the sense "avoid" or "refrain from" is frequently used in an expression such as *I cannot help but think.* In formal writing use either *I cannot help thinking* or *I cannot but think.* Another idiomatic use of *help* is exemplified by this sentence: Don't change it any more than you can *help* (any more than you have to). Some grammarians condemn this usage on the ground that *help* in this sense means "avoid" and logically requires a negative.

here. In constructions introduced by *here is* and *here are,* the number of the verb is governed by the subject, which appears after the verb: *Here is* the annual *report; Here are* the quarterly *reports.*

historic, historical. *Historic* and *historical* are differentiated in usage, although their senses overlap. *Historic* refers to what is important in history: The *historic* first voyage to outer space. It is also used in regard to what is famous or interesting because of its association with persons or events in history: Edison's *historic* lab. *Historical* refers to whatever existed in the past, whether regarded as important or not: a *historical* character. Events are *historical* if they happened, *historic* only if they are regarded as important. *Historical* refers also to anything concerned with history or the study of the past: a *historical* society; a *historical* novel.

hopefully. The use of *hopefully* to mean "it is to be hoped" (*Hopefully,* we'll exceed last year's sales volume) can be justified by analogy to the similar uses of *happily* and *mercifully.* However, it is best to avoid using *hopefully* this way because many people object to it.

how. The use of *as how* for *that* in sentences (They said *as how* they would go) should be avoided. Similarly, the expressions *seeing as how* and *being as how* should be avoided in business writing.

however. *However* is redundant in combination with *but.* One or the other should be used: We had an invitation *but* didn't go; We had an invitation; *however,* we didn't go. The use of *however* as the first word of a sentence is generally acceptable.

identical. Some authorities specify *with* as the preferred preposition after *identical.* But either *with* or *to* is acceptable in business: a model identical *with* [or *to*] last year's.

idle. *Idle* may be used in the transitive sense "to make idle." The following example is acceptable: The dock strike had *idled* many crews and their ships.

if. *If* may be substituted for *whether* to introduce a clause indicating uncertainty after a verb such as *ask, doubt, know, learn,* or *see*: We shall soon learn *if* [*whether*] it is true. *If* should be avoided when it may be ambiguous: Please inform the registrar *if* you intend to be present. (Does it mean *whether or not* you intend to be or *only if* you intend to be?) Often *if not* is also ambiguous: The discovery offered persuasive, *if not* conclusive evidence. This could mean "persuasive and perhaps conclusive" or "persuasive but not conclusive." Traditionally, the subjunctive (*if I were*) is used for a situation contrary to fact: *If* I *were* the president, I *would* [or *should*] make June 1 a national holiday. The indicative is required when the situation described by the *if* clause is assumed to be true: If I *was* short with you a moment ago, it is only because I wasn't paying attention. When an *if* clause is preceded by *ask* or *wonder,* use the indicative: He *asked if* Napoleon *was* a great general. Using *would have* in place of the subjunctive in contrary-to-fact *if* clauses is incorrect: *If I had been* [not *If I would have been*] promoted.

immigrate. See **migrate, emigrate, immigrate.**

impact. *Impact* (verb) is sometimes used transitively: These taxes *impact* small businesses. It is also used intransitively with *on*: Social pathologies, common to the inner city, *impact* most heavily *on* a plant operating in such a location. Some authorities consider the preceding example unacceptable.

imply. See **infer, imply.**

important. The following sentence may be written with the adjective *important*: The shareholders' opinion is evident; *more important,* it will prevail. It also may be written with an adverb: The shareholders' opinion is evident; *more importantly,* it will prevail. Most grammarians prescribe the adjective form, in which *important* stands for "what is important."

impractical, impracticable. *Impractical* can refer to that which is not sensible or prudent: Your suggestion that we use balloons to convey messages across town is *impractical. Impracticable* applies to that which is not capable of being carried out or put into practice: Building a highway to the moon is *impracticable.* A plan may be *impractical* if it involves undue cost or effort and still not be *impracticable.* The distinction between these words is subtle, and *impractical* is often used where *impracticable* would be more precise.

infer, imply. *Infer* is sometimes confused with *imply,* but the distinction between the two words is useful. To *imply* is "to state indirectly." To *infer* is "to draw a conclusion." One should write: The quarterly report *implies* that sales are down because of the recession. Because of that implication, investors have *inferred* that we have something to hide, and our stock has fallen three points.

inflammable. See **flammable, inflammable.**

input. *Input* is technical and business jargon referring to information fed into a computer. Careful writers avoid it in other contexts, particularly in formal writing and international correspondence: The nominee declared that he had no *information* [not *input*], as far as he knew, in the adoption of the plank on abortion.

inside, inside of. *Inside* and *inside of* have the same meaning. *Inside* is generally preferred, especially in writing, when the reference is to position or location: *inside* the warehouse. *Inside of* is used more acceptably when the reference is to time: The 300-page report was photocopied *inside of* 10 minutes. *Better:* the 300-page report was photocopied *in less than* 10 minutes.

insure. See **assure, ensure, insure.**

intense, intensive. *Intensive* is often used interchangeably with *intense.* However, it refers especially to the strength or concentration of an activity when imposed from without. Thus one speaks of *intense* dislike but *intensive* study.

intrigue. *Intrigue* is fully established as a noun and a verb in all meanings except "to arouse the interest or curiosity of." In that sense it has been resisted by writers on usage, who regard it as an unneeded French substitute for available English words, such as *interest, fascinate, pique,* or *puzzle.* Nevertheless, it has gained increasing acceptance, probably because no single English word has precisely the same meaning. The following example is therefore acceptable: The announcement of a special press conference *intrigued* the financial writers in the manner of a good suspense novel.

its, it's. *Its,* the possessive form of the pronoun *it,* is never written with an apostrophe. The contraction *it's* (for *it is* or *it has*) is always written with an apostrophe.

joint. See **reciprocal, joint.**

kind. The use of the plurals *these* and *those* with *kind* (*these kind* of films) has been defended by some as a sensible idiom but should be avoided in writing. Substitute *this* (or *that*) *kind of* or *these* (or *those*) *kinds of* and see that the following nouns and verbs agree in number with *kind: This kind of* film *has had* a lot of success in foreign markets. *Those are* the *kinds of* books that capture the public imagination. When *kind of* is used to mean "more or less," it is properly preceded by the indefinite article *a* in formal writing: *a kind of* genius [not *kind of a* genius]. The use of *kind of* to mean "somewhat" (We were *kind of* sleepy) should be avoided.

kudos. *Kudos* is one of those words, like *congeries,* that looks plural but is historically singular. So it is correctly used with a singular verb: *Kudos is* due the committee for organizing a successful company picnic.

lack. As an intransitive verb meaning "to be deficient," *lack* is used chiefly in the present participle with *in*: You will not be *lacking in* support from the finance committee. In the sense "to be in need of something," it requires no preposition but is sometimes used with *for*: You will not *lack* [or *lack for*] support from the finance committee. In that example, *lack* is preferred over *lack for*. In some cases, however, the two phrasings can convey different meanings: The millionaire *lacks* nothing [has everything]; The millionaire *lacks for* nothing [has everything he needs].

latter. *Latter,* as used in contrast to *former,* refers to the second of two: Jones and Smith have been mentioned for transfer to our London office, but the *latter* may decline the post. *Latter* is not appropriate when more than two are named: Jones, Smith, and Kowalski have been nominated. Kowalski should then be referred to as *the last, the last named,* or preferably, simply *Kowalski.*

lay, lie. *Lay* ("to put, place, or prepare") and *lie* ("to recline or be situated") are frequently confused. *Lay* is a transitive verb and takes an object. *Lay* and its principal parts (*laid, laid, laying*) are correctly used in the following examples: Please *lay* the books on the floor; The messenger *laid* [not *lay*] the computer printouts on the desk; The dining room table *was laid* for four; He was *laying* the tray down when I came in. *Lie* is an intransitive verb and does not take an object. *Lie* and its principal parts (*lay, lain, lying*) are correctly used in the following examples: The founder of the company often *lies* [not *lays*] down after lunch; When I *lay* [not *laid*] down, I fell asleep; The rubbish had *lain* [not *laid*] in the dumpster for a week; I *was lying* [not *laying*] in bed when I received the call; The valley *lies* to the east. There are a few exceptions to these rules. The idioms *lay low* and *lay for* and the nautical sense of *lay* (*lay* at anchor), though intransitive, are well established.

leave alone, let alone. *Leave alone* may be substituted for *let alone* in the sense of "to refrain from disturbing or interfering": *Leave* the secretaries *alone* and they will produce; *Left alone,* they were quite productive.

Those who do not accept these examples generally believe *leave alone* should be restricted to the sense "to depart and leave one in solitude": They were *left alone* in the wilderness. In formal writing *leave* is not an acceptable substitute for *let* in the sense "to allow or permit." Only *let* is acceptable in these examples: *Let* me be; *Let* us not quarrel; *Let* matters stand.

lend. See **loan, lend.**

less. See **fewer, less.**

let's. In colloquial speech *let's* is sometimes used as a mere indicator that a suggestion is being proffered, and its connection with the more formal *let us* has become correspondingly attenuated. One hears usages like *Let's us go, Don't let's get all excited,* and *Let's get yourself ready.* These usages should all be avoided in business writing.

lie. See **lay, lie.**

lighted, lit. *Lighted* and *lit* are equally acceptable as past tense and past participle of *light.* Both forms are well established as adjectives also: a *lighted* (or *lit*) cigarette.

like. *Like* should be avoided as a conjunction: The machine responds *as* [not *like*] it should. Constructions like *looks like, sounds like,* and *tastes like* are less offensive, but *as if* should be substituted in business writing: It looks *as if* there will be no action on the bill before Congress recesses. There is less objection to the use of *like* as a conjunction when the verb following it is not expressed: The new senator took to politics *like* a duck to water.

likewise. *Likewise* is not a conjunction and cannot take the place of a connective such as *and* or *together with*: The mayor risked his credibility, *likewise* his honor. *Better:* The mayor risked his credibility *and* (or *and likewise*) his honor.

literally. *Literally* means "in a manner that accords precisely with the words." It is often used as if it meant "figuratively" or "in a manner of speaking," which is almost the opposite of its true meaning: The boss was *literally* breathing fire.

loan, lend. *Loan* is used as a verb, especially in business, although some hold that *lend* is the preferred form in all writing. *Lend* is preferred over *loan* in the following examples: One who *lends* money to a friend may lose a friend; When I refused to *lend* my car, I was kicked out of the carpool. Many phrases and figurative uses require *lend*: *lend* an ear; distance *lends* enchantment.

lost. The phrase *lost to* can sometimes be ambiguous: As a result of poor preparation, the court battle was *lost to* the defense attorney. Was it lost by the defendant's attorney or lost by the plaintiff's attorney to the defendant's attorney? Unless the context makes the meaning clear, the sentence should be reworded: As a result of poor preparation, the court battle was *lost by* the defense attorney.

majority. When *majority* refers to a particular number of votes, it takes a singular verb: Her *majority* was five votes. When it refers to a group of persons or things that are in the majority, it may take either a plural or singular verb, depending on whether the group is considered as a whole or as a set of people considered individually. When, for example, we refer to an election accomplished by a group as a whole, we say The *majority elects* the candidate *it wants*. When we speak, for example, of something done individually, such as living within five miles of an office, we say The *majority* of our employees *live* within five miles of the office. *Majority* is often preceded by *great* (but not by *greater*) in emphatically expressing the sense of "most of": The *great majority* has decided not to throw good money after bad. The phrase *greater majority* is appropriate only when considering two majorities: A *greater majority* of the workers has accepted this year's contract than accepted last year's.

man. Unless they are referring to a male human being, business writers should substitute a nonsexist reference, such as *one, man or woman, human, person, police officer, firefighter, humankind,* and *member of Congress*: Every *citizen* [not *man*] should have a right to work.

masterful. *Masterful* means "strong-willed, imperious, domineering": a *masterful* approach. It also is used, as is *masterly,* in the sense "having the skill of a master." But the distinction between the two words should be respected: a *masterly* sales presentation.

materialize. *Materialize* as an intransitive verb has the primary sense "to assume material form" or, more generally, "to take effective shape": If our plans *materialize,* we will be ready to corner the market. Although *materialize* is widely used informally in the sense "appear" or "happen" (Three more witnesses testified, but no new evidence *materialized*), such usage should be avoided.

may. See **can, may.**

means. In the sense "financial resources," *means* takes a plural verb: Our *means are* adequate for this acquisition. In the sense "a way to an end," it may take a singular or plural verb; the choice of a modifier such as *any* or *all* generally determines the number of the verb: *Every means was* tried; There *are several means* at our disposal.

meantime, meanwhile. *Meantime* is more common than *meanwhile* as a noun: In the *meantime,* we made plans for an unfavorable Federal Communications Commission ruling. In expressing the same sense as "in the meantime" as a single adverb, *meanwhile* is more common than *meantime*: Meanwhile, we made plans for an unfavorable ruling.

might. In many Southern varieties of English *might* is used in a "double" construction with *could*: We *might could* build over there. Less frequently, one hears *may can* and *might should.* These constructions are not familiar to the majority of Americans in other regions or to individuals in other countries and hence should be avoided in business writing.

migrate, emigrate, immigrate. *Migrate* is used with reference to both the place of departure and the destination and can be followed by *from* or *to.* It is said of persons, animals, and birds and sometimes implies a lack of permanent settlement, especially as a result of seasonal or periodic movement. *Emigrate* pertains to a single move by a person and implies permanence. It refers specifically to the place of *departure* and emphasizes movement *from* that place. If the place is mentioned, the preposition is *from*: Since many people have *emigrated from* Russia, we see a new demand for Russian-language books. *Immigrate* also pertains to a single move by persons and likewise implies permanence. But it refers to *destination,* emphasizes movement there, and is followed by *to*: Many illegal aliens have *immigrated to* the United States in recent months.

minimize. According to traditional grammar, *minimize* can mean only "to make as small as possible" and is therefore an absolute term, which cannot be modified by *greatly* or *somewhat,* which are appropriately used only with verbs like *reduce* and *lessen.* The informal use of *minimize* to mean "to make smaller than before," which can be so modified, should be avoided in business writing.

mobile. See **movable, mobile.**

most, mostly. The adverb *most* is sometimes used informally in the sense of "almost": *Most* all the clients accepted the provisions in the contract. However, this usage should be avoided in business writing. In the sense "very," as an intensive where no explicit comparison is involved, *most* is acceptable both in writing and in speech: a *most* ingenious solution. The adverb *mostly* means "for the greatest part, mainly," or "generally, usually": The trees are *mostly* evergreens. In writing one should say: *for the most part* [not *mostly*] in sentences like *For the most part,* Northern Telecom is the supplier of our communications equipment.

movable, mobile. Something is *movable* if it can be moved: *movable* office furniture; a *movable* partition. It is *mobile* if it is designed for easy transportation (a *mobile* electric generating unit) or if it moves frequently (a *mobile* drilling rig).

mutual, common. *Mutual* is often used to describe a relation between two or more things, and in this use it can be paraphrased with expressions involving *between* or *each other*: their *mutual* relations, meaning "their relations with each other" or "the relations between them." *Common* describes a relationship shared by the members of a group to something else (their *common* interest in accounting) or in the expression *common knowledge,* "the knowledge shared by all." The phrase *mutual friend,* however, refers to a friend of each of the several members of a group: The business partners were originally introduced by a *mutual friend.*

nauseous, nauseated. Traditionally, *nauseous* means "causing nausea"; *nauseated* means "suffering from nausea." The use of *nauseous* in the sense of *nauseated* should be avoided: She was *nauseated* after eating in the cafeteria; His behavior is *nauseous.*

need. The *regular form* of *need* must be agree with its subject and is followed by *to*: He needs *to* go. The *irregular form* primarily occurs in questions, negations, and *if* clauses. It does not agree with its subject and is not followed by *to*: He need not go; *Need it be* done in a hurry? The irregular form means something like "to be obliged to": You *needn't* come (you are under no obligation to come). In this case there is an externally imposed obligation on the subject *you.* If there were no externally imposed obligation, the regular form could be used: Since I was there when it happened, I *don't need* to hear [not *needn't hear*] the television news account.

neither. *Neither* is construed as singular when it occurs as the subject of a sentence: *Neither* of the reports *is* finished. Accordingly, a pronoun with *neither* as an antecedent also must be singular: *Neither* of the doctors in the lawsuit *is* likely to reveal *his or her* identity.

no. When *no* introduces a compound phrase, its elements should be connected with *or* rather than with *nor*: The candidate has *no* experience *or* interest in product development; *No* modification *or* change in operating procedures will be acceptable to them.

nominal. *Nominal* in one of its senses means "in name only." Hence a *nominal payment* is a token payment, bearing no relation to the real value of what is being paid for. The word is often extended in use, especially by sellers, to describe a low or bargain price: We acquired 600,000 barrels of new oil reserves at a *nominal* extra cost.

no sooner. *No sooner,* as a comparative adverb, should be followed by *than,* not *when*: *No sooner* had I arrived *than* I had to leave for an emergency meeting; I had *no sooner* made an offer *than* they said the property had been sold to another person.

not. Care should be taken with the placement of *not* and other negatives in a sentence to avoid ambiguity. *All issues are not speculative* could be taken to mean either "all of the issues are not speculative" or "not all of the issues are speculative." *We didn't sleep until noon* could mean either "We went to sleep at noon" or "We got up before noon."

nothing. *Nothing* takes a singular verb, even when it is followed by a phrase containing a plural noun or pronoun: *Nothing* except your fears *stands* in your path.

number. As a collective noun *number* may take either a singular or a plural verb. It takes a singular verb when it is preceded by the definite article *the*: *The number* of skilled workers *is* small. It takes a plural verb when preceded by the indefinite article *a*: *A number* of the workers *are* unskilled.

odd. *Odd,* when used to indicate a few more than a given number, should be preceded by a hyphen to avoid ambiguity: *thirty-odd* salespeople in the showroom. *Odd* in that sense is used only with round numbers.

off. *Off* should not be followed by *of* or *from*: The speaker stepped *off* [not *off of* or *off from*] the platform. Nor should *off* be used for *from* to indicate a source in a sentence: I got a loan *from* [not *off*] the credit union.

on, upon. To indicate motion toward a position, both *on* and *onto* can be used: The dog jumped *on* [*onto*] the counter. *Onto* is more specific, however, in indicating that the motion was initiated from an outside point, such as from the floor. In constructions where *on* is an adverb attached to a verb, it should not be joined with *to* to form the single word *onto*: The meeting moved *on to* [not *onto*] the next subject. In their uses to indicate spatial relations, *on* and *upon* are often interchangeable: The container was resting *on* [or *upon*] the flatcar. To indicate a relation between two things, however, instead of between an action and an end point, *upon* cannot always be used: Hand me the book *on* [not *upon*] the file cabinet. Similarly, *upon* cannot always be used in place of *on* when the relation is not spatial: We will be in Des Moines *on* [not *upon*] Tuesday.

one another. See **each other, one another.**

onetime, one-time. *Onetime* (single word) means "former." *One-time* (hyphenated) means "only once." Thus a *onetime employee* is a former employee; a *one-time mayor* was mayor only once.

only. When used as an adverb, *only* should be placed with care to avoid ambiguity. Generally, this means having *only* adjoin the word or words that it limits: Dictators respect *only force*; they are not moved by words. Dictators *only respect* force; they do not worship it. She picked up the receiver *only when* he entered, not before. She *only picked up* the receiver when he entered; she didn't dial the number. Occasionally, placement of *only* earlier in the sentence seems more natural: The committee can [*only*] make its decision by Friday of next week *only* if it receives a copy of the latest report. Placement of *only* after *can* would serve the rhetorical function of warning the reader that a condition on the statement follows. *Only* is often used as a conjunction equivalent to *but* in the sense "were it not that": They would have come, *only* they were snowed in. This usage should be avoided in business writing.

oral. See **verbal, oral.**

ought. *Ought to* is sometimes used without a following verb if the meaning is clear: Should we begin soon? Yes, we *ought to.* The omission of *to* (No, we *ought* not), however, is not standard. Usages like *one hadn't ought to come* and *one shouldn't ought to say that*, which are common in certain varieties of American English, should be avoided in business writing.

owing to. See **because, due to, owing to.**

pair. *Pair* as a noun can be followed by a singular or plural verb. The singular is always used when *pair* denotes the set taken as a single entity: This *pair* of shoes *is* a year old. A plural verb is used when the members are considered as individuals: The *pair are* working more harmoniously now. After a numeral other than *one, pair* itself can be either singular or plural, but the plural is more common: Six *pairs* of stockings *are* defective.

parent. The use of *parent* as a verb is generally unacceptable. Since there is no acceptable one-word substitute for it, paraphrases like *perform the duties of parenthood* are recommended.

party. A person may be called a *party* in the sense of "participant": a *party* to the industrial espionage ring. But except in legal usage, *party* should not be used as a general synonym for *person*: The *person* [not *party*] who stole $12,000 worth of inventory was taken into custody.

pass. The past tense and past participle of *pass* is *passed:* They *passed* [or *have passed*] right by the front gate. *Past* is the corresponding adjective (in centuries *past*), adverb (drove *past*), and preposition (*past* midnight; *past* the crisis).

peer. *Peer* is sometimes misused in the sense of "a superior": That manager is the *equal*, if not the *peer*, of any executive on the committee. Since *peer* refers to an *equal*, not a superior, it is redundant in that sentence. *Peer* is properly used in the expressions *peer group* and *a jury of one's peers.*

people, persons. Traditionally, *people* and *persons* have been distinguished in usage. *People* is the proper term when referring to a large group of individuals, collectively and indefinitely: *People* use a wide variety of our products at work and at home. *Persons* is applicable to a specific and relatively small number: Two *persons* were fired. In modern usage, however, *people* is also acceptable with any plural number: I counted two *people*. The possessive form is *people's* (the *people's* rights) except when *people* is used in the plural to refer to two or more groups considered to be political or cultural entities: the Slavic *peoples'* history.

per. *Per* is used with reference to statistics and units of measurement: *per* mile; *per* day; *per* person. In nontechnical writing, it is preferable to substitute *a* or *each* for *per*: a dozen persons *a* [or *each*] day. Its more general use, as in *per* the terms of this contract, should be avoided in business writing.

percent, percentage. *Percent* is usually written as one word in business material and should be spelled out in nontechnical work: 20 *percent.* The number of a noun that follows it or is understood to follow it governs the number of the verb: Twenty *percent* of the stock *is* owned by a conglomerate; Forty-seven *percent* of our sales *come* from consumer appliances. *Percentage,* when preceded by *the,* takes a singular verb: The *percentage* of unskilled workers *is* small. When preceded by *a,* it takes either a singular or plural verb, depending on the number of the noun in the prepositional phrase that follows: A small *percentage* of the workers *are* unskilled; A large *percentage* of the defective press run *was* never shipped. When the word *of* follows, *percentage* should be used rather than *percent*: *percentage of* sales.

perfect, perfectly. *Perfect* has been traditionally considered an absolute term, like *unique, chief,* and *prime,* and is not subject to comparison with *more, less, almost,* and other modifiers of degree. The comparative form nonetheless is used in the United States Constitution in the phrase *a more perfect union.* It is generally regarded as correct when *perfect* is used to mean "ideal for the purposes": A *more perfect spot* for our broadcasting station could not be found. *Perfectly* is used informally as a mere intensive denoting "quite," "altogether," or "just": *perfectly good; perfectly dreadful.* This use should be avoided in business writing.

permit. *Permit of* is sometimes used to mean "to allow for": *permits of* two interpretations. But the usage should be avoided in business writing.

person. *Person* is increasingly used to create compounds that may refer to either a man or a woman: *chairperson; spokesperson; anchorperson; salesperson.* These forms can be used when reference is to the position itself, regardless of who might hold it: The committee should elect a new *chairperson* at its meeting. They are also appropriate when speaking of the specific individual holding the position: She was the best *anchorperson* the local station had ever had. In such cases referring to *he* or *she,* the alternatives *anchorwoman* and *spokesman* also would be acceptable and might be preferred by the holder of the position.

persons. See **people, persons.**

personality. *Personality,* meaning "a celebrity" or "a notable," is widely used in speech and journalism. But it should be avoided in this sense in business writing.

persuade. See **convince, persuade.**

plead. In strict legal usage one is said to *plead guilty* or *plead not guilty* but not to *plead innocent*. In nonlegal contexts, however, *plead innocent* is sometimes used.

plus. When *plus* is used after a singular or plural subject, the verb traditionally remains singular: Two *plus* two *equals* four; Our production efficiency *plus* their excellent distribution system *results* in a new industry leader. *Plus* is sometimes used loosely as a conjunction to connect two independent clauses: We had terrible weather this year, *plus* the recession affected us adversely. This use should be avoided in business writing.

P.M. See **ante meridian.**

poor. In formal usage *poor* should be used as an adjective, not an adverb: a *poor* person. It should not be used to qualify a verb: *did poor; never worked poorer*. *Poorly* and *more poorly* are required in such examples.

practical, practicable. *Practical* describes that which is sensible and useful: a *practical* approach. *Practicable* means "usable" and "workable": Your idea is *practicable*. The distinction, however, is often subtle, and many writers use *practical* in both cases. This example illustrates the traditional distinction: It might be *practicable* to build a bullet train between New York and Omaha, but it would not be *practical*.

practically, virtually. The primary sense of *practically* is "in a way that is practical": handle the project *practically*. It has also become almost interchangeable with *virtually*, meaning "in fact or to all purposes": The city was *practically* (or *virtually*) paralyzed by the strike. Thus a man whose liabilities exceed his assets may be said to be *practically bankrupt*, even though he has not been legally declared insolvent. By a slight extension of this meaning, however, *practically* is often used to mean "nearly" or "all but": They had *practically* closed the deal by the time I arrived. Such use should be avoided in business writing.

precipitate, precipitant, precipitous. *Precipitate* (adjective) and *precipitately* often refer to rash, overhasty human actions: a *precipitate* decision. *Precipitant* (adjective) and *precipitantly* are also used in the foregoing sense, with stress on rushing forward or falling headlong (literally or figuratively): *precipitant* action. *Precipitous* and *precipitously* are used primarily of physical steepness (a *precipitous* slope) or in the figurative extensions of such literal uses (a *precipitous* drop in interest rates).

premiere. *Premiere* is primarily used as a noun meaning "the first public performance": the *premiere* of the new movie. It is generally unacceptable as a verb despite its wide use in the world of entertainment.

presently. *Presently* is used primarily in the sense "soon": She will arrive *presently.* It is also used in the sense "at the present time": He is *presently* [*now*] living in Chicago. Writers who use the word should take care that the meaning is clear from the context.

principle, principal. *Principal* and *principle* are often confused but have no meanings in common. *Principle* is only a noun, and all its senses are abstract: *principles* of nuclear physics. *Principal* is both a noun and an adjective. As a noun (aside from its specialized meaning in law and finance), it generally denotes a person who holds a high position or plays an important role: a meeting between all the *principals* in the transaction. As an adjective it has the related sense "chief" or "leading": *principal* candidates.

protagonist. *Protagonist* denotes the leading figure in a theatrical drama or, by extension, in any work or undertaking. Sometimes in modern usage the sense of singularity is lost: There are three *protagonists* in the takeover fight. This watered-down meaning should be avoided. *Protagonist* is also used to indicate a champion or advocate, a use that should be avoided.

prove, proved, proven. The regular form *proved* is the preferred past participle: You have *proved* your point; The theory has been *proved* by our physicists. The alternative *proven* in such examples is unacceptable to many experts. *Proven* is a Scots variant made familiar through its legal use: The charges were not *proven.* But *proven* is more widely used as an adjective directly before a noun: a *proven* talent; a *proven* point.

quick, quickly. Both *quick* and *quickly* can be used as adverbs. *Quick* is more frequent in conversation: Come *quick!* In writing the slightly more formal *quickly* is preferred: When the signal was relayed to our parts center, we responded *quickly.* In the latter example, *quick* would be unacceptable to most experts.

quote, cite. *Quote* (transitive verb) is appropriate when words are being given exactly as they were originally written or spoken: He *quoted* the first paragraph of the report. When the reference is less exact, *cite* is preferable: He *cited* an advertising study. *Quote* (noun) as a substitute for *quotation* should be avoided: the *quotation* [not *quote*] from Milton.

raise, rise. *Raise* is properly used as a transitive verb: *Raise* the loading bay doors. For intransitive uses, *rise* is standard: The platform *rises.* However, *raise* is sometimes used as an intransitive verb: The window *raises* easily. *Raise* (noun), rather than *rise,* is now standard in the United States for an increase in salary, although one still speaks of *a rise in prices.*

rare, scarce. *Rare* and *scarce* are sometimes interchangeable, but *scarce* carries an additional implication that the quantities involved are insufficient or inadequate. Thus we speak of *rare books* or of *the rare qualities* of someone we admire but of increasingly *scarce* oil reserves.

rarely, seldom. The use of *ever* after *rarely* or *seldom* is considered redundant: He *rarely* [not *rarely ever*] makes a mistake. The following constructions, using either *rarely* or *seldom,* are standard, however: *rarely if ever*; *rarely or never* [not *rarely or ever*].

rather. *Rather* is usually preceded by *should* or *would* in expressing preference: They *would rather* not diversify the company. But *had* is equally acceptable: I *had rather* be dead than be unemployed. In a contraction such as *he'd,* either *would* or *had* can be understood: He'd rather [He *would* or *had rather*] be dead than be unemployed. As a modifier, *rather* is frequently unnecessary and overused: *rather* nice; *rather* cold; *rather* important.

reciprocal, joint. *Reciprocal,* like *mutual,* described earlier, can apply to relations between the members of a group, often with reference to an exchange of goods or favors: *reciprocal* trade. *Joint* is often used to describe an undertaking in which several partners are involved: The *joint* efforts of federal and local officials will be required to eradicate acid rain.

refer/reference. See **allude/allusion, refer/reference.**

regard, respects. *Regard* is traditionally singular in the phrase *in* (or *with*) *regard to* (not *in regards to*). *Regarding* and *as regards* are used in the same sense "with reference to" but are not as widely acceptable. In the same sense *with respect to* is acceptable, but *respecting* is not. *Respects* is sometimes preferable to *regards* in the sense "particulars": In some *respects* [not *regards*] we are similar to our competition.

relatively. *Relatively* is appropriate when a comparison is stated or implied: The first question was *relatively* easy (that is, in comparison to the others). *Relatively* should not be used to mean simply "fairly": I am *fairly* [not *relatively*] sure of it.

repel, repulse. The verbs *repel* and *repulse* both have the physical sense of "to drive back or off." They also may apply to rebuffing or rejecting discourteously, but only *repel* is used in the sense of "to cause distaste or aversion": Your arrogance *repelled* us; He *repulsed* with rudeness all of our attempts to help him.

replete. *Replete* means "abundantly supplied": a takeover battle *replete* with scandal, mudslinging, and threats. It should not be used to mean simply "complete" or "equipped": a club *complete* [not *replete*] with pool, tennis courts, and golf courses.

responsible. Some usage experts believe that *responsible* should be used only with reference to persons, since only persons can be held accountable. The word is widely used, however, with reference to things: Defective welding was *responsible* for the buckled axle.

restive, restless. *Restive* and *restless* are used as equivalent terms. *Restive,* however, implies more than simply "nervous" or "fidgety." It implies resistance to some sort of restraint. Thus a patient who is sleeping poorly may be *restless,* but the same patient is *restive* only if kept in bed against his or her will.

rise. See **raise, rise.**

sacrilegious. The adjective *sacrilegious* is often misspelled through confusion with *religious.* It refers to gross irreverence toward something sacred: His profanity in church was *sacrilegious.*

said. As an adjective *said* is seldom appropriate to any but legal writing, where it is equivalent to *aforesaid*: the *said* tenant (named in a lease); *said* property. In similar contexts in general usage, *said* should be omitted: *the tenant; the property.*

same. Only in legal writing is *the same* or just *same* used as a substitute for *it* or *them.* In general writing one should be specific: The charge is $5. Please send *your payment* [not *the same*] today.

scarce. See **rare, scarce.**

scarcely. *Scarcely* has the force of a negative; therefore, it is not properly used with another negative: I *could scarcely* believe it [*not* I *couldn't scarcely* believe it]. A clause following *scarcely* is introduced by *when* or, less often, by *before* but not by *than*: The meeting had *scarcely* begun *when* [or *before*] it was interrupted.

seasonal, seasonable. *Seasonal* and *seasonable,* though closely related, are differentiated in usage. *Seasonal* applies to what depends on or is controlled by the season of the year: a *seasonal* rise in unemployment. *Seasonable* applies to what is appropriate to the season (*seasonable* clothing) or timely (a *seasonable* intervention in the dispute). Rains are *seasonal* if they occur at a certain time of the year. They are *seasonable* at any time if they save the crops.

see that. The phrase *see where* sometimes occurs in conversation as an informal equivalent of *see that*: I *see that* [*see where*] everything is running smoothly at the grain elevator. The same applies to *read where*. These informal usages should be avoided in business writing.

seldom. See **rarely, seldom.**

semimonthly. See **bimonthly, semimonthly.**

set, sit. Originally, *set* meant "to cause (something) to sit," so it is now in most cases a transitive verb: The worker *sets* his shovel down; One *sets* the table. *Sit* is generally an intransitive verb: They *sit* at the microphone. There are some exceptions: The sun *sets* [not *sits*]; A hen *sets* [or *sits*] on her eggs.

shall, will. In formal writing *shall* is used in the first person to indicate futurity: I *shall* leave tomorrow. In the second and third persons the same sense of futurity is expressed by *will*: He *will* come this afternoon. Use of the auxiliaries *shall* and *will* is reversed when the writer wants to indicate conditions, such as determination, promise, obligation, command, compulsion, permission, or inevitability: I *will* leave tomorrow. In contemporary writing *will* is used in all three persons to indicate futurity: We *will* be in New York next week. *Shall* is still used in first-person interrogatives (*Shall* we go? Where *shall* we have our sales conference this year?) and in a few set phrases (We *shall* overcome). In writing, a condition other than mere futurity is often expressed more clearly by an alternative to *shall* or *will,* such as *must* or *have to* (indicating determination, compulsion, or obligation) or by use of an intensifying word, such as *certainly* or *surely,* with *shall* or *will.* Informally, contractions such as *I'll, we'll,* and *you'll* are generally used without distinction between the functions of *shall* and *will* as formally defined.

should, would. Traditionally, the rules governing the use of *should* and *would* were based on the rules governing the use of *shall* and *will.* These rules have been eroded even more in the case of *should* and *would.* Either *should* or *would* is now used in the first person to express conditional futurity: If I had known that, I *should* [or *would*] have made a different reply. In the second and third persons only *would* is acceptable: If he had known that, he *would* have made a different reply. *Would* cannot always be substituted for *should,* however. *Should* is used in all three persons in a conditional clause: *if I* [or *you* or *he* or *she*] *should decide to go. Should* is also used in all three persons to express duty or obligation (the equivalent of *ought to*): *I* [or *you* or *he* or *she*] *should go. Would* is used to express volition or promise: I agreed that I *would* do it. Either *would* or *should* is possible as an auxiliary with *like, be inclined, be glad, prefer,* and related verbs: I *would* [or *should*] like to call your attention to an oversight in the accountant's report. But *would* is more common than *should. Should have* is sometimes incorrectly written *should of* by writers who have mistaken the source of the spoken contraction *should've.*

since. See **as, since.**

sit. See **set, sit.**

slow, slowly. *Slow* is sometimes used as an informal variant of the adverb *slowly* when it comes after the verb: We drove the car *slow.* But *slowly* should be used in business writing. *Slow* is often used informally when brevity and forcefulness are sought: Drive *slow! Slow* is also the established idiomatic form with certain senses of common verbs: The watch runs *slow;* Take it *slow.*

so. The conjunction *so* is followed by *that* when it introduces a clause stating the purpose of or reason for an action: The supervisor stayed late *so that* [*in order that*] he could catch up on his paperwork. *So* can stand alone, however, when it is used to introduce a clause that states the result or consequence of something: The canning process kills much of the flavor of the food, *so* salt is added.

so . . . as. See **as . . . as, so . . . as.**

sometime. *Sometime* as an adjective is properly used to mean "former." It is also used colloquially with the meaning "occasional": the team's *sometime* pitcher. This latter use, however, should be avoided in business writing.

stratum. The standard singular form is *stratum;* the standard plural is *strata* (or sometimes *stratums*) but not *stratas.*

take. See **bring, take.**

tend. *Tend* is an informal variant of *attend* in the phrase *tend to,* meaning "to apply one's attention to": A special session of the legislature has been called to *tend to* [*attend to*] the question of a windfall profits tax. This usage should be avoided in international correspondence.

than, as. In comparisons a pronoun following *than* or *as* may be taken as either the subject or the object of a "missing" verb whose sense is understood: John is older *than* I [*am*]. The nominative *I* is required since the verb *am* is implied. *But*: It does not surprise me *as much as him*. The use of the objective *him* can be justified by analogy to the sentence It does not surprise me *as much as* [it surprises] *him*.

this, that. *This* and *that* are both used as demonstrative pronouns to refer to a thought expressed earlier: The door was unopened; *that* [or *this*] in itself casts doubt on the guard's theory. *That* is sometimes prescribed as the better choice in referring to what has gone before (as in the preceding example). When the referent is yet to be mentioned, only *this* is used: *This* is what bothers me — we have no time to consider late applications. *This* is often used in speech as an emphatic variant of the indefinite article *a*: *This* friend of mine inquired about working here; I have *this* terrible headache. But such informal usage should be avoided in business writing.

tight. *Tight* as an adverb appears after the verb when it follows verbs such as *squeeze, shut, close, tie,* and *hold*: hold on *tight*; close it *tight*. In most cases the adverb *tightly* also may be used in this position: close it *tightly*. In a few cases *tight* is the only form that may be used: sit *tight*; sleep *tight*. Before a verb only *tightly* is used: The money supply will be *tightly* controlled.

together with. *Together with,* like *in addition to,* is often employed following the subject of a sentence or clause to introduce an addition. The addition, however, does not alter the number of the verb, which is governed by the subject: The chairman [singular], *together with* two aides, *is* expected in an hour. The same is true of *along with, as well as, besides, in addition to,* and *like*: Common sense *as well as* training *is* a requisite for a good job.

too. *Too* preceded by *not* or another negative is frequently used informally as a form of understatement to convey humor or sarcasm: The workers were *not too* pleased with the amount of their raises; This applicant is *not too* bright. *Not too*, when used to mean approximately "not very," is also considered informal: Passage of the bill is *not* now considered *too* likely. Such informal use should be avoided in business writing. *Too* can often be eliminated from such sentences without loss; but if deletion gives undue stress to the negative sense, the writer may find *not very* or *none too* preferable choices: The applicant is *not very* bright. *Too* is often used in writing in place of *moreover* or *in addition* to introduce a sentence: There has been a cutback in oil production; *Too*, rates have been increasing. This usage also should be avoided in business writing.

torn. *Torn*, never *tore*, is the standard past participle of the verb *tear*. I have *torn* the book.

tortuous, torturous. Although *tortuous* and *torturous* have a common Latin source, their primary meanings are distinct. *Tortuous* means "twisting" (a *tortuous* road) or by extension "extremely strained or devious" (*tortuous* reasoning). *Torturous* refers primarily to the pain of torture. However, *torturous* also can be used in the sense of "twisted" or "strained," and *tortured* is an even stronger synonym: *tortured reasoning*.

transpire. *Transpire* has long been used in the sense "to become known": It soon *transpired* that they intended to gain a controlling interest in the corporation. The meaning "to happen" or "to take place" has come into use more recently: The board wondered what would *transpire* next. This latter use should be avoided in business writing, particularly in international correspondence.

try and, try to. *Try and* is common in informal conversation for *try to*, especially in established combinations such as *try and stop me* and *try and get some rest*. In most contexts, however, it is not interchangeable with *try to* unless the level is clearly informal. The following is unacceptable in business writing: It is a mistake to *try and* force compliance with a regulation that is so unpopular.

type. *Type* is followed by *of* in constructions like *that type of leather*. The variant form omitting *of*, as in *that type leather*, is generally unacceptable. *Type* is most appropriate when reference is being made to a well-defined or sharply distinct category: that *type* of chassis; this *type* of aspirin. When the categorization is vaguer or less well accepted, *kind* or *sort* is preferable. See also **kind**.

under way. See **way, under way, aweigh.**

unexceptional, unexceptionable. *Unexceptional* is often confused with *unexceptionable.* When the desired meaning is "not open to objection" or "above reproach," the term is *unexceptionable*: *unexceptionable* arguments. *Unexceptional* should be used to mean "not exceptional": an *unexceptional* student.

uninterested. See **disinterested, uninterested.**

upon. See **on, upon.**

various. *Various,* sometimes appearing as a collective noun followed by *of,* is unacceptable usage: He spoke to *various of* the members. It is correct in the sense "of diverse kinds": for *various* reasons.

verbal, oral. In the sense "by word of mouth," *verbal* is synonymous with *oral.* In other senses *verbal* has to do with words, whether written or spoken: *verbal* communication (for example, as opposed to gestures). *Verbal,* when applied to terms such as *agreement, promise, commitment,* and *understanding,* is well established as a synonym of *oral.* But anyone who fears misunderstanding may use *oral* instead: *oral* [*verbal*] agreement.

virtually. See **practically, virtually.**

wait on, wait for. *Wait on* is correctly used in the sense "to serve." *Wait for* is used to mean "awaiting": We will *wait for* the purchaser's decision.

want. When *want* is followed immediately by an infinitive construction, it does not take *for*: I *want you* to go [not *want for you*]. When *want* and the infinitive are separated in the sentence, however, *for* is used: What I *want* is *for you* to finish that one first; I *want* very much *for you* to take the company's offer.

-ward, -wards. Since the suffix *-ward* indicates direction, there is no need to use *to the* with it: The cargo ship is sailing *westward* [or *to the west*].

way, under way, aweigh. *Way,* not *ways,* is the generally accepted form in writing when the term refers to distance: a long *way* to go. The phrase *under way* (meaning "in motion" or "in progress") is written as two words or as one (*underway*), including reference to the nautical (not *under weigh*). Confusion sometimes arises because an anchor is *weighed* and, when off the bottom, is *aweigh*.

well. See **good, well.**

what. When *what* is the subject of a *clause,* it is singular if it is taken as equivalent to *that which* or *the thing which*: *What* seems to be a mechanical problem in the stamping equipment *is* creating defective panels. It is plural if it is equivalent to *those which* or *the things which*: *What were* at first minor incidents have now become major problems in the chemical disposal system. When a *what* clause is the subject of a *sentence,* it is usually plural if the clause indicates plurality. But the conditions governing this choice are complicated, and an authority, such as *The American Heritage Dictionary of the English Language,* should be consulted for further study.

whatever. *Whatever* (pronoun) and *what ever* are used in questions and statements: *Whatever* [or *what ever*] made them say that? Both forms are used, although the one-word form is more common. (The same is true of *whoever, whenever, wherever,* and *however* when used in corresponding senses.) For the adjective only the one-word form is used: Take *whatever* office supplies you need. When the phrase preceding a restrictive clause is introduced by *whatever, that* should not be used: *whatever* book *that* you want to look at. *Better*: *Whatever* book you want to look at will be sent to your office.

when. In informal usage *when* is used to mean "a situation or event in which": A dilemma is *when* you don't know which way to turn. This usage, however, should be avoided in business writing.

where. When *where* refers to "the place *from* which," it requires the preposition *from*: *Where* did you come *from?* When it refers to "the place *to* which," it requires no preposition: *Where* did they go [*to*]? When *where* refers to "the place *at* which," it also requires no preposition: *Where* are they [*at*]?

which. *Which* sometimes refers to an entire preceding statement rather than to a single word: The drilling failed to turn up any new reserves, *which* disturbed the geologist. In this acceptable example the reference is clear. But when *which* follows a noun, the antecedent may be in doubt and ambiguity may result: The inspector filed the complaint, *which* was a surprise. If *which* is intended to refer to the entire first clause rather than to *complaint,* the desired sense would be expressed more clearly by this construction: We learned that the inspector had filed the complaint, and that discovery came as a surprise to us.

whose. *Whose,* as the possessive form of a relative pronoun, can refer to both persons and things. Thus it functions as the possessive of both *who* and *which.* The following example, in which *whose* refers to an inanimate object, is acceptable: The car, *whose* design is ultramodern, is typical of the new styles. (The alternative possessive form *of which* is also used in referring to things but is sometimes cumbersome in application.)

why. *Why* is redundant in *the reason why*: The reason [*why*] they opposed the new policy is not clear. The sentence could also be recast: Their reasons for opposing the new policy are not clear.

will. See **shall, will.**

win. *Win* used as a noun in the sense of "victory" or "success" is frequently seen in sports reporting and other informal contexts. It should not be used in this sense in business writing: An impressive *victory* [not *win*] in the primary would strengthen his position greatly.

-wise. The suffix *-wise* has long been used to mean "in the manner or direction of": *clockwise, likewise, otherwise,* and *slantwise.* It is particularly overused as business jargon meaning "with relation to" and attachable to any noun: *saleswise, inflationwise.* Generally considered vague and pretentious, the *-wise* suffix should be avoided in all forms of domestic and international communication: The report is not encouraging *saleswise*; *Taxwise,* however, it is an attractive arrangement. Rephrase such sentences: The report is not encouraging *in terms of potential sales*; For *tax savings,* however, it is an attractive arrangement.

with. *With* does not have the conjunctive force of *and.* Consequently, in the following example the verb is governed by the singular subject and remains singular: The governor, *with* his aides, is expected at the trade show on Monday.

would. See **should, would.**

wreak. *Wreak* is sometimes confused with *wreck,* perhaps because the *wreaking* of damage may leave a *wreck*: The storm *wreaked* havoc along the coast. The past tense and past participle of *wreak* is *wreaked,* not *wrought,* which is an alternative past tense and past participle of *work.* Thus: The Bible says God *wreaked* punishment on sinners. But Samuel F. B. Morse properly asked "What hath God *wrought?*"

Cliches

Cliches are overused, trite expressions that weaken messages and detract from their effectiveness. They also cause the writer to appear unimaginative and unprofessional. They are especially troublesome in international correspondence since foreign readers tend to translate everything literally. Secretaries can be of immense help to their employers by remaining alert to cliches that may inadvertently be used in conventional and electronic messages. The following list contains examples of the kinds of expressions that should never be used in business.

a little (of that) goes a long way
add insult to injury
agonizing reappraisal
agree to disagree
albatross around one's neck
all in a day's work
all in all
all in the same boat
all (*or* other) things being equal
all things considered
all things to all men (*or* people)
all work and no play
armed to the teeth
as luck would have it
as the crow flies
at a loss for words (*or* never at a loss . . .)
at one fell swoop
at this point in time
axe to grind
bag and baggage
battle royal
beat a dead horse
beat a hasty retreat
beat around the bush
beg to disagree

bend (*or* lean) over backward
best foot forward
best-laid plans
best of all possible worlds
best of both worlds
better late than never
bite off more than one can chew
bite the bullet
black-and-white issue
boggle the mind
bolt from the blue
bone of contention
bright future
budding genius
by leaps and bounds
by the same token
case in point
clear as a bell
clear as mud
dead giveaway
dead in the water
die is cast
draw the line
easier said than done
far be it from me
few and far between
few well-chosen words
fill the bill
first and foremost
food for thought
foot in the door
foot the bill
foregone conclusion
frame of reference
get a jump on the competition
get down to brass tacks
get one's feet wet
get (*or* start) the ball rolling
grain of salt

graphic account
grind to a halt
handwriting on the wall
hard row to hoe
have a foot in the door
high and dry
hit the nail on the head
in no uncertain terms
in on the ground floor
in the final (*or* last) analysis
in the long run
it goes without saying
it is interesting to note
it stands to reason
keep a low profile
last but not least
leave no stone unturned
let well enough alone
light at the end of the tunnel
make a long story short
meaningful dialogue
method in one's madness
mince words
miss the boat
moment of truth
moot question (*or* point)
more easily said than done
more than meets the eye
necessary evil
needs no introduction
neither here nor there
no sooner said than done
not worth its salt
nothing new under the sun
of a high order
on the ball (*or* stick)
on the other hand
open and shut case
opportunity knocks

other side of the coin
over a barrel
part and parcel
pillar to post
plain and simple
play hardball
play it by ear
pull no punches
red-letter day
render a decision
rest assured
save for a rainy day
second to none
shot in the arm
show one's hand
small world
strictly speaking
sweet smell of success
take a dim view of
take a raincheck
take it easy
take the bull by the horns
that is to say
throw caution to the wind
tip the scales
too little, too late
tried and true
uncharted waters
up to one's ears
usually reliable source(s)
viable option
view with alarm
wash one's hands of
well worth one's while (*or* trouble)
when all is said and done
when you come right down to it
without a doubt
without further ado
worst-case scenario

Redundant Expressions

Redundancy — needless repetition of words and ideas — is one of the principal obstacles to writing clear, precise prose. The following list gives some common redundant expressions. The elements that are italicized in the phrases should be deleted.

anthracite *coal*
old antique
ascend *upward*
assemble *together*
pointed barb
first beginning
big *in size*
bisect *in two*
blend *together*
capitol *building*
close *proximity*
coalesce *together*
collaborate *together* or *jointly*
fellow colleague
congregate *together*
connect *together*
consensus *of opinion*
courthouse *building*
habitual custom
descend *downward*
doctorate *degree*
endorse a check *on the back*
erupt *violently*
explode *violently*
real fact
passing fad
few *in number*
founder *and sink*
basic fundamental
fuse *together*
opening gambit
gather *together*
free gift
past history

hoist *up*
current or *present* incumbent
new innovation
join *together*
knots *per hour*
large *in size*
merge *together*
necessary need
universal panacea
continue to persist
individual person
advance planning
chief or *leading* or *main* protagonist
original prototype
protrude *out*
recall *back*
recoil *back*
new recruit
recur *again* or *repeatedly*
temporary reprieve
revert *back*
short *in length* or *height*
shuttle *back and forth*
skirt *around*
small *in size*
tall *in height*
two twins
completely unanimous
visible *to the eye*
from whence

BUSINESS STYLE GUIDE

The importance of using proper capitalization, punctuation, and other points of style cannot be overemphasized. Improper or inconsistent use can result in unprofessional documents that will detract not only from your company's image but from the writer's image and yours as well.

The key to excellence in business writing is impeccable use of the language so that your documents will be admired for their sound construction, their attractive packaging, and their appropriate, consistent style. Making certain that a document is styled correctly and consistently is a task often delegated to the secretary. The following sections, therefore, contain style guidelines to help you produce attractive, professional documents. For information about researching, organizing, and typing specific documents, such as a report, refer to Chapter 6.

The style recommended in this chapter is one suitable for a variety of offices. If you work in an office that must follow a style tailored for your work or your particular profession, however, purchase a copy of a suitable style manual. Your local library and local bookstore should be able to direct you to style guides prepared for various disciplines, such as physics, biology, chemistry, mathematics, and education. General style books suitable for a variety of professional activity are also available, for example, the *Chicago Manual of Style* and the *Prentice Hall Style Manual.* Or your company may have its own in-house style guide. Whichever guide you select, follow it consistently.

If you are preparing material for outside periodical or book publishers, ask them for a copy of their house style and formatting and submission requirements. Many such organizations have specific guidelines for manuscript preparation and for disk submission as well as for writing style.

GUIDE TO CAPITALIZATION AND PUNCTUATION

You should use an American style of capitalization and punctuation whether you are writing for a domestic or a foreign audience. In exact quotations, however, follow the style of the original writer. In international correspondence, follow the style of your foreign contacts in writing personal names, company names, and addresses.

Capitalization

The following guidelines apply to the capitalization of words, terms, and other expressions in *most* cases. But in matters of style, be alert to the many exceptions to the rule that are evident. *Most* software languages, for instance, are styled in all capitals (*BASIC*), but a *few* should have only an initial capital (*Pascal*).

Beginnings

1. Capitalize the first word of a sentence.

   Personal income increased 0.9 percent in December.

2. Capitalize the first word of a direct quotation, but lowercase the first word of a split quotation.

   "It is not a matter of what they want," commented the spokesperson, "but a question of timing and tactics."

3. Capitalize the first word of every line in a poem in traditional verse, unless the poet has intentionally lowercased it.

   The quiet mind is richer than
      a crown. . . .
   A mind content both crown and
      kingdom is.
                     — Robert Greene,
                     Farewell to Folly

Proper Names

1. Capitalize proper names, such as the names of deities, people or words used in personification, corporations, organizations and their members, councils and congresses, and historical periods and events. Lowercase general references that do not include the proper names.

God, Allah, the Messiah
Death, the Grim Reaper
Pope John Paul III, the pope
United Airlines, the airline
First Lutheran Church, the church
Republican Party, the party, a Republican
Civil Rights Commission, the commission
U.S. government, the federal government, the government
General Assembly of Illinois, Illinois legislature, the assembly
War on Poverty
Reconstruction

2. Capitalize the names of places including structures, geographic divisions, districts, regions, and locales. Lowercase general references that stand alone or precede the proper name.

Wall Street
New York State, the state of New York, the state
North Pole
the South, southern, southerner (general), Southerner (Civil War context), turn south on I–17
George Washington Bridge, the bridge
the Sunbelt
China
New England
Division Street, the street

3. Capitalize the names of rivers, lakes, mountains, seas, and oceans, but lowercase general references to them.

Atlantic Ocean, the ocean
Mississippi River, the river
Arkansas and Mississippi rivers
Lake Superior, the lake
Blue Ridge Mountains, the mountains

4. Capitalize the names of ships, airplanes, and space vehicles, but lowercase general references to them.

USS *Enterprise,* the *Enterprise,* the spaceship
Sputnik II, the satellite
Voyager, the space shuttle

the *Concorde*, the airplane
a Boeing 727, an airplane

5. Capitalize the names of nationalities, races, tribes, and languages. Lowercase general references that are not part of the proper name.

Americans, American citizens
Caucasians, white people
French, French culture
Spaniard, Spanish language
African-American, black
Native American (American Indian)

6. Capitalize words derived from proper names when used in their primary sense, but lowercase most derivatives. (*Note*: Numerous exceptions apply to this guideline. Often, the choice is up to the writer.)

European cities
British royalty
Arabic numerals (*or* arabic numerals)
Dutch oven (*or* dutch oven)
morocco leather
french fries (*or* French fries)
Roman numerals, roman type

Titles

1. Capitalize titles of people when they precede their names or when the title represents an epithet. Lowercase most titles when they follow the names or are used alone (but see exceptions).

Mr. Eldon Waterbury; Eldon Waterbury, Esq.
Professor Janice Croft; Janice Croft, professor of biological sciences; the professor
Secretary of State Warren Christopher; Mr. Secretary; Warren Christopher, the secretary of state; the secretary
General C. V. Roswell, General Roswell, the general (*General of the Army* and *Fleet Admiral* are both capitalized after a name to avoid confusion with other generals and admirals.)
Elizabeth II, queen of England; Her Majesty, Queen Elizabeth; the queen
The Great Emancipator
George Herman "Babe" Ruth

2. Capitalize the important words in titles of publications, awards, and artistic and musical works. Lowercase most general references to the type of publication or work (but see exceptions).

> *Secretarial Science,* the book
> "How to Write with a Word Processor," the chapter
> *The Secretary,* the magazine
> Bible (specific religious book), biblical, the pharmacist's "bible" (an important book)
> Scriptures, scriptural
> Talmud, talmudic (*or* Talmudic)
> Koran, Koranic
> Nobel Prize in literature, Nobel Peace Prize
> *A Sidewalk Cafe at Night* (Van Gogh)
> *Gone With the Wind,* the movie
> *The Wall Street Journal,* the newspaper
> Adagio from the Fifth Symphony
> Piano Concerto no. 5

Education

1. Capitalize the names of institutions and their divisions, but lowercase general references to them.

> University of Hawaii, the university
> School of Medicine, the medical school
> Physical Education Department, phys. ed. department, the department

2. Capitalize the names of classes, but lowercase general references to members. Capitalize the official names of programs or courses, but lowercase general descriptions.

> Senior Class
> a senior
> Economics 102, the economics course
> Secretarial Business Program, the program

3. Capitalize educational degrees and honors when they follow a name. Lowercase general references to degrees.

> James V. Roulette, Doctor of Law; a doctor of law
> Victoria Johnson, M.D.
> Henry Snowden, Fellow of the Royal Academy; a fellow

Days and Time

1. Capitalize the days of the week, months of the year, holidays, and holy days. Lowercase period designations and numerical periods that are not part of a proper name, and lowercase recent cultural periods.

Monday	Middle Ages
March	Iron Age
Fourth of July	Victorian era
Labor Day	nuclear age
election day	space age
Passover	colonial period
Ramadan	antiquity, ancient Greece
twentieth century	A.D., B.C. (*or* A.D., B.C.)
Tenth Dynasty	Age of Reason

2. Capitalize proper nouns in time zones, but lowercase the other words referring to time, time zones, and seasons.

mountain standard time (mst)
Pacific standard time (Pst)
Greenwich mean time (Gmt)
a.m., p.m. (*or* A.M., P.M.)
10 o'clock, ten o'clock
spring
winter solstice

Law

1. Capitalize the formal names of specific courts, but lowercase general references to a type of court or general references to any court except the U.S. Supreme Court (but see exceptions).

U.S. Supreme Court, the Court
Arizona Supreme Court, the court
the U.S. Court of Appeals for the Seventh Circuit, the court of appeals, the circuit court, the court
traffic court
New York Court of Appeals, the Court of Appeals (the highest state court, capitalized to distinguish it from the U.S. court of appeals, which is not the highest U.S. court)

2. Capitalize the important words in treaties, laws, and cases. Lowercase most general references to the document or event.

> U.S. Constitution, the Constitution
> Ohio Constitution, the constitution
> Fifth Amendment, the amendment
> Civil Rights Act of 1964
> Social Security (*or* social security)
> a drug-reform law
> Labor Management Relations Act
> *Miranda* v. *Arizona,* the *Miranda* case, the case
> Franklin's case, Franklin's trial

Military Service

1. Capitalize the names of military branches and organizations, but lowercase general references to them.

> United States Air Force, the air force
> United States Marine Corps, the Marine Corps, the marines
> Second Battalion, the battalion
> Joint Chiefs of Staff
> armed forces
> Allied forces, the Allies (world wars)

2. Capitalize the formal names of battles and wars, but lowercase general references to the involvement.

> World War I, First World War, the war
> Vietnam War, the war
> Korean conflict
> invasion of Kuwait

3. Capitalize military awards, but lowercase general references to an honor or award.

> Purple Heart
> Navy Cross
> Croix de Guerre (*or* croix de guerre)
> Distinguished Service Cross
> military honor

Business

1. Capitalize the official names of or trademarks for equipment and software, but lowercase general references to equipment, programs, and procedures.

Rawlins Computer Systems
486 computer
Microsoft Word Version 6.0, word processing software
MKDIR, the command
Lotus 1-2-3, the program
Pascal, the language
Filesaver, the database
format instructions

2. Capitalize registered trademark names, but the circled symbol ® or the symbol ™ may be omitted.

Xerox copier
Bufferin buffered aspirin
Kleenex tissue
Ping-Pong table tennis
Dacron polyester

Science

1. Capitalize geologic time designations and words such as *Lower* that refer to a time within a period. Lowercase *period* in most cases, and lowercase most adjectives such as *late* that are used descriptively.

Paleozoic era
Quaternary period
Pliocene epoch
Lower Jurassic
Middle Pliocene
Ice Age, an ice age
Piedmont Lowland, the lowland

2. Capitalize official names in astronomy, but lowercase general references to types of bodies and phenomena.

Mars, the planet
Earth (planet), earth (soil)

North Star
the Galaxy, a galaxy
aurora borealis, northern lights

3. Capitalize the proper nouns in chemistry and physics theorems and laws. Capitalize *Law* in popular, fictitious names and laws, but otherwise lowercase the names of chemical elements and general references to laws and principles. For the capitalization of chemical symbols, consult an appropriate chemistry handbook or style guide.

iron, Fe
the Pythagorean theorem
Einstein's theory of relativity
Boyle's law
Murphy's Law

4. Capitalize the proper nouns in the names of diseases, the proper nouns in the brand names of drugs, and the genus names of infectious organisms. Lowercase generic names and general medical terms.

Hodgkin's disease
Fertinic (brand name), ferrous gluconate (generic name)
chronic fatigue syndrome
Trichinella spiralis, the disease trichinosis
Phthirus (lice), *P. pubis*

5. Generally, capitalize family, order, and genus names, and lowercase species names. Capitalize the proper nouns in common names.

Eschscholtzia californica, E. californica, California poppy
Cervus elaphus, C. elaphus, elk
the family Mutillidae
the order Mecoptera
black-eyed Susan
Canada thistle
rainbow trout
Cooper's hawk

Numbers

Capitalize names that contain numerical designations, but lowercase general references to the names, and lowercase general references to numbers.

Thirteenth Precinct, the precinct
Room 2020
Chapter 2 (or chapter 2)
Fifth Avenue, the avenue
line 16
size 10
fourteen people

Abbreviations

Capitalize abbreviations of official names and personal or professional titles preceding names, but lowercase initialisms that have no proper nouns, and lowercase abbreviations of common nouns.

Oct.
Tues.
Dr. Jones
1600 Pennsylvania Ave.
FBI
OPEC
asap (as soon as possible)
mgr.

Punctuation

The purpose of punctuation is to make what is written clearer and less subject to misinterpretation. Although the trend is toward less punctuation in matters such as abbreviations, business writers know that misunderstandings are costly and believe that punctuation should be used whenever it is correct to use it. Those who deal with an international audience in particular use punctuation to guide foreign readers through each sentence. In spite of the recognized value of punctuation, however, it must be used correctly. Misplaced or overused punctuation can be just as confusing as too little punctuation. The following guidelines apply to the fourteen basic marks of punctuation.

Apostrophe (')

1. Use an apostrophe to indicate the possessive case of singular and plural nouns, indefinite pronouns, and surnames combined with designations such as *Jr.* and *II.*

Mrs. Black's office is at the end of the hall.
That could be anyone's pen.
Donald Harris II's term on the board is almost over.

2. Use an apostrophe to indicate joint possession when used with the last of two or more nouns in a series.

Standard and Poor's data
Coke and Pepsi's competition
Jane and Bob's law firm

3. Use an apostrophe to indicate individual possession when used with each of two or more nouns in a series.

Tom's and Nancy's suggestions (two separate suggestions)
Smith's, Roe's, and Doe's reports (three separate reports)

4. Use an apostrophe to indicate the plurals of figures, letters, or words when this is not clear without the apostrophe.

poorly formed a's and e's, 6's and 7's
But: 1900s, 88s and 99s, MBAs

5. Use an apostrophe to indicate omission of letters in contractions.

isn't (is not)
it's (it is)
wouldn't (would not)

6. Use an apostrophe to indicate omission of figures in dates.

the class of '94
fiscal year '95–'96

Brackets [ ]

1. Use brackets to enclose words or passages in quotations to indicate insertion of material written by someone other than the original writer.

"Justice Potter did not think it [increasing the Court's membership to ease the work load for each justice] would solve the problem."

2. Use brackets to enclose material inserted within matter that is already in parentheses.

(The return on equity [ROE] is 35 percent.)

Colon (:)

1. Use a colon to introduce words, phrases, or clauses that explain, amplify, or summarize what has preceded.

There are two choices: use temporary help or use part-time help.

2. Use a colon to introduce a long quotation.

Said the chairman: "The deficit is our principal consideration. Business is hesitant to expand when the country is burdened with runaway inflation, and when there is no expansion, there is no increase in employment."

3. Use a colon to introduce a list.

The report outlined results of the increase in trauma disorders, including the following:

- More than 80 percent of the population suffers from back ailments.
- The greatest risk of back strain is between ages thirty-five and fifty-five.
- Repetitive actions are the major cause of back injuries.

4. Use a colon to separate chapter and verse numbers in references to biblical quotations.

Romans 12:6
Ecclesiastes 9:11

5. Use a colon to separate city from publisher and dates from page numbers in footnotes and bibliographies.

Boston: Houghton Mifflin, 1994.
Atlantic, 132, no. 3 (1989): 41–92.

6. Use a colon to separate hour and minute in time designations.

3:45 P.M.
a 7:30 meeting

7. Use a colon after the salutation in a business letter.

Ladies and Gentlemen:
To whom it may concern:
Dear Ms. Kane:

Comma (,)

1. Use a comma to separate the clauses of a compound sentence connected by a coordinating conjunction.

> The title of the book has not been decided, and the release date has not been set.

The comma may be omitted in short compound sentences.

> We have prepared the case and we are ready to present it.

2. Use a comma to separate items in a series.

> The program explains how to overcome obstacles of worker resistance, resentment, and skepticism.

3. Use a comma to separate two or more adjectives modifying the same noun if *and* could be used between them.

> The company selected a bold, modern letterhead design.

4. Use a comma to set off a nonrestrictive clause or phrase (one that if eliminated would not affect the meaning of the sentence).

> The classified section, which gets larger every year, has more than 200,000 business listings.

Commas should not be used when the clause is restrictive (essential to the meaning of the sentence).

> The classified section that was published in 1994 has more than 200,000 business listings.

5. Use a comma to set off words or phrases that are in apposition to (that are equivalent to) a noun or noun phrase.

> Marilyn Stowe, former president of Stowe Industries, will be the keynote speaker.

A comma should not be used if such words or phrases precede the noun they modify.

> Former president of Stowe Industries Marilyn Stowe will be the keynote speaker.

6. Use a comma to set off transitional words and short expressions that require a pause in reading or speaking.

> Therefore, the new product announcement will be delayed.

7. Use a comma to set off words used to introduce a sentence if needed for clarity.

> At best, the shipment will be ready by August 1.

8. Use a comma to set off a subordinate clause or a long phrase that precedes a principal clause.

> If we underestimate the competitive drive of the other members, we could lose our market share.

9. Use a comma to set off short quotations and sayings.

> "That's typical," said the mayor, responding to his opponent's charges.

10. Use a comma to indicate omission of a word or words.

> To err is human; to forgive, divine.

11. Use a comma to set off the year from the month in full dates.

> I began the study on February 6, 1995, after receiving the grant.

Omit the comma when only the month and the year are used.

> I began the study in February 1995 after receiving the grant.

12. Use a comma to set off city and state in geographic names.

> The product was tested in Princeton, New Jersey, and other eastern locations.

13. Use a comma to separate series of four or more figures into thousands, millions, and so on.

> Every time bulk diesel fuel goes up a penny, it costs us $100,000.

14. Use a comma to set off words used in direct address.

> Mr. Stone, would you be able to open the meeting while Ms. McKenzie takes a long-distance call?

15. Use a comma to separate a question from the rest of the sentence.

> That's a remarkable improvement, isn't it?

16. Use a comma to set off any sentence elements that might be misunderstood if the comma were not used.

When the report is in, the committee will vote on the resolution.

17. Use a comma after the salutation in a personal letter and the complimentary close in a business or personal letter.

Dear Lee,
Sincerely,

18. Use a comma to set off some titles, degrees, and honorifics from surnames and from the rest of a sentence.

Sandra Maynard, Esq.
John Kennedy, Jr.
Susan P. Green, M.D., presented the case.

Dash (—)

1. Use a dash to indicate a sudden break or change in continuity.

Last year, the Hyatt Wonder World attracted more than 500,000 people — more than Thomas Jefferson's Monticello — at $14 a head for adults.

2. Use a dash to set apart a defining or emphatic phrase.

Only one service — day care — improved in 1994.

3. Use a dash to set apart parenthetical material.

The East Coast division's income from retail ads was three times as much as from other ads — $6 million versus $2 million.

4. Use a dash to mark an unfinished sentence.

"I demand we take a vote on — " the shareholder insisted before his microphone was shut off.

5. Use a dash to set off a summarizing phrase or clause.

The real measure of employee satisfaction is intangible — it can't be counted in dollars and cents.

6. Use a dash to set off the name of an author or source, as at the end of a quotation.

> The good of the people is the chief law.
>
> — Cicero

Ellipsis Points (. . .)

1. Use three spaced periods to indicate the omission of words or sentences within quoted matter.

> "It is . . . very hard to . . . please everybody." (Publilius Syrus)

2. Use four spaced periods to indicate the omission of words at the end of a sentence.

> "Antisthenes used to say that envious people were devoured by their own disposition. . . ." (Diogenes Laertius)

3. Use three to five spaced periods centered on a line alone to indicate the omission of one or more lines of poetry or one or more paragraphs.

> Vice itself lost half its
> evil by losing all its grossness.
>
> . . . . .
>
> Kings will be tyrants from
> policy, when subjects are
> rebels from principle.
>
> — Edmund Burke

4. Use three spaced periods to catch the reader's attention in certain types of writing, such as advertising copy.

> Your representative owes you the highest ethical standards . . . something we at Variety Industries take very seriously.

Exclamation Point (!)

1. Use an exclamation point after an emphatic or exclamatory sentence. (But overuse will cause it to lose its effectiveness.)

> No, never! We will not yield a single microinch!

2. Use an exclamation point after an emphatic interjection.

Great!

Hyphen (-)

1. Use a hyphen in word division to indicate that part of a word or more than one syllable has been carried over from one line to the next.

Complex information isn't easily reduced to outline form.

2. Use a hyphen to join the elements of some compounds.

cost-effectiveness
all-powerful
jack-of-all-trades

3. Use a hyphen to join the elements of some compound modifiers preceding nouns.

a cattle-feeding enterprise
a heavy-duty press

4. Use a suspended hyphen to indicate that two or more compounds share a single base.

three- and four-ton stamping machines
eight- and ten-year-old foundries

5. Use a hyphen to separate the prefix and root in some combinations such as a prefix preceding a proper noun, a prefix ending in a vowel when the root begins with the same vowel, and a prefix that must be hyphenated to indicate a different meaning or pronunciation.

pro-Democrat
anti-intelligence
re-form (to form again)

6. Use a hyphen as a substitute for the word *to* between figures or words in tabular material.

1-2 years
$25-$30

7. Use a hyphen to separate the parts of compound numbers from twenty-one through ninety-nine.

fifty-seven clients
thirty-one messages

Parentheses ( )

1. Use parentheses to enclose material that is not an essential part of the sentence and that if not included would not alter its meaning.

Kansas City television (KCTV-5) anchor Wendall Anschutz said he would ask the source.

2. Use parentheses to enclose letters or figures to indicate subdivisions in some series.

It seems our choices are to (a) launch a counteroffensive marketing campaign, (b) press ahead to get our new model out six months ahead of schedule, or (c) run like hell.

3. Use parentheses to enclose figures following and confirming written-out numbers, especially in legal documents.

Cauldren, Inc., will provide service for three (3) machines described as follows:

4. Use parentheses to enclose abbreviations of written-out words when the abbreviations are used for the first time in a text and may be unfamiliar to the reader.

According to Martin Costell, administrator of the National Office Organization (NOO), the new directory will sell for $45.

Period (.)

1. Use a period to end a complete declarative or mild imperative sentence.

Hotline telephone numbers are becoming increasingly popular.
Please sign here.

2. Use a period between the letters of or after some abbreviations. (*Note:* The trend is to omit periods after abbreviations that are forms of contractions [*nat'l*], after most technical [*cos* for cosine] and metric [*mm*] abbreviations unless the term spells another word such as *cot.* [*cot = bed*], after and between letters of initialisms such as *aka* [also known

as], and after and between the letters of acronyms such as BASIC [computer language].)

Inc.	Jan.
etc.	Ltd.
Calif.	ave.

Since abbreviation style differs among businesses, follow the style preferred in your company, or consult a modern dictionary of abbreviations.

Question Mark (?)

1. Use a question mark after a direct question.

Are you going to the conference?

But use a period when the remark is really a statement.

Would you please take care of this. (Please take care of this.)

2. Use a question mark to indicate uncertainty or a query such as a question to an author about something in his or her manuscript.

Ferdinand Magellan (1480?–1521)
OK?

Quotation Marks (" ", ' ')

1. Use double quotation marks to enclose direct quotations. Put commas and periods inside closing quotation marks; put semicolons and colons outside. Other punctuation, such as exclamation points and question marks, should be put inside the closing quotation marks only if it is part of the matter quoted.

"I believe Plautus was right," he said, "that sometimes it's better to take a loss."

Did he really say "It's a waste of time"?

2. Use double quotation marks to enclose words or phrases to clarify their meaning or to indicate that they are being used in a special way.

The human "robots" in the pressroom point to boredom as their worst enemy.

3. Use double quotation marks to set off the translation or meaning of a term.

The French word *oeuvre* means "work(s)," such as the work of an artist.

4. Use double quotation marks to enclose the titles of articles, chapters in books, essays and unpublished papers, short stories, television and radio episodes, songs and short musical pieces, and short poems.

"Economic Courtship" (article)
"Word Processing" (chapter)
"The Structure of Datalinks" (thesis)
"Maude and Her Prince" (short story)
"Mark I" (television episode)
"Forever" (song)
"The Dancer" (short poem)

5. Use single quotation marks to enclose a quotation within a quotation.

Mason often turned to Byron in his analysis: "I concede the motivation, but I also recognize the admonition of Lord Byron that 'fame is the thirst of youth.'"

When quotations are set off as extracts, the opening and closing quotation marks are omitted, and any single quotation marks within the quotation would be changed to double quotation marks.

Mason often turned to Byron in his analysis:

I concede the motivation, but I also recognize the admonition of Lord Byron that "fame is the thirst of youth."

Semicolon (;)

1. Use a semicolon to separate the clauses of a compound sentence having no coordinating conjunction.

Some employees resigned in protest; others formed a grievance committee to fight the new policy.

2. Use a semicolon to separate the clauses of a compound sentence in which the clauses contain internal punctuation, even when the clauses are joined by a conjunction.

The toys are assembled in Kansas City, Missouri; Peoria, Illinois; and Des Moines, Iowa; and they are warehoused in Peoria.

3. Use a semicolon to separate elements of a series in which the items already contain commas.

> The meetings are scheduled for December 6, 1994; March 17, 1995; and May 2, 1995.

4. Use a semicolon to separate clauses of a compound sentence joined by a conjunctive adverb such as *nonetheless, however,* or *hence.*

> We will produce the product; however, it will cost $15, not $12.

Virgule or Slash (/)

1. Use a virgule to separate successive divisions in an extended date. (But note that a hyphen, or, when writing for publication, an en dash, is more common.)

> the fiscal year 1994/95 (1994–95)
> the term 1991/1995 (1991–1995)

2. Use a virgule to represent the word *per* in tabular material, invoices, and similar copy.

> 6/doz.
> rev./sec.

3. Use a virgule to mean *or* between the words *and* and *or* and sometimes between other words to indicate possible options or words of equal value.

> and/or
> owner/operator
> book/catalog

GUIDE TO COMPOSITION

Many secretaries compose their own messages and revise and refine the messages of others. The art of composition involves skills beyond the use of proper punctuation and capitalization. It involves the development of sentences and paragraphs; the proper use of alternative typefaces, particularly italics; and the careful and consistent spelling of words and numbers as well as the proper use of symbols and other technical expressions in both text and illustrations. Secretaries who prepare manuscripts for desktop publishing or other composition (see Chapter 4) need to mark their manuscripts in a way that will be understood by editorial personnel and compositors. Table 11.1 on pages 378–379 lists the appropriate marks to use in preparing material for composition.

Sentence and Paragraph Development

Sentence Style   In regard to style, there are two types of sentences — the periodic and the cumulative. The *periodic sentence* places the main idea at the very end, so that the previous matter serves as a buildup. The *cumulative sentence* puts the main point first, followed by supporting data or commentary.

> *Periodic*: The most interesting aspect of secretarial life has nothing to do with secretarial tasks or skills *but is, very simply, a matter of diversity.*

> *Cumulative*: *Diversity is the most interesting aspect of secretarial life,* and this quality is not a prerequisite of, or a procedural guideline relative to, any individual secretarial task.

Problems in Sentence Development   There are four kinds of sentence structure (simple, compound, complex, and compound-complex), as explained in Chapter 10. When the proper punctuation or the appropriate coordinating conjunction is omitted between independent clauses, the result is a run-on sentence.

> The automobile had faulty brakes it was therefore recalled.

This problem can be corrected by restating the sentence in one of the following ways.

> The automobile had faulty brakes, and it was therefore recalled.
> The automobile had faulty brakes; therefore, it was recalled.
> Since the automobile had faulty brakes, it was recalled.
> The automobile, having faulty brakes, was recalled.

Another impediment to the proper development of a complete sentence with a subject and predicate, as described in Chapter 10, is the comma fault. The comma fault occurs when two independent clauses are separated by a comma instead of being linked by a coordinating conjunction.

> The chemical industry in the United States has contributed much to our economy, it should not be condemned on the basis of isolated instances of pollution.

Table 11.1   Examples of Selected Proofreaders' Marks

MARK	INSTRUCTION
Copper is highly toxic *to* many aquatic organisms.	Insert indicated letter, word, phrase, or sentence.
Copper is highly toxic#to many aquatic organisms.	Insert space.
Copper is highly toxic to many aquatic organisms⊙	Insert period.
Copper is highly toxic to many aquatic organisms and . . .	Insert punctuation (or subscript).
We have measured the mussels sensitivity to copper.	Insert apostrophe (or superscript).
Copper is highly toxic to many aquatic organisms.5	Raise to superscript.
Copper (29Cu) is highly toxic to many aquatic organisms.	Lower to subscript.
Copper is highly toxic to to many aquatic organisms.	Delete.
Copper is highly toxic to all *many* aquatic organisms.	Delete and insert.
Copper is highly toxic to many aquatic organisms.	Close space.
Copper is highly toxic to many aquatic organisms.	Delete and close.
Copper is highly toxic to many aquatic organisms. STET	Let it stand.
copper is highly toxic to many aquatic organisms. *U.C.*	Capitalized letter.
Copper is highly toxic to many aquatic Organisms. *lc.*	Lowercase letter.
Copper is highly toxic to many AQUATIC organisms.	Lowercase word.

Table 11.1, continued

MARK	INSTRUCTION
Copper is highly toxic to many aquatic organisms.	Transpose letters.
Copper is highly to toxic many aquatic organisms.	Transpose words.
¶ Copper is highly toxic to many aquatic organisms.	Begin new paragraph.
No ¶ Copper is highly toxic to many aquatic organisms.	No new paragraph.
Copper is highly toxic to many ⌐ aquatic organisms.	Move left as indicated.
Copper is highly toxic to many aquatic organisms. ⌐	Move right as indicated.
Copper is highly toxic to many aquatic organisms.	Raise as indicated.
Copper is highly toxic to many aquatic organisms.	Lower as indicated.
⌐APPENDIX A ⌐	Center.
Copper is highly toxic to ⌐ many aquatic organisms.	Run in.
APPENDIX A	Italics or underscore.
APPENDIX A	Boldface.

The following sentences illustrate ways to eliminate the comma fault.

The chemical industry in the United States has contributed much to our economy, *and* it should not be condemned on the basis of isolated instances of pollution.

The chemical industry in the United States has contributed much to our economy. It should not be condemned on the basis of isolated instances of pollution.

The chemical industry in the United States has contributed much to our economy; it should not be condemned on the basis of isolated instances of pollution.

The United States chemical industry, having contributed much to our economy, should not be condemned on the basis of isolated instances of pollution.

Once a sentence has been properly composed, it should be organized along with other sentences to form logical paragraphs that lead readers from beginning to end in an orderly, intelligent fashion.

Paragraph Style　A paragraph is a distinct division of a written work that expresses a thought or point relevant to the whole but is complete in itself; it may consist of a single sentence or several sentences. A paragraph should contain a topic sentence expressing the main thought, which is developed and supported by the other sentences of the paragraph.

Although it is possible for the topic sentence to be placed anywhere within the paragraph, it is most often found at the beginning as a statement that is enlarged upon by the sentences that follow. A topic sentence at the end of a paragraph usually functions as a cohesive summation of the ideas and arguments in the sentences leading up to it. The topic sentence is the cement binding a paragraph together into a coherent whole.

Paragraphing can be easy if you follow a few simple guidelines.

- Keep your paragraphs unified, with every sentence related to the main topic; avoid needless digressions from the main point that will destroy unity.

- Avoid overshort or overlong paragraphs. A short one may not cover a topic adequately, and a long one may be uninviting and difficult to assimilate.

- When preparing letters and business reports, split long paragraphs into shorter ones and combine short paragraphs into a single longer one.

- Remember that transitional words and phrases (such as conjunctive adverbs) are an invaluable aid in guiding the reader from one sentence to another.

The following are topic sentences that begin a series of paragraphs arranged in a logical order, with one point smoothly moving to the next.

In 1995 a series of mishaps led us to examine problems of customer dissatisfaction.

The first step was to talk extensively with the people involved in direct customer contact.

We learned that the most helpful ideas were coming from secretaries throughout the company.

The next step was to develop a series of "what if" proposals.

Another way of achieving smooth transition is repetition of key words. The key words serve as guides to the reader.

You can apply the same principle to sentences as applied to *words*: short is beautiful.

Also, just as you can count letters in a *word,* you can count *words* in a sentence to evaluate length.

Keeping the vocabulary limited to a finite number of terms that are used over and over again reinforces the message and enables the reader to understand the material more easily. But you can develop your paragraphs in any number of ways to make them lucid and effective. You might, for example, start with a definition.

The term *office automation* refers to the use of a computer in an office environment to facilitate normal operating procedures. The impact of office automation upon workflow can be very small or very great, depending on the extent to which organizational structures are affected.

The first sentence defines *office automation.* The second sentence in the paragraph then goes on to talk about the impact of office automation in the workplace. Here are several other ideas to employ in paragraph development.

- Using a technique such as comparison, contrast, or analogy, you could make two points and discuss first one and then the other.

- You could also use cause and effect whereby you would describe the situation or state of affairs and then discuss the underlying causes that prompted the problem or condition.

- Or you could first describe the underlying causes and then build up to the result or consequence.

- You could include examples by way of support or illustration for an idea or point of view that you have already expressed.

- When categories are involved, you could set down classes or sets relating to a topic and define each one as a means of introducing the main topic to which the categories pertain.

No firm rule exists for the particular pattern(s) you choose. Your topic will suggest logical ways to move from one paragraph to another. The most important point is that the movement be smooth and understandable in a way that will help the reader gain as much as possible from the discussion.

Use of Italics

Regular text is traditionally set in a light or medium roman type face. Certain words and phrases, however, such as a heading, might be set in boldface at the discretion of the typist, designer, or compositor. Other words and phrases might be set in an italic face, and certain guidelines apply to the use of italics in styling business material.

1. Use italics to indicate the titles of books, plays, and long poems.

the book *Silent Spring*
the play *Phantom of the Opera*
the epic poem *Paradise Lost*

2. Use italics to indicate the titles of magazines and newspapers.

Time magazine and *The Wall Street Journal* both carried the report.

3. Use italics to indicate the titles of motion pictures and radio and television series.

the movie *The Lion King*
the television series *Murphy Brown*

4. Use italics to indicate the titles of long musical compositions.

Beethoven's *Emperor* Concerto
William Tell Overture

5. Use italics to indicate the names of paintings and sculptures.

the painting *American Gothic*
the sculpture *The Thinker*

6. Use italics to indicate words, letters, or numbers that are referred to as such.

the word *pueblo*
the letter *A*
the number *4*

7. Use italics to indicate unfamiliar foreign words and phrases.

bleich (German: pale)
raiz (Portuguese: root)

8. Use italics to indicate the names of plaintiff and defendant in legal citations (the *v.* or *vs.,* meaning "versus," may be either roman or italic).

Franklin v. *Madison*
Miranda vs. *Arizona*

9. Use italics to emphasize a word or phrase (but avoid overuse).

Too many of those studies *weren't* being implemented.

10. Use italics to indicate the Latin names of genus, species, subspecies, and varieties in botanical and zoological nomenclature. (Do not italicize phyla, classes, orders, or families.)

the genus *Homo*
the species *alba*
the subspecies *macrothrix*
the variety *hirta*

11. Use italics to indicate the names of ships and planes but not the abbreviation preceding the name.

USS *Rover*
Apollo II

12. Use italics for letter symbols in mathematical expressions.

$(6n - m)\log a,\ \exp[(2x - y)/4]$

$x^1 + x^2 + \ldots + x^3$

Spelling

Spelling errors and inconsistencies detract from the professional appearance and effectiveness of a message. Although a computer spellchecker will locate many such problems, it cannot distinguish between correctly spelled but misused words such as *to* in place of *too,* and the spelling program may have a different style than that of your company. Perhaps your spell-checker selects *micro-unit* (hyphenated), whereas your company follows the modern trend to write most prefixes and base words closed (*microunit*). Also, your spelling program probably does not include all of the terms you use every day — hence the need for an up-to-date dictionary.

Although numerous spelling rules exist, they are so complex and so riddled with exceptions that many secretaries would rather double check doubtful spellings in a reliable dictionary. Nevertheless, the following guidelines may be helpful.

General Rules

Nouns. To make most singular nouns plural, add *s* or *es* without changing the original spelling of the singular part.

offices
boxes
McCoys
Harrises

For certain irregular nouns, the singular form is made plural by changing the spelling.

alumnus, alumni
brother-in-law, brothers-in-law

In other cases, both singular and plural forms are spelled the same.

corps, corps
deer, deer

Some nouns ending in *s* are plural in form but may function as either singular or plural or as both in number.

politics, politics
mathematics, mathematics

Possessives. Add an apostrophe and *s* to a word if it already ends with an *s* sound and if using a possessive form creates a new syllable.

the boss's office
the witness's statement

If the possessive form is hard to pronounce with the newly created syllable, add only the apostrophe and omit the *s*.

Mr. Phillips' proposal
for appearance' sake
Los Angeles' population

When the plural form of a noun has a different spelling from the singular form, add both an apostrophe and *s*.

children's playground
women's program

Otherwise, in most cases add an apostrophe but omit the *s*.

cars' features
computers' memory

Add an apostrophe but omit the *s* when a word ending is pronounced as *eez*.

Yerkes' law
Euripides' life

Compounds. Compounds are spelled in three ways: open (separate words without a hyphen), closed (one word without a hyphen), and hyphenated (words connected with a hyphen). Since no firm rule exists for most compounds, writers should consult a current dictionary when in doubt.

Latin America
paperwork
know-how

Compound adjectives are usually hyphenated before a noun, except for very familiar compounds such as *public relations,* but are written open after a noun.

the well-written paper
the paper that is well written

Prefixes. In contemporary writing, most prefixes are added to a base word without using a hyphen; a few, however, such as *ex-,* meaning "former," are always hyphenated, and some, such as those creating a double vowel that is hard to read, are also hyphenated. Any prefix that precedes a capitalized word must also be hyphenated.

> counterproductive
> ex-senator
> semi-independent
> pro-American

Suffixes. In some cases when a form is added to the end of a word, the final consonant of the base word is doubled; in other cases it is not. Since no general rule exists to account for all cases, consult a modern dictionary when in doubt.

> management
> cancellation

Foreign Terms. The plural of many words of foreign origin is different from the regular English plural, and some terms have Anglicized plurals. Consult a modern dictionary when in doubt. The following are examples of preferred English plurals.

> appendix, appendixes
> formula, formulas
> focus, focuses

Some foreign words may require one of the nine principal diacritical marks.

acute	´
breve	˘
cedilla	ç
circumflex	^
dieresis	¨
grave	`
haček	ˇ
macron	‾
tilde	˜

Unfamiliar foreign terms are usually italicized (underlined in manuscript copy). Some foreign terms, however, have become Anglicized in business usage and are commonly written without diacritical marks and without italics (or underlining). Some style guides, such as the *U.S. Government Printing Office Style Manual,* do not use accents on or italicize the following terms. Other guides, such as *The American Heritage Dictionary of the English Language,* may retain the accents. Follow the preferred style in your office.

aba ca	critiquing
aide memoire	debacle
a la carte	debris
a la king	debut
a la mode	debutante
angstrom	decollete
apertif	dejeuner
applique	denouement
apropos	depot
auto(s)-da-fe	dos-a-dos
blase	eclair
boutonniere	eclat
brassiere	ecru
cabana	elan
cafe	elite
cafeteria	entree
caique	etude
canape	facade
cause celebre	faience
chateau	fete
cliche	fiance
cloisonne	fiancee
comedienne	frappe
comme ci comme ca	garcon
communique	glace
confrere	grille
consomme	gruyere
cortege	habitue
coulee	ingenue
coup de grace	jardiniere
coup d'etat	litterateur
coupe	materiel
crepe	matinee
crepe de chine	melange
critique	melee

menage
mesalliance
metier
moire
naive
naivete
nee
opera bouffe
opera comique
papier mache
piece de resistance
pleiade
porte cochere
porte lumiere
portiere
pousse cafe
premiere
protege
puree

rale
recherche
regime
risque
role
rotisserie
roue
saute
seance
smorgasbord
soiree
souffle
suede
table d'hote
tete-a-tete
tragedienne
vicuna
vis-a-vis

Word Division   When the right margin of a letter or document is so uneven that it is unattractive, you may decide to divide some very long words at the end of a line. The rules for word division at the end of a line are as complex as those for spelling and also have numerous exceptions. Spelling dictionaries and regular dictionaries indicate the division of words by syllables. In addition, the following guidelines apply to most types of business writing.

Words Not to Divide. Single-syllable words and words with fewer than five letters should not be divided.

stayed (*not* stay-ed)
into (*not* in-to)

A single letter should not be separated from the beginning or end of the word, and vowels that are pronounced together should not be separated.

abate (*not* a-bate)
ready (*not* read-y)
re-ceive (*not* rece-ive)

Common Divisions. If possible, divide a word *after* a single-letter syllable within the word.

busi-ness (*not* bus-iness)
posi-tive (*not* pos-itive)

When two vowels within a word are pronounced separately, divide *between* them.

experi-ence (*not* exper-ience)
situ-ation (*not* situa-tion)

When there are two consonants between two vowels, divide the word between the consonants if it does not change the pronunciation.

im-por-tant
ad-van-tage

Always keep at least two letters and the hyphen on the top line and at least three characters, one of which could be a punctuation mark, on the bottom line.

re- (top line) new (bottom line)
remind- (top line) er: (bottom line)

If possible, divide words with affixes *at* the prefix or suffix, and divide compounds *between* the principal parts.

non-essential
trust-worthy
all-important

Generally, divide gerunds and present participles *before* the *-ing* ending, but if the final consonant is doubled, divide *between* the double letters. If the base word ends with a double consonant, however, divide *after* the two letters.

learn-ing
control-ling
fill-ing

When you pronounce the *le* syllable as *ul* in a word such as *handle,* divide the word *before* that syllable.

whis-tling
siz-zling

Do not divide an abbreviation unless it already has a hyphen.

asap (*not* as-ap)
AFL-CIO

If it is necessary to divide a name, divide only between the first name or initial and the last name.

Jennifer C. / Brewster
S. M. / Cantor

If a title precedes the name, divide *after* the title.

President / Aaron Beil
Dr. / G. D. Shriner

If it is necessary to divide long numbers, divide only *at* a comma, with at least two digits before and after.

3,912,-076 people
$209,-765

Divide dates only *between* day and year.

August 16, / 1994
February 1, / 1995

Divide places only *between* city and state or state and ZIP code.

Mill Valley, / CA 94941
Mill Valley, CA / 94941

Divide streets *between* words, not within words and not after the street number.

1927 Second / Street
421 Citrus / Grove Boulevard
421 Citrus Grove / Boulevard

Divide numbered or lettered items in a series only *before* the number or letter.

(1) pens, / (2) pencils, and (3) erasers
(a) computers, (b) faxes, and / (c) copiers

Numbers and Symbols

Numbers. In general business writing, spell out numbers from *zero* through *ninety-nine* and large round numbers, such as *one thousand.* But if a sentence or paragraph has a large uneven number, such as *107,* use figures for all other numbers within the same category. (If your office has another style, however, follow it.)

forty-seven applicants
371 tons of iron ore
For the three shop positions, there were 75 women applicants and
121 men applicants.

In scientific and technical writing, spell out numbers from zero to nine or ten, and use figures if any other larger numbers are used within the same category.

nine applicants
11 tons of iron ore
For the three shop positions, there were 7 women applicants and 13
men applicants.

Use figures to express specific dates, measures, hours, addresses, page numbers, and coordinates.

10 percent (*or* 10%)
January 22, 1995
80° (*or* 80 degrees) north latitude
4:00 P.M.
30 Rockefeller Plaza
p. 12
vol. 3 (*or* volume 3)
76 tons
0.5 microns
2.5 ml

When a sentence begins with a number, always spell it out.

Fifteen thousand feet of wire was lost.
But: We lost 15,000 feet of wire.

However, if a calendar year falls at the beginning of a sentence, use figures but add an introductory phrase before it so that the sentence does not begin with a figure.

Next year, 1996, promises to have sales that are double this year's earnings.

Fiscal year 1996 may have sales that are double this year's earnings.

Spell out approximations or numbers used casually.

We hiked a couple miles yesterday.
Thanks a million.

Spell out ordinals in text, but ordinals in correspondence address blocks may be spelled out or written in figures (see Chapter 5 for guidelines).

the twentieth century
the tenth meeting
Fifth Avenue
31 East 14 Street

Sometimes numbers form part of a corporate name or a set phrase. Style corporate names and phrases associated with them exactly as shown on letterhead or in reference works such as *Thomas Register.*

Ten Speed Press
20th Century-Fox Studios
42nd Street Photo
Pier 1 Imports
Saks Fifth Avenue
Fortune 500

When possible, round off very large numbers and use the word *million* or *billion* in place of numerous zeros.

$116.7 million in sales
a $200 billion federal deficit

But if digits must be used in one instance in a sentence, use them for the other large numbers too.

$116,700,000 in sales and $2,000,000 in returns
a $3,000,000 business with an inventory of $1,691,421

Decimals, ratios, and percentages are usually written as figures.

2.6 and 0.9 percent
5:1 ratio
100 to 1 odds

A zero should be used in front of a decimal fraction *only* if the quantity could or might exceed 1.00. Omit the zero if it will never exceed one.

0.6 factor
R = .12

Common fractions and general references to fractional amounts are usually spelled out in text unless the reference would be too long or awkward.

a two-thirds margin
8½ by 11 inches

Inclusive numbers may be abbreviated in footnotes, invoices, and other nontext material.

pp. 100–109, 109–10, 1186–87, 1301–1400
A.D. 36–42, 430–22 B.C., 1890–1900, 1990–96

Symbols. Signs and symbols are usually spelled out in general business writing, but the symbolic representation is more often used in technical and scientific writing.

General: 4 (*or* four) feet and 6 (*or* six) inches
Technical: 4' 6"

General: 12 percent
Technical: 12%

When a measurement is stated using an abbreviation or symbol, a figure should be used with it.

60 mm (*not* sixty mm)
$5 (*not* $5 dollars or five $)

The next sections have tables illustrating common technical signs, symbols, and abbreviations.

Mathematical Material

Scientific Notation. Because scientists often deal with very large or small numbers, they have developed a special *scientific notation* that enables them to name such numbers without using an excessive number of zeros. This notation is based on powers of 10 (10^n, where the exponent n is any number). For example, the number 1,000 (one followed by three zeros) is written more compactly as 10^3 ("ten to the third power") because $10 \times 10 \times 10 = 1,000$.

You can see the usefulness of this notation when you consider a larger number such as *one billion* (1,000,000,000 or one followed by nine zeros). In scientific notation, this is written as 10^9. Using this notation, you can quickly write numbers as large as you please without bothering to count zeros, even numbers that are so large that they have no name, such as 10^{28} ("ten to the 28th power"), or one followed by 28 zeros.

You can also use this notation to write numbers less than one. The general form is 10^{-n} (read as "ten to the minus n"), where the minus sign means 1 divided by 10^n, or $1/10^n$. For example, *one billionth* is written 10^{-9} ($1/10^9$).

You can combine this notation with decimal numbers to express numbers that lie between powers of ten. This is done by multiplying the base number by another number, or in general, $m \times 10^n$. For example, 240,000 may be written 2.4×10^5. This system of notation is very useful when you use the metric system of measurement, which is based on units of ten.

Mathematical Expressions. In typing mathematical material, you not only will be dealing with signs and symbols that may be unfamiliar, but you also may be working with handwritten drafts that are barely legible. The most effective way of coping with this situation is to familiarize yourself with the subject matter you will be dealing with. If your office prepares much mathematical material, you will no doubt have a technical style guide explaining the presentation of such material. For limited work in this area, a general guide, such as the *Chicago Manual of Style*, which has a section on mathematical expressions, may be helpful.

If you cannot identify a symbol in a handwritten draft, you can leave a space with a question mark or ask the author. In the latter case it is preferable, if there are several questionable symbols, to mark them for clarification in a single conference with the author.

If you are preparing a manuscript to be typeset, make a list of all symbols and other unusual expressions used in the manuscript. A compositor will find this very helpful, and many journals require that such a list accompany any article submissions. Since house styles vary, follow the specifications of the individual journal in preparing a manuscript. As is the case with any document, neatness, legibility, and accuracy are paramount.

Mathematical expressions consist of various signs and symbols, including the following:

- *Letter symbols*: The letters in a mathematical expression may stand for variables (whose values range over a set of numbers), constants (whose numerical values are fixed and must be specified in a particular context), abbreviations of English words, or other kinds of symbols such as index numbers. The meaning of each letter, abbreviation, or symbol should be clearly defined the first time it is used in a manuscript, with an indication of whether it is a variable, a constant, or another kind of symbol. Letters of the Greek alphabet also are used in mathematical expressions. (Greek letters are used for certain kinds of quantities for historical reasons.) See Table 11.2 on page 396.

- *Fences*: Fences, sometimes called *symbols of inclusion,* are the punctuation marks of mathematics. Their role is to prevent ambiguity by setting off from one another the different terms in a mathematical expression. Fences include left and right parentheses ( ), brackets [ ], braces { }, and other specialized symbols. The accepted convention for the order in which fences are used is $\{[( )]\}$. If more fences are needed, this order may be repeated with larger fences: $\{[(n + 2) (n + 1)^2 - 2n + (a - 1)^3]u\} - n^2$.

- *Signs of operation*: Signs of operation, sometimes called *operators* or *operational signs,* indicate specific mathematical operations, such as addition (+), subtraction (−), multiplication (×), or division (÷). The signs × and ÷ are usually implicit. Instead of writing $a \times b \times c$, you could write abc. Another way of indicating multiplication is by writing a^3 instead of aaa ("a cubed" or "a to the third power"). Similarly, in division, instead of writing $x \div y$, you could use the fractional form x/y ("x divided by y" or "x over y").

Operations are also indicated by the superscript (exponent) of a quantity. For example, a^n ("a raised to the nth power" or "a to the nth") means n of the quantities a multiplied together. The symbol for root of a quantity ($\sqrt{\ }$) is called the *radical* symbol, as in $\sqrt{x}$, read as "the square root of x."

Other signs stand for more complicated processes such as *differentiation* and *integration*. These are operations that change the *form* of a function. If an equation in functional form is $y = f(x)$, differentiation could be expressed as $dy/dx = f'(x)$. Because *integration* is the reverse of differentiation, it is sometimes known as

Table 11.2   Greek Alphabet

UPPERCASE	LOWERCASE	NAME
A	α	alpha
B	β	beta
Γ	γ	gamma
Δ	δ	delta
E	ε	epsilon
Z	ζ	zeta
H	η	eta
Θ	θ	theta
I	ι	iota
K	κ	kappa
Λ	λ	lambda
M	μ	mu
N	ν	nu
Ξ	ξ	xi
O	o	omicron
Π	π	pi
P	ρ	rho
Σ	σ, ς	sigma
T	τ	tau
Υ	υ	upsilon
Φ	φ	phi
X	χ	chi
Ψ	ψ	psi
Ω	ω	omega

antidifferentiation. Integration may be thought of as a procedure that sums up an infinite number of elements whose size becomes gradually smaller; it is indicated by the symbol $\int$.

Other signs of operation are the *product sign* Π (capital Greek *pi*) and the *summation symbol* $\sum$ (capital Greek *sigma*). They are used when a series of mathematical terms is multiplied or added, respectively. *Trigonometric functions* specify operations performed on letter symbols that represent angles, for example: $x = \sin\theta$, $y = \cos\theta$, and $z = \tan\theta$, where *sin* = "sine," *cos* = "cosine," *tan* = "tangent," and θ is an angle.

Another sign is the *factorial* symbol !, as in $n!$ (read as "n factorial"). The ! indicates the product of all the integers (whole numbers) from n to 1. For examples of mathematical operators, see Table 11.3 on page 398.

- *Signs of relation:* In contrast to signs of operation, signs of relation indicate the relationships among the various terms in a mathematical expression. In addition to the equality sign, other often-used signs of relation play similar roles. For example, $<$ and $>$ mean "less than" and "greater than," respectively; the expression $a < b$ is read as "a is less than b," and $a > b$ is read as "a is greater than b." For examples, see Table 11.4 on pages 399–400.

Spacing of Symbols. Proper spacing of mathematical symbols is important both to avoid ambiguity and to give a clean, uniform appearance to a manuscript. Unless you know that an author is meticulous about writing mathematics, you cannot rely on what you see, either in a handwritten draft or in one that has been typed by the author. You may be more familiar with the rules than the author is and thus can provide a valuable service.

Use *no space* in the following cases:

- Between quantities multiplied together when no multiplication sign is used: xy or $2ab$.

- Between a symbol and its subscript and superscript: x^n, x^{2y+c}, or Q_{max}.

- Before and after fences: $(2x + b)(6y + c)$ or $[(x^2 - 2y^2)(x + 2)]u_i$.

- In names of functions or between names of multiplied functions: $f(x)$ or $f(x)f(y)$.

Table 11.3   Common Mathematical Operators

+	plus
−	minus
±	plus or minus
∓	minus or plus
×	multiplication sign
Σ	summation
Π	product symbol
∂	backcurling delta (partial differential sign)
∇	del (vector operator)
∇	bold del
∀	inverted sans serif aye (for all)
∃	inverted sans serif ee (there exists)
∧	wedge, roof (outer product sign; conjunction sign)
∨	inverted wedge or roof (disjunction sign)
∩	intersection sign
∪	union sign
√	radical
∫	integral
∮	contour integral

- Between a sign and its quantity in signed quantities: ±6, −7, +10.
- When a sign of relation is used with a single quantity: "a value >6," "a length of ~3 meters."

Use *one space* in the following cases:

- Before and after a binary sign of operation (an operation involving two quantities): $a + b$ or $a − b$ (note that this is different from a signed quantity). An exception is when a binary operator or

Table 11.4 Common Mathematical Signs of Relation

$=$	equals; double bond
$\neq$	not equal to
$\triangleq$	corresponds to
$\equiv$	identically equal to; equivalent to; triple bond
$\not\equiv$	not identically equal to; not equivalent to; not always equal to
$\sim$	asymptotically equal to; of the order of magnitude of
$\approx$	approximately equal to
$\simeq$	approximately equal to
$\cong$	congruent to; approximately equal to
$\propto$	proportional to; variation
$<$	less than
$>$	greater than
$\not<$	not less than
$\not>$	not greater than
$\ll$	much less than
$\gg$	much greater than
$\leq$	less than or equal to
$\geq$	greater than or equal to
$\lesssim$	less than or approximately equal to
$\gtrsim$	greater than or approximately equal to
$\subset$	included in, a subset of
$\supset$	contains as a subset
$\not\subset$	not included in, not a subset of
$\subseteq$	contained within
$\supseteq$	contains
$\in$	an element of

Table 11.4, continued

∋	contains as an element
∉	not an element of
→	approaches, tends to; yields; is replaced by
↔	mutually implies
⊥	perpendicular (to)
‖	parallel (to)

sign of addition appears in a superscript, subscript, or limit, in which case no spaces are used: u^{n-1}, $\sum\limits_{i=1}^{\infty}$.

- Before and after a sign of relation: $a = 2b$, $x < y$, $g \subset r$.

- Before and after abbreviations that are set in roman type: $2 \sin \theta$, $\log b$, $2x \exp 4y$. An exception to this is when the abbreviation is preceded or followed by an expression in fences or a superscript or subscript. In such case, use no space: $(6n - m)\log a$, $\exp[(2x - y)/4]$, $\sin^2\theta$.

- Before and after a unary sign of operation (an operation on one expression):

$$\omega\int_0^{\infty} (6x^2 - 4y)\ dx,\ iq\,\frac{\partial\psi}{\partial t},\ \sum_{n=1}^{\infty} x_n,\ \text{or}\ \frac{dy}{dx}\ f(x).$$

Note: if an expression includes limits, count one space before and after the beginning and end of the limit: $\lim\limits_{y\to\infty} f(x)$.

If limits are written as superscripts or subscripts, count one space after the last character to the right:

$$g(t) = \frac{1}{2\pi i}\int_{a-i\infty}^{a+i\infty} e^{xt}f(x)\ dx.$$

- After commas in sets of symbols: $(r,\ \theta,\ \phi)$ and $f(x, y)$.

Use *three spaces* between elements in the following cases:

- Between two or more equations that are in sequence on the line: $z = a^2 + b^2 + c^2$, $x = 2a + 3b + c$.

- Between an equation and a condition on that equation: $d = u_a k \quad (a = 1, 2, 3, \ldots, n)$.

- Between an equation and any parenthetical unit of measure: $a = v/t \quad (m \cdot s^{-2})$.

- Between an equation and a following phrase in a displayed expression: $f(x) \to 0 \quad$ as $x \to \infty$.

Breaking Equations. To avoid awkwardness as well as to conserve space, equations or expressions set in text are often formatted differently from equations set on a separate line (displayed). For example, in text, an equation containing a fraction should be typed with the solidus (slash) instead of a horizontal fraction bar: $h^2/4\pi^2 ke^2 m = a_0/Z$.

Displayed equations are often numbered. The rule of thumb is that if a displayed equation is subsequently cited, it should be numbered. All numbered equations should be displayed, but not all displayed equations need be numbered. If they will not fit on a single line, lengthy displayed equations may be broken (carried over to the next line). An equation should be broken, if at all possible, only preceding a sign of relation (equal, less than, etc.) or preceding a sign of operation (plus, minus, integral symbol, etc.). The second line may be a standard indent and the equation number flush right.

$$u'(t) = b^0 a_0^{-1} \sum_{r=1}^{\infty} \exp(s_r t) p_r t \quad \text{(line break can come here)}$$

$$- b_1 a_0^{-1} \sum_{r=1}^{\infty} \exp[s_r(t - \omega)] p_r(t - \omega). \tag{2}$$

Fractions, expressions within fences, and expressions within a radical sign ($\sqrt{\ }$) should not be broken unless absolutely necessary. Do not break an expression containing an integral sign until d (variable) occurs.

$$\overline{K}(s, t) = -K(s, t) + \int_a^b K(s, r)K(r, t)\, dr$$

$$- \int_a^b \int_a^b K(s, r)K(r, w)K(w, t)\, dr\, dw.$$

Where Lists. Displayed equations are often followed by lists that define the symbols they contain, called "where lists" since they are preceded by the word *where*. When a list is lengthy (say, four or more lines) or itself contains built-up expressions, it should be displayed separately and the definitions aligned with the equal sign. The symbol definitions should be listed in the same order in which they appear in the equation. For example, an author might say:

We may write:

$$F^{3/4} = \left(\frac{bW_v - c}{2yL}\right)^m,$$

where b = proportionality constant,
          W_v = vapor mass rate,
          c = intercept as $W_v = 0$,
          $2yL$ = cross-sectional area normal to flow,
          L = tube length per crosspass,
          m = positive exponent.

Chemical Material

Chemical Notation. Chemists generally divide all chemical compounds into two major kinds, inorganic compounds and organic compounds. *Inorganic compounds* are those that are composed of elements other than the element carbon (atomic number 12). *Organic compounds* are those that contain carbon atoms. The reason for this division is twofold. Historically, the first carbon compounds studied were products of the human body; hence, they were called organic compounds. Second, because of its chemical properties, the element carbon forms a countless variety of different compounds, and the molecules of carbon compounds can be very large. Such compounds have given rise to a separate field of study.

The language of chemistry includes certain essential terms and principles. For example:

- The basic unit of matter is the *atom.*

- There are many different kinds of atoms, and each kind is called an *element.*

- The chemical properties of an element are governed by its atomic structure; for example, every atom has a central part, the *nucleus,* in which most of its mass (or weight) is concentrated.

- The nucleus consists of two kinds of particles: the *proton,* which has one positive unit of electrical charge, and the *neutron,* which is electrically neutral.

- The number of protons in the nucleus is called its *atomic number.*

- The total number of neutrons and protons in a nucleus is called its *atomic mass number.*

- In nature, the nuclei of atoms of the same element can contain different numbers of neutrons (such atoms are called *isotopes*). The *average* mass of an element as it is found in nature is called the *atomic weight.*

- The nucleus is surrounded by a swarm of much lighter, fast-moving particles called *electrons,* each of which carries one negative unit of electrical charge; the electrons are bound to the nucleus by the attractive force between their negative charges and the positive charge on the nucleus.

- As we increase the number of protons and electrons in an atom, the number of electrons in the valence shell repeats in a regular pattern, and atoms having the same number of valence electrons tend to have similar chemical properties. This periodic pattern enables us to group elements with similar chemical properties (see the periodic table of the elements on pp. 404–405).

The periodic table of elements lists the names of the elements, their chemical symbols, and their atomic numbers. Since a chemical symbol is not an abbreviation, it is *not* followed by a period.

Inorganic Chemistry. The *name* of a chemical element appearing in text should be spelled out the first time it is used. The name of an element is not capitalized (unless it is the first word in a sentence):

Oxygen and hydrogen react to form water.

However, the first letter of each chemical *symbol* is always capitalized; the second letter, if there is one, is never capitalized.

The material was found to consist of C, H, Cl, and Br.

Indicating the atomic number, atomic mass number, ionic charge, and number of atoms of an element in a compound is done by the use of appropriate index numbers (superscripts and subscripts) attached to the chemical symbol. As in mathematical notation, there is no space between a chemical symbol and its index number.

PERIODIC TABLE OF THE ELEMENTS

The first periodic table was devised by Dmitri Mendeleev in 1869. At that time only 63 elements were known. Mendeleev left empty spaces in his table to make the known elements fit in the correct columns. He correctly predicted that the spaces would later be filled in as more elements were discovered. The modern periodic table is essentially Mendeleev's chart with some improvements.

The periodic table arranges the chemical elements in two ways. The first is by atomic number, the number of protons in the atomic nucleus of an element. The elements are arranged so that their atomic numbers increase reading across each row, or period, from left to right. The second is by chemical families. Each column, or group, contains elements with similar chemical properties.

The lanthanide series (elements 57–71) and the actinide series (elements 89–103) are composed of elements with Group 3b chemical properties. They are placed below the main body of the table to make it easier to read. Elements 104–109 have been isolated experimentally but they have not been officially named.

An alphabetical list of the elements with their symbols and atomic numbers appears below the periodic table for ease in locating a particular element.

	Group 1a	Group 2a	Group 3b	Group 4b	Group 5b	Group 6b	Group 7b	Group 8	Group 8
1	1 **H** Hydrogen								
2	3 **Li** Lithium	4 **Be** Beryllium							
3	11 **Na** Sodium	12 **Mg** Magnesium							
4	19 **K** Potassium	20 **Ca** Calcium	21 **Sc** Scandium	22 **Ti** Titanium	23 **V** Vanadium	24 **Cr** Chromium	25 **Mn** Manganese	26 **Fe** Iron	27 **Co** Cobalt
5	37 **Rb** Rubidium	38 **Sr** Strontium	39 **Y** Yttrium	40 **Zr** Zirconium	41 **Nb** Niobium	42 **Mo** Molybdenum	43 **Tc** Technetium	44 **Ru** Ruthenium	45 **Rh** Rhodium
6	55 **Cs** Cesium	56 **Ba** Barium	57–71* **Lanthanides**	72 **Hf** Hafnium	73 **Ta** Tantalum	74 **W** Tungsten	75 **Re** Rhenium	76 **Os** Osmium	77 **Ir** Iridium
7	87 **Fr** Francium	88 **Ra** Radium	89–103** **Actinides**	104	105	106	107	108	109

*Lanthanides	57 **La** Lanthanum	58 **Ce** Cerium	59 **Pr** Praseo-dymium	60 **Nd** Neodymium	61 **Pm** Promethium	62 **Sm** Samarium	63 **Eu** Europium

**Actinides	89 **Ac** Actinium	90 **Th** Thorium	91 **Pa** Protactinium	92 **U** Uranium	93 **Np** Neptunium	94 **Pu** Plutonium	95 **Am** Americium

Element	Symbol	No.	Element	Symbol	No.	Element	Symbol	No.
Actinium	Ac	89	Cadmium	Cd	48	Erbium	Er	68	Indium	In	49
Aluminum	Al	13	Calcium	Ca	20	Europium	Eu	63	Iodine	I	53
Americium	Am	95	Californium	Cf	98	Fermium	Fm	100	Iridium	Ir	77
Antimony	Sb	51	Carbon	C	6	Fluorine	F	9	Iron	Fe	26
Argon	Ar	18	Cerium	Ce	58	Francium	Fr	87	Krypton	Kr	36
Arsenic	As	33	Cesium	Cs	55	Gadolinium	Gd	64	Lanthanum	La	57
Astatine	At	85	Chlorine	Cl	17	Gallium	Ga	31	Lawrencium	Lr	103
Barium	Ba	56	Chromium	Cr	24	Germanium	Ge	32	Lead	Pb	82
Berkelium	Bk	97	Cobalt	Co	27	Gold	Au	79	Lithium	Li	3
Beryllium	Be	4	Copper	Cu	29	Hafnium	Hf	72	Lutetium	Lu	71
Bismuth	Bi	83	Curium	Cm	96	Helium	He	2	Magnesium	Mg	12
Boron	B	5	Dysprosium	Dy	66	Holmium	Ho	67	Manganese	Mn	25
Bromine	Br	35	Einsteinium	Es	99	Hydrogen	H	1	Mendelevium	Md	101

Group 8	Group 1b	Group 2b	Group 3a	Group 4a	Group 5a	Group 6a	Group 7a	Group 0
								2 **He** Helium
			5 **B** Boron	6 **C** Carbon	7 **N** Nitrogen	8 **O** Oxygen	9 **F** Fluorine	10 **Ne** Neon
			13 **Al** Aluminum	14 **Si** Silicon	15 **P** Phosphorus	16 **S** Sulfur	17 **Cl** Chlorine	18 **Ar** Argon
28 **Ni** Nickel	29 **Cu** Copper	30 **Zn** Zinc	31 **Ga** Gallium	32 **Ge** Germanium	33 **As** Arsenic	34 **Se** Selenium	35 **Br** Bromine	36 **Kr** Krypton
46 **Pd** Palladium	47 **Ag** Silver	48 **Cd** Cadmium	49 **In** Indium	50 **Sn** Tin	51 **Sb** Antimony	52 **Te** Tellurium	53 **I** Iodine	54 **Xe** Xenon
78 **Pt** Platinum	79 **Au** Gold	80 **Hg** Mercury	81 **Tl** Thallium	82 **Pb** Lead	83 **Bi** Bismuth	84 **Po** Polonium	85 **At** Astatine	86 **Rn** Radon

64 **Gd** Gadolinium	65 **Tb** Terbium	66 **Dy** Dysprosium	67 **Ho** Holmium	68 **Er** Erbium	69 **Tm** Thulium	70 **Yb** Ytterbium	71 **Lu** Lutetium
96 **Cm** Curium	97 **Bk** Berkelium	98 **Cf** Californium	99 **Es** Einsteinium	100 **Fm** Fermium	101 **Md** Mendelevium	102 **No** Nobelium	103 **Lr** Lawrencium

Name	Symbol	Number	Name	Symbol	Number	Name	Symbol	Number	Name	Symbol	Number
Mercury	Hg	80	Platinum	Pt	78	Samarium	Sm	62	Thorium	Th	90
Molybdenum	Mo	42	Plutonium	Pu	94	Scandium	Sc	21	Thulium	Tm	69
Neodymium	Nd	60	Polonium	Po	84	Selenium	Se	34	Tin	Sn	50
Neon	Ne	10	Potassium	K	19	Silicon	Si	14	Titanium	Ti	22
Neptunium	Np	93	Praseodymium	Pr	59	Silver	Ag	47	Tungsten	W	74
Nickel	Ni	28	Promethium	Pm	61	Sodium	Na	11	Uranium	U	92
Niobium	Nb	41	Protactinium	Pa	91	Strontium	Sr	38	Vanadium	V	23
Nitrogen	N	7	Radium	Ra	88	Sulfur	S	16	Xenon	Xe	54
Nobelium	No	102	Radon	Rn	86	Tantalum	Ta	73	Ytterbium	Yb	70
Osmium	Os	76	Rhenium	Re	75	Technetium	Tc	43	Yttrium	Y	39
Oxygen	O	8	Rhodium	Rh	45	Tellurium	Te	52	Zinc	Zn	30
Palladium	Pd	46	Rubidium	Rb	37	Terbium	Tb	65	Zirconium	Zr	40
Phosphorus	P	15	Ruthenium	Ru	44	Thallium	Tl	81			

- The atomic number is indicated by a lower-left index number: $_1H$, $_8O$, $_{12}Mg$, $_{50}Sn$. (The atomic number is usually omitted in a chemical formula, as it is unique to an element.)

- The atomic mass number is indicated by an upper-left index number: ^1H, ^{16}O, ^{24}Mg, ^{118}Sn. Another way of indicating the atomic mass number of an element, usually when it stands alone or is mentioned in text, is to place it after the name or chemical symbol of the element: uranium 238, curium 247, carbon 14.

To determine the number of neutrons in a nucleus, subtract the atomic number from the atomic mass number. Hence the isotope ^{235}U has 143 neutrons (235 minus 92) and ^{238}U has 146 neutrons (238 minus 92).

- Ionic charge is indicated by an upper-right index number: H^+, F^-, O^{2-}, Fe^{3+}, Co^{3+}, U^{5+}, Mn^{4+}. If an ion has only one plus or minus charge, the numeral *1* is omitted.

When an atom gives up valence electrons, it is said to be *oxidized* or in an *oxidation state*. Some atoms can give up different numbers of valence electrons. The *oxidation number*, which specifies how many electrons have been given up, is indicated by a roman numeral in parentheses following the chemical symbol: Fe(II), Fe(III), Co(III), U(V), Mn(IV). There is no space between the chemical symbol and the parenthetical numeral.

- The number of atoms of an element in a molecule is indicated by a lower-right index number: H_2, O_2, $C_{16}H_{34}$, K_2CO_3.

- The same notation, with some additional features, is used for chemical compounds or molecules. Such an expression is known as a *chemical formula*. For example, the formula for the water molecule, which consists of two atoms of hydrogen and one atom of oxygen, is expressed in chemical notation by H_2O.

Organic Chemistry. Because a carbon atom can form covalent bonds with as many as four other atoms, it is known as a *tetravalent* element. The spatial orientation of other atoms when they bond to carbon, and the number of bonds they form with carbon, strongly affect the properties of the resulting molecule.

For example, two molecules containing carbon may have the same chemical formula (with regard to the total number of atoms in the molecule) but quite different physical or chemical properties because of the way the other atoms are attached to the carbon atoms. For this reason, formulas describing carbon compounds are often given in *structural* form. A *structural formula* displays the spatial relationships among the atoms in a unique and unambiguous way.

In general, a carbon atom can bond to its neighbors in four ways; each kind of bond is represented by a special notation.

1. A single bond, in which two electrons are shared, is represented by a single line drawn from the carbon atom to another atom.

$$
\begin{array}{c}
\text{H} \\
| \\
\text{H} - \text{C} - \text{H} \\
| \\
\text{H}
\end{array}
$$

2. A double bond, in which four electrons are shared, is represented as follows.

$$
\begin{array}{ccc}
\text{H} & & \text{H} \\
\diagdown & & \diagup \\
& \text{C} = \text{C} & \\
\diagup & & \diagdown \\
\text{H} & & \text{H}
\end{array}
$$

3. A triple bond, in which six electrons are shared, is represented as follows.

$$
\text{H} - \text{C} \equiv \text{C} - \text{H}
$$

4. A hydrogen bond is represented by a dotted line in which a hydrogen atom bonded to atom A in one molecule makes an additional bond to atom B in either the same or another molecule.

$$
\begin{array}{c}
\text{O} \\
\diagup \diagdown \\
\text{H} \quad \text{H} \\
\vdots \\
\text{O} \\
\diagup \diagdown \\
\text{H} \quad \text{H}
\end{array}
$$

The Metric System   The metric system, also called the International System of Units (SI), is a standardized system of expressing units of measurement. SI units have been officially adopted in nearly every country in the world because of their simplicity and ease of manipulation. Although the use of metric weights and measures was legalized in the United States as long ago as 1866, Americans have in general preferred the traditional English system of measurement (such as *foot, pound,* and *degree Fahrenheit*), and conversion to SI has been slow.

Base Units. Table 11.5 gives the SI base and supplemental units and their abbreviations. You may find that the SI units for mass (the kilogram), length (the meter), and time (the second) are the most familiar. However, the other base units (and their derived units) are used extensively in scientific literature. Each SI base unit has been defined with great precision in terms of measurable physical quantities. As measuring techniques become more precise, the base units occasionally have been redefined by decision of international scientific meetings. To deal with very large and very small measurements, SI provides prefixes for the base units. Table 11.6 gives the SI prefixes, their equivalents in scientific notation, and their official symbols.

Table 11.5   SI Base and Supplemental Units

QUANTITY	UNIT	SYMBOL
length	meter	m
mass	kilogram	kg
time	second	s
electric current	ampere	A
thermodynamic temperature	kelvin	K
amount of substance	mole	mol
luminous intensity	candela	cd
plane angle	radian	rad
solid angle	steradian	sr

Table 11.6   SI Prefixes

SYMBOL	PREFIX	MULTIPLICATION FACTOR
E	exa	10^{18}
P	peta	10^{15}
T	tera	10^{12}
G	giga	10^{9}
M	mega	10^{6}
k	kilo	10^{3}
h	hecto	10^{2}
da	deca	10^{1}
d	deci	10^{-1}
c	centi	10^{-2}
m	milli	10^{-3}
µ	micro	10^{-6}
n	nano	10^{-9}
p	pico	10^{-12}
f	femto	10^{-15}
a	atto	10^{-18}

Conversion from U.S. Customary Units to SI. Tables 11.7, 11.8, and 11.9 on pages 410–411 list some common SI units and U.S. customary equivalents. To convert from U.S. customary to SI, you would multiply the number of U.S. customary units by the equivalent in SI units. For example, to convert 6 miles to kilometers, multiply 6 by 1.609 to obtain 9,654 meters, or 9.654 kilometers.

SI Style. Because a small change in the way SI units are written or typed can change their meaning completely, it is important to style them correctly. Adherence to a few simple rules can avoid confusion.

Table 11.7 Measurement

Length

U.S. Customary Unit	U.S. Equivalents	Metric Equivalents	Metric Unit	Number of Meters	U.S. Equivalent
inch	1/12 foot	2.540 centimeters	kilometer	1,000	0.621 mile
foot	1/3 yard, 12 inches	0.305 meter	hectometer	100	109.361 yards
yard	3 feet, 36 inches	0.914 meter	decameter	10	32.808 feet
rod	5½ yards, 16½ feet	5.029 meters	meter	1	39.370 inches
mile (statute, land)	1,760 yards, 5,280 feet	1.609 kilometers	decimeter	0.1	3.937 inches
mile (nautical, international)	1.151 statute miles	1.852 kilometers	centimeter	0.01	0.394 inch
			millimeter	0.001	0.039 inch

Area

U.S. Customary Unit	U.S. Equivalents	Metric Equivalents	Metric Unit	Square Meters	U.S. Equivalent
square inch	0.007 square foot	6.452 square centimeters	square kilometer	1,000,000	0.386 square mile
			hectare	10,000	2.471 acres
square foot	144 square inches	929.030 square centimeters	are	100	119.599 square yards
			deciare	10	11.960 square yards
square yard	1,296 square inches, 9 square feet	0.836 square meters	centare	1	10.764 square feet
acre	43,560 square feet, 4,840 square yards	4,047 square meters	square centimeter	0.0001	0.155 square inch
square mile	640 acres	2.590 square kilometers			

Volume and Capacity

U.S. Customary Unit	U.S. Equivalents	Metric Equivalents	Metric Unit of Volume	Cubic Meters	U.S. Equivalent
cubic inch	0.00058 cubic foot	16.387 cubic centimeters	decastere	10	13.079 cubic yards
			stere	1	1.308 cubic yards
cubic foot	1,728 cubic inches	0.028 cubic meter	decistere	0.10	3.531 cubic feet
cubic yard	27 cubic feet	0.765 cubic meter	cubic centimeter	0.000001	0.061 cubic inch

U.S. Customary Liquid Measure	U.S. Equivalents	Metric Equivalents	Metric Unit of Capacity	Liters	U.S. Equivalent
fluid ounce	8 fluid drams, 1.805 cubic inches	29.574 milliliters	hectoliter	100	2.838 bushels (dry), 26.42 gallons (liquid)
pint	16 fluid ounces, 28.875 cubic inches	0.473 liter	decaliter	10	1.135 pecks (dry), 2.642 gallons (liquid)
quart	2 pints, 57.75 cubic inches	0.946 liter	liter	1	.908 quart (dry), 1.057 quarts (liquid)
gallon	4 quarts, 231 cubic inches	3.785 liters	deciliter	0.10	.182 pint (dry), .211 pint (liquid)
barrel	varies from 31 to 42 gallons, established by law or usage		centiliter	0.01	.338 fluid ounce
			milliliter	0.001	.271 fluid dram

U.S. Customary Dry Measure	U.S. Equivalents	Metric Equivalents
pint	½ quart, 33.6 cubic inches	0.551 liter
quart	2 pints, 67.2 cubic inches	1.101 liters
peck	8 quarts, 537.605 cubic inches	8.810 liters
bushel	4 pecks, 2,150.421 cubic inches	35.239 liters

Weight and Mass

U.S. Customary Unit (Avoirdupois)	U.S. Equivalents	Metric Equivalents	Metric Unit	Number of Grams	U.S. Equivalent
grain	0.037 dram, 0.002285 ounce	64.799 milligrams	metric ton	1,000,000	1.102 tons
			quintal	100,000	220.462 pounds
dram	27.344 grains	1.772 grams	kilogram	1,000	2.205 pounds
ounce	16 drams, 437.5 grains	28.350 grams	hectogram	100	3.527 ounces
			decagram	10	0.353 ounce
pound	16 ounces, 7,000 grains	453.592 grams	gram	1	0.035 ounce
ton (short)	2,000 pounds	0.907 metric ton (1,000 kilograms)	decigram	0.10	1.543 grains
			centigram	0.01	0.154 grain
ton (long)	1.12 short tons, 2,240 pounds	1.016 metric tons	milligram	0.001	0.015 grain

Table 11.8   Metric Conversion Chart

When You Know	Multiply By	To Find		When You Know	Multiply By	To Find
LENGTH				**VOLUME**		
millimeters	0.04	inches		milliliters	0.20	teaspoons
centimeters	0.39	inches		milliliters	0.07	tablespoons
meters	3.28	feet		milliliters	0.03	fluid ounces
meters	1.09	yards		liters	4.23	cups
kilometers	0.62	miles		liters	2.11	pints
inches	25.40	millimeters		liters	1.06	quarts
inches	2.54	centimeters		liters	0.26	gallons
feet	30.48	centimeters		cubic meters	35.31	cubic feet
yards	0.91	meters		cubic meters	1.31	cubic yards
miles	1.61	kilometers		teaspoons	4.93	milliliters
AREA				tablespoons	14.79	milliliters
square centimeters	0.16	square inches		fluid ounces	29.57	milliliters
square meters	1.20	square yards		cups	0.24	liters
square kilometers	0.39	square miles		pints	0.47	liters
hectares (10,000m²)	2.47	acres		quarts	0.95	liters
square inches	6.45	square centimeters		gallons	3.79	liters
square feet	0.09	square meters		cubic feet	0.03	cubic meters
square yards	0.84	square meters		cubic yards	0.76	cubic meters
square miles	2.59	square kilometers		**SPEED**		
acres	0.40	hectares		miles per hour	1.61	kilometers per hour
MASS AND WEIGHT				kilometers per hour	0.62	miles per hour
grams	0.035	ounce		**TEMPERATURE**		
kilograms	2.20	pounds		When You Know	Use This Formula	To Find
tons (1,000 kg)	1.10	short tons		degrees Fahrenheit	(°F − 32) ÷ 1.8	degrees Celsius
ounces	28.35	grams		degrees Celsius	(°C × 1.8) + 32	degrees Fahrenheit
pounds	0.45	kilograms				
short tons (2,000 lb)	0.91	metric tons				

Table 11.9   Scientific Measurement Units

Quantity	SI Unit	Symbol	Derivation	Other Units
acceleration	meter per second squared	m/s^2		
angular acceleration	radian per second squared	rad/s^2		
angular velocity	radian per second	rad/s		
density	kilogram per cubic meter	kg/m^3		
electric capacitance	farad	F	(A·s/V)	
electric charge	coulomb	C	(A·s)	electrostatic unit (esu) = 3.34×10^{-10}C
electric current	ampere	A		
electric field strength	volt per meter	V/m		
electric resistance	ohm	Ω	(V/A)	
energy, work, quantity of heat	joule	J	(N·m)	electronvolt (eV) = 1.60219×10^{-19}J calorie (cal) = 4.184 J British thermal unit (Btu) = 1,054.35 J erg = 10^{-7} J foot-pound (ft-lb) = 1.35582 J
flux of light	lumen	lm		
force	newton	N	$(kg \cdot m/s^2)$	dyne (dyn) = 10^{-5} N
frequency	hertz	Hz	(s^{-1})	formerly cycle per second (cps, c/sec)
illumination	lux	lx	(lm/m^2)	
inductance	henry	H	(V·s/A)	
length	meter	m		angstrom (Å) = 10^{-10} m
luminance	candela per square meter	cd/m^2		
magnetic field strength	ampere per meter	A/m		oersted (Oe) = $(1/4\pi) \times 10^3$ A/m
magnetic flux	weber	Wb	(V·s)	maxwell (Mx) = 10^{-8} Wb
magnetic flux density	tesla	T	(Wb/m^2)	gauss (G) = 10^{-4} T
magnetomotive force	ampere-turn	At		
mass	kilogram	kg		
power	watt	W	(J/s)	horsepower (hp) = 745.7 W
pressure	newton per square meter	N/m^2		atmosphere (atm) = 1.01325×10^5 N/m² bar = 10^5 N/m²
velocity	meter per second	m/s		
voltage, potential difference, electromotive force	volt	V	(W/A)	

- Write the full names of SI units in lowercase letters (unless being the first word in a sentence). Some SI units (*newton, kelvin, watt, pascal*) are named after famous scientists; if so, the *symbol* begins with an uppercase letter: N, K, W, Pa. An exception is the (non-SI but commonly used) unit for temperature, the degree Celsius, which is always capitalized.

- Do not italicize SI units because they are not mathematical symbols.

- Do not put a period after SI symbols, except at the end of a sentence; they are *not* abbreviations.

- Do not mix unit names and their symbols. For example, do not write "km/second." Write either "km/s" or "kilometers per second."

- Do not pluralize symbols; for example: 800 km, *not* 800 kms. Full unit names are pluralized normally, by adding an *s*: meters, kilograms.

- Always space between a symbol and its numerical value: 500 s, not 500s (which appears to be the plural of 500). The exception is the degree Celsius (°C), where the degree and Celsius symbols are written flush with the numerical value (40°C).

- When a prefix symbol (M, G, etc.) is combined with a unit symbol, do not leave a space between them: GHz, *not* G Hz.

- Derived units involving multiplication, such as newton meter, should be separated from one another with a raised dot (N·m) or, if your typing element lacks this symbol, with a period (N.m).

- Derived units involving division can be written using either the solidus (/) or the negative exponent combined with the dot multiplier. For example, kilograms per cubic meter may be written: kg/m^3 or $kg \cdot m^{-3}$. When preparing a manuscript for a journal, consult its style specifications on this point. Whatever style is used, it is best to be consistent.

- When numerical values are written in SI, use a space rather than a comma to separate groups of three digits to the left and to the right of the decimal point. Thus *ten thousand* is typed 10 000 rather than 10,000 and *one millionth* is 0.000 000 1 rather than 0.000,000,1. Numbers with only four digits to the right or left of the decimal point are written without either a space or a comma: 9856 and 0.0011. In decimal numbers less than one, the decimal point is *always* preceded by a zero: 0.068, not .068. (This SI style should not be confused with traditional business style: 1,342,784.69.)

CHAPTER

12

Few businesses can exist without meetings to exchange information and decide upon necessary actions. But participants need not be assembled in one location for a meeting to take place. Other alternatives to a face-to-face discussion include document conferencing and teleconferencing, described later in this chapter. Often such alternatives are more time- and cost-efficient methods of discussion and decision-making than face-to-face meetings.

When a meeting or conference has been proposed, many factors should be considered to determine whether the meeting is truly necessary. You may not be in a position to make such a determination; however, you will have information about schedules and other matters that can be very helpful to executives.

Generally, the person in charge will have to decide if there is a real objective for the meeting or conference and what will be accomplished as a result. If no concrete actions will be taken or if the participants will not leave the meeting better informed, the meeting may be unnecessary. But once it is decided that the meeting is necessary, the strategies described in the next sections will help to make it more efficient, controlled, and effective.

TYPES OF MEETINGS

On-Site Meetings

The most common meetings are the frequent on-site staff and executive meetings held in most businesses. As described in the section "The Secretary's Duties," you may be expected to prepare and distribute notices and agendas for these meetings, collect files and other information, take notes, and prepare the formal minutes.

On-site meetings might include some or all of the following:

- Sales and other departmental meetings held at corporate head-quarters. These meetings may involve hotel, restaurant, travel, and entertainment arrangements as indicated in later sections.

- Shareholders' and directors' meetings. These meetings, whether on-site or in other locations, are more formal than routine departmental and staff meetings.

- Regularly scheduled management and executive committee meetings.

- Special (not regularly scheduled) staff, management, and executive meetings.

- Employee meetings, such as those called by management to make important announcements to all personnel.

Refer to the section "Meeting Arrangements" for a description of large conferences and other meetings held in facilities away from the company offices.

Informal Meetings

Conventional Meetings. Most staff, departmental, and executive meetings are informal. The meeting notice and the agenda do not follow a prescribed pattern, and the minutes may consist only of informal notes and a follow-up letter to participants from the person in charge confirming any decisions that were made. Even in such an informal atmosphere, though, the person conducting a meeting needs to have a list of matters to discuss and needs to guide the discussion and maintain order among the participants. The secretary's role in this type of meeting is often defined more by office practices than by formal meeting procedure.

Roundtable Meetings. Although only small meetings are usually informal, some organizations occasionally hold companywide roundtable meetings — with no agenda and no assigned speakers. In these open-space meetings the participants, seated in a large circle, decide what to talk about. Typically, someone leads off with a comment or question, and later the participants can sign up for smaller, individual discussion groups. Although the company may set up some ground rules, such as how long someone may speak, the success of the meeting depends in part on the mature, orderly behavior of the participants.

This type of unstructured meeting is not suitable when a particular outcome is desired or when on-the-spot decisions must be made. But since it encourages the free exchange of ideas, it can be useful for collecting a wide range of information and discovering more about the participants' interests and needs.

Formal Meetings   A formal meeting follows prescribed rules, beginning with the purpose for holding the meeting. Each step thereafter must also meet the requirements of the organization. Often an organization's bylaws state who shall call a meeting, when and where it may be held, who is entitled to attend, what form of notice must be given, how many votes are required to pass an issue, how the minutes shall be maintained, and so on. Some formal meetings are large, for example, a convention (see "Meeting Arrangements") or a shareholders' meeting for a large corporation. Others are small, for example, a directors' meeting.

Shareholders' Meeting. Invitations to shareholders' meetings are very formal and are usually printed. They are issued on behalf of the company officers about four weeks before the event or at a set time stipulated in the company's bylaws. A proxy form usually accompanies the invitations, for use by the shareholders who cannot attend in person. The corporate secretary or general counsel usually handles invitations to these kinds of meetings. The office secretary, however, assists in making arrangements for the printing and mailing.

Directors' Meetings. Directors' meetings are usually either formal or semiformal, depending on the size of the organization. Unlike a shareholders' meeting, a directors' meeting may not require a printed notice or proxy. But like a shareholders' meeting, a directors' meeting often must be held as directed by the organization's bylaws. For more about your duties and procedures, refer to the section "The Secretary's Duties."

Teleconferencing

People who need to discuss something or make decisions about something can do so in many ways, including communication by telephone or electronic mail. The teleconference is a sophisticated version of electronic communication and telecommunication designed primarily to link participants in groups of all sizes for discussion and decision-making.

Teleconferences may consist of audio or video transmission. A small *audioconference*, for example, might involve three people in different cities who use the long-distance operator to connect them simultaneously by telephone, with each being charged for the cost of a person-to-person call. (For more about basic telephone communication, refer to Chapter 8.) As soon as television cameras are added, the teleconference becomes a *videoconference*. When computers are used to link people who simultaneously exchange and view each other's documents on screen, the conference becomes a *document conference*.

Document Conferencing In a *document conference*, meeting participants use their computers, with conferencing software, and modems to call each other over their network lines. Once a connection has been established among all participants, the same document can be called up on everyone's computer screen. Using a keyboard or mouse, a participant can then change the document while the others watch the changes being made on their own screens. Users select or are given different color "pens" to differentiate their annotations from those of the other participants.

When the participants also have a full duplex teleconferencing device (a participant can speak without clipping off another's voice) or when they have speakerphones or modems with voice capability, they can also *discuss* the document being displayed on everyone's screen.

Like any type of conference, a document conference also requires preparation and planning. Participants must be notified of the time and place of the intended computer link and should be advised about the material or documents to be displayed or discussed. Secretaries are usually actively involved in preparing schedules and sending notices, as well as processing the hard-copy printouts resulting from the document conference.

Videoconferencing

Types of Videoconferencing. The term *videoconferencing* covers a wide range of long-distance visual conferencing. Some offices, for example, are equipped with Picturephone systems enabling two or more users who have this equipment to see each other as they talk over the telephone. This type of visual conferencing is most suitable for a few participants who remain in their individual offices and converse with others as they would do in a regular telephone conversation. When larger groups are involved, a meeting room specially equipped with television cameras and electronic visual aids is usually required. Some hotel chains offer such facilities. A firm also can rent or build its own videoconferencing system using transmission facilities provided by communication companies.

One-Way Transmission. Videoconferencing may involve one- or two-way television transmission. One-way transmissions are essentially private television transmissions to a select audience and are used for activities such as announcing new policies to a company's national sales force (see illustration). The salespeople meet in a videoconferencing room in their city and watch corporate management's televised presentation. Questions can be fielded through a telephone hookup. The advantages to videoconferencing are that everyone gets the message at the same time and executives are not tied up for weeks putting on traveling road shows to educate a sales force.

Two-Way Transmission. Two-way videoconferencing involves smaller but more elaborate facilities. The standard configuration is a sound-proof room with a conference table and one or more wide-screen television monitors on a wall at one end of the table. Two cameras are often used, either to provide coverage from different angles or to project charts or other written material on the screen. Fax machines also may be included. The cost of two-way videoconferencing can be high, but

Videoconferencing

One-way videoconferencing at a hotel videoconferencing facility.
Courtesy of Hilton Hotels Corporation.

its advantage is its cost-effectiveness over executive travel time to an off-site location.

Service Companies. The yellow pages of many telephone directories list teleconferencing service companies that will set up the type of conferencing arrangement you need, providing the equipment as well as the transmission link between the locations you designate. Some will provide a tape recording of the proceedings or supply someone to record the proceedings using a stenorecorder or telerecorder device similar to that used in a courtroom. If you are helping with the arrangements for a teleconference, get cost estimates and a list of services and equipment provided from several teleconference service companies. Programs or agendas, as well as meeting notices, must be distributed to participants in sufficient time for them to make arrangements to attend.

PARLIAMENTARY PROCEDURE

Parliamentary procedure refers to the steps that meeting participants take to adhere to the rules, precedents, and customary practices that apply to meeting conduct. Together, these "rules, precedents, and customary practices" are known as *parliamentary law.* Secretaries who conduct meetings of assistants and other coworkers, or who attend and take minutes at other meetings, need to be familiar with proper parliamentary procedure. Although very small, informal meetings usually dispense with formal motions and standard parliamentary practice, more formal meetings must follow parliamentary guidelines.

The most familiar, detailed guide is *Robert's Rules of Order,* available in various paperback editions. Smaller, quick-reference guides are also available, for example *How to Run a Meeting* (Plume, 1994), based on the larger *New Robert's Rules of Order* (Signet, 1989). These and similar guides describe the conduct of meetings according to parliamentary rules similar to those used by the U.S. House of Representatives.

Duties of Officers

President The president, or chair (*also*: chairman, chairperson), opens a meeting and calls it to order, announcing business in the order listed on the agenda. The presiding officer also puts motions to a vote and announces the results. If points of order arise, the presiding officer decides those questions (subject to possible appeal by any two members). A chair may vote when voting is by ballot or, otherwise, only when his or her vote is needed to change the outcome. In addition to conducting the meetings, a president may have many other duties, such as signing legal documents and representing the organization at ceremonial functions.

Vice President   The vice president, or vice chairman, assists the president and assumes the chair when the president is absent. Vice presidents often head various committees and handle special assignments for the organization.

Secretary   The secretary (*also*: clerk, recording secretary) maintains the organization's official records and often must sign all important papers. When both the president and vice president are absent, the secretary calls the meeting to order and asks the group to elect a chair pro tem. When the position of secretary and treasurer are combined, the secretary also has the financial responsibilities described for the treasurer. The most important duty of the secretary, however, is the recording of the proceedings and the preparation and maintenance of the minutes. Thus if your job is to take and type the minutes, this task will usually be done according to the instruction of the elected corporate secretary.

Treasurer   The treasurer maintains the organization's financial records, including the checkbook and checking or savings accounts. The treasurer also must pay all bills and arrange for the filing of tax returns and the handling of the necessary bookkeeping and auditing activities. Usually, the treasurer must prepare monthly or quarterly financial reports and present them at the appropriate meetings. (Some organizations hire outside management, and the treasurer then would supervise the financial services that management provides.) If you work for the treasurer of an organization, part of your duties will consist of helping to maintain the necessary records and typing and distributing the treasurer's periodic financial reports.

Committees   Although not officers of the organization, committee chairs often perform the same duties as those of a regular chair while the committee is in session. Often committee chairs are appointed by the president, or the first person named to serve on a committee may become its chair. In other cases the committee members elect their own chair. Frequently, the person elected or chosen names another committee member as secretary to record the proceedings of committee meetings and prepare minutes, which should be kept separate from the minutes of the parent organization.

Introducing Business

Business is introduced and transactions decided by way of *motions*. A member, after being recognized by the chair, "moves" that some resolution be approved or that some action be taken.

I move that we adopt the following resolution: RESOLVED That . . .

The chair then asks for a second to the motion ("I second the motion") and asks for discussion. The names of the persons moving and seconding are often omitted in a very informal meeting.

It has been moved [by . . .] and seconded [by . . .] that we adopt the following resolution: . . . Is there any discussion?

After discussion appears to be over, the chair puts the question to a vote by voice, show of hands, secret ballot, or other approved method.

Is there any further discussion? [*none requested*] All those in favor of the motion to . . . say aye; those opposed, no. [*pause for vote*] The noes have it. The motion has failed.

Motions   In formal meetings motions are stated formally, and the rules developed for *Robert's Rules of Order* or another approved parliamentary guide must be followed. Numerous restrictions and qualifications apply to the important motions that are used, and a secretary should have a rules-of-order book available for reference *during* the meeting.

Classes of Motions   Generally, there are four classes of motions.

- A *privileged motion* is the highest ranking motion and takes precedence over any other motion currently being discussed. You might, for example, ask the chair to return to the specified order of business or set the time for adjournment.

- A *subsidiary,* or *secondary, motion* is one that is applied to another motion currently being considered as a means of disposing of the other motion. Hence you might move to table (lay aside) the other motion.

- An *incidental motion* is one that arises from or is prompted by another motion and has to be decided before a vote can be taken on the other motion. You might, for example, move to withdraw the other motion.

- A *main,* or *principal, motion* is any motion used to introduce business. You might, for example, move that a person be appointed to study recycling in the office. The description of this type of motion (*principal*) is misleading because main, or principal, motions yield to *all* other motions and are therefore of *lower* rank than the other three types of motions.

THE SECRETARY'S DUTIES

Meeting Preparation

The secretary's role in planning and participating in any meeting that involves his or her supervisor(s) is instrumental to ensuring a successful meeting. Once your supervisor has instructed you to set up a meeting, you should determine the date, time, and place the meeting is to be held. Often these criteria will depend on the availability of a meeting room. You may be required to shop around for a room, present alternatives to the executive, and proceed with plans according to his or her decision.

Next, you need to know who should attend the meeting and if any of the participants is required to bring specific documents or present a report. You will also need to know what your recourse should be if one or more of the people on the attendance list are unable to attend. Can the meeting take place without those people? Should the meeting be postponed to a time more convenient to them? Can a substitute sit in for those unable to attend? You also need to know what, if any, audiovisual or other equipment will be needed during the meeting.

Although guests may be invited, or the meeting may be declared open to the public or to all employees, usually only those who are essential to the objective of a meeting should attend. Ten to twelve people at the most should attend a discussion-style meeting. However, if the intent is to give or hear a speech, with or without a question-and-answer period, the number of participants need be restricted only by seating and space availability.

The Agenda

Preliminary Agenda. After determining the number of participants, prepare an agenda. For some meetings a preliminary (or working) agenda is circulated to the prospective participants. In some cases the host may want to solicit agenda topics from those participants. Use of a preliminary agenda enables the host to cut out as much extraneous subject matter as possible. The final agenda is developed from the preliminary model and often is distributed to the participants in advance so that they will be prepared to discuss and act on the various topics.

How to Set Up an Agenda. Type the agenda double- or triple-spaced in numbered or unnumbered outline style. Include as much or as little detail as the executive requires. In a large organization it is helpful to include the names of people presenting reports or any other detail that may be helpful to the participants. The illustration on page 424 is an agenda for a small informal staff meeting. Excessive detail is omitted since the participants work together, know each other, and are generally familiar with the meeting activity.

Meeting Notice

Types of Notification. Once you have done the preliminary work for the meeting, you are ready to inform the participants. Seven to ten business days are considered appropriate notification for an in-house staff or executive meeting.

Depending on the level of formality in your company or the nature of the meeting, you may telephone the participants' offices and then confirm the verbal notification in writing by mailing or faxing a brief letter stating the date, time, location, nature of the meeting along with the agenda, and any special requests of the individual. For example, alert the participants or presenters about any special materials they should bring with them. Also, ask the participants to let you know if they will attend, and notify the chair of any prospective absentees as soon as you receive the replies.

Sometimes only the members of high-level corporate committees receive copies of the agenda and the minutes of previous meetings. In such cases you would send only a brief memo to the presenters and other participants, informing them of the date, time, and location of the meeting and the time at which presenters are expected to make their presentation(s).

Agenda

AGENDA

Editorial Meeting

April 14, 1995

1. Call to order

2. Roll call

3. Minutes of previous meeting (corrections, omissions)

4. Directors' report

5. Publisher's report

6. Production manager's report

7. Unfinished business

   a. Works in progress

   b. Proposals before the board

   c. Staff

8. New business

   a. Budget

   b. New proposals

9. Announcements (including date of next meeting)

10. Adjournment

A meeting of the Publishing Committee will be held at 9:00 a.m., Tuesday, May 23, 1995, in the Board Room on the 30th floor. Mr. Smith would like to have you give your report between 9:15 and 9:45 a.m. Please telephone this office (extension 721) if you have any questions. If you are unable to attend, please let Mr. Smith or me know by Friday, May 12. Thank you very much.

If you work in the office of the company president, you may be called on to issue formal notices of forthcoming meetings to the board of directors. These gatherings usually occur at a set time during the fiscal year, and the procedures in preparing for them are predetermined. Examine previous notices in the files for content and format.

Directors' Address List. Keep a current list of the directors' full names, corporate and home addresses, corporate titles, and telephone and fax numbers. Notify them of the meeting, preferably in writing, at least two or three weeks in advance or in accordance with the provisions of the company's bylaws. Keep a separate list of the directors in order of seniority on the board, with notations about the date on which they were notified of the meeting and a check mark indicating whether or not each person will or will not be able to attend. Total the number of attendees to determine whether a quorum will be present.

Other Arrangements. You also may have to make arrangements for outside sites for shareholders' meetings. With directors' meetings you may have to make hotel reservations for those living out of town, and you may be expected to arrange dinners and lunches for them. This is very likely if your position is in the office of the president or the chair and chief executive officer.

Meeting-Room Preparation Before the meeting begins, check the room for temperature and proper ventilation, a supply of pens and paper, water and glasses, wastebaskets, brochures or other handouts, coat and hat racks, and the setup of fax machines, computers, visual aids, and any special equipment that you ordered. Many meetings are now nonsmoking, so ashtrays may be unnecessary. If you are having refreshments, check that tables or serving carts are available for snacks and beverages.

If you have prepared a meeting file (reports, pertinent correspondence, and so on) for your boss or anyone else, present it before the meeting or bring it to the meeting room, whichever the recipient prefers. (*Hint*: If you must present a variety of material, arrange it in color-coded folders so that the participant can quickly locate different items during the meeting.)

If place cards on the meeting table indicate where each person will sit, quickly draft a seating chart for your use later in identifying who is speaking as you take notes. If place cards are not used, wait until everyone is seated to prepare the chart.

The Minutes

Preparation   If you are required to take the minutes of the meeting, bring along both pens and writing paper and a tape recorder and blank cassettes. Arrive at the meeting site before everyone else does to ensure that everything is ready. To take the minutes, you should have plenty of materials (paper, cassettes, and so on) to get through a lengthy dictation session. (Refer to Chapter 4 for more about dictation and transcription procedures.) Make sure you have a copy of the agenda, as well as any reports, financial statements, or other documents that may be referred to during the meeting.

What to Record   The most difficult part of taking minutes is deciding what information has to be written down verbatim, what can be paraphrased, and what is nonessential for the official record. Minutes are meant to be concise, factual, and objective records of what has happened during a meeting. Therefore, you cannot allow personal preferences to influence your note-taking, and you cannot give more weight to what certain people say and not record the pertinent remarks of others. You must be able to interpret statements for what is truly being said, not what you hear by way of the deliverer's voice inflections, intonations, or mannerisms.

It can be very difficult to discriminate from among all the opinions and facts just what should be recorded in the minutes, and to record the proceedings fairly, it is necessary to take a disinterested position. As a recorder you must listen carefully *and* take down information even when more than one person is talking at the same time, making sure that you attribute all statements to their correct sources.

Motions and Resolutions. In corporate or organizational meetings, it is necessary to record motions and resolutions verbatim as well as the names of those who made them. You may want to have blank copies of forms to use for this purpose on which you fill in names and motions.

Motion #1: _____

_____

_____

_____

_____

Made by: _____
Seconded by: _____

Recording Guidelines. To begin your note-taking session, follow these guidelines.

- Write down the date, location, and time the meeting begins.

- Record the names of those present and absent (if the number is less than twenty). A quorum check is necessary for larger meetings.

- Identify the type of meeting (such as regular, weekly, annual, special, or executive).

- Identify the presiding officer.

- Record the action. When the meeting begins, key your notes to match numbered items (if any) on the agenda. If the discussion is "works in progress" and this subject is item *a* under *7. Unfinished Business,* key your notes *7a* and record the discussion. This relieves you of writing *7. Unfinished Business: a, works in progress.* When you type your notes, you simply refer to your agenda to transcribe the key *7a.*

- Record the time of adjournment.

Since the minutes serve as official records of meetings, it is imperative that they be objectively recorded and conscientiously transcribed into a final, formal document.

Drafts

Preparation. When you sit down at your computer or typewriter, you should have the following materials accessible:

- The agenda

- Your notes and recorded cassettes

- *Robert's Rules of Order* or a similar reference book on parliamentary procedure

- Any reports or other documents distributed at the meeting

- Verbatim copies of motions and resolutions

- The constitution or bylaws of the group (if applicable)

Format Guidelines. Prepare the draft according to these general guidelines. To determine the specific format, examine previous copies of the minutes in the files, and follow the format established for your organization.

- Double-space the draft, even if the final version will be single-spaced, so that handwritten corrections can be made between the lines.

- Number the pages consecutively at the top or bottom of the pages.

- Identify the meeting and date at the top of the page.

- Identify the participants (if no more than twenty) and the presiding officer in the first paragraph, and state when the meeting was called to order.

- Use subheads for different topics if warranted by the length and complexity of the document.

- Conclude with the time of adjournment.

- Assemble all attachments for inclusion with the final copy.

For more about document preparation, see Chapters 4 and 6.

Copy Distribution. It is good practice (and usually required) to present the presiding officer and the corporate secretary with a printout of the draft. If this is not feasible, present the draft to your supervisor before preparing the final copy. Either person will be able to help you find misinterpretations or extremely sensitive material that should not be published.

Final Copy   The final copy may be single- or double-spaced. Check copies of previous minutes for your organization's preferred style. The paper used also depends on precedent. Some groups have specially printed stationery for official minutes, while others use ordinary white bond paper.

Most minutes today, particularly those of an informal meeting, are written in a narrative style, and it is especially important that your summaries of the discussions succinctly express the scope of the conversations. See the illustration in this section for an example of the official minutes of an editorial scheduling meeting.

MEETING ARRANGEMENTS

The arrangements for an in-house staff or executive meeting are usually relatively simple. They may involve informally notifying participants, typing a brief agenda, reserving the company conference room or asking to use someone's office, and ordering coffee or other beverages and snacks (if any).

By contrast, the arrangements for a convention or other large off-site meeting are time-consuming and very complex, usually involving a team of planners and arrangers, each with a specific duty such as program development or speaker invitations. The secretaries to the members of the team must help to prepare and maintain records of schedules, deadlines, hotel and other arrangements, registrations, and anything else pertinent to the particular meeting.

With the appropriate word processing, calendar, and desktop publishing software, most of the planning and publishing activities can be handled within the company. For more information about handling such activities electronically, see Chapters 4 through 9.

Hotel Services

Setting up a formal meeting may be simple or complicated, depending on the nature of the event and the kind of planning you do. The easiest and most direct way to plan off-site meetings is to get in touch with the hotel, convention center, or other facility where the event will be held.

Get bids from at least three hotels based on the data in your list of advance information (see below) as well as any other information supplied by the meeting planners. The authorized committee can then decide which hotel is the most competitive.

Meeting Arrangement and Coordination Major domestic and foreign hotels and conference centers have individuals responsible for setting up and coordinating meeting arrangements. They are trained to suggest innovative arrangements and handle a myriad of details that

Minutes

Editorial Scheduling Meeting
ABC PUBLISHERS
October 16, 1995

Call to Order: The weekly editorial scheduling meeting of Friday, October 16, convened at 10 a.m. in the conference room. The presiding officer was Amanda Billings. Members of the staff present included Robert Desmond, Carl Edwards, Denise Jameson, Martha Nichols, and Philip Thompson. Roger Lochman was unable to attend.

Minutes: The minutes of the previous meeting, held on Monday, October 9, were read and accepted. There were no corrections or omissions.

Finances: Amanda Billings reported that the corporation is looking to the office products line to balance the shortfall in sales expected in the Secondary Education Division. She asked that everyone keep this goal in mind when ambitious schedules are established for new projects.

Robert Desmond informed the staff that he is preparing an analysis of the titles in progress in relation to their marketability, production costs, production schedules, and longevity. He requested that each editor submit a summary of costs to date for freelance services.

Billings requested that Desmond and Carl Edwards submit a preliminary budget for 1996 to her by December 1.

Production: Edwards emphasized the need for constant, even workflow so that both editorial and production functions will proceed efficiently. He will be free to meet with any editors who wish to discuss flow of manuscript to composition.

Scheduling: Billings reminded everyone that they must submit their appropriate sections of the formal publishing plans for the office products line to her by October 23.

Submissions: The staff voted to reject a manuscript entitled *Dictionaries: Friends or Foes?* that was circulated among them during September. The vote was unanimous.

Minutes, continued

Editorial Scheduling Meeting
October 16, 1995   2

Personnel: Denise Jameson raised the question again about when a new editor will be hired to replace Tom Westman. It was pointed out that because of the ambitious schedules and short-handed staff, this situation should be addressed as soon as possible.

Next Meeting: The next meeting of the editorial staff will be held on Friday, October 23.

Adjournment: The meeting was adjourned at 11:30 a.m.

_____

Secretary

_____

Presiding Officer

---

would overwhelm most sponsoring organizations. Nevertheless, some meetings may require that all arrangements be made by the sponsoring organization. Regardless of whether this is the case or whether the hotel or conference site representative does the coordinating, it is extremely important that all possible requirements be known well in advance of the event.

Advance Information

Information the Hotel Coordinator Will Need. Even when you use hotel services, some activities must be planned early so that you can tell the hotel coordinator the following essential things:

- The date(s) of the meeting
- The estimated number of participants and overnight room requirements
- The size of the meeting rooms and dining rooms needed
- The desired seating plans
- The meals (number, locations, times, and menus) required
- The special equipment required and in which rooms
- The nonbusiness events (tours, dances, and so on) that are planned
- The registration and information booth requirements
- The airport courtesy car requirements
- The security requirements
- Any other special needs

Deadlines. You must know well in advance the inclusive dates of the event, since sites are sometimes reserved years in advance. The number of participants also must be confirmed in advance, for this figure affects all other planning — the budget for the entire event, the number of hotel reservations required, the selection of conference and dining rooms, the type of seating, the group rates for meals, and so forth.

Determine with the hotel the final cutoff date for receipt of acceptances and changes in the list of participants and stick to it. Otherwise, chaos will ensue — rooms will not be available, the hotel staff will be upset, and participants arriving without reserved rooms will be angry.

Meeting Activity Sheet

COMPANY LETTERHEAD

TO:	International Hotel	DATE:	February 1, 1995

TO: International Hotel   DATE: February 1, 1995

FROM: Janice Sale   SUBJECT: Affiliates' Meeting
       Executive Assistant to
           Martin Miller   INCLUSIVE
       UBC TV Network   DATES: May 1–4, 1995
       45 Green Mountain Tower
       City, ST 98765
       123-555-7890

DAY-BY-DAY ACTIVITY CHART

Date	Time	Room	Activity	Setup	Attendees	Equip.	Meals
5/4	9:00 a.m.– noon	Blue	Ratings review	Panel plan seats for 200	200	1 dais mike, 25 aisle mikes, 4 video machines	
	10:30 a.m.– 10:45 a.m.	Red	Break	4 buffet tables	200		Fruit bowl, pastries, coffee, tea, milk, juice
	1:00 p.m.– 2:00 p.m.	Lilac	Lunch	20 round tables each seating 10 people	200		Vichyssoisse, veal roast, green salad, rolls, apple pie, coffee, tea, milk

Meeting Activity Sheet, continued

Continuation Page Letterhead

Date	Time	Room	Activity	Setup	Attendees	Equip.	Meals
	2:15 p.m.–5:00 p.m.	Sand	New programs	Same as 9–12	200		
	3:45 p.m.–4:00 p.m.	Red	Break	Same as 10:30–10:45	200		Cheese, crackers, coffee, tea, milk, juice
	6:00 p.m.–7:30 p.m.	White	Cocktail party	4 buffet tables, 4 open bars	200		See attached bar and hors d'oeuvres lists

Give the hotel representatives detailed information on a day-by-day chart showing exactly what is expected of them. Base your chart on the agenda that the executive has written for the meeting. See the illustration on pages 433–434 for a sample of one day's activities for a television affiliates meeting.

Conference Package

Mailing Arrangements   A detailed conference package, with a program and registration forms, must be mailed to all prospective participants in sufficient time for them to respond. For many meetings it is necessary to make the first mailing several months before the meeting date, especially if a bulk third-class postal mail or other relatively slow delivery method is used. Some meeting planners select a particular airline as the "official airline" for the conference, and in return the airline may fund or handle the mailing of the conference package.

What to Include   A conference package should include some or all of this information.

- Program
- Registration materials, including a return confirmation form, nametag, and meal tickets
- A map indicating the location of the meeting site
- Ground transportation data
- Information about hotel check-in and check-out times, room reservations and costs, meal plans, and payment procedures
- Description of planned entertainment and a summary of available activities and points of interest
- Activities available for spouses of meeting participants
- Description of available exercise and sports facilities
- List of doctors in the area
- Any other information a participant will need to know

Meeting Room

Seating Plans   Various seating plans should be studied in relation to the nature of the meeting and the number of participants. Is it a panel

Seating Plans for Meetings

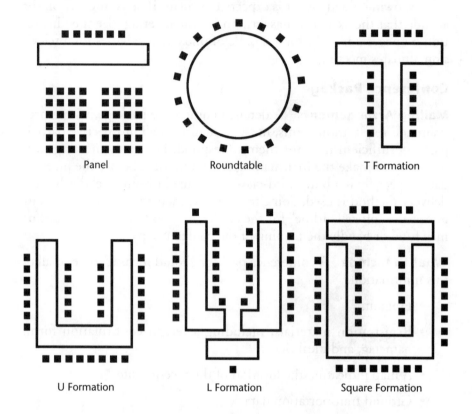

Panel   Roundtable   T Formation

U Formation   L Formation   Square Formation

discussion? A formal sales presentation? An informal brainstorming session? A meeting at which an important person will give a speech? The illustration above suggests possible seating plans.

Consider round tables for meals. Such tables allow for more relaxed conversation. The long rectangular tables of the T and U formations are more appropriate for formal gatherings, especially those during which video or slide shows are to be presented.

Supplies and Equipment   Ensure that all tables are covered, if appropriate, and set with water pitchers, glasses, pens, and writing pads. Ashtrays should be placed only in areas where smoking is permitted. If place cards are used, check them against your seating charts just before the meeting begins.

If audiovisual equipment, screens, flip charts and markers, slide projectors, lecterns, microphones, computers, recorders, or video machines are needed, give the hotel a list of these items and then ensure later that they are on hand in the right rooms at the right times. If you are using overhead projectors, you should find out the dimensions of the screens so that the people preparing the transparencies will tailor them to fit the equipment. If the hotel cannot supply all the equipment you need, check the yellow pages for equipment rentals. *Reconfirm* delivery of all rental equipment.

Refreshments Companies usually plan morning and afternoon breaks during meetings, and tables should be set up in appropriate places for them. For the morning break, usually lasting fifteen minutes, you may offer coffee, tea, juice, and milk as well as snacks. Ensure that decaffeinated coffee is available. Avoid serving only sweet rolls at the morning break. A large crystal bowl of melon balls mixed with various other fresh fruits is a welcome alternative or at least an interesting supplement to the rolls. Hot turnovers are also appealing. Consult with the hotel or an outside caterer for ideas.

Your Role at a Large Conference

Preconference Checks If you attend a large meeting, you will fulfill many responsibilities that are usual for an *expediter* or a *troubleshooter*. Devise checklists on which you have noted the particulars of the meeting plans for each day. Go to the meeting rooms and check the seating, the ventilation, the place cards, the positioning of the equipment, and the arrangements for morning and afternoon break refreshments. If other members of the conference team have this assignment, you may simply accompany them and offer assistance as needed.

Stay in contact with the hotel staff members assigned to your company's event, and work closely with them to resolve any last-minute problems. If registration is to take place the night before and early on the first official day of the meeting, be at the desk along with the other participants so that you can assist in getting the participants settled.

Speaker Presentations You may be asked to assist a speaker with a projector or other equipment during a presentation. Take time in advance to familiarize yourself with the equipment so that the presentation will run smoothly and professionally. If possible, rehearse the presentation at least once before it is given, especially if you are using a projector keyed to a running tape recorder. Be sure that all electrical cords are out of the way; speakers have been known to become entangled in such wiring and fall while walking back and forth during presentations.

Hospitality Suites   If the company has booked a hospitality suite for informal gatherings between events, request that the housekeeping staff clean and air the room at least one time, and preferably two times, during the day. Stale air and odors combine to create an unpleasant atmosphere for people who want to use the suite for telephone calls, small informal meetings, or simply relaxation.

Special Services   You may have to arrange for special secretarial or translation services. Discuss these problems with the hotel; if no help is forthcoming, check the yellow pages for temporary secretaries and for foreign-language translators or schools. Universities are also good sources for translators, as is the U.S. State Department, which maintains a list of qualified people to accompany foreign visitors on government-sponsored itineraries.

Special Security Requests   The meeting may feature someone from the private, political, governmental, or entertainment sector as a keynote speaker or performer. If so, talk to that person's staff and the hotel staff about any special security arrangements required.

Travel Arrangements   For information on making travel arrangements to attend meetings both within the country and in other countries, see Chapter 13.

INTERNATIONAL AND DOMESTIC TRAVEL

In many companies, a significant percentage of executive time is spent in travel, sometimes both domestic and foreign travel. Secretaries to executives who travel have additional responsibilities involving both travel arrangements and follow-up activities after the trip.

TRAVEL PREPARATIONS

Sources of Information

The information you need to make arrangements for a trip is available through a wide variety of sources from travel agents to transportation companies to printed and electronic guides. Of all the sources, though, none is as important as the travel agent.

Travel Agent Your company may have its own in-house travel department or travel officer, or you may use a commercial agency. If you are seeking outside services, look for an agent who is willing to spend time with you both to understand your business and to help you make the best possible arrangements. Don't hesitate to shop around and examine the agent's reputation by checking with other clients of the agent or even the Better Business Bureau.

Ask if the agent is a member of the American Society of Travel Agents (ASTA) and if he or she has a Certified Travel Counselor rating. Find out if the agency uses a modern computerized system and whether it specializes in business travel. Ask whether it can open a company account and if it will provide the type of account summaries your office requires, and ask if the agency charges for its services.

Make a list of the special services that you need, including unusual requests, and determine whether the agency can handle everything you need. Ask what kind of ongoing service will be provided, such as mileage-accumulation reporting and application for frequent-flier benefits. Even after you select an agent, continue to compare prices and services with other agents from time to time to be certain you are getting the best possible rates and service.

Transportation Companies   Although businesses make most or all travel arrangements through commercial travel agencies or in-house travel departments, you may still want to call airlines, Amtrak, or other transportation companies (use the toll-free 800 numbers) to find out something pertaining to a particular company or schedule. You can find the numbers of major airlines and other transportation companies (rail, ship, bus, car rental, and so on) in the yellow pages. Any numbers that you call frequently should be added to your electronic and print desk telephone list.

Electronic Systems   A number of electronic sources of information are available to users who have the right equipment. Your company may, for example, lease a computerized travel system that will display flight numbers and other travel information meeting the guidelines you specify: perhaps your boss travels only the first week of every month and prefers all flights to be between 6 P.M. and 1 A.M.

You can also subscribe to an electronic travel service in the same way that you subscribe to a shopping service or a financial service. With a modem and the right software you can access the service to receive flight schedules, hotel and restaurant information, and other data about travel. In some cases you can make reservations by computer and either pick up your ticket at the terminal or have it delivered. Some general database subscriber services also provide travel data along with numerous other types of information.

Printed Guides   Although printed guides cannot give you up-to-the-minute information, you may want to build a library of travel guides for general reference. For instance, you should have a travel guide for each city and country your boss regularly visits. Additionally, you may need road maps, hotel guides, and other local information available in guide books or through the chamber of commerce of each city.

Schedules and Timetables. Useful publications include the *Official Airline Guide* (OAG), which contains airline schedules and other information. A North American edition and a World edition are updated periodically. An electronic edition and a pocket print version are also available. The *Official Railway Guide*, a print edition, is similar except that it contains rail timetables for Amtrak and trains in Mexico and Canada, as well as information on commuter rail services in selected large cities. The *Thomas Cook Continental Timetable* (Europe) and the *Thomas Cook Overseas Timetable* have rail schedules for numerous other countries.

Hotel Guides. The *OAG Travel Planner Hotel and Motel Redbook*, published periodically, has information on hotels, airlines, car rental agencies, and railroads, with miscellaneous other data such as city and county maps and currency conversion rates. Examples of other books with information about hotels are the *Hotel and Travel Index* and the *Official Hotel and Resort Guide*. To examine any one of these publications before adding it to your company library, ask your travel agent and local reference librarian if they have copies available. Also visit a bookstore to view numerous travel guides and books on other countries.

Country Information. For a variety of information on other countries, consider both the books that are written about a particular country and the world fact books and guides that cover all countries, such as the *World Factbook, World Travel Guide*, and *Statesman Year-Book*, available in most library reference rooms. You can also subscribe to the State Department's *Background Notes* or the David M. Kennedy Center for International Studies' (Brigham Young University's) *Culturgrams*. Both are newsletter-style reports on major countries of the world.

Reservations

Even though most business reservations are made through a commercial travel agent or an in-house travel officer, you must always collect certain information that the agent will need.

- What is the destination?

- How many stopovers will there be and where?

- What means of transportation does the executive prefer (e.g., air, rail, car)?

- What time of day or night does the executive prefer to travel?

- What type of commuter connections does the executive prefer (e.g., bus shuttle, air shuttle)?

- What car rental or courtesy car service will the executive need?

- What type of hotel/motel accommodations does the executive prefer?

- What are the estimated arrival and departure dates and times?

- What travel documents are needed (if international trip)?

- How much luggage is allowed?

- What payment or billing method will the executive use?

- What is the currency exchange rate (for international trip)?

- What special requirements does the executive have (e.g., translator, telecommunications facilities, disabilities assistance)?

- What portable equipment and supplies will the executive want to take along?

Make a checklist and collect as much information as possible before you call or visit the travel agent. The agent may point out other information that he or she needs to make the most appropriate overall arrangements, including air and rail connections, ground transportation, and suitable hotel accommodations. If you make any portion of the arrangements yourself, such as car rental or hotel accommodations, coordinate the times, dates, and locations with the main portion of the trip being arranged by the travel agent.

What the Travel Agent Will Do   Most agents, depending on agency size and proximity to your office, will set up an account for billing purposes, will make all travel and travel-related arrangements, will deliver the tickets to your office or arrange for airport ticket pickup, and will assist you with international documentation such as visas and tourist cards. They also will provide itinerary sheets with day-by-day reservations and accommodations information.

Fares and Other Costs   Hotels offer a corporate rate to those who request it. Meals may or may not be included. They are included under the American plan, but only breakfast is included under the Continental plan. No meals are included under the European plan. Fares, too, can vary greatly depending on the day of the week, the time of day, the month of the year, the length of stay, the class of travel (e.g., first class), and the nature of the flight (one way or roundtrip).

Business travelers are often limited in flexibility as to travel time, and many companies require that personnel use a business, economy, or other discount class of travel. (Find out if snacks or meals are provided.) So your options regarding reservations may also be limited. The travel agency will provide all cost estimates for the arrangements it makes. For any other information you need, call the toll-free numbers of hotels and transportation companies.

Special Conveniences and Services

Many executives belong to airline clubs, which provide specially equipped lounges at major airports. There, passengers can have beverages and snacks, use the telephone, plug in a notebook computer or portable fax, and work while waiting for the flight to be announced.

Transportation and Accommodations Services Your boss may want to know whether telephones will be available on the airline or Amtrak train that is used. Many executives also need special electronic and telecommunications facilities at their hotels. Large hotels generally have the appropriate jacks as well as computer and fax equipment and services. Those that offer frequent-stay benefits often provide extra services for business travelers, including late check-outs and car rental discounts as well as room upgrades. Most hotels provide a wide range of other services, such as tour arrangements and reservations for theater performances.

Small Package Service When documents need to be shipped while an executive is traveling, you can use one of the overnight courier services described in Chapter 9. Most international passenger airlines also have a small package service whereby a package can be shipped on the next flight for a nominal fee. Special customs clearances are included, but the package must be picked up promptly at the destination. Inquire at the airline for further information.

Business Assistance

Throughout the world the traveler will rarely be too far from communication with an embassy or consulate where expert assistance in arranging local business contacts can be obtained. Many international cities also have U. S. Chamber of Commerce offices that can be helpful. Major sources of information in the United States include the U.S. Department of Commerce, U.S. Department of State, U.S. Small Business Administration, Export-Import Bank of the United States, Overseas Private Investment Corporation, and the U.S. Trade and Development Program. Ask your local reference librarian to direct you to current telephone numbers and addresses.

You can find information and guidance on business matters, such as the use of translators and interpreters, from the economic or commercial attaché of any United States embassy or consulate, special overseas trade office, or Chamber of Commerce office abroad. Most hotels can also help you make arrangements for special assistance, such as translation services. Many executives, however, prefer to have a company employee with this capability accompany them, rather than rely on a foreign translator who may not have the company's best interests in mind.

Packing and Luggage

Packing   Your travel agent or airline reservations office can provide up-to-date weather information and can offer suggestions about the type of clothing that will be needed at the destination. Printed and electronic guides also offer general climatic summaries, and the country profiles at the end of this chapter also provide brief climatic descriptions.

Some countries, such as those in the Middle East and parts of Africa, have very strict clothing requirements, especially for women. Study a guide to the area where the executive will be traveling for information about social and religious customs affecting attire. Your travel agent also may be able to advise you about the pertinent customs.

Some executives maintain a prepacked flight bag and overnight kit or, if this is not feasible, a series of packing lists — one for overnighters, another for two-or three-day trips, and still another for trips of four days or more. If you have not prepared such lists before, ask the executive to dictate the desired items, and be prepared to add your own suggestions. Prepacking or at least maintaining packing lists is a method that has been used for years by military personnel. It saves much time and last-minute rushing.

A prepacked travel briefcase is another way of expediting takeoff. Include in it things such as a copy of the itinerary, an appointment book, an address book, writing and mailing materials, notebook computer and supplies, dictation equipment with cassettes, a calculator, and miscellaneous supplies such as stamps, paper clips, and cellophane tape.

Travelers in other countries should remember that throughout Europe, the Mediterranean, and the Far East the standard electric current is generally 220 volts/50 hertz, and the plugs to appliances as well as the electrical outlets differ markedly from ours. Therefore, if an electric appliance such as a shaver or hair dryer is carried along, the executive should take a lightweight, all-purpose transformer and plug adapter, available at most department or hardware stores.

Luggage   Executives usually prefer luggage of a size and weight that can be carried on board the flight. Ask the travel agent or check with the airline for regulations concerning size, weight, and amount of carry-on luggage. With carry-on luggage, there is no need to wait at the baggage claim area upon arrival. If luggage is to be checked, the executive needs to allow additional time for airport check-in. Ask the travel agent or airline office about minimum check-in times. The travel agent or airline office also can tell you the maximum weight allowable and pieces that can be checked. This point applies especially to long trips or to trips in which the executive may have to transport special product samples in oversize bags.

Appointment Schedules and Itineraries

Appointment Schedule   A traveling executive needs a schedule of all appointments that have been arranged. Set up a tentative schedule with your computer, and continue to edit in changes until the last possible moment. Although you should use any format for the schedule that your boss prefers, appointment schedules are often prepared in table or list format, providing the following information:

Name, company, address, and telephone number
City and state or city and country
Date and time
Comments

If extensive comments or reminders are required concerning the appointments, you may want to have a separate sheet for each appointment or include only a couple appointments per page.

Appointment Schedule
October 9, 1995

Name, Co., Address, Phone No.: . . .

City, State, Country: . . .

Date and Time: . . .

Comments and Reminders: . . .

If the information for the various appointments is brief, you could set up four columns across the sheet and type in the appropriate data for all of the appointments under the column headings.

NAME, CO., ADDRESS, PHONE NO.	CITY, STATE, COUNTRY	DATE AND TIME	COMMENTS AND REMINDERS

It is always helpful to note on the appointment schedule the time differences, if any, so that the executive will know what time it is at the home office. If something should arise during a business meeting that warrants a telephone call, the executive can decide when to place the call.

If pertinent, use the "Comments and Reminders" space to include the name, address, and telephone number of the limousine service (if any); the name of the driver (if known); and the name, address, and telephone number of the place where the appointment will take place, if it differs from the contact's company address.

Host Data. The "Comments and Reminders" section can also be used to summarize notes about the person or company the executive will visit. Sometimes information can be obtained from business directories in your local library's reference room. Some information can be obtained from the person who originally set up or suggested the meeting. Another source of information is the international edition of *Who's Who.* If the host is a government official, the local consulate or embassy can usually provide appropriate personal background information. Having some knowledge of a foreign colleague's interests, social and religious customs, and family can be of great assistance in getting a meeting off to a pleasant, diplomatic start.

File Material. Some of the information the executive needs, such as a report or brochure, may be too extensive to summarize on the appointment schedule or on an itinerary. In that case you may want to collect the information that is needed and organize it by topic in individual file folders. When practical, make photocopies of file material and leave the original in the files. If more than two folders are used, color-code the labels to help the executive locate information quickly and easily.

Itinerary An itinerary is an essential document for the executive who travels. Frequently, the travel agent prepares the itinerary, which you can annotate if you have additional information that you would like to include. If you prepare the itinerary, set it up in your computer so that changes can be made at the last minute. Use column headings such as the following, and fill in the appropriate information below the headings. Include a footnote that explains whether all times that are listed are standard, daylight, or something else.

Date
Place of departure (city and terminal)
Departure time
Destination (city and terminal)
Arrival time
Type of transportation (plane, train, etc.)
Accommodation (flight, car, room number, etc.)
Meal/snack service
Car rental (type, agency, location, telephone)
Other ground transportation (shuttle bus, limousine, location, etc.)
Hotel (name, address, telephone)

Ask your boss if he or she would like any other information on the itinerary; if so, include it within these categories or additional categories.

INTERNATIONAL TRAVEL

The executive who travels in other countries must consider all of the things just mentioned in this chapter as well as a host of other matters, such as a passport, foreign currency, a language translator, and customs. The secretary's role becomes particularly important in helping the executive prepare for the international aspect of a trip. Because of the complexity of international travel, business travelers rarely attempt to make arrangements without the assistance of a travel agent.

Travel Documents

Passport A valid U.S. passport is needed when the executive is traveling in other countries. Although a few countries, such as Canada and Mexico, do not require it, almost all other countries do.

Passport applications should be presented in person to a clerk of a federal court, a state court authorized to naturalize aliens, an agent of the State Department, or a post office that has the authority to issue passports. If the executive already has a passport, it may be renewed by mail. To apply for a passport, a traveler must submit proof of citizenship, proof of identity, two photographs, and the required fee. The Superintendent of Documents offers a free booklet, *Your Trip Abroad,* which explains what travel documents are needed. If you have additional questions, ask your travel agent for assistance or inquire at the nearest passport office.

Visa and Tourist Card   Many countries require a visa or tourist card for entry. The visas are issued by the embassies and consulates of the various countries for a small fee or free of charge. Be certain to check with the appropriate consulate or embassy or with your travel agent to learn which visas or tourist cards are required for a particular trip. Regulations can change without notice. Since consulates are not located in all U.S. cities, allow sufficient time for securing the proper visa application forms, completing them, and applying by mail, especially if several visas are required. It is helpful to keep a current District of Columbia telephone book if the executive frequently travels in other countries. You can find the addresses and telephone numbers of all embassies in Washington in that directory. For addresses of overseas consular offices, ask your local reference librarian for directories that have this information, for example, the *Congressional Directory.* The Superintendent of Documents also sells a publication called *Key Officers of Foreign Service Posts.*

Health Documents and Medications   If the executive is taking special medication, he or she should carry enough of the medication for the duration of the trip, as well as a doctor's certificate verifying the need for the medication. The family physician can provide information relating to prescription refills in case of an emergency. It is a good idea to take along extra medication just in case a business trip lasts longer than expected or inclement weather or other circumstances delay the return schedule. Items such as passports, visas, and medication should never be packed in luggage that is to be checked, in case the luggage does not arrive on the same flight or is lost.

Under World Health Organization regulations many countries require that visitors be vaccinated against smallpox, cholera, and yellow fever. Although some vaccinations are not required by the World Health Organization, they may be recommended for the traveler's protection. Consult your local Public Health Service or your travel agent.

All vaccinations must be contained in a World Health Organization certificate, obtainable from the Public Health Service in your city.

Should the executive be concerned with the possibility of becoming ill during a foreign trip, you or the executive should contact Intermedic or the International Association for Medical Assistance to Travelers (IAMAT) before departure. Both organizations, located in New York City, publish international directories of English-speaking physicians.

International Driving Permit Executives who plan to rent a car while traveling in other countries must have a current international driving permit. Applications, available from the American Automobile Association and the American Automobile Touring Alliance, should be submitted along with a valid U.S. driver's license, two passport photos, and the required fee. Ask your travel agent for assistance if you have further questions.

Business Letters The executive may want to have individuals, banks, and other sources write letters of introduction, letters granting credit, or other letters that will be helpful while conducting business in other countries. The Department of Commerce has commercial and market information that may be helpful in deciding what type of introductory letters will be needed. Foreign commercial officers in U.S. embassies and consulates can also provide help with business introductions.

Currency

Foreign Currency Before leaving home, the executive will need some currency of the host country. Most banks maintain international departments and will exchange dollars for foreign currency. Thus upon arrival the executive does not have to wait at the airport for a bank to open or queue up to exchange currency. Taxis, buses, and trains are ready to depart for town and hotel or for connections to other cities away from the airport, and with local currency in hand the executive will have no delay in getting out of the airport area. Also, with local currency available upon arrival, the executive will have money for tipping porters and bellhops, taking transportation, and using pay telephones.

The bank, when exchanging dollars into foreign currency, will usually provide a guide on the foreign currency purchased, such as denominations and conversion rates. Conversion rates are based on the current buying rate and therefore fluctuate. One day's rate may be slightly more or less on another day. Conversion from dollars to local currency also can be accomplished after arrival at most major cities abroad. Banks and currency exchange booths are located in major airports throughout the world. However, banking hours vary in different countries. The executive should be prepared by having at least a small amount of foreign currency on hand before departing. Most hotels abroad can exchange dollars if necessary, but the conversion rate there may not be as attractive as it is in the United States since the hotels must pay a percentage to have dollars converted back into the local currency.

Additional Funds and Credit An executive should also have one or more company or personal credit cards and an appropriate supply of traveler's checks. These checks can be purchased from banks or from issuers such as American Express Company. They are available in various denominations from as little as $10 to as much as several thousand dollars. For additional funds a letter of credit can be purchased from a bank, usually in an amount of $1,000 or more, on which the traveler can draw at foreign banks.

Language

Translators and Interpreters Although English is widely used around the world for business dealings, the executive who knows the language in other countries has an advantage. Even the use of a few common words and phrases will please the hosts. Unless the executive is fluent in the other language, however, a translator or interpreter will be needed, and these arrangements should be made before the executive leaves the United States, as described earlier. The U.S. embassy or consulate in the host country is often a more reliable source of assistance in finding outside translators than a hotel or other foreign source. In addition, the executive should have a foreign language dictionary and phrase book for each country as well as a pocket electronic foreign dictionary.

Language Courses If the company plans major commitments to a given country or area of the world, the executive may be required to take a language course. Adult education language classes are offered by most universities, colleges, and high schools in the evenings and on weekends. Private and semiprivate classes are available through most language schools, which are advertised in the yellow pages. Self-teaching cassettes and records are also available, as is private instruction from tutors. The amount of international corporate involvement will determine the amount of fluency required; but learning a foreign language is never a wasted talent, and most executives believe it will serve them well.

Assisting the Executive   You can help in many ways by finding sources of information on language (books, tapes, schools, and so on), by locating advertisements of electronic and print phrase dictionaries, and also by learning something of the language along with the executive. In addition, you will probably be required to order a supply of business cards for the executive for the trip. The information on each card should also be printed in the language of the host country on the *reverse* side of the card. Find a printer who is able to handle foreign language material.

Security

Security is a concern for any traveler both in the United States and in other countries. Most potential problems, however, can be avoided if commonsense precautions are taken.

Established Patterns   Established patterns or routines are the greatest threats to personal security and safety. Hence a regular route and time of travel should not be followed. Frequent changes of direction, travel time, and mode of transportation, coordinated within an overall protection plan, will make it more difficult for a potential abductor or attacker to plan an ambush or interception.

Release of Travel Information   One of the most important things to remember is *not* to announce travel plans. Keep all such arrangements confidential. For instance, travel information concerning the executive or the executive's family should not be released to the media. Information for the local newspapers (top executives and their families are newsworthy) can be carried after the *return* from a trip. Press releases with photographs and travel details could create unnecessary exposure and should be evaluated very carefully. Telephone calls, mail, or personal inquiries from unknown sources or persons seeking travel information or personal data about the executive and the family should be refused.

Hotel Reservations   Whenever possible, especially in the case of high-level executives of multinational organizations, bookings for hotels, rental cars, limousines, or chauffeur services should be made in the name of the manager of the local office in the host country, in the company name only, or in a name other than the executive's (perhaps in the name of an associate traveling with the executive). This procedure will preclude unnecessary interest on the part of unknown people in the travel plans and whereabouts of the executive.

Executive-Staff Cooperation   An important safeguard is encouraged by clear and open communication between the executive and the secretary and other staff members. Arrangements and agreements between the executive, the secretary, and other staff should be made with a view toward ensuring that everyone is continually aware of *all* itineraries, changes in itineraries (regardless of when any changes are made), and arrival times, destinations, departure times, excursions, and so forth. The more you know about where an executive should be at any time, the easier it will be for you to recognize that something is wrong if the executive is long overdue.

Transportation   Upon arrival at a destination terminal, travelers sometimes fail to check whether taxis have identification numbers and shuttle drivers have valid identification. A traveler should not hesitate to ask for identification if any doubts exist. When possible, passengers also should verify the fare before leaving.

Mass transit in some countries is faster than taxis and shuttles, but it can be dangerous at night. When using mass transit, travelers should avoid shoulder bags that can easily be pulled off; instead, carry tokens or fare cards in a secure pocket. Especially, executives should avoid displayed identification that would reveal where they are staying.

Luggage Identification Tags   Airline regulations require that personal identification be carried on the outside of all checked luggage in the event that the luggage is misdirected at some point during the journey. Top executives should not put luggage tags bearing a residence address or even an office address on their luggage. No one besides the family and close associates needs to know that the executive is going on a trip.

For travel identification, executives should use one of the many commercial identification tags that bear only a name and an identification number. Some of the private clubs maintained by the airlines issue special luggage tags with a name (initials only rather than first names) and the traveler's identification number. If the luggage is misdirected en route and is subsequently found, the airline locating the luggage will contact the other airline's office whose luggage identification tags are on the suitcases to determine how to reroute or return them. Special tags are also issued by various credit card companies. These companies follow the same basic procedures with regard to the data on the tags. The offices issuing the cards maintain the utmost security concerning their clients.

If the executive has to have an address on the identification tag, it is recommended that the corporate address be used, but not the company name or executive title. Also, tags with a lift-up cover will help to hide the traveler's name and address.

Accommodations   Travelers should take certain precautions in their hotels and the surrounding area. Before taking a drive or walk, for example, it is a good idea to ask the concierge if and where it is safe to be out alone. Even in recommended areas, the visitor needs to be alert to anyone who might be following and to pickpockets and thieves that run or drive past, snatching purses and packages before the traveler realizes what has happened. Important documents should be kept in the hotel safe and only photocopies carried in pockets or purses. Items that are taken along in a car should be locked in the trunk, and a well-lit parking area should be selected.

Travel guides recommend that guests register using only initials and ask for two keys, which suggests that the guest isn't alone. Speak in terms of *we*: "We prefer a nonsmoking room." Refuse rooms by an exit or elevator, but also avoid rooms in a sparsely populated wing. Test all locks, and be certain the emergency exit is *un*locked; take the room key with you when you go out. Above all, don't hesitate to express concerns or ask hotel personnel for assistance.

Foreign Political Atmosphere   Evaluate the political atmosphere of a foreign government and the mood of its populace as they relate to Americans or American enterprise. If political or economic unrest is evident, confer with the government's foreign affairs office or with our State Department before departure. You can access the State Department's traveler information by telephone (202-647-5252) or fax (202-647-3000).

Suggest that the executive check in with foreign governmental representatives upon arrival. When possible, give the U.S. embassy or consulate in the host country a copy of the executive's itinerary, at least on a per-city basis. Take the advice of the embassy or consulate personnel about any special security procedures.

For each country on the executive's itinerary, prepare a list of phrases in the local language, such as "I need the police (or doctor, telephone, ambulance, hospital, U.S. embassy, and so on)." Include *numerals* in the host country's language on the same list. For instance, 1, 2, 3, 4, and so forth are fine in most countries, but Egypt, China, Japan, and most Middle Eastern countries have different numeral systems.

Prepare instructions on the use of local pay telephones; telephone services in many countries are not the same as services in the United States. The local consulate of the country being visited or the United States embassy or consulate there will be of valuable assistance in this regard. Also, remind the executive to keep a supply of local currency in coins for use with the pay telephones.

Customs

Executives who travel to other countries should be aware of the customs regulations covering purchases brought back to the United States. Some items that the executive takes along also may have to be declared before entering the destination country.

Ask your travel agent for detailed information, and contact the nearest U.S. Customs office for current information. Request a free copy of *Know Before You Go, Customs Hints for Returning U.S. Residents*. Travel guides also may have Customs information for the countries covered in the guides.

TRIP FOLLOW-UP

Meet with the executive and go over the itinerary sheet as soon as possible after the trip is over. Having kept a copy of the itinerary and having made pertinent notes as the executive has called in during the trip, your own follow-up tasks now should be easier.

Expense Reports

No doubt the executive will have made notes on the itinerary regarding expenses. If additional currency exchanges took place while the executive was traveling, the rates will usually differ, either from day to day or from city to city. This factor will affect the bottom line of the expense reports. In converting foreign currency to dollars, use the currency conversion rate that was charged.

Remember to take into consideration tips for porters at airports and hotels and doormen at hotels and clubs. Any cash paid out as tips should be noted. If you remind the executive about the tips, other cash expenses that are not supported by receipts may come to mind at the same time.

If payment for hotels, meals, or limousines was made with a major credit card, it is advisable to complete as much of the expense report as possible and hold it, pending receipt of the credit card charges. (The credit card accounting office converts the foreign currency to dollars for billing.) If your company prefers that all expenses be submitted immediately upon return, always mention in the expense report that a supplemental expense record will follow as soon as all credit card billings have been received.

Follow-up Correspondence

While going over the itinerary with the executive after the trip, request all business cards that the executive has received during the course of the trip. Add the names, addresses, corporate titles, and telephone numbers of the card bearers to the executive's electronic and print address lists. During the review, make a note of any letters of appreciation that should be written. Were any special arrangements made by a host, such as limousine transportation, flowers or fruit baskets in the hotel room, dinners at the host's home or at a club or restaurant, or special tours? A short note of thanks will suffice.

Dear Mr. Giraud:

My sincere thanks for the courtesies you extended to me during my recent visit to Paris. The welcome that I received from your fine staff on check-in made me feel at home. It was especially thoughtful of you to provide the excellent bottle of wine, which made the long journey much less tiring.

The kindness of your personnel was greatly appreciated, and I am looking forward to returning to Paris soon.

Sincerely yours,

Martin I. Benson

President

If the executive called in during the trip, review any notes made during the conversations. Will some time elapse before plans or agreements made abroad can be put into final form? If so, a note to this effect is called for, thereby reassuring the foreign business colleague that although some work still may be pending, the arrangements discussed are nevertheless proceeding.

Dear Mr. Johnson:

Thank you again for spending time with me on Thursday, January 19, to discuss our proposal. I have given the information and changes to our legal staff for incorporation into the final analysis. As soon as these changes have been approved by the Board, I will write to you again.

The many courtesies and kindnesses that were extended to me during our discussions were greatly appreciated. Thank you very much.

Sincerely yours,

Martin I. Benson

President

For more about preparing correspondence, refer to Chapter 5.

Written Reports

While reviewing the itinerary, take the opportunity to type all notes or comments made by the executive. Prepare these notes immediately for the executive's review, together with a list of all business cards received. The executive will then have raw travel data in a readable, well-organized format for reference in writing any posttrip reports.

As soon as the executive has given you the full information for the posttrip report, prepare a draft for editing, additions, and other changes. Chapter 6 provides formatting and preparation guidelines for business reports, and Chapter 11 provides a guide to proper business style.

COUNTRY PROFILES

In a global economy, secretaries need to become more familiar with the different countries and regions of the world that their employers visit. Toward this end, the profiles that are presented here list the following information for nearly two hundred countries:

Official name
Capital
Nationality
Language
Religion
Currency
Location
General holidays
Religious holidays

Some countries, such as Tajikistan, are newly emerging republics, and others, such as Bosnia, are in political and economic turmoil. Information in such cases should be considered tentative, often incomplete, and subject to change. Some of the new democracies, for example, are planning to issue their own currencies and in time will develop their own general and religious holidays. Even in many stable, established countries, occasional social, political, and economic change should be expected.

Some of the following information varies from year to year. Certain national and other general holidays, for example, may be observed on different days each year. The dates for religious holidays vary so extensively, in fact, that they are not given in the country profiles. The dates for general holidays, however, are given, since variations are usually minor. But in all cases the data in these profiles should be used as a *general* guide. Any specific facts should be confirmed through an appropriate source, such as a U.S. embassy, before making firm travel plans based on them.

Afghanistan, Republic of
Capital: Kabul
Nationality: Afghan(s)
Language: Pashto (majority), Dari, Persian, Turki, other
Religion: Sunni Muslim (majority), Shiite Muslim, Hindu, Jewish, Christian
Currency: afghani (Af) = 100 puls
Location: Southwest Asia
General Holidays: Apr. 27, Revolution Day; May 1, Workers' Day; Aug. 19, Independence Day
Religious Holidays: Leilat al-Meiraj, Eid al-Fitr, Eid al-Adha, Ashoura, Prophet's Birthday

Albania, Republic of
Capital: Tirana
Nationality: Albanian(s)
Language: Albanian (official: Tusk dialect), Greek

Religion: Sunni Muslim (majority), Greek Orthodox, Roman Catholic
Currency: lek (ALL) = 100 quindars
Location: Southeast Europe
General Holidays: Jan. 1, New Year's Day; Jan. 11, Proclamation of Republic; May 1, Labor Day; Nov. 28, Independence Day; Nov. 29, Liberation Day

Algeria, People's Democratic Republic of

Capital: Algiers
Nationality: Algerian(s)
Language: Arabic (official), French, Berber dialects, English in major business centers
Religion: Sunni Muslim
Currency: Algerian dinar (DZD) = 100 centimes
Location: North Africa
General Holidays: Jan. 1, New Year's Day; May 1, Labor Day; Jul. 5, Independence Day; Nov. 1, Anniv. of Outbreak of Revolution
Religious Holidays: Id al-Fitr, Id al-Adha, Islamic New Year, Ashoura, Mawlid an-Nabi

Andorra, Principality of

Capital: Andorra la Vella
Nationality: Andorran(s)
Language: Catalan (official), French, Spanish
Religion: Roman Catholic
Currency: franc (FFr) = 100 centimes; peseta (Pta) = 100 céntimos
Location: Southwest Europe
General Holidays: Jan. 1, New Year's Day; Sep. 8, National Day; Dec. 31, New Year's Eve
Religious Holidays: Epiphany, Good Friday, Easter, Easter Monday, Christmas Day

Angola, People's Republic of

Capital: Luanda
Nationality: Angolan(s)
Language: Portuguese (official), Bantu
Religion: Animist (majority), Roman Catholic, Protestant
Currency: kwanza (AKZ) = 100 lwei
Location: Southwest Africa
General Holidays: Feb. 4, MPLA Anniversary; Aug. 1, Angolan Armed Forces Day; Sep. 17, Day of National Hero; Nov. 11, Independence Day; Dec. 10, Anniv. of Founding of MPLA; Dec. 25, Family Day

Antigua and Barbuda

Capital: St. John's
Nationality: Antiguan(s)

Language: English
Religion: Anglican (majority), Roman Catholic, other Christian
Currency: East Caribbean dollar (EC$) = 100 cents
Location: East Caribbean Sea
General Holidays: Jan. 1, New Year's Day; May (varies), Labor Day; Jul. 1,
    Caricom Day; Aug. 3-4, Carnival; Nov. 1, Independence Day
Religious Holidays: Good Friday, Easter Monday, Whit Monday, Christmas Day

Argentina (Argentine Republic)

Capital: Buenos Aires
Nationality: Argentine(s)
Language: Spanish (official), English, German, French, Italian
Religion: Roman Catholic
Currency: peso (ARP), formerly austral (ARA) = 100 centavos
Location: Southeast South America
General Holidays: Jan. 1, New Year's Day; May 1, Labor Day; May 25, National
    Day; Jun. (varies), Assertion Day of Argentinian Rights; Jun. (varies), Flag
    Day; Jul. 9, Independence Day; Aug. 17, San Martín's Death; Sep. 21,
    Student Day; Oct. 12, Discovery of America Day
Religious Holidays: Maundy Thursday, Good Friday, Feast of Immaculate
    Conception, Christmas Day

Armenia, Republic of

Capital: Yerevan
Nationality: Armenian(s)
Language: Armenian (official), Russian, Kurdish, Azerbaijani, English, German
Religion: Armenian Apostolic, Russian Orthodox, Protestant, Muslim
Currency: ruble (Rub) = 100 kopeks (new currency to be introduced)
Location: Between Europe and Asia

Australia, Commonwealth of

Capital: Canberra
Nationality: Australian(s)
Language: English
Religion: Protestant/Anglican, Roman Catholic, other
Currency: Australian dollar (A$) = 100 cents
Location: Indian and Pacific Oceans
General Holidays: Jan. 1, New Year's Day; Jan. 26, Australia Day; Apr. 25,
    ANZAC Day; Jun. (varies), Queen's Birthday
Religious Holidays: Good Friday, Easter Monday, Christmas Day, Boxing Day

Austria, Republic of

Capital: Vienna
Nationality: Austrian(s)

Language: German; English required in schools
Religion: Roman Catholic
Currency: Austrian schilling (Sch) = 100 groschen
Location: West-central Europe
General Holidays: Jan. 1, New Year's Day; May 1, Labor Day; Oct. 26, National Day
Religious Holidays: Epiphany, Easter, Easter Monday, Ascension Day, Whit Monday, Corpus Christi, Assumption, All Saints' Day, Immaculate Conception, Christmas Day, St. Stephen's Day

Azerbaijan, Republic of
Capital: Baku
Nationality: Azerbaijani(s) or Azeri(s)
Language: Azerbaijani (official), Russian, Armenian, Turkish, local dialects
Religion: Shiite Muslim (majority), Sunni Muslim, Russian Orthodox, Armenian Apostolic
Currency: manat
Location: Between Europe and Asia
General Holidays: May 28, Independence Day

Bahamas, Commonwealth of the
Capital: Nassau
Nationality: Bahamian(s)
Language: English
Religion: Baptist, Anglican, Roman Catholic, other
Currency: Bahamian dollar (Ba$) = 100 cents
Location: Caribbean Sea
General Holidays: Jan. 1, New Year's Day; Jun. (1st Fri.), Labor Day; Jul. 10, Independence Day; Aug. (1st Mon.), Emancipation Day; Oct. 12, Discovery Day
Religious Holidays: Good Friday, Easter Monday, Whit Monday, Christmas Day

Bahrain, State of
Capital: Manama
Nationality: Bahraini(s)
Language: Arabic (official), English, Farsi, Urdu
Religion: Sunni Muslim (majority), Shiite Muslim, Christian, Baha'i, Hindu, Parsee
Currency: Bahraini dinar (BHD) = 1,000 fils
Location: Middle East
General Holidays: Dec. 16, National Day
Religious Holidays: Prophet's Birthday, Eid al-Fitr, Eid al-Adha, Islamic New Year, Ashoura

Bangladesh, People's Republic of
Capital: Dhaka
Nationality: Bangladeshi(s)
Language: Bangla (official), English
Religion: Muslim (majority), Hindu, Buddhist, Christian
Currency: taka (BDT) = 100 poishas
Location: South Asia
General Holidays: Feb. 21, Martyrs' Day; Mar. 26, Independence Day; Apr. 15, Bengali New Year's Day; May 1, May Day; Nov. 7, National Integrity Day; Dec. 16, Victory Day
Religious Holidays: Christmas Day, Eid ul-Fitr, Eid ul-Azha, Muharram, Eid-i-Milad-un-Nabi

Barbados
Capital: Bridgetown
Nationality: Barbadian(s)
Language: English (official), local Bajan Creole
Religion: Anglican (majority), Methodist, Roman Catholic
Currency: Barbados dollar (BBD) = 100 cents
Location: Caribbean Sea
General Holidays: Jan. 1, New Year's Day; Jan. 21, Errol Barrow Day; May 1, Labor Day; Aug. (varies), Kadooment Day; Oct. (varies), United Nations Day; Nov. 30, Independence Day
Religious Holidays: Good Friday, Easter Monday, Whit Monday, Christmas Day, Boxing Day

Belarus, Republic of
Capital: Minsk
Nationality: Belarussian(s)
Language: Belarussian (official), Russian, Polish, Eastern Slavonic
Religion: Roman Catholic, Eastern Orthodox, Muslim, Jewish
Currency: taler
Location: Northeast Europe
General Holidays: Jul. 27, Independence Day

Belgium, Kingdom of
Capital: Brussels
Nationality: Belgian(s)
Language: Flemish (official, over 50 percent) and French (official, about 30 percent), German
Religion: Roman Catholic (majority), Protestant, Jewish
Currency: Belgian franc (BFr) = 100 centimes
Location: Northwest Europe
General Holidays: Jan. 1, New Year's Day; May 1, May Day; Jul. 21, Independence Day; Nov. 11, Armistice Day; Nov. 15, King's Birthday

Religious Holidays: Easter Monday, Ascension Day, Whit Monday, Assumption, All Saints' Day, Christmas Day, Boxing Day

Belize
Capital: Belmopan
Nationality: Belizean(s)
Language: English (official), Spanish, Maya, Carib
Religion: Roman Catholic (majority), Protestant
Currency: Belizean dollar (B$) = 100 cents
Location: Northeast Central America
General Holidays: Jan. 1, New Year's Day; Mar. 9, Baron Bliss Day; May 1, Labor Day; May 24, Commonwealth Day; Sep. 10, National Day; Sep. 21, Independence Day; Oct. 13, Pan American Day; Nov. 19, Garifuna Day
Religious Holidays: Good Friday, Holy Saturday, Easter Monday, Christmas Day, Boxing Day

Benin, Republic of
Capital: Porto Novo
Nationality: Beninese
Language: French (official), English, Bariba, Fulani, Fon, Yoruba
Religion: Animist (majority), Roman Catholic, Muslim
Currency: CFA franc (CFA Fr) = 100 centimes
Location: West Africa
General Holidays: Jan. 1, New Year's Day; Jan. 16, Martyrs' Day; May 1, Workers' Day; Oct. 26, Armed Forces Day; Nov. 30, National Day; Dec. 31, Harvest Day
Religious Holidays: Good Friday, Easter Monday, Eid al-Fitr, Ascension Day, Whit Monday, Tabaski (Eid al-Adha), Assumption, All Saints' Day, Christmas Day

Bhutan, Kingdom of
Capital: Thimphu
Nationality: Bhutanese
Language: Dzongkha (official), Sharchop Kha, Nepalese, English
Religion: Buddhist (majority), Hindu
Currency: Ngultrum (Re) = 100 chetrums
Location: South Asia
General Holidays: Nov. 11, Birthday of Jigme Singye Wangchuk; Dec. 17, National Day of Bhutan
Religious Holidays: Wesak/Buddha Day, Thimphu Tsechu

Bolivia, Republic of
Capital: Sucre
Nationality: Bolivian(s)
Language: Spanish (official), Quechua, Aymara, English
Religion: Roman Catholic (majority), Protestant

Currency: boliviano (B$) = 100 centavos
Location: Central South America
General Holidays: Jan. 1, New Year's Day; (varies), Carnival; Mar. 23, Dia del Mar (Sea Day); Mar. 19, Father's Day; May 1, Labor Day; May 27, Mother's Day; Aug. 6, Independence Day
Religious Holidays: Good Friday, Corpus Christi, All Saints'/All Souls' Day, Christmas Day

Bosnia-Herzegovina (Republic of Bosnia and Herzegovina)
Capital: Sarajevo
Nationality: Bosnian(s) and Herzegovine(s)
Language: Serbo-Croatian
Religion: Eastern Orthodox, Roman Catholic, Muslim
Currency: dinar (D) = 100 para
Location: Southeast Europe

Botswana, Republic of
Capital: Gaborone
Nationality: Motswana (sing.) Batswana (pl.)
Language: English (official), Setswana
Religion: Christian, indigenous
Currency: pula (Pu) = 100 thebes
Location: South-central Africa
General Holidays: Jan. 2, New Year's Day; Jul. 16, President's Day; Sep. 30, Botswana Day
Religious Holidays: Good Friday, Easter Monday, Ascension Day, Christmas Day, Boxing Day

Brazil, Federative Republic of
Capital: Brasília
Nationality: Brazilian(s)
Language: Portuguese (official), French, German, Italian, English
Religion: Roman Catholic
Currency: cruzeiro (Cr) = 100 centavos
Location: Northeast-central South America
General Holidays: Jan. 1, New Year's Day; Jan. 20, Foundation of Rio de Janeiro; Jan. 25, Foundation of São Paolo; Feb. (varies), Carnival; Apr. 21, Tiradentes Day; May 1, Labor Day; Sep. 7, Independence Day; Nov. 15, Proclamation of Republic
Religious Holidays: Easter, Ascension Day, Corpus Christi, Nossa Senhora de Aparecida, All Souls' Day, Christmas Day

Brunei Darussalam, State of
Capital: Bandar Seri Begawan
Nationality: Bruneian(s)
Language: Malay (official), Chinese, English

Religion: Muslim (official; mostly Sunni), Christian, Buddhist, Confucian
Currency: Brunei dollar (Br$) = 100 cents
Location: Southeast Asia
General Holidays: Jan. 1, New Year's Day; (varies), Chinese New Year; May 1,
    Anniv. of Royal Brunei Regiment; Jul. 15, Sultan's Birthday
Religious Holidays: Anniv. of Revelation of Koran, Hari Raya Puasa, Eid al-Fitr,
    Hari Raya Haji, Feast of Sacrifice, Eid al-Adh, Muslim New Year, Mouloud
    (Prophet's Birthday), Christmas Day

Bulgaria, Republic of

Capital: Sofia
Nationality: Bulgarian(s)
Language: Bulgarian (official), Turkish, Macedonian, Russian, French, German,
    English
Religion: Bulgarian (Eastern) Orthodox (majority), Muslim, Roman Catholic,
    Protestant, Jewish, Gregorian-Armenian
Currency: lev (Lv) = 100 stotinki
Location: Southeast Europe
General Holidays: Jan. 1, New Year's Day; Mar. 3, Liberation Day; May 1, Labor
    Day; May 24, Education Day; Sep. 9, National Day
Religious Holidays: Orthodox Easter, Christmas Day

Burkina Faso

Capital: Ouagadougou
Nationality: Burkinabe
Language: French (official), tribal languages
Religion: Animist (majority), Muslim, Roman Catholic
Currency: CFA franc (CFA Fr) = 100 centimes
Location: West Africa
General Holidays: Jan. 1, New Year's Day; May 1, Labor Day; Aug. 4, National
    Day
Religious Holidays: Eid al-Fitr, Easter Monday, Ascension Day, Whit Monday,
    Eid al-Adha, Assumption, Mouloud (Prophet's Birthday), All Saints' Day
    (Toussaint), Christmas Day

Burundi, Republic of

Capital: Bujumbura
Nationality: Burundian(s)
Language: French (official), Kirundi, Swahili
Religion: Roman Catholic (majority), Protestant, animist
Currency: Burundi franc (BurFr) = 100 centimes
Location: Central Africa
General Holidays: Jan. 1, New Year's Day; Feb. 5, Unity Day; May 1, Labor Day;
    Jul. 1, Independence Day; Sep. 3, Anniv. of Third Republic; Sep. 18,
    Victory Day (UPRONA)

Religious Holidays: Easter Monday, Ascension Day, Assumption, All Saints' Day, Christmas Day

Cambodia, State of
Capital: Phnom Penh
Nationality: Cambodian(s) (Kampuchean[s])
Language: Khmer (official), French, Chinese, Vietnamese
Religion: Theravada Buddhist (majority), Muslim, Christian
Currency: riel (CRI) = 100 sen
Location: Southeast Asia
General Holidays: Jan. 7, Liberation of Phnom Penh; Apr. 17, Victory over American Imperialism Day; May 1, Labor Day; May 20, Day of Hatred; Sep. 22, Feast of Ancestors; Nov. (varies), Full Moon Water Festival
Religious Holidays: Buddhist New Year

Cameroon, Republic of
Capital: Yaoundé
Nationality: Cameroonian(s)
Language: French and English (official), numerous local African languages
Religion: Animist, Christian, Muslim
Currency: CFA franc (CFA Fr) = 100 centimes
Location: West-central Africa
General Holidays: Jan. 1, New Year's Day; Feb. 11, Youth Day; May 1, Labor Day; May 20, National Day; Jun. 11, Festival of Sheep
Religious Holidays: Good Friday, Easter Monday, Eid al-Fitr, Ascension Day, Eid al-Adha, Assumption, Christmas Day

Canada
Capital: Ottawa
Nationality: Canadian(s)
Language: English, French
Religion: Roman Catholic (majority), United Church, Anglican, other
Currency: Canadian dollar (Can$) = 100 cents
Location: Northern North America
General Holidays: Jan. 1, New Year's Day; May (varies), Victoria Day; Jul. 1, Canada Day; Sep. 7, Labor Day; Oct. (varies), Thanksgiving Day; Nov. 11, Remembrance Day
Religious Holidays: Good Friday, Easter Monday, Christmas Day, Boxing Day

Cape Verde, Republic of
Capital: Praia
Nationality: Cape Verdean(s)
Language: Portuguese (official), Criuolo, English, French
Religion: Roman Catholic (majority), Protestant
Currency: Cape Verde escudo (CVE) = 100 centavos

Location: Atlantic Ocean off North and West Africa
General Holidays: Jan. 1, New Year's Day; Jan. 20, National Heroes' Day; Mar. 8, Women's Day; May 1, Labor Day; Jun. 1, Children's Day; Jul. 5, Independence Day; Sep. 12, Day of Nation
Religious Holidays: Christmas Day

Central African Republic
Capital: Bangui
Nationality: Central African(s)
Language: French (official), Sangho, Arabic, Hansa, Swahili
Religion: Animist, Muslim, Christian
Currency: CFA franc (CFA Fr) = 100 centimes
Location: Central Africa
General Holidays: Jan. 1, New Year's Day; Mar. 29, Anniv. of Death of Barthélemy Boganda; May 1, Labor Day; Jun. 30, National Day of Prayer; Aug. 13, Independence Day; Dec. 1, National Day
Religious Holidays: Easter Monday, Ascension Day, Whit Monday, Assumption, All Saints' Day, Christmas Day

Chad, Republic of
Capital: N'djaména
Nationality: Chadian(s)
Language: French and Arabic (official), Chadian Arabic, Sara, numerous tribal languages
Religion: Muslim, animist, Christian
Currency: CFA franc (CFA Fr) = 100 centimes
Location: North-central Africa
General Holidays: Jan. 1, New Year's Day; May 1, Labor Day; May 25, Liberation of Africa Day; May 25, Anniv. of OAU's Foundation; Aug. 11, Independence Day; Nov. 28, Proclamation of Republic; Dec. 1, Victory of Deby over Habré Day
Religious Holidays: Eid al-Fitr, Easter Monday, Whit Monday, Eid al-Adha, Assumption, Mouloud (Prophet's Birthday), All Saints' Day, Christmas Day

Chile, Republic of
Capital: Santiago
Nationality: Chilean(s)
Language: Spanish (official), English
Religion: Roman Catholic (majority), Protestant
Currency: Chilean peso (Ch$) = 100 centavos
Location: Southwest South America
General Holidays: Jan. 1, New Year's Day; May 1, Labor Day; May 21, Navy Day; Sep. 18, Independence Day; Sep. 19, Army Day; Oct. 12, Columbus Day

Religious Holidays: Good Friday, Easter Saturday, Corpus Christi, St. Peter and St. Paul's Day, Assumption, All Saints' Day, Immaculate Conception, Christmas Day

China, People's Republic of
Capital: Beijing
Nationality: Chinese
Language: Mandarin Chinese (official), Chinese, local dialects
Religion: (officially atheist), Buddhist (majority), Taoist, Confucian, Protestant, Roman Catholic
Currency: yuan (¥) = 10 jiao/mao or 100 fen
Location: East Asia
General Holidays: Jan. 1, New Year's Day; Jan./Feb. (varies), Chinese New Year; Mar. 8, International Working Women's Day; Apr. 4–6, Quing Ming Festival; Jul. 1, Founding of Communist Party of China; Aug. 1, Army Day; Oct. 1–2, National Days

Colombia, Republic of
Capital: Bogotá
Nationality: Colombian(s)
Language: Spanish (official), English, local Indian dialects
Religion: Roman Catholic (majority), Jewish, Protestant
Currency: Colombian peso (Col$) = 100 centavos
Location: Northwest South America
General Holidays: Jan. 1, New Year's Day; May 1, Labor Day; Jul. 20, Independence Day; Aug. 7, Battle of Boyacá; Oct. 12, Columbus Day; Nov. 14, Independence of Cartagena
Religious Holidays: Epiphany, St. Joseph's Day, Holy Thursday, Good Friday, Ascension Day, Corpus Christi, Feast of Sacred Heart, Saints Peter and Paul, Assumption, All Saints' Day, Feast of Immaculate Conception, Christmas Day

Comoros, Federal Islamic Republic of the
Capital: Moroni
Nationality: Comoran(s)
Language: French and Arabic (official), Comoran (blend of Arabic and Swahili), Shaafi Muslim, Malagasu
Religion: Sunni Muslim (majority), Roman Catholic
Currency: Comoran franc (CFA Fr) = 100 centimes
Location: Indian Ocean
General Holidays: Jul. 6, Independence Day; Nov. 27, Anniv. of Pres. Abdallah's Assassination
Religious Holidays: Leilat al-Meiraj, Eid al-Fitr, Eid al-Adha, Muslim New Year, Ashoura, Mouloud (Prophet's Birthday)

Congo, Republic of the
Capital: Brazzaville
Nationality: Congolese
Language: French (official), Lingala, Kikongo, other
Religion: Animist (majority), Roman Catholic, Protestant, Muslim
Currency: CFA franc (CFA Fr) = 100 centimes
Location: West Africa
General Holidays: Jan. 1, New Year's Day; Feb. 5, Général Denis Sassou-Ngeusso
    Day; Mar. 6, National Tree Day; Mar. 8, Women's Day; Mar. 18, Anniv.
    of Marien Ngouabi's Death; May 1, Labor Day; Jun. 22, Birthday of
    Popular Army; Jul. 31, Revolution Day; Aug. 13–14, Anniv. of Aug. 1963
    Revolution; Aug. 15, Independence Day; Dec. 25, Children's Day; Dec. 31,
    Foundation Day
Religious Holidays: Good Friday, Easter Monday, Christmas Day

Costa Rica, Republic of
Capital: San José
Nationality: Costa Rican(s)
Language: Spanish (official), English
Religion: Roman Catholic
Currency: Costa Rican colón (CRC) = 100 centimos
Location: Central America
General Holidays: Jan. 1, New Year's Day; May 1, Labor Day; Jul. 25, Annexation
    of Guanacaste; Sep. 15, Independence Day; Oct. 12, Columbus Day;
    Dec. 1, Abolition of Armed Forces
Religious Holidays: Maundy Thursday, Good Friday, Ascension Day, Corpus
    Christi, St. Peter and St. Paul's Day, Virgin of Los Angeles, Assumption,
    Feast of Immaculate Conception, Christmas Day

Croatia, Republic of
Capital: Zagreb
Nationality: Croatian(s)
Language: Serbo-Croatian
Religion: Roman Catholic
Currency: Croatian dinar (D) = 100 para
Location: Southeast Europe
General Holidays: May 30, Independence Day

Cuba, Republic of
Capital: Havana
Nationality: Cuban(s)
Language: Spanish (majority), French, English
Religion: Roman Catholic
Currency: Cuban peso (Cub$) = 100 centavos

Location: Northwest Caribbean Sea
General Holidays: Jan. 1, Liberation Day; May 1, Labor Day; Jul. 25–27, Revolution Day; Oct. 10, Wars of Independence Day

Cyprus, Republic of
Capital: Nicosia
Nationality: Cypriot(s)
Language: Greek (majority), Turkish, English, German, French
Religion: Greek Orthodox (majority), Muslim, Maronite Latin
Currency: Cyprus pound (C£) = 100 cents
Location: East Mediterranean Sea
General Holidays: Jan. 1, New Year's Day; Apr. 1, Greek-Cypriot Independence Day; May 1, May Day; Jun. 15, Kataklysmos; Oct. 1, Cyprus Independence Day; Oct. 28, Greek Independence Day
Religious Holidays: Epiphany, Good Friday, Easter, Assumption, Christmas Day

Czech Republic
Capital: Prague
Nationality: Czech(s)
Language: Czech (official), Slovak, Hungarian, Romany, Russian, German, English
Religion: Roman Catholic (majority), Protestant, Orthodox, other
Currency: koruna (Kcs) = 100 haler(u)
Location: Central Europe
General Holidays: Jan. 1, New Year's Day; May 1, Labor Day; May 8, National Liberation Day; Jul. 5, National Day; Oct. 28, Independence Day
Religious Holidays: Easter Monday, St. Cyril and St. Methodius Day, Christmas Day

Denmark, Kingdom of
Capital: Copenhagen
Nationality: Dane(s)
Language: Danish (official), Faroese, Greenlandic, German, French, English
Religion: Evangelical Lutheran (majority), Roman Catholic
Currency: Danish krone (DKr) = 100 øre
Location: North Europe
General Holidays: Jan. 1, New Year's Day; Apr. 16, Queen Margrethe's Birthday; May 15, General Prayer Day; Jul. 5, Constitution Day
Religious Holidays: Maundy Thursday, Good Friday, Easter Monday, Ascension Day, Whit Monday, Christmas Day

Djibouti, Republic of
Capital: Djibouti
Nationality: Djiboutian

Language: Arabic and French (official), Afar, Somali, English
Religion: Muslim (majority), Roman Catholic, Protestant, Greek Orthodox
Currency: Djibouti franc (DjFr) = 100 centimes
Location: Northeast Africa
General Holidays: Jan. 1, New Year's Day; May 1, Workers' Day; Jun. 27,
    Independence Day
Religious Holidays: Eid al-Fitr, Eid al-Adha, Islamic New Year, Prophet's Birthday,
    Christmas Day

Dominica, Commonwealth of
Capital: Rosean
Nationality: Dominican(s)
Language: English (official), French patois, Creole French, Cocoy
Religion: Roman Catholic (majority), Anglican, Methodist
Currency: East Caribbean dollar (EC$) = 100 cents
Location: East Caribbean Sea
General Holidays: Jan. 1, New Year's Day; Feb./Mar. (varies), Masquerade
    Carnival; May 1, May Day; Nov. 4, Independence Celebrations; Nov. 5,
    Community Service Day
Religious Holidays: Good Friday, Easter Monday, Whit Monday, Christmas Day,
    Boxing Day

Dominican Republic
Capital: Santo Domingo
Nationality: Dominican(s)
Language: Spanish (official), English
Religion: Roman Catholic (majority), Protestant, Jewish
Currency: Dominica peso (RD$) = 100 centavos
Location: Caribbean Sea
General Holidays: Jan. 1, New Year's Day; Jan. 21, La Altagracia; Jan. 26, Duarte's
    Birthday; Feb. 27, Independence Day; Apr. 14, Pan-American Day; May 1,
    Labor Day; Jul. 16, Foundation of Sociedad de la Trinitaria; Aug. 16,
    Restoration Day; Sep. 24, Las Mercedes; Oct. 12, Columbus Day; Oct. 24,
    United Nations Day
Religious Holidays: Epiphany, Good Friday, Corpus Christi, All Saints' Day,
    Christmas Day

Ecuador, Republic of
Capital: Quito
Nationality: Ecuadorian(s)
Language: Spanish (official), Quechua, other Indian dialects
Religion: Roman Catholic
Currency: sucre (Su) = 100 centavos
Location: Northwest South America
General Holidays: Jan. 1, New Year's Day; May 1, Labor Day; May 24, Anniv.
    of Battle of Pichincha; Jul. 24, Anniv. of Birth of Simón Bolívar; Aug. 10,

Independence Day; Oct. 9, Anniv. of Independence of Guayaquil; Oct. 12,
Día de la Raza; Nov. 3, Anniv. of Independence of Cuenca; Dec. 6,
Foundation of Quito
Religious Holidays: Good Friday, Easter Saturday, Christmas Day

Egypt, Arab Republic of
Capital: Cairo (El Qahira)
Nationality: Egyptian(s)
Language: Arabic (official), English, French
Religion: Muslim (majority; mostly Sunni), Coptic church, other Christian
Currency: Egyptian pound (E£) = 100 piastres
Location: Northeast Africa
General Holidays: Jan. 1, New Year's Day; Apr. 25, Sinai Liberation Day; May 1,
Workers' Day; Jun. 18, Evacuation Day; Jul. 23, Revolution Day; Oct. 6,
Army Forces Day; Dec. 23, Victory Day
Religious Holidays: Leilat al-Meraj (Ascension of Mohammed), Eid al-Fitr, 1st
Bairam, Sham el-Nassim (Coptic Easter Monday), Eid al-Adha, 2nd Bairam,
Islamic New Year, Prophet's Birthday

El Salvador, Republic of
Capital: San Salvador
Nationality: Salvadoran(s)
Language: Spanish (official), Nahua, English
Religion: Roman Catholic (majority), other Christian
Currency: colón (ES$) = 100 centavos
Location: Western Central America
General Holidays: Jan. 1, New Year's Day; May 1, Labor Day; Jun. 22,
School Teachers' Day; Jun. 29–30, Bank Holiday (banks only);
Aug. 1–6, August Festivities (banks and commerce, Aug. 3-6); Sep. 15,
Independence Day; Oct. 12, Columbus Day; Nov. 5, First Call for
Independence
Religious Holidays: Easter, Corpus Christi, All Souls' Day, Christmas Day

Equatorial Guinea, Republic of
Capital: Malabo
Nationality: Equatorial Guinean(s)
Language: Spanish (official), pidgin English, Fang, Bubi, other African
dialects
Religion: Roman Catholic (majority), animist
Currency: CFA franc (CFA Fr) = 100 centimes
Location: West Africa
General Holidays: Jan. 1, New Year's Day; May 1, International Labor Day;
Jun. 5, President's Birthday; Aug. 3, Armed Forces Day; Aug. 15,
Constitution Day; Oct. 12, Independence Day
Religious Holidays: Good Friday, Corpus Christi, Immaculate Conception,
Christmas Day

Estonia, Republic of
Capital: Tallinn
Nationality: Estonian(s)
Language: Estonian (official), Russian, English, German, Finnish
Religion: Protestant (majority; mostly Lutheran), Orthodox
Currency: ruble (Rub) = 100 kopeks, to be replaced with kroon
Location: Northeast Europe
General Holidays: Jan. 1, New Year's Day; May 1, May Day
Religious Holidays: Good Friday, Easter Monday, Christmas Day

Ethiopia, People's Democratic Republic of
Capital: Addis Ababa
Nationality: Ethiopian(s)
Language: Amharic (official), English, Arabic, Tigrinya, Orominga
Religion: Muslim, Ethiopian Orthodox, Coptic, animist
Currency: Ethiopian birr (ETB) = 100 cents
Location: Northeast Africa
General Holidays: Mar. 2, Battle of Adowa Day; Apr. 6, Victory Day;
    May 1, May Day; Sep. 11, New Year's Day (Julian 1984); Sep. 12,
    Revolution Day
Religious Holidays: Christmas Day, Epiphany, Eid al-Fitr, Easter Monday
    (Christian), Palm Monday (Coptic church), Eid al-Adha, Mouloud
    (Prophet's Birthday), Feast of Masgel (Coptic)

Fiji, Republic of
Capital: Suva
Nationality: Fijian(s)
Language: English (official), Fijian, Hindustani
Religion: Methodist, Hindu, Roman Catholic, Muslim
Currency: Fiji dollar (F$) = 100 cents
Location: Western South Pacific Ocean
General Holidays: Jan. 1, New Year's Day; Jun. 11, Queen's Birthday;
    Jul. 30, Bank Holiday; Oct. 8, Independence Day; Nov. 12, Prince of
    Wales Birthday
Religious Holidays: Good Friday, Easter Monday, Prophet's Birthday, Diwali,
    Christmas Day

Finland, Republic of
Capital: Helsinki
Nationality: Finn(s)
Language: Finnish (majority) and Swedish (both official), Lapp, English
Religion: Evangelical Lutheran (majority), Eastern Orthodox, other Christian,
    Jewish, Muslim
Currency: markka (F Mk) = 100 penni(a)
Location: North Europe

General Holidays: Jan 1, New Year's Day; Apr. 30–May 1, May Day Eve and May Day; Jun. 19–20, Midsummer's Eve and Day; Dec. 6, Independence Day
Religious Holidays: Epiphany, Good Friday, Easter, Ascension Day, Whitsun, All Saints' Day, Christmas Eve, Christmas Day, Boxing Day

France (French Republic)
Capital: Paris
Nationality: Frenchman, Frenchwoman
Language: French (official), English, regional dialects
Religion: Roman Catholic (majority), Protestant, Jewish, Muslim
Currency: franc (FFr) = 100 centimes
Location: West Europe
General Holidays: Jan. 1, New Year's Day; May 1, Labor Day; May 8, VE (Victory in Europe) Day; Jul. 14, Bastille Day; Nov. 11, Remembrance Day
Religious Holidays: Easter Monday, Ascension Day, Whit Monday, Assumption, All Saints' Day, Christmas Day

Gabon (Gabonese Republic)
Capital: Libreville
Nationality: Gabonese
Language: French (official), Fang, Myene, Bateke, Bapounou, Eschira, Bandjabi
Religion: Christian (majority), Muslim, animist
Currency: CFA franc (CFA Fr) = 100 centimes
Location: West Africa
General Holidays: Aug. 17, Independence Day
Religious Holidays: Major Islamic, Major Christian

The Gambia, Republic of
Capital: Banjul
Nationality: Gambian(s)
Language: English (official), Mandinka, Fulu, Wollof, Jola, Serahule
Religion: Muslim (majority), Christian, animist
Currency: Gambian dalasi (Di) = 100 bututs
Location: West Africa
General Holidays: Jan. 1, New Year's Day; Feb. 18, Independence Day; May 1, Labor Day
Religious Holidays: Eid al-Fitr, Easter, Eid al-Adha, Assumption, Mouloud (Prophet's Birthday), Christmas Day

Georgia, Republic of
Capital: Tbilisi
Nationality: Georgian(s)
Language: Georgian (official), Russian, Armenian, ethnic languages
Religion: Georgian Orthodox, Muslim, Jewish
Currency: ruble (Rub) = 100 kopeks (new currency to be introduced)

Location: Between Europe and Asia
General Holidays: Apr. 9, Independence Day

Germany, Federal Republic of

Capital: Berlin (seat of government: Bonn)
Nationality: German(s)
Language: German (official), Sorbian, English, French
Religion: Protestant, Roman Catholic
Currency: deutsche mark (DM) = 100 pfennigs
Location: West-central Europe
General Holidays: Jan. 1, New Year's Day; May 1, Labor Day; Oct. 3, Day of Unity; Nov. 18, Day of Prayer and Repentance
Religious Holidays: Epiphany, Easter, Ascension Day, Whit Monday, Corpus Christi, Assumption, All Saints' Day, Christmas Day

Ghana, Republic of

Capital: Accra
Nationality: Ghanaian
Language: English (official), Akan, Moshi-Dagomba, Ewe, Ga, Fante, Twi
Religion: Christian, Muslim, indigenous beliefs
Currency: cedi (C) = 100 pesewas
Location: West Africa
General Holidays: Jan. 1, New Year's Day; Mar. 6, Independence Day; May 1, May Day; Jun. 4, Anniv. of 1979 Uprising; Jul. 1, Republic Day; Dec. 31, Revolution Day
Religious Holidays: Good Friday, Easter Monday, Christmas Day

Greece (Hellenic Republic)

Capital: Athens
Nationality: Greek(s)
Language: Greek (official), English, French, German, Italian, Turkish
Religion: Greek Orthodox (majority), Muslim, Roman Catholic
Currency: drachma (Dr) = 100 leptae
Location: Southeast Europe
General Holidays: Jan. 1, New Year's Day; Mar. 25, Independence Day; May 1, Labor Day; Oct. 28, Ochi Day
Religious Holidays: Epiphany, Orthodox Easter, Day of Holy Spirit, Assumption, Christmas Eve, Christmas Day, St. Stephen's Day

Grenada

Capital: St. George's
Nationality: Grenadian(s)
Language: English (official), French patois
Religion: Roman Catholic (majority), Anglican, Protestant
Currency: East Caribbean dollar (EC$) = 100 cents
Location: Southeast Caribbean Sea

General Holidays: Jan. 1, New Year's Day; Feb. 7, Independence Day; May 1, Labor Day; Aug. 3–4, Emancipation Day; Aug. 7–11, Carnival; Oct. 25, Thanksgiving Day
Religious Holidays: Easter, Whit Monday, Corpus Christi, Christmas Day

Guatemala, Republic of
Capital: Guatemala City
Nationality: Guatemalan(s)
Language: Spanish (official), English, Indian dialects
Religion: Roman Catholic (majority), Protestant, Mayan
Currency: quetzal (Q) = 100 centavos
Location: Central America
General Holidays: Jan. 1, New Year's Day; May 1, Labor Day; Jun. 30, Anniv. of Revolution; Sep. 15, Independence Day; Oct. 12, Columbus Day; Oct. 20, Revolution Day; Dec. 31, New Year's Eve
Religious Holidays: Epiphany, Easter, Assumption (Guatemala City only), All Saints' Day, Christmas Eve, Christmas Day

Guinea, Republic of
Capital: Conakry
Nationality: Guinean(s)
Language: French (official), Susu, Malinke, Fula
Religion: Muslim (majority), Christian, animist
Currency: Guinea franc (FG)
Location: West Africa
General Holidays: Jan. 1, New Year's Day; Apr. 3, Anniv. of Second Republic; May 1, Labor Day; Oct. 2, Independence Day; Nov. 1, Armed Forces Day
Religious Holidays: Assumption, End of Ramadan Feast, Tabaski, Christmas Day

Guinea-Bissau, Republic of
Capital: Bissau
Nationality: Guinea-Bissauan(s)
Language: Portuguese (official), Creole, French, African languages
Religion: Animist (majority), Muslim, Christian
Currency: peso (GBP) = 100 centavos
Location: Northwest Africa
General Holidays: Jan. 1, New Year's Day; Jan. 20, National Hero's Day; Mar. 8, Women's Day; May 1, Labor Day; Aug. 3, Martyrs of Colonialism Day; Sep. 24, Independence Day; Nov. 14, Readjustment Day
Religious Holidays: Eid al-Fitr/Korité, Eid al-Adha/Tabaski, Christmas Day

Guyana, Co-operative Republic of
Capital: Georgetown
Nationality: Guyanese
Language: English (official), Hindi, Urdu, Amerindian
Religion: Christian (majority), Hindu, Muslim

Currency: Guyana dollar (Guy$) = 100 cents
Location: Northeast South America
General Holidays: Jan. 1, New Year's Day; Feb. 23, Republic Day; May 1, Labor Day; Jul. 5, Caribbean Day; Aug. 1, Freedom Day
Religious Holidays: Youman Nabi, Phagwah, Good Friday, Easter Monday, Eid al Alzha, Divali, Christmas Day, Boxing Day

Haiti, Republic of
Capital: Port-au-Prince
Nationality: Haitian(s)
Language: French (official), Creole, French patois
Religion: Roman Catholic (majority; with voodoo influence), Protestant
Currency: gourde (Gde) = 100 centimes
Location: Caribbean Sea
General Holidays: Jan. 1, New Year's Day; Jan. 2, Heroes of Independence Day; Apr. 14, Pan-American Day; May 1, Agricultural and Labor Day; May 18, Flag Day; May 22, National Sovereignty Day; Oct. 24, United Nations Day; Nov. 18, Army Day; Dec. 5, Discovery Day
Religious Holidays: Shrove Monday and Tuesday, Good Friday, Assumption, All Souls' Day, Christmas Day

Honduras, Republic of
Capital: Tegucigalpa
Nationality: Honduran(s)
Language: Spanish (official), English, Indian dialects
Religion: Roman Catholic (majority), Mormon, Evangelist
Currency: lempira (L) = 100 centavos
Location: Central America
General Holidays: Jan. 1, New Year's Day; Apr. 14, Day of Americas; May 1, Labor Day; Jun. 11, Day of Student; Sep. 15, Independence Day; Oct. 3, Birth of General Morazán; Oct. 12, Discovery of America Day; Oct. 21, Armed Forces Day; Dec. 31, New Year's Eve
Religious Holidays: Maundy Thursday, Good Friday, Christmas Day

Hungary (Hungarian Republic)
Capital: Budapest
Nationality: Hungarian(s)
Language: Hungarian (official: Magyar), German, French, English
Religion: Roman Catholic (majority), Protestant, Eastern Orthodox, Jewish
Currency: forint (Ft) = 100 fillér
Location: East-central Europe
General Holidays: Jan. 1, New Year's Day; Mar. 15, Anniv. of 1848 uprising against Austrian rule; May 1, Labor Day; Aug. 20, Constitution Day; Oct. 23, Proclamation Day of Republic
Religious Holidays: Easter, Christmas Day

Iceland, Republic of
Capital: Reykjavík
Nationality: Icelander(s)
Language: Icelandic (official), Danish, English
Religion: Evangelical Lutheran (majority), other Protestant, Roman Catholic
Currency: Icelandic krona (IKr) = 100 aurar
Location: Atlantic Ocean near Arctic Circle
General Holidays: Jan. 1, New Year's Day; Apr. (varies), First Day of Summer; May 1, Labor Day; Jun. 17, National Day; Aug. (varies), Merchants Holiday; Dec. 31, New Year's Eve
Religious Holidays: Maundy Thursday, Good Friday, Easter Monday, Ascension Day, Whit Monday, Christmas Day

India, Republic of
Capital: New Delhi
Nationality: Indian(s)
Language: Hindi and fourteen other official languages, English, other
Religion: Hindu (majority), Muslim, Sikh, Christian, Buddhist
Currency: rupee (RS) = 100 paise
Location: Indian and Asian subcontinent
General Holidays: Jan. 1, New Year's Day; Jan. 26, Republic Day; Aug. 15, Independence Day; Oct. 2, Mahatma Gandhi's Birthday; Nov. 10, Guru Nannak's Birthday
Religious Holidays: Eid al-Fitr, Good Friday, Mahabir Jayanti, Buddha Purnima, Eid uz-Zuha, Muharram (Islamic New Year), Dussehra, Diwali, Christmas Day

Indonesia, Republic of
Capital: Jakarta (Java)
Nationality: Indonesian(s)
Language: Bahasa Indonesia (official), Dutch, English, numerous local dialects
Religion: Muslim (majority), Protestant, Roman Catholic, Hindu
Currency: rupiah (Rp) = 100 sen
Location: Between Southeast Asia and Australia
General Holidays: Jan. 1, New Year's Day; Aug. 17, Independence Day
Religious Holidays: Eid al-Fitr, Good Friday, Ascension Day, Waisak Day, Eid al-Adha, Islamic New Year, Mouloud (Prophet's Birthday), Christmas Day

Iran, Islamic Republic of
Capital: Tehran
Nationality: Iranian(s)
Language: Persian (official: Farsi), Arabic, Turkish, English, French, German
Religion: Muslim (official; mostly Shiite), Christian, Jewish, Zoroastrian, Baha'i
Currency: Iranian rial (RL) = 1/10 toman (1 toman = 10 rial)
Location: West Asia and the Middle East

General Holidays: Feb. 11, National Day (Fall of Shah); Mar. 20, Oil National-
ization Day; Mar. 21–24, Ruz (Iranian New Year); Apr. 1, Islamic Republic
Day; Apr. 2, Revolution Day

Religious Holidays: Leilat al-Meiraj, Eid al-Fitr, Birthday of Twelfth Imam, Eid
al-Adha, Ashoura, Martyrdom of Imam Ali, Mouloud (Prophet's Birthday)

Iraq, Republic of

Capital: Baghdad
Nationality: Iraqi(s)
Language: Arabic (official), Kurdish (official in Kurdish areas), Assyrian,
Armenian
Religion: Muslim (majority; mostly Shiite), Christian, Druze
Currency: Iraqi dinar (ID) = 20 dirhams = 1,000 fils
Location: West Asia and the Middle East
General Holidays: Jan. 1, New Year's Day; Jan. 6, Army Day; Jul. 14,
Republic Day
Religious Holidays: Leilat al-Meiraj, Eid al-Fitr, Eid al-Adha, Muslim New Year,
Ashoura, Mouloud (Prophet's Birthday)

Ireland, Republic of

Capital: Dublin
Nationality: Irishman, Irishwoman (sing.), Irish (pl.)
Language: Irish (Gaelic) and English (both official)
Religion: Roman Catholic (majority), Protestant, Anglican
Currency: Irish pound (IR£) = 100 pence (penny)
Location: North Atlantic Ocean
General Holidays: Jan. 1, New Year's Day; Jun., Aug., Oct. (Mondays), Bank
holidays
Religious Holidays: St. Patrick's Day, Good Friday, Easter Monday, Christmas
Day, St. Stephen's Day

Israel, State of

Capital: Jerusalem
Nationality: Israeli(s)
Language: Hebrew and Arabic (official), English, French, Spanish, German,
Yiddish, Polish, Hungarian, Russian
Religion: Jewish (majority), Muslim (mostly Sunni), Christian, Druze
Currency: New Israel shekel (NIS) = 100 agorot (sing. agora)
Location: West Asia
General Holidays: Feb. 6, Arbor Day; May 7, Independence Day
Religious Holidays: National Day of Remembrance, Shabbat, Rosh Hashana
Tishri, Yom Kippur Tishri, Succot Tishri, Simhat Torah Tishri, Hanukka
Kislev 25-Tevet, Tu B'Shevat Shevat, Purim Adar, Pessah Nissan,
Independence Day Iyar, Lag Ba'Omer Iyar, Jerusalem Liberation Day Iyar,
Shavu'ot Sivan, Tisha B'Av Av

Italy (Italian Republic)
Capital: Rome
Nationality: Italian(s)
Language: Italian (official), German, French, Slovenian, English
Religion: Roman Catholic (majority), Protestant
Currency: Italian lira (Lit) = 100 centisimi
Location: West and South Europe
General Holidays: Jan. 1, New Year's Day; Apr. 25, Liberation Day;
    May 1, Labor Day; May 12, Festival of Tricolor; Nov. 5, National
    Unity Day
Religious Holidays: Epiphany, Easter Monday, Assumption, All Saints' Day,
    Immaculate Conception, Christmas Day, St. Stephen's Day

Ivory Coast (Côte d'Ivoire), Republic of the
Capital: Abidjan
Nationality: Ivorian(s)
Language: French (official), Dioula, Baoule, other African languages
Religion: Indigenous (majority), Muslim, Christian
Currency: CFA franc (CFA Fr) = 100 centimes
Location: West Africa
General Holidays: Jan. 1, New Year's Day; May 1, Labor Day; Nov. 15, Peace
    Day; Dec. 7, National Day
Religious Holidays: Eid al-Fitr, Easter Monday, Ascension Day, Whit Monday,
    Eid al-Adha, Assumption, All Saints' Day, Christmas Day

Jamaica
Capital: Kingston
Nationality: Jamaican(s)
Language: English (official), French patois, Creole
Religion: Protestant (majority), Roman Catholic, Jewish, Muslim, Hindu,
    Baha'i
Currency: Jamaican dollar (J$) = 100 cents
Location: North Caribbean Sea
General Holidays: Jan. 1, New Year's Day; May 25, Labor Day; Aug. 3,
    Independence Day; Oct. 19, National Heroes' Day
Religious Holidays: Ash Wednesday, Good Friday, Easter Monday, Christmas Day,
    Boxing Day

Japan
Capital: Tokyo
Nationality: Japanese
Language: Japanese (official), some English in large urban areas
Religion: Shintoist and Buddhist (majority), Christian
Currency: Japanese yen (¥) = 100 sen
Location: West Pacific Ocean

General Holidays: Jan. 1, New Year's Day; Jan. 15, Coming of Age Day; Feb. 11, National Foundation Day; Mar. (varies), Vernal Equinox; Apr. 29, Greenery Day; May 3, Constitution Memorial Day; May 5, Children's Day; Sep. 15, Respect for Aged Day; Sep. (varies), Autumn Equinox; Oct. 10, Health and Sports Day; Nov. 3, Culture Day; Nov. 23, Labor Thanksgiving Day; Dec. 23, Birthday of Emperor

Jordan, Hashemite Kingdom of

Capital: Amman
Nationality: Jordanian(s)
Language: Arabic (official), English, French
Religion: Sunni Muslim (majority), Shiite Muslim, Christian
Currency: Jordan dinar (JD) = 1,000 fils
Location: West Asia and the Middle East
General Holidays: Jan. 1, New Year's Day; Jan. 15, Arbor Day; Mar. 22, Arab League Day; May 1, Labor Day; May 25, Independence Day; Jun. 10, Arab Revolt and Army Day; Aug. 11, Accession of King Hussein; Nov. 14, King Hussein's Birthday
Religious Holidays: Leilat al-Meiraj, Easter, Eid al-Fitr, Eid al-Adha, Islamic New Year, Mouloud (Prophet's Birthday), Christmas Day

Kazakhstan, Republic of

Capital: Alma-Ata
Nationality: Kazakh(s)
Language: Kazakh (official), Russian, Uighur, regional dialects
Religion: Sunni Muslim, Eastern Orthodox
Currency: ruble (Rub) = 100 kopeks (new currency to be introduced)
Location: Central Asia
General Holidays: Dec. 16, Day of the Republic

Kenya, Republic of

Capital: Nairobi
Nationality: Kenyan(s)
Language: Swahili and English (official), Kikuyu, Luo, other indigenous languages
Religion: Protestant, Roman Catholic, Muslim, indigenous beliefs
Currency: Kenyan shilling (KSh) = 100 cents
Location: East Africa
General Holidays: Jan. 1, New Year's Day; May 1, Labor Day; Jun. 1, Madaraka Day (birth of republic); Oct. 20, Kenyatta Day; Dec. 12, Independence Day
Religious Holidays: Eid al-Fitr, Good Friday, Easter Monday, Eid al-Adha, Christmas Day, Boxing Day

Kirghizia (Kyrgyzstan), Republic of

Capital: Frunze
Nationality: Kirghiz (Kyrgyz)

Language: Kirghizian (official), Russian, ethnic languages
Religion: Sunni Muslim
Currency: ruble (Rub) = 100 kopeks (new currency to be introduced)
Location: Central Asia
General Holidays: Aug. 31, Independence Day

Kiribati, Republic of
Capital: Tarawa
Nationality: Kiribatian(s)
Language: English and Swahili (both official), Kiribati, Gilbertese
Religion: Roman Catholic, Protestant, Baha'i, Seventh-Day Adventist
Currency: Australian dollar (A$) = 100 cents
Location: Central Pacific Ocean
General Holidays: Jan. 1, New Year's Day; Jul. 12, Independence Day; Aug. 4, Youth Day
Religious Holidays: Easter, Christmas Day

Korea (North) (Democratic People's Republic of Korea)
Capital: Pyongyang
Nationality: Korean(s)
Language: Korean
Religion: (no official religion), Buddhist, Confucian, Christian, Chundo Kyo
Currency: won (NKW) = 100 chon
Location: East Asia
General Holidays: Jan. 1, New Year's Day; Feb. 16, Kim Jong Il's Birthday; Mar. 8, International Women's Day; Apr. 15, Kim Il Sung's Birthday; May 1, May Day; Aug. 15, Liberation Day; Sep. 9, Independence Day; Oct. 10, Korean Workers' Party Day; Dec. 27, Constitution Day

Korea (South) (Republic of Korea)
Capital: Seoul
Nationality: Korean(s)
Language: Korean (official), English
Religion: Mahayana Buddhist, Confucian, Daoist, Chundo Kyo, Christian, folk religions
Currency: won (SKW) = 10 hwan = 100 chun
Location: East Asia
General Holidays: Jan. 1–2, New Year; Feb. (varies), Folklore Day; Mar. 1, Independence Movement Day; Apr. 5, Arbor Day; May 5, Children's Day; Jun. 6, Memorial Day; Jul. 17, Constitution Day; Aug. 15, Liberation Day; Sep. 10–12, Thanksgiving Day; Oct. 3, National Foundation Day
Religious Holidays: Buddha's Birthday, Christmas Day

Kuwait, State of
Capital: Kuwait City
Nationality: Kuwaiti(s)
Language: Arabic (official), English
Religion: Muslim (majority), Christian, Hindu, Parsee
Currency: Kuwaiti dinar (KD) = 1,000 fils
Location: Middle East
General Holidays: Jan. 1, New Year's Day; Feb. 25, National Day
Religious Holidays: Ascension Day, Eid al-Fitr, Waqfa, Eid al-Adha, Islamic New
  Year, Birth of Prophet

Laos (Lao People's Democratic Republic)
Capital: Vientiane
Nationality: Lao
Language: Lao (official), French, English, Vietnamese
Religion: Buddhist (majority), Confucian, Christian, animist
Currency: Laotian kip (LAK) = 100 att
Location: Southeast Asia
General Holidays: Jan. 1, New Year's Day; (varies), Lao New Year (Water Festival);
  May 1, Labor Day; Dec. 2, National Day
Religious Holidays: Buddhist Memorial Day

Latvia, Republic of
Capital: Riga
Nationality: Latvian(s)
Language: Latvian (official), Russian, ethnic languages
Religion: Protestant (majority: Lutheran), Roman Catholic
Currency: ruble (Rub) = 100 kopeks (new currency to be introduced)
Location: Northeast Europe
General Holidays: Jan. 1, New Year's Day; May 1, May Day; Nov. 18,
  National Day
Religious Holidays: Good Friday, Easter Monday, St. John's Day, Christmas Day

Lebanon, Republic of
Capital: Beirut
Nationality: Lebanese
Language: Arabic and French (both official), Armenian, English, Kurdish
Religion: Muslim (majority: Shiite), Roman Catholic, other Christian, Jewish
Currency: Lebanese pound (L£) = 100 piastres
Location: West Asia and the Middle East
General Holidays: Jan. 1, New Year's Day; Mar. 22, Arab League Anniv.; Nov. 22,
  Independence Day; Dec. 31, Evacuation Day
Religious Holidays: Leilat al-Meiraj, Feast of St. Marron, Eid al-Fitr, Easter,
  Ascension Day, Eid al-Adha, Islamic New Year, Ashoura, Assumption,
  Mouloud (Prophet's Birthday), All Saints' Day, Christmas Day

Lesotho, Kingdom of

Capital: Masera
Nationality: Mesotho (sing.), Basotho (pl.)
Language: Sesotho and English (both official), Zulu, Xhosa
Religion: Roman Catholic (majority), Lesotho, Evangelical, Anglican
Currency: loti (LSM) = 100 lisente
Location: South Africa
General Holidays: Jan. 1, New Year's Day; Jan. 20, Army Day; Mar. 12, Moshoeshoe's Day; Mar. 21, Tree Planting Day; Jul. (varies), Family Day; Jul. 17, King's Birthday; Oct. 4, Independence Day; Oct. 5, National Sports Day
Religious Holidays: Good Friday, Easter Monday, Ascension Day, Christmas Day, Boxing Day

Liberia, Republic of

Capital: Monrovia
Nationality: Liberian(s)
Language: English (official), Bassa, Kpelle, Kru, other African languages
Religion: Indigenous (majority), Muslim, Christian
Currency: Liberian dollar (L$) = 100 cents
Location: West Africa
General Holidays: Jan. 1, New Year's Day; Feb. 11, Armed Forces Day; Mar. 12, Decoration Day; Mar. 15, JJ Robert's Birthday; Apr. 12, National Redemption Day, Anniv. of 1980 coup; May 14, National Unification Day; Jul. 26, Independence Day; Aug. 24, Flag Day; Nov. 6, Thanksgiving Day; Nov. 12, National Memorial Day; Nov. 29, Pres. Tubman's Birthday
Religious Holidays: Good Friday, Fast and Prayer Day, Christmas Day

Libya (Great Socialist People's Libyan Arab Republic)

Capital: Tripoli
Nationality: Libyan(s)
Language: Arabic (official), English, Italian
Religion: Sunni Muslim
Currency: Libyan dinar (LD) = 1,000 dirhams
Location: North Africa
General Holidays: Mar. 28, British Evacuation Day; Jun. 11, Evacuation Day; Sep. 1, Revolution Day; Oct. 7, Evacuation Day
Religious Holidays: Leilat al-Meiraj, Eid al-Fitr, Eid al-Adha, Islamic New Year, Ashoura, Mouloud (Prophet's Birthday)

Liechtenstein, Principality of

Capital: Vaduz
Nationality: Liechtensteiner(s)
Language: German (official), Alemannic dialect, English
Religion: Roman Catholic (majority), Protestant, other
Currency: Swiss franc (SFr) = 100 centimes

Location: West-central Europe
General Holidays: Jan. 1, New Year's Day; May 1, Labor Day
Religious Holidays: Epiphany, Shrove Tuesday, St. Joseph Day, Good Friday,
    Easter Monday, Ascension Day, Whit Monday, Corpus Christi, Assumption,
    Nativity of Our Lady, Immaculate Conception, Christmas Day, Boxing Day

Lithuania, Republic of
Capital: Vilnius
Nationality: Lithuanian(s)
Language: Lithuanian (official), Polish, English, Russian, ethnic dialects
Religion: Roman Catholic (majority), Evangelical Lutheran, Evangelical
    Reformist, Jewish
Currency: ruble (Rub) = 100 kopeks, to be replaced with litas
Location: Northeast Europe
General Holidays: Jan. 1, New Year's Day; Feb. 16, Day of Independence; May 1,
    May Day; Jul. 6, National Day (Mindaugas Coronation)
Religious Holidays: Good Friday, Easter Monday, Christmas Day

Luxembourg, Grand Duchy of
Capital: Luxembourg
Nationality: Luxembourger(s)
Language: Luxembourgish (official: a German-Moselle-Frankish dialect), French,
    German
Religion: Roman Catholic (majority), Protestant, Jewish
Currency: Luxembourg franc (LFr) = 100 centimes
Location: West Europe
General Holidays: Jan. 1, New Year's Day; Feb. (varies), Carnival Monday; May 1,
    May Day; Jun. 23, National Day; Sep. (varies), Fair Day
Religious Holidays: Shrove Tuesday, Easter Monday, Ascension Day, Whit
    Monday, Assumption, All Saints' Day, All Souls' Day, Christmas Day,
    St. Stephen's Day

Macedonia, Republic of
Capital: Skopje
Nationality: Macedonian(s)
Language: Macedonian (official), Turkish, Serbo-Croatian
Religion: Eastern Orthodox, Muslim, Roman Catholic
Currency: dinar (D) = 100 para (Yugoslav currency)
Location: South-central Europe
General Holidays: Aug. 2, St. Elijas Day

Madagascar, Democratic Republic of
Capital: Antananarivo
Nationality: Malagasy
Language: French and Malagasy (both official)
Religion: Animist (majority), Christian, Muslim

Currency: Malagasy franc (MGF) (1 ariary = 5 francs)
Location: West Indian Ocean
General Holidays: Jan. 1, New Year's Day; Mar. 29, Martyrs of 1947 Day; May 1,
  Labor Day; Jun. 26, Independence Day; Dec. 30, Anniv. of Democratic
  Republic of Madagascar
Religious Holidays: Good Friday, Easter Monday, Ascension Day, Whit Monday,
  Assumption, All Saints' Day, Christmas Day

Malawi, Republic of

Capital: Lilongwe
Nationality: Malawian(s)
Language: English and Chichewa (both official), Tombuka, local languages
Religion: Protestant (majority), Roman Catholic, Muslim, Hindu
Currency: kwacha (MK) = 100 tambala
Location: Southeast Africa
General Holidays: Jan. 1, New Year's Day; Mar. 3, Martyrs' Day; May 14,
  Kamuzu Day (Pres. Banda's Birthday); Jul. 6, Republic Day; Oct. 17,
  Mothers' Day; Dec. 21, National Tree Planting Day
Religious Holidays: Good Friday, Easter Monday, Christmas Day,
  Boxing Day

Malaysia, Federation of

Capital: Kuala Lumpur
Nationality: Malaysian(s)
Language: Malay (official), English, Chinese, Tamil, Iban, Mandarin and Hakka
  dialects, tribal languages
Religion: Muslim (majority), Buddhist, Taoist, Confucian, Hindu, Christian
Currency: ringgit (M$) = 100 sen
Location: Central Southeast Asia
General Holidays: Jan. 1, New Year's Day; Feb. (varies), Chinese New Year; May
  1, Labor Day; Jun. (varies), Yang di-Pertuan Agong's Birthday; Aug. 31,
  National Day
Religious Holidays: Hari Raya Puasa (Eid al-Fitr), Wesak Day, Hari Raya Haji
  (Eid al-Adha), Maal Hijrah, Mouloud (Prophet's Birthday), Deepavali,
  Christmas Day

Maldives, Republic of the

Capital: Malé
Nationality: Maldivian(s)
Language: Dhivehi (official), English
Religion: Sunni Muslim
Currency: Maldivian rufiyaa (MRF) = 100 laari
Location: Indian Ocean
General Holidays: Jan. 1, New Year's Day; Feb. (varies), Martyr's Day; Jul. 26,
  Independence Day; Aug. 29–30, National Day; Nov. 3 ,Victory Day;
  Nov. 10, Fisheries' Day; Nov. 11–12, Republic Day; Nov. 28, Huravee Day

Religious Holidays: Ramadan, Eid al-Fitr, Hajj Day, Eid al-Adha, Islamic New
Year, Prophet Mohammed's Birthday

Mali, Republic of
Capital: Bamako
Nationality: Malian(s)
Language: French (official), Bambara, Arabic, other local languages
Religion: Muslim (majority), Christian, animist
Currency: CFA franc (CFA Fr) = 100 centimes
Location: Northwest Africa
General Holidays: Jan. 1, New Year's Day; Jan. 20, Army Day; May 1, Labor
Day; May 25, Day of Africa; Sep. 22, Independence Day; Nov. 19,
Liberation Day
Religious Holidays: Easter Monday, Ramadan, Tabaski, Prophet's Baptism,
Mawloud, Christmas Day

Malta, Republic of
Capital: Valleta
Nationality: Maltese
Language: Maltese and English (official), Italian
Religion: Roman Catholic
Currency: Maltese lira (liri, Lm) = 100 cents
Location: Mediterranean Sea
General Holidays: May 1, Malta Labor Day; Sep. 8, Our Lady of Victories Feast
Day; Sep. 21, Independence Day; Dec. 13, Republic Day
Religious Holidays: St. Paul's Shipwreck, St. Peter and St. Paul Feast Day,
Assumption, Immaculate Conception

Marshall Islands, Republic of the
Capital: Majuro
Nationality: Marshallese
Language: English (official), Marshallese, Malay-Polynesian dialects, Japanese
Religion: Protestant
Currency: U.S. dollar (US$) = 100 cents
Location: West Pacific Ocean
General Holidays: Jan. 1, New Year's Day; Mar. (varies), Memorial and Nuclear
Victim's Day; May 1, Constitution Day; Jul. 4, Fisherman's Day; Sep. 4,
Workers' Day; Oct. 21, Independence Day; Nov. 17, President's Day;
Dec. 4, Kamolo (Thanksgiving) Day
Religious Holidays: Christmas Day

Mauritania, Islamic Republic of
Capital: Nouakchott
Nationality: Mauritanian(s)
Language: Arabic and French (official), local dialects

Religion: Muslim
Currency: Mauritanian ouguiya (U) = 5 khoums
Location: Northwest Africa
General Holidays: Jan. 1, New Year's Day; May 1, Labor Day; May 25, African
    Liberation Day, Anniv. of OAU's foundation; Nov. 28, National Day
Religious Holidays: Leilat al-Meiraj, Korité (Eid al-Fitr), Tabaski (Eid al-Adha),
    Islamic New Year, Mouloud (Prophet's Birthday)

Mauritius, Republic of
Capital: Port Louis
Nationality: Mauritian(s)
Language: English (official), Creole, French, Hindi, Urdu, Hakka, Bojpoori,
    Arabic, Chinese
Religion: Hindu (majority), Christian, Muslim
Currency: Mauritian rupee (MRe) = 100 cents
Location: Southwest Indian Ocean
General Holidays: Jan. 1–2, New Year; Feb. (varies), Chinese Spring Festival (New
    Year); Mar. 12, Independence Day; May 1, Labor Day
Religious Holidays: Cavadee, Maha Shivaratree, Ougadi, Eid al-Fitr, Good Friday,
    Ganesh Chaturti, Divali, All Saints' Day, Christmas Day

Mexico (United Mexican States)
Capital: Mexico City
Nationality: Mexican(s)
Language: Spanish (official), English
Religion: Roman Catholic (majority), Protestant
Currency: Mexican peso (Mex$) = 100 centavos
Location: Southern North America
General Holidays: Jan. 1, New Year's Day; Feb. 5, Constitution Day; Mar. 21,
    Birth of Benito Juárez; May 1, Labor Day; May 5, Anniv. of Battle of
    Puebla; Sep. 16, Independence Day; Oct. 12, Día de la Raza; Nov. 1,
    President's Annual Message; Nov. 20, Anniv. of Mexican Revolution
    of 1910
Religious Holidays: St. Anthony's Day, Good Friday, Easter Monday, Corpus
    Christi, Assumption, All Saints' Day, All Souls' Day, Day of Our Lady of
    Guadalupe, Christmas Day

Micronesia, Federated States of
Capital: Kolonia
Nationality: Micronesian(s)
Language: English (official), Japanese, local languages
Religion: Protestant (majority), Roman Catholic
Currency: U.S. dollar (US$) = 100 cents
Location: West Pacific Ocean
General Holidays: Jan. 1, New Year's Day; Mar. (varies), Yap Day; May (varies),
    Federated States of Micronesia Day; Sep. 8, Liberation Day (Kosrae); Sep. 11,

Liberation Day (Pohnpei); Sep. 23, Charter Day (Chuuk); Nov. 3, Independence Day; Nov. 8, Constitution Day (Pohnpei); Dec. 24, Yap Constitution Day
Religious Holidays: Christmas Day

Moldova, Republic of
Capital: Kishinev
Nationality: Moldovian(s)
Language: Romanian (official), Moldovian, Russian, ethnic languages
Religion: Eastern Orthodox, Russian Orthodox
Currency: ruble (Rub) = 100 kopeks (leu to be introduced)
Location: Southeast Europe
General Holidays: Aug. 27, Independence Day

Monaco, Principality of
Capital: Monaco
Nationality: Monacan(s) or Monégasque(s)
Language: French (official), English, Italian, Monégasque
Religion: Roman Catholic (majority), Anglican
Currency: French franc (FFr) = 100 centimes
Location: West Europe
General Holidays: Jan. 1, New Year's Day; May 1, Labor Day; Nov. 19, Monaco National Day
Religious Holidays: Feast of St. Dévote (Principality's patron saint), Easter Monday, Ascension Day, Whit Monday, Corpus Christi, Assumption, All Saints' Day, Immaculate Conception, Christmas Day

Mongolia, State of
Capital: Ulan Bator
Nationality: Mongolian(s)
Language: Mongolian Khalkha (official), Russian, Turkic, Chinese, local dialects
Religion: Tibetan Buddhist (majority), Muslim
Currency: tugrik (Tug) = 100 mongos
Location: Central Asia
General Holidays: Jan. 1, New Year's Day; 1st 2 days of 1st lunar month, Tsagaan Sar (Mongolian New Year); Mar. 8, Women's Day; Jul. 11–13, Naadam (anniv. of revolution); Nov. 26, Constitution Day

Morocco, Kingdom of
Capital: Rabat
Nationality: Moroccan(s)
Language: Arabic (official), Berber, French, Spanish
Religion: Muslim (majority), Christian, Jewish
Currency: Moroccan dirham (DH) = 100 centimes
Location: Northwest Africa

General Holidays: Jan. 1, New Year's Day; Mar. 3, Feast of Throne; May 1, Labor Day; Jul. 9, Youth Day; Aug. 14, Oued Eddahab Day; Nov. 6, Green March Day; Nov. 18, Independence Day

Religious Holidays: Eid el-Seghir (Eid al-Fitr), Eid el-Kebir (Eid al-Adha), Muslim New Year, Ashoura, Mouloud (Prophet's Birthday)

Mozambique, Republic of

Capital: Maputo
Nationality: Mozambican(s)
Language: Portuguese (official), local African languages
Religion: Indigenous beliefs (majority), Christian, Muslim, Hindu
Currency: Mozambique metical (M) = 100 centavos
Location: Southeast Africa
General Holidays: Jan. 1, New Year's Day; Feb. 3, Mozambican Heroes' Day; Apr. 7, Mozambican Women's Day; May 1, Workers' Day; Jun. 25, Independence Day; Sep. 7, Lusaka Agreement (Victory Day); Sep. 25, Armed Forces Day; Dec. 25, Family Day

Myanmar, Union of (formerly Burma)

Capital: Yangon (formerly Rangoon)
Nationality: Burmese
Language: Burmese (official), English, more than a hundred other languages and dialects
Religion: Theravada Buddhist (majority), Hindu, Muslim, Christian, animist
Currency: kyak (Kt) = 100 pyas
Location: Southeast Asia
General Holidays: Jan. 4, Independence Day; Feb. 12, Union Day; Mar. 2, Peasants' Day; Mar. (varies), Full moon of Tabaung; Mar. 27, Armed Forces Day; Apr. 13–15, Maha Thingyan (water festival); Apr. 16, Burmese New Year; May 1, Workers' Day; May (varies), Full moon of Kason; Jul. (varies), Full moon of Waso; Jul. 19, Martyrs' Day; Oct. (varies), Full moon of Thadingyut; Nov. (varies), Devali; Tazaungdaing Festival; Dec. 3, National Day
Religious Holidays: Eid al-Adha, Christmas Day

Namibia, Republic of

Capital: Windhoek
Nationality: Namibian(s)
Language: English (official), Afrikaans, German, indigenous languages
Religion: Christian (majority), indigenous beliefs
Currency: rand (R) = 100 cents (Namibian to be introduced)
Location: Southwest Africa
General Holidays: Jan. 1, New Year's Day; Mar. 21, Independence Day; May 1, Workers' Day; Aug. 26, Namibia Day; Dec. 10, Human Rights Day
Religious Holidays: Good Friday, Easter Monday, Ascension Day, Christmas Day

Nauru, Republic of
Capital: No city; government in Yaren District
Nationality: Nauruan(s)
Language: Nauruan (official), English, French
Religion: Protestant (majority), Roman Catholic
Currency: Australian dollar (A$) = 100 cents
Location: South-central Pacific Ocean
General Holidays: Jan. 1, New Year's Day; Jan. 31, Independence Day; Oct. 26, Angam Day
Religious Holidays: Easter, Christmas Day, Boxing Day

Nepal, Kingdom of
Capital: Kathmandu
Nationality: Nepalese
Language: Nepali (official), twenty other languages and numerous dialects
Religion: Hindu (majority), Buddhist, Muslim, Christian
Currency: Nepalese rupee (Rs) = 100 paisa
Location: Central Asia
General Holidays: [*Note:* All holidays subject to date change (lunar calendar).] Martyrs' Day, King Tribhuvan Memorial and National Democracy Day, Women's Day, New Year's Day, Mother's Day, Teacher's Day, Father's Day, UN Day, Her Majesty's Birthday, King Mahendra Memorial and Constitution Day, His Majesty's Birthday
Religious Holidays: Prithvi Jayanti, Basant Panchami, Shivaratri, Fagupurnima, Ghode Jatra (Kathmandu Valley only), Chaitra Ashtami, Ram Nawani, Buddha Jayanti, Janai Purnima, Gai Jatra (Kathmandu Valley only), Krishnashtami, Teej, Rishi Panchami, Indra Jatra (Kathmandu Valley only), Ghatasthapana, Dashain festival, Tihar festival, Balachaturdashi

Netherlands, Kingdom of the
Capital: Amsterdam
Nationality: Dutchman, Dutchwoman
Language: Dutch (official), English, French, German
Religion: Roman Catholic, Protestant, unaffiliated
Currency: gulden (Gld) = 100 cents
Location: Northwest Europe
General Holidays: Jan. 1, New Year's Day; Apr. 30, Queen's Birthday; May 5, National Liberation Day
Religious Holidays: Good Friday, Easter Monday, Ascension Day, Whit Monday, Christmas Day

New Zealand
Capital: Wellington
Nationality: New Zealander(s)
Language: English (official), Maori

Religion: Christian (majority), Hindu, Confucian, other
Currency: New Zealand dollar (NZ$) = 100 cents
Location: South Pacific Ocean
General Holidays: Jan. 1, New Year's Day; Jan. 2, 2d January; Feb. 6, Waitangi
Day (National Day); Apr. 25, ANZAC Day; Jun. 4, Queen's Birthday;
Oct. 22, Labor Day
Religious Holidays: Good Friday, Easter Monday, Christmas Day, Boxing Day

Nicaragua, Republic of
Capital: Managua
Nationality: Nicaraguan(s)
Language: Spanish (official), English, indigenous Indian languages
Religion: Roman Catholic
Currency: Nicaraguan córdoba (C$) = 100 centavos
Location: Central America
General Holidays: Jan. 1, New Year's Day; May 1, Labor Day; Jul. 19, Anniv. of
Triumph of Revolution; Sep. 15, Independence Day
Religious Holidays: Holy Thursday, Good Friday, Easter, Christmas Day, Feast of
Immaculate Conception

Niger, Republic of
Capital: Niamey
Nationality: Nigerian(s)
Language: French (official), Hausa, Djerma, Manga, Zarma, Tuareg
Religion: Muslim (majority), Christian, animist
Currency: CFA franc (CFA Fr) = 100 centimes
Location: West Central Africa
General Holidays: Jan. 1, New Year's Day; Apr. 15, Anniv. of 1974 coup; May 1,
Labor Day; Aug. 3, Independence Day; Dec. 18, Republic Day
Religious Holidays: Eid al-Fitr, Easter Monday, Eid al-Adha, Islamic New Year,
Mouloud (Prophet's Birthday), Christmas Day

Nigeria, Federal Republic of
Capital: Abuja
Nationality: Nigerian(s)
Language: English (official), Hausa, Yoruba, Ibo, more than 250 other local
languages
Religion: Muslim (majority), Christian, numerous local religions
Currency: naira (N) = 100 kobo
Location: West Africa
General Holidays: Jan. 1, New Year's Day; May 1, Workers' Day; Oct. 1,
National Day
Religious Holidays: Good Friday, Easter Monday, Christmas Day, Boxing Day,
Eid al-Fitr, Eid al-Kabir, Prophet's Birthday

Norway, Kingdom of
Capital: Oslo
Nationality: Norwegian(s)
Language: Norwegian (official), Lappish, English
Religion: Evangelical Lutheran (majority), Roman Catholic, other Christian
Currency: Norwegian krone (NKr) = 100 øre
Location: North Europe
General Holidays: Jan. 1, New Year's Day; May 1, Labor Day; May 17, Norwegian Constitution Day
Religious Holidays: Holy Thursday, Good Friday, Easter Monday, Ascension Day, Whit Monday, Christmas Day, St. Stephen's Day

Oman, Sultanate of
Capital: Muscat
Nationality: Omani(s)
Language: Arabic (official), English, Baluchi, Urdu, Indian dialects
Religion: Ibadhi Muslim (majority), Sunni Muslim, Shiite Muslim, Hindu
Currency: Omani rial (RO) = 1,000 baiza
Location: Middle East
General Holidays: Nov. 18, National Day; Nov. 19, Sultan's Birthday
Religious Holidays: Leilat al-Meiraj (Ascension of Prophet), Eid al-Fitr, Eid al-Adha, Muharram, Islamic New Year, Ashoura, Mouloud (Prophet's Birthday)

Pakistan, Islamic Republic of
Capital: Islamabad
Nationality: Pakistani(s)
Language: Urdu and English (official), Punjabi, Sindhi, Pashto, Saraiki, Baluchi, other
Religion: Sunni Muslim (majority), Shiite Muslim, Hindu, Christian
Currency: Pakistan rupee (Re) = 100 paisa
Location: South Asia
General Holidays: Mar. 23, Pakistan Day; May 1, Labor Day; Aug. 14, Independence Day; Sep. 6, Defense of Pakistan Day; Sep. 11, Anniv. of Death of Quaid-i-Azam; Nov. 9, Iqbal Day; Dec. 25, Quaid-i-Azam's Birthday
Religious Holidays: Good Friday, Easter Monday, Eid al-Fitr, Eid al-Adha, Islamic New Year, Ashoura, Eid-e-Milad-un-Nabi (Prophet's Birthday), Christmas Day, Boxing Day

Panama, Republic of
Capital: Panama City
Nationality: Panamanian(s)
Language: Spanish (official), English
Religion: Roman Catholic (majority), Protestant
Currency: balboa (Ba) = 100 centesimos
Location: South Central America

General Holidays: Jan. 1, New Year's Day; Jan. (varies), National Martyrs' Day; May 1, Labor Day; Aug. 15, Foundation of Panama City (Panama City only); Oct. 12, Columbus Day; Nov. 1, National Anthem Day; Nov. 3, Independence from Colombia Day; Nov. 4, National Flag Day; Nov. 5, Independence Day (Cólon only); Nov. 10, First Call of Independence; Nov. 28, Independence from Spain; Dec. (varies), Mother's Day

Religious Holidays: Shrove Tuesday, Good Friday, All Souls' Day, Immaculate Conception, Christmas Day

Papua New Guinea

Capital: Port Moresby
Nationality: Papua New Guinean(s)
Language: English (official), pidgin English, Motu, more than seven hundred other languages and dialects
Religion: Christian (majority), indigenous beliefs
Currency: kina (K) = 100 toea
Location: South Pacific Ocean
General Holidays: Jan. 1, New Year's Day; Jun. 1, Queen's Birthday; Jul. 23, Remembrance Day; Sep. 16, Independence Day and Constitution Day
Religious Holidays: Good Friday, Easter Monday, Christmas Day, Boxing Day

Paraguay, Republic of

Capital: Asunción
Nationality: Paraguayan(s)
Language: Spanish (official), Guarani
Religion: Roman Catholic (majority), Mennonite, other Protestant
Currency: guaraní (G), replacing peso (1 guaraní = 100 pesos)
Location: Central South America
General Holidays: Jan. 1, New Year's Day; Feb. (varies), Carnaval; Mar. 1, Heroes' Day; May 1, Labor Day; May 15, Independence Day; Jun. 12, Peace of Chaco; Aug. 15, Founding of Asunción; Aug. 25, Constitution Day; Sep. 29, Battle of Boquerón; Oct. 12, Columbus Day
Religious Holidays: Epiphany, San Blás (national saint), Maundy Thursday, Good Friday, Ascension Day, Corpus Christi, All Saints' Day, Immaculate Conception, Christmas Day

Peru, Republic of

Capital: Lima
Nationality: Peruvian(s)
Language: Spanish and Quechua (official), Aymara, English
Religion: Roman Catholic
Currency: nuevo sol (PES) = 100 centavos, replacing inti (1,000 soles = 1 inti)
Location: Western South America
General Holidays: Jan. 1, New Year's Day; May 1, Labor Day; Jun. 24, Day of Peasant; Jul. 28–29, Independence Day; Oct. 8, Battle of Angamos

Religious Holidays: Shrove Tuesday, Maundy Thursday, Good Friday, St. Peter and St. Paul's Day, Santa Rosa of Lima Day, All Saints' Day, Immaculate Conception, Christmas Day

Philippines, Republic of the
Capital: Manila
Nationality: Filipino(s)
Language: Filipino and English (both official), more than a hundred other languages and dialects
Religion: Roman Catholic (majority), Protestant, Muslim, Buddhist
Currency: Philippine peso (PP) = 100 centavos
Location: Pacific Ocean and South China Sea
General Holidays: Jan. 1, New Year's Day; Feb. 25, Freedom Day; Apr. 9, Bataan Day; May 1, Labor Day; May 6, Araw ng Kagitingan; Jun. 12, Independence Day; Aug. 27, National Heroes' Day; Sep. 11, Barangay Day; Sep. 21, National Thanksgiving Day; Nov. 30, Andres Bonifacio Day; Dec. 30, Rizal Day; Dec. 31, Last Day of the Year
Religious Holidays: Maundy Thursday, Good Friday, Easter Monday, All Saints' Day, Christmas Day

Poland (Polish Republic)
Capital: Warsaw
Nationality: Pole(s)
Language: Polish (official), German, French, English
Religion: Roman Catholic (majority), Orthodox, Protestant
Currency: zloty (Zl) = 100 groszy
Location: East-central Europe
General Holidays: Jan. 1, New Year's Day; May 1, Labor Day; May 3, National Day; May 9, Victory Day; Nov. 11, Independence Day
Religious Holidays: Easter Monday, Corpus Christi, Assumption, All Saints' Day, Christmas Day

Portugal, Republic of
Capital: Lisbon
Nationality: Portuguese
Language: Portuguese
Religion: Roman Catholic (majority), Protestant
Currency: escudo (Esc) = 100 centavos
Location: Southwest Europe
General Holidays: Jan. 1, New Year's Day; Feb. 7, Carnival; Apr. 25, Liberty Day; May 1, Labor Day; Jun. 10, Portugal Day; Oct. 5, Portuguese Republic; Dec. 1, Portuguese Independence
Religious Holidays: Good Friday, Corpus Christi, St. Anthony's Day (only Lisbon), Assumption, All Saints' Day, Immaculate Conception, Christmas Day

Qatar, State of
Capital: Doha
Nationality: Qatari(s)
Language: Arabic (official), English
Religion: Muslim
Currency: Qatari riyal (QR) = 100 dirhams
Location: Middle East
General Holidays: Feb. 22, Accession of HH The Emir; Sep. 3, National Day
Religious Holidays: Leilat al-Meiraj, First Day of Ramadan, Eid al-Fitr, Eid al-Adha, Islamic New Year

Romania
Capital: Bucharest
Nationality: Romanian(s)
Language: Romanian (official), German, Hungarian, French, English
Religion: Romanian Orthodox (majority), Roman Catholic, Lutheran, Muslim, Jewish
Currency: leu (lei) = 100 ban(i)
Location: Southeast Europe
General Holidays: Jan. 1–2, New Year; May 1–2, Romanian Labor Day; Aug. 23–24, Romanian Independence Day; Dec. 31, Day of Republic
Religious Holidays: Orthodox Easter, Good Friday, Easter Monday, Christmas

Russia (Russian Federation)
Capital: Moscow
Nationality: Russian(s)
Language: Russian (official), ethnic languages
Religion: Russian Orthodox (majority), Muslim, Buddhist, Jewish
Currency: ruble (Rub) = 100 kopeks
Location: Northeast Europe and North Asia
General Holidays: Jun. 12, Independence Day
Religious Holidays: Russian Orthodox Easter, Russian Orthodox Christmas Day

Rwanda, Republic of
Capital: Kigali
Nationality: Rwandan(s)
Language: Kinyarwanda and French (both official), Kiswahili
Religion: Roman Catholic (majority), Protestant, Muslim, animist
Currency: Rwanda franc (RwFr) = 100 centimes
Location: Central Africa
General Holidays: Jan. 1, New Year's Day; Jan. 28, Democracy Day; May 1, Labor Day; Jul. 1, National Day; Jul. 5, Peace and National Unity Day; Aug. 1, Harvest Day; Sep. 25, Referendum Day; Oct. 26, Armed Forces Day
Religious Holidays: Easter Monday, Ascension Day, Pentecost Monday, Assumption, All Saints' Day, Christmas Day

Saint Kitts and Nevis, Federation of
Capital: Basseterre
Nationality: Kittsian(s), Nevisian(s)
Language: English
Religion: Anglican, Roman Catholic, Protestant
Currency: East Caribbean dollar (EC$) = 100 cents
Location: East Caribbean Sea
General Holidays: Jan. 1, New Year's Day/Carnival Day; May 4, Labor Day;
    Jun. 13, Queen's Birthday; Aug. 3, Emancipation Day; Aug. 4, Culturama
    (Nevis only); Sep. 19, Independence Anniv.
Religious Holidays: Good Friday, Easter Monday, Whit Monday, Christmas Day,
    Boxing Day

Saint Lucia
Capital: Castries
Nationality: Saint Lucian(s)
Language: English (official), French patois
Religion: Roman Catholic (majority), Protestant
Currency: East Caribbean dollar (EC$) = 100 cents
Location: Southeast Caribbean Sea
General Holidays: Jan. 1–2, New Year; Feb. 22, Independence Day; Feb. 22–23,
    Carnival; May 1, Labor Day; Aug. 3, Emancipation Day; Oct. 5,
    Thanksgiving Day; Dec. 13, National Day
Religious Holidays: Good Friday, Easter Monday, Whit Monday, Corpus Christi,
    Christmas Day

Saint Vincent and the Grenadines
Capital: Kingstown
Nationality: St. Vincentian(s) or Vincentian(s)
Language: English, French patois
Religion: Roman Catholic, Anglican, Methodist, other Christian
Currency: East Caribbean dollar (EC$) = 100 cents
Location: East Caribbean Sea
General Holidays: Jan. 1, New Year's Day; Jan. 22, St. Vincent and the
    Grenadines Day; May 4, Labor Day; Jul. 6, Caricom Day; Jul. (varies),
    Carnival Tuesday; Aug. 3, Emancipation Day; Oct. 27, Independence Day
Religious Holidays: Good Friday, Easter Monday, Whit Monday, Christmas Day

San Marino, Republic of
Capital: San Marino
Nationality: Sanmarinese
Language: Italian
Religion: Roman Catholic
Currency: Italian lira (L) and national coins
Location: West Europe

General Holidays: Jan. 1, New Year's Day; Feb. (varies), Liberation Day; Mar. (varies), Anniv. of Arengo; Apr. 1, Captains-Regent Investiture; May 1, Labor Day; Jul. 28, Anniv. of Fall of Fascism; Sep. 3, San Marino Day and Republic Day; Oct. 1, Captains-Regent Investiture

Religious Holidays: St. Joseph's Day, Easter Monday, Corpus Christi, Assumption, All Saints' Day, Commemoration of Dead, Immaculate Conception, Christmas Day, St. Stephen's Day

São Tomé and Príncipe, Democratic Republic of

Capital: São Tomé
Nationality: São Toméan(s)
Language: Portuguese (official), French, English, local dialects
Religion: Roman Catholic (majority), Protestant
Currency: dobra (Db) = 100 centimos
Location: Off west coast of Africa
General Holidays: Jan. 1, New Year's Day; Feb. 4, Martyr's Day; May 1, Workers' Day; Jul. 12, Independence/National Day; Sep. (varies), Armed Forces Day; Sep. 30, Farmer's Day; Dec. 21, People's Popular Power Day
Religious Holidays: Shrove Tuesday, Good Friday, Easter Monday, Ascension Day, Corpus Christi, Assumption, All Saints' Day, Christmas Day

Saudi Arabia, Kingdom of

Capital: Riyadh
Nationality: Saudi(s)
Language: Arabic (official), English
Religion: Sunni Muslim (majority), Shiite Muslim
Currency: Saudi Arabian rial (SAR) = 100 halalas
Location: Middle East
Religious Holidays: Leilat al-Meiraj, Eid al-Fitr, Eid al-Adha, Islamic New Year, Ashoura, Mouloud (Prophet's Birthday)

Senegal, Republic of

Capital: Dakar
Nationality: Senegalese
Language: French (official), Wolof, other local languages
Religion: Muslim (majority), Roman Catholic, Protestant, indigenous beliefs
Currency: CFA franc (CFA Fr) = 100 centimes
Location: Northwest Africa
General Holidays: Jan. 1, New Year's Day; Apr. (varies), National Day; May 1, Labor Day; Jul. 14, Day of Association
Religious Holidays: Good Friday, Easter Monday, Eid al-Fitr, Ascension Day, Whit Monday, Eid al-Adha, Assumption, Mouloud (Prophet's Birthday), All Saints' Day, Christmas Day

Seychelles, Republic of
Capital: Victoria
Nationality: Seychellois
Language: Creole (official), French, English
Religion: Roman Catholic (majority), Anglican, Muslim
Currency: Seychelles rupee (SR) = 100 cents
Location: West Indian Ocean
General Holidays: Jan. 1–2, New Year; May 1, Labor Day; Jun. 5, Liberation
   Day; Jun. 29, Independence Day
Religious Holidays: Good Friday, Easter Monday, Corpus Christi, Assumption,
   All Saints' Day, Immaculate Conception, Christmas Day

Sierra Leone, Republic of
Capital: Freetown
Nationality: Sierra Leonean(s)
Language: English (official), Krio, other local languages
Religion: Animist (majority), Muslim, Christian
Currency: leone (Le) = 100 cents
Location: West Central Africa
General Holidays: Jan. 1, New Year's Day; Apr. 27, Independence Day
Religious Holidays: Eid al-Fitr, Good Friday, Easter Monday, Eid al-Adha,
   Mouloud (Prophet's Birthday), Christmas Day

Singapore, Republic of
Capital: Singapore
Nationality: Singaporean(s)
Language: English (official), Mandarin Chinese, Malay, Tamil
Religion: Chinese: Buddhist and atheist (majority), Malays: Muslim (majority),
   Christian, Hindu, Sikh, Taoist, Confucian
Currency: Singapore dollar (S$) = 100 cents
Location: Southwest Asia
General Holidays: Jan. 1, New Year; Feb. (varies), Chinese New Year; May 1,
   Labor Day; Aug. 9, National Day
Religious Holidays: Hari Raya Puasa, Good Friday, Vesak Day, Hari Raya Haji,
   Deepavali, Christmas Day

Slovakia (Slovak Republic)
Capital: Bratislava
Nationality: Slovak(s)
Language: Slovak (official), Czech, Hungarian, Polish
Religion: Roman and Greek Catholic (majority), Protestant, Jewish, Orthodox
Currency: Slovak koruna (Sk)
Location: Central Europe
General Holidays: May 9, National Liberation Day; Aug. 29, Slovak National
   Uprising

Slovenia, Republic of
Capital: Ljubljana
Nationality: Slovene(s)
Language: Slovenian (official), Macedonian, Serbo-Croatian, Hungarian, Italian
Religion: Roman Catholic (majority), Eastern Orthodox, Muslim, Jewish
Currency: tola(r)
Location: South-central Europe
General Holidays: Jun. 25, Independence Day

Solomon Islands
Capital: Honiara
Nationality: Solomon Islander(s)
Language: English (official), Pidgin English, more than a hundred indigenous languages
Religion: Anglican, Roman Catholic, South Sea Evangelical, other Protestant
Currency: Solomon Islands dollar (SI$) = 100 cents
Location: Southwest Pacific Ocean
General Holidays: Jan. 1, New Year's Day; Jun. 5, Queen's Official Birthday; Jul. 7, Independence Day
Religious Holidays: Good Friday, Easter, Whit Monday, Christmas Day

Somalia (Somali Democratic Republic)
Capital: Mogadishu
Nationality: Somali(s)
Language: Somali (official), Arabic, Swahili, Italian, English
Religion: Sunni Muslim (majority), Roman Catholic
Currency: Somali shilling (SoSh) = 100 cents
Location: East Africa
General Holidays: Jan. 1, New Year's Day; May 1, Labor Day; Jun. 26, Independence Day; Jul. 1, Foundation of Republic; Oct. 21–22, Anniv. of 1969 Revolution
Religious Holidays: Eid al-Fitr, Eid al-Adha, Ashoura, Mouloud (Prophet's Birthday)

South Africa, Republic of
Capital: Cape Town (legislative), Pretoria (administrative)
Nationality: South African(s)
Language: Afrikaans and English (both official), Zulu, Xhosa, Sesotho, other African languages
Religion: Christian (majority), Hindu, Muslim, Jewish
Currency: rand (R) = 100 cents
Location: South Africa

General Holidays: Jan. 1, New Year's Day; Apr. 6, Founders' Day; May 1, Labor Day; May 31, Republic Day; Oct. 10, Kruger Day; Dec. 16, Day of Vow

Religious Holidays: Good Friday, Ascension Day, Christmas Day, Day of Good Will

Spain, Kingdom of

Capital: Madrid
Nationality: Spaniard(s)
Language: Castilian Spanish (official), Catalan, Galician, Basque
Religion: Roman Catholic
Currency: peseta (Pta) = 100 centimos
Location: Southwest Europe
General Holidays: Jan. 1, New Year's Day; May 1, Labor Day; Jun. 24, King Juan Carlos' Saint's Day; Oct. 12, National Day; Dec. 6, Constitution Day
Religious Holidays: Three Kings' Day, Maundy Thursday (except Barcelona), Good Friday, Easter Monday (Barcelona and Palma de Mallorca only), Corpus Christi, St. James of Compostela, Assumption, All Saints' Day, Immaculate Conception (except Barcelona), Christmas Day, Boxing Day (Barcelona and Palma de Mallorca only)

Sri Lanka, Socialist Republic of

Capital: Colombo
Nationality: Sri Lankan(s)
Language: Sinhala and Tamil (both official), English
Religion: Buddhist (majority), Hindu, Christian, Muslim
Currency: Sri Lankan rupee (SLRe) = 100 cents
Location: Indian Ocean
General Holidays: Feb. 4, National Day; May 1, May Day; May 22, National Heroes Day; All full moon days ("poya" days)
Religious Holidays: Tamil Thai Pongal Day, Good Friday, Maha Sivarathri Day, Sinhala and Tamil New Year's Eve and Day, Id al-Fitr, Id al-Adha, Prophet's Birthday, Deepawali Festival Day, Christmas Day

Sudan, Republic of

Capital: Khartoum
Nationality: Sudanese
Language: Arabic (official), English, numerous local dialects
Religion: Sunni Muslim (majority), Christian, animist
Currency: Sudanese pound (Sud£) =100 piastres
Location: Northeast Africa
General Holidays: Jan. 1, Independence Day; Apr. 6, Uprising Day, anniv. of 1985 coup; May 1, Labor Day; Jul. 1, Decentralization Day
Religious Holidays: Eid al-Fitr, Sham an-Nassim (Coptic Easter Monday), Eid al-Adha, Islamic New Year, Mouloud (Prophet's Birthday), Christmas Day

Suriname, Republic of
Capital: Paramaribo
Nationality: Surinamer(s)
Language: Dutch (official), English, Sranan Tongo (Taki-Taki), Hindi, Javanese,
  Chinese, French, Spanish
Religion: Christian (majority), Hindu, Muslim, indigenous beliefs
Currency: Suriname guilder (SGld) = 100 cents
Location: Northern South America
General Holidays: Jan. 1, New Year's Day; Feb. 25, Revolution Day; May 1,
  Labor Day; Jul. 1, National Union Day; Nov. 25, Independence Day
Religious Holidays: Phagwa, Eid al-Fitr, Easter, Christmas Day

Swaziland, Kingdom of
Capital: Mbabane
Nationality: Swazi(s)
Language: English and Siswati (both official)
Religion: Christian (majority), animist
Currency: lilangeni (E) = 100 cents
Location: South Africa
General Holidays: Jan. 1, New Year's Day; Apr. 19, King's Birthday; Apr. 25,
  National Flag Day; Jul. 22, Public Holiday; Aug. or Sep. (varies), Reed
  Dance; Sep. 6, Independence Day
Religious Holidays: Good Friday, Easter Monday, Ascension Day, Christmas Day,
  Boxing Day, Incwala

Sweden, Kingdom of
Capital: Stockholm
Nationality: Swede(s)
Language: Swedish (majority), Lapp, Finnish, English, German
Religion: Evangelical Lutheran (majority), Roman Catholic, other Protestant,
  Muslim, Jewish
Currency: krona (SKr) = 100 öre
Location: Northeast Europe
General Holidays: Jan. 1, New Year's Day; May 1, Labor Day; Jun. 20, Midsum-
  mer's Day
Religious Holidays: Epiphany, Good Friday, Easter Monday, Ascension Day,
  Whit Monday, All Saints' Day, Christmas Day

Switzerland (Swiss Confederation)
Capital: Bern
Nationality: Swiss
Language: German (official), French, Italian, Romansh
Religion: Roman Catholic, Protestant
Currency: Swiss franc (SFr) = 100 rappen or centimes

Location: West Europe
General Holidays: Jan. 1–2, New Year; May 1, Labor Day; Aug. 1, National Day
Religious Holidays: Good Friday, Easter Monday, Ascension Day, Whit Monday,
    Christmas Day

Syria (Syrian Arab Republic)
Capital: Damascus
Nationality: Syrian(s)
Language: Arabic (official), French, English, Kurdish, Armenian
Religion: Sunni Muslim (majority), Christian, other Muslim
Currency: Syrian pound (S£) = 100 piastres
Location: Middle East
General Holidays: Jan. 1, New Year's Day; Mar. 8, Revolution Day; Jul. 23,
    Egypt's Revolution Day; Sep. 1, Union of Syria, Egypt and Libya; Oct. 6,
    Beginning of Oct. War; Nov. 16, National Day
Religious Holidays: Leilat al-Meiraj, Eid al-Fitr, Easter (Greek Orthodox), Eid
    al-Adha, Islamic New Year, Mouloud (Prophet's Birthday), Christmas Day

Taiwan (Republic of China)
Capital: Taipei
Nationality: Chinese
Language: Mandarin Chinese (official), Taiwanese dialects, English, Japanese
Religion: Buddhist (majority), Taoist, Confucian, Christian
Currency: New Taiwan dollar (NT$) = 100 cents
Location: Southeast Asia
General Holidays: Jan. 1, National Holiday and Founding Day; Feb. (varies),
    Chinese New Year; Mar. 29, Youth Day; Apr. 5, Ching Ming, Tomb-
    Sweeping Day; Jun. 5, Dragon Boat Festival; Sep. 11, Mid-Autumn Moon
    Festival; Sep. 28, Teachers' Day; Oct. 10, Double Tenth National Day;
    Oct. 25, Retrocession Day; Oct. 31, Birthday of Chiang Kai-shek; Nov. 12,
    Dr. Sun Yat-sen's Birthday; Dec. 25, Constitution Day
Religious Holidays: Confucius' Birthday

Tajikistan, Republic of
Capital: Dushanbe
Nationality: Tajik(s)
Language: Tajik (official), Russian, Uzbek, ethnic languages
Religion: Sunni Muslim, Russian Orthodox, Jewish
Currency: ruble (Rub) = 100 kopeks (new currency to be introduced)
Location: Southeast Central Asia
General Holidays: Sep. 9, Independence Day

Tanzania, United Republic of
Capital: Dodoma
Nationality: Tanzanian(s)

Language: Swahili and English (both official), Bantu, other African languages
Religion: Christian, Muslim, Hindu, indigenous beliefs
Currency: Tanzanian shilling (TSh) = 100 cents
Location: East Africa
General Holidays: Jan. 1, New Year's Day; Jan. 12, Zanzibar Revolution Day; Feb. 5, Chama Cha Mapinduzi Day; Apr. 26, Union Day; May 1, Labor Day; Jul. 7, Saba Saba Peasants' Day; Dec. 9, Independence Day
Religious Holidays: Eid al-Fitr, Easter, Eid al-Haji, Maulidi (Prophet's Birthday), Christmas Day

Thailand, Kingdom of
Capital: Bangkok
Nationality: Thai
Language: Thai (official), English, Malay, Tachew Chinese
Religion: Theravada Buddhist (majority), Muslim, Christian
Currency: bhat (Bt) = 100 satangs
Location: Southeast Asia
General Holidays: Jan. 1, New Year's Day; Feb. (varies), Chinese New Year; Apr. 6, Chakri Day; Apr. 12–14, Songkran (Water Festival); May 1, Labor Day; May 5, Coronation Day; May 14, Royal Ploughing Ceremony; Jul. 15, Khao Phansa; Aug. 12, Queen's Birthday; Oct. 13, Chulalongkorn Day; Dec. 5, King's Birthday; Dec. 10, Constitution Day; Dec. 31, New Year's Eve
Religious Holidays: Makha-buja Day, Visakha Puja, Asalha Puja

Togo, Republic of
Capital: Lomé
Nationality: Togolese
Language: French (official), Ewe, Mina, Dagomba, Kabyè
Religion: Traditional and animist (majority), Christian, Muslim
Currency: CFA franc (CFA Fr) = 100 centimes
Location: West Africa
General Holidays: Jan. 1, New Year's Day; Jan. 13, Liberation Day; Jan. 24, Day of Victory; Apr. 24, Victory Day; Apr. 27, Independence Day; May 1, Labor Day; Sep. 24, Anniv. of failed attack on Lomé
Religious Holidays: Eid al-Fitr, Easter Monday, Ascension Day, Whit Monday, Eid al-Adha (Tabaski), Assumption, All Saints' Day, Christmas Day

Tonga, Kingdom of
Capital: Nuku'alofa
Nationality: Tongan(s)
Language: Tongan and English (both official)
Religion: Wesleyan Church, Roman Catholic, Anglican
Currency: pa'anga (T$) = 100 senti
Location: South Pacific Ocean

General Holidays: Jan. 1, New Year's Day; Apr. 25, Anzac Day; May 4,
Crown Prince's Birthday; Jun. 4, Independence Day; Jul. 4, HM
the King's Birthday; Nov. 4, Constitution Day; Dec. 4, King George
Tupou I Day
Religious Holidays: Easter, Christmas Day, Boxing Day

Trinidad and Tobago, Republic of
Capital: Port of Spain
Nationality: Trinidadian(s), Tobagonian(s)
Language: English (official), Hindi, French, Spanish, Chinese
Religion: Roman Catholic, Hindu, Protestant, Muslim
Currency: Trinidad and Tobago dollar (TT$) = 100 cents
Location: Southeast Caribbean Sea
General Holidays: Jan. 1, New Year's Day; Feb./Mar. (varies), Carnival; Jun. 19,
Labor Day; Aug. 1, Emancipation Day; Aug. 31, Independence Day;
Sep. 24, Republic Day
Religious Holidays: Eid al-Fitr, Good Friday, Easter Monday, Whit Monday,
Corpus Christi, Divali, Christmas Day

Tunisia, Republic of
Capital: Tunis
Nationality: Tunisian(s)
Language: Arabic (official), French, English
Religion: Muslim (majority), Roman Catholic, Protestant, Jewish
Currency: Tunisian dinar (TD) = 1,000 millimes
Location: North Africa
General Holidays: Jan. 1, New Year's Day; Mar. 20, Independence Day; Mar. 21,
Youth Day; Apr. 9, Martyr's Day; May 1, Labor Day; Jul. 25, Republic Day;
Aug. 13, Women's Day; Nov. 7, New Era Day
Religious Holidays: Aid el-Seghir, Aid el-Kebir, Ras El Am Hejri (Muslim New
Year's Day), Mouloud (Prophet's Birthday)

Turkey, Republic of
Capital: Ankara
Nationality: Turk(s)
Language: Turkish (official), Kurdish, Arabic, French, German, English
Religion: Sunni Muslim (majority), Christian, Jewish
Currency: Turkish lira (TL)
Location: Southeast Europe and West Asia
General Holidays: Jan. 1, New Year's Day; Apr. 23, National Independence and
Children's Day; May 1, Spring Day; May 19, Atatürk's Commemoration
Day, Youth and Sports Day; Aug. 30, Victory Day; Oct. 28–29,
Republic Day
Religious Holidays: Feast of Ramazan, Kurban Bayrami (Feast of Sacrifice)

Turkmenistan, Republic of
Capital: Ashkhabad
Nationality: Turkmen
Language: Turkmenian (official), Russian, ethnic languages
Religion: Sunni Muslim (majority), shamanism, Sufi mysticism
Currency: ruble (Rub) = 100 kopeks (new currency to be introduced)
Location: Southwest Central Asia
General Holidays: Oct. 27, Independence Day

Tuvalu
Capital: Fongafale
Nationality: Tuvaluan(s)
Language: Tuvaluan, English
Religion: Protestant (majority), other Christian
Currency: Australian dollar (A$) = 100 cents (also Tuvaluan dollar = 100 cents)
Location: South and West Pacific Ocean
General Holidays: Jan. 1, New Year's Day; Mar. (varies), Commonwealth Day; Jun. 15, Queen's Birthday; Aug. 3, National Children's Day; Oct. 1–2, Tuvalu Day; Nov. 14, Prince of Wales' Birthday
Religious Holidays: Easter, Christmas Day, Boxing Day

Uganda, Republic of
Capital: Kampala
Nationality: Ugandan(s)
Language: English (official), Luganda, Swahili, other African languages
Religion: Christian (majority), animist, Muslim
Currency: Uganda shilling (USh) = 100 cents
Location: Central and East Africa
General Holidays: Jan. 1, New Year's Day; Mar. 25, Anniv. of formation of UNLF; May 1, Labor Day; Jun. 3, Martyrs' Day; Oct. 9, Independence Day
Religious Holidays: Leilat al-Meiraj, Eid al-Fitr, Easter, Eid al-Adha, Christmas Day

Ukraine, Republic of
Capital: Kiev
Nationality: Ukrainian(s)
Language: Ukrainian (official), Russian, ethnic languages
Religion: Ukrainian Orthodox, Roman Catholic, Protestant, Jewish, Muslim
Currency: ruble (Rub) = 100 kopeks (new currency to be introduced)
Location: Southeast Central Europe
General Holidays: Aug. 24, Independence Day

United Arab Emirates
Capital: Abu Dhabi
Nationality: Emirian(s)
Language: Arabic (official), Hindi, Urdu, Farsi, English
Religion: Sunni Muslim (majority), Shiite Muslim, Christian, Hindu
Currency: dirham (Dh) = 100 fils
Location: Middle East
General Holidays: Aug. 6, Accession of HH Shaikh Zayed; Dec. 2,
    National Day
Religious Holidays: Lailat al-Mi'raj, Beginning of Ramadan, Eid al-Fitr,
    Eid al-Adha, Islamic New Year, Mouloud (Prophet's Birthday)

United Kingdom of Great Britain
and Northern Ireland
Capital: London
Nationality: Briton(s), British (collective pl.)
Language: English (official), Welsh, Gaelic, ethnic languages
Religion: Protestant (majority), other Christian, Jewish, Muslim, Hindu
Currency: pound sterling (£) = 100 pence (penny)
Location: Northwest Europe
General Holidays: England: May (1st Mon.), May Day; May (4th Mon.), Spring
    Holiday; Aug. (4th Mon.), Summer Bank Holiday *Northern Ireland:* May
    (1st Mon.), May Day; Jul. (2nd Fri.), Orangemen's Day; Aug. (4th Mon.),
    Summer Bank Holiday *Scotland:* Jan. 2, Bank Holiday; May (3rd Mon.),
    Victoria Day; Aug. (1st Mon.), Bank Holiday; Sep. (3rd Mon.), Autumn
    Holiday
Religious Holidays: England and Scotland: Good Friday, Easter Monday, Christ-
    mas Day, Boxing Day *Northern Ireland:* St. Patrick's Day, Good Friday,
    Easter Monday, Easter Tuesday, Christmas Day, Boxing Day

Uruguay, Oriental Republic of
Capital: Montevideo
Nationality: Uruguayan(s)
Language: Spanish (official), English
Religion: Roman Catholic (majority), Protestant, Jewish
Currency: Uruguayan nuevo peso (UN$) = 100 centésimos
Location: Southeast South America
General Holidays: Jan. 1, New Year's Day; Apr. 19, Landing of 33; May 1,
    Labor Day; May 18, Battle of Las Piedras; Jun. 19, Artigas' Birthday;
    Jul.18, Constitution Day; Aug. 25, Independence Day; Oct. 12,
    Columbus Day
Religious Holidays: Epiphany, All Souls' Day, Blessing of Waters,
    Christmas Day

Uzbekistan, Republic of
Capital: Tashkent
Nationality: Uzbek(s)
Language: Uzbek (official), Russian, ethnic languages
Religion: Sunni Muslim, Orthodox Christian, Jewish
Currency: ruble (Rub) = 100 kopeks (new currency to be introduced)
Location: Central Asia
General Holidays: Sep. 1, Independence Day

Vanuatu, Republic of
Capital: Vila
Nationality: Vanuatuan(s)
Language: English and French (official), Pidgin English (Bislama), local dialects
Religion: Christian
Currency: vatu (VT) = 100 centimes
Location: Southwest Pacific Ocean
General Holidays: Jan. 1, New Year's Day; May 4, Labor Day; Jul. 30, Independence Day; Oct. 5, Constitution Day; Nov. 29, Unity Day
Religious Holidays: Easter, Ascension Day, Assumption, Christmas Day

Venezuela, Republic of
Capital: Caracas
Nationality: Venezuelan(s)
Language: Spanish (official), English, French, Portuguese, German, Indian dialects
Religion: Roman Catholic (majority), Protestant
Currency: bolívar (VBO) = 100 centimos
Location: Northern South America
General Holidays: Jan. 1, New Year's Day; Feb. (varies), Carnival; Apr. 19, Declaration of Independence; May 1, Labor Day; Jun. 24, Carabobo Day; Jul. 5, Independence Day; Jul. 24, Bolívar's Birthday; Oct. 12, Día de la Raza
Religious Holidays: Good Friday, Easter Monday, Christmas Day

Vietnam, Socialist Republic of
Capital: Hanoi
Nationality: Vietnamese
Language: Vietnamese (official), Khmer, Chinese, Russian, French, English
Religion: Buddhist (majority), Confucian, Taoist, Roman Catholic
Currency: new dong (ND)
Location: Southeast Asia
General Holidays: Jan. 1, New Year's Day; Feb. (varies), Têt (Lunar New Year); Apr. (varies), Emperor-Founder Hung Vuong; Apr. 30, Liberation of Saigon; May 1, May Day; Sep. 2–3, National Day
Religious Holidays: Easter, Vu Lan, Christmas Day

Western Samoa, Independent State of
Capital: Apia
Nationality: Western Samoan(s)
Language: Samoan (official), English
Religion: Congregational Church, Roman Catholic, Methodist, Mormon
Currency: Western Samoa dollar (S$) or tala (WST) = 100 sene
Location: South Pacific Ocean
General Holidays: Jan. 1–2, New Year's Day; Apr. 25, Anzac Day; Jun. 1–3, Independence Day; Nov. 19, National Women's Day
Religious Holidays: Good Friday, Easter Monday, Whit Monday, Christmas Day, Boxing Day

Yemen, Republic of
Capital: Sana'a
Nationality: Yemini(s)
Language: Arabic (official), English
Religion: Muslim (majority), Christian, Hindu
Currency: Yemen riyal (YR) = 100 fils and Yemeni dinar (YD) = 1,000 fils
Location: Middle East
General Holidays: Jan. 1, New Year's Day; May 1, Labor Day; Jun. 13, Corrective Movement Anniv.; Oct. 14, National Day
Religious Holidays: Leilat al-Miraj, Eid al-Fitr, Eid al-Adha, Muharram, Islamic New Year, Mouloud (Prophet's Birthday)

Yugoslavia, Federal Republic of (Serbia and Montenegro)
Capital: Belgrade
Nationality: Yugoslav(s)
Language: Serbo-Croatian (official), Macedonian, Slovenian, Albanian, Hungarian
Religion: Eastern Orthodox (majority), Roman Catholic, Muslim
Currency: Yugoslav new dinar (D) = 100 para
Location: South-central Europe

Zaire, Republic of
Capital: Kinshasa
Nationality: Zairian(s)
Language: French (official), Swahili, Lingala, other African dialects
Religion: Roman Catholic (majority), Protestant, Muslim, local traditional beliefs
Currency: zaire (Z) = 100 makuta
Location: Central Africa
General Holidays: Jan. 1, New Year's Day; Jan. 4, Day of Martyrs of Independence; May 1, Labor Day; May 20, Anniv. of Mouvement Populaire de la Révolution; Jun. 24, Fishermen's Day; Jun. 30, Independence Day; Aug. 1, Parents' Day; Oct. 14, Youth Day; Oct. 27, Three-Z Day (anniv. of country's change of name to Zaire; Nov. 17, Army Day; Nov. 24, Anniv. of Second Republic
Religious Holidays: Christmas Day

Zambia, Republic of

Capital: Lusaka
Nationality: Zambian(s)
Language: English (official), about seventy native languages
Religion: Christian (majority), Muslim, Hindu, indigenous beliefs
Currency: Zambian kwacha (ZK) = 100 ngwee
Location: South Central Africa
General Holidays: Jan. 1, New Year's Day; Mar. 11, Youth Day; May 1, Labor
    Day; May 24, Africa Freedom Day; Jul. 5, Heroes' Day; Jul. 8, Unity Day;
    Aug. 5, Farmers' Day; Oct. 24, Independence Day
Religious Holidays: Easter, Christmas Day

Zimbabwe, Republic of

Capital: Harare
Nationality: Zimbabwean(s)
Language: English (official), numerous indigenous languages
Religion: Christian (majority), Hindu, Muslim, indigenous beliefs
Currency: Zimbabwe dollar (Z$) = 100 cents
Location: South Africa
General Holidays: Jan. 1, New Year's Day; Apr. 18, Independence Day; May 1,
    Workers' Day; May 25, Africa Day; Aug. 11–12, Heroes' Day
Religious Holidays: Good Friday through Easter Monday, Christmas Day,
    Boxing Day

ACCOUNTING AND DATA PROCESSING

CHAPTER

14

The evolution of the practice of accounting as a means of enabling businesses to keep track of past events and provide them with useful information for making future decisions has been essential to business expansion. The most important advance has been the introduction of computer technology (see Chapter 1) to improve and vastly accelerate the handling of accounting and data processing activities. With a computer, for example, journals and ledgers can be maintained more efficiently. Financial reports can be prepared and modified with far less typing and retyping than was previously necessary. Complex calculations can be made more rapidly and easily using spreadsheet software, and tax returns can be prepared with far greater efficiency using tax-preparation software.

Every business must handle certain financial and tax matters and subsequently keep records of these transactions as well as report them to various persons and groups outside the organization, including government agencies. A secretary is often required to perform many of the daily functions related to these types of financial transactions.

BASIC ACCOUNTING PRINCIPLES

Accounting is called the "language of business." The first step in mastering any language is to learn its rules and the meanings of its terms. Present-day accounting practice has produced a number of generally accepted principles that standardize both terminology and methods of recording the activities of the business. This standardization allows a company's accounting reports to be meaningful to managers, bankers, stockholders, creditors, government agencies, and others interested in its financial reports. These generally accepted principles provide the language of business that is understood by a diverse group of individuals.

Dual-Aspect Concept

Assets and Liabilities   Business accounting deals with the relationship between two aspects of business ownership: assets and liabilities. The items of value that a company owns are called *assets*. A company's assets are entered into the records at their original cost to the company, indicating that the value of the assets is equal to their cost. Over time, certain items owned by a company increase or decrease in value. Once an asset is recorded at its original cost, however, it is almost never adjusted to a current market value. Such adjustment could require continual revaluation to reflect the almost daily changes in the real or current market values of a company's numerous assets.

Assets owned by a company may include the following:

- Cash (in the bank as well as petty cash)

- Accounts receivable

- Marketable securities (stocks, bonds, certificates of deposit)

- Prepaid items (insurance, rent deposits)

- Property, plant, and equipment (land, buildings, equipment, furniture, fixtures)

- Inventory (raw materials, work in process, finished goods)

The money or funds used to acquire assets is provided either by the owners or the creditors of the company. *Creditors* are individuals or companies that lend money or extend credit to a business for a certain period. When this occurs, they acquire a claim of that amount against the business. Because a business will use its assets to pay off these claims, the claims are *claims against assets*. If a business refuses to pay a claim, the person to whom it is due can sue the business in a court of equity. Thus *all* claims against assets are called *equities*. A court of equity will usually hold the business liable for the amount of the claim.

Basic Accounting Equation   An understanding of claims helps explain the accounting term for the equity of a creditor: *liability*. Any asset not claimed by a creditor will be claimed by the owners of the business. These claims are called *owners' equity*. The total of all claims cannot exceed what there is to be claimed. This leads to the dual-aspect concept, also known as the basic accounting equation.

Assets = Liabilities + Owners' Equity

Monetary Concepts

An accounting system records only those events that can be expressed in terms of dollars, for example, the purchase of land or equipment or the sale of inventory for cash or on account. The morale and health of company personnel cannot be expressed in dollar terms, and the accounting system does not consider such factors. Thus a company's accounting records do not reveal all the facts, or even all the important facts, about a business.

The Business Entity

Accounting records are maintained for the business entity, as opposed to the persons who own, operate, or are otherwise associated with the business. Records reflect only what is happening to the company and not the personal transactions entered into by the people related to the company. For example, if the owner of a business buys a home, this purchase has no bearing on what is happening to the business, since the owner is an entity distinct from the business entity. A business may be operated under any one of several legal forms, such as a corporation, a partnership (two or more owners), or a proprietorship (one owner). Regardless of legal status, the business-entity concept applies.

The Accrual Principle

The accrual principal is based on the fact that the net income of a business is related not to the flow of cash but rather to changes in the owners' equity resulting from operations of a business. Revenue of a business adds to the owners' equity, and expenses decrease the owners' equity. The difference between revenue and expenses is the company's net income. See later sections of this chapter for additional explanations.

Two other generally accepted principles also relate to the accrual concept.

- The *realization concept* states that *revenue* is recognized when goods are delivered or when services are performed. It does not specifically relate to when cash is received for the sale of goods or services.

- The *matching concept* states that expenses of a period are costs associated with the revenues or activities of that period. The expenses do not relate to the actual cash disbursements for those expenses.

Most entities account for revenues and expenses as well as cash receipts and cash payments. Many individuals and some small businesses keep track only of cash receipts and cash payments. This type of accounting is called *cash accounting.* If you record your deposits, the checks you write, and your balance in a bank account, you are doing cash accounting. To measure the income of a period, a company must measure revenues and expenses, and this requires the use of accrual accounting. Accrual accounting is the only method that measures true changes in owners' equity.

ACCOUNTING REPORTS

Balance Sheet

Format   Accounting information is given to third parties outside the company on three main financial statements. Secretaries who type such reports must follow the format required by their employers and store this format in their computers for subsequent use. One report, called the *balance sheet,* shows a company's assets and liabilities and owners' equity at a given time. It presents the company's financial position at a specific moment, while recognizing that events may subsequently occur that will change certain aspects of the items of value that a company owns, as well as claims against those assets by creditors and owners.

The illustration of a balance sheet on page 514 is fairly typical, although it is also common to find the assets listed on the left-hand side and the liabilities on the right-hand side of a page. In any event, the dual-aspect principle is followed, and the total dollar amount of assets will equal the total amount of liabilities and owners' equity. The totals, however, do not indicate the company's financial condition. It is only after analysis of the various accounts listed on the balance sheet that you can come to any conclusions about the financial health of a company.

Balance Sheet

Andrew Manufacturing Company
Balance Sheet
December 31, 1993

ASSETS

Current Assets			
Cash			$ 10,000
Marketable Securities			13,000
Accounts Receivable, net			72,000
Inventories			101,000
Prepaid Insurance			3,000
Total Current Assets			199,000
Fixed Assets			
Land		$120,000	
Buildings		500,000	
Furniture and Fixtures		73,000	
Equipment		104,000	
		797,000	
Less: Accumulated Depreciation		407,000	
Total Fixed Assets			390,000
Other Assets			
Long-Term Investments		93,000	
Long-Term Receivables		10,000	
Goodwill, net		72,000	
Other Assets		17,000	
Total Other Assets			192,000
TOTAL ASSETS			$781,000

LIABILITIES & OWNERS' EQUITY

Current Liabilities			
Accounts Payable			$ 53,000
Bank Loan Payable			100,000
Accrued Wages and Salaries Payable			7,000
Current Portion of Mortgage Payable			5,000
Taxes Payable			10,000
Total Current Liabilities			175,000
Long-Term Liabilities			
Mortgage Payable		$200,000	
Bonds Payable		150,000	
Total Long-Term Liabilities			350,000
Total Liabilities			525,000
Owners' Equity			
Common Stock		100,000	
Retained Earnings		156,000	
Total Owners' Equity			256,000
TOTAL EQUITIES			$781,000

Balance Sheet Accounts   A balance sheet showing a number of items becomes more useful when the items are classified into significant groups of assets and liabilities. It would be possible to list each individual account receivable, each inventory item owned, each piece of equipment, and each account payable, but this usually provides much more detail than is needed for a balance sheet analysis. For the practical purpose of making the balance sheet more informative, items are grouped into classifications. There is no limit to the number of classifications, but the ones in the illustration are common.

Current Assets. The first balance sheet classification is current assets. The current assets classification includes cash and other assets that can reasonably be expected to be realized in cash or sold or consumed during the normal operating period of the business, usually one year. Current assets can be subclassified as indicated in the following list:

- *Cash*: This includes all cash owned by a company, including cash in the bank (in a checking or savings account) and petty cash. The amount of cash a company has will change through the receipt of cash for sales and the payment of bills with cash (or checks). An adequate amount of cash is vital to a company's survival, and sufficient amounts should be available to meet the immediate needs of the company's operations.

- *Marketable securities*: If a company has more cash on hand than is needed for the immediate future, it may use the excess cash to purchase short-term investments, such as certificates of deposit or stock or indebtedness of other companies. The investing company earns short-term returns such as interest or dividends just as an individual's savings account in a bank earns interest. These investments can be readily sold in the marketplace and converted back into cash on very short notice.

- *Accounts receivable*: This account often constitutes a large portion of a company's current assets and represents amounts of money owed to the company by its regular customers. It is collectible within the next twelve months. This account is reported as its net value, which means that the actual value of the receivables has been reduced by an amount equivalent to the company's expectations of receivables that will not be paid. A company maintains detailed records of accounts receivable by customer in a subsidiary accounts receivable ledger. This subsidiary record has a page devoted to each customer and lists all sales "on account" as well as cash collections related to these sales. The total of every page balance in the subsidiary ledger is shown as the amount owed to the company as total accounts receivable.

- *Inventories*: Inventories often represent the largest portion of current assets for a company. For manufacturing firms, inventories include raw materials to be converted into a finished product, work-in-process inventories that include partially completed products, and finished products ready for sale. Inventories generally cannot be converted into cash as quickly as receivables, since it takes time for the goods to be sold (usually resulting in an account receivable) and for the cash to be collected.

- *Prepaid items*: This represents prepayments for resources such as rent, interest, insurance, and deposits that will be used up during the next twelve months. Since they have not yet been used up or consumed, they still are assets (items of value) to the company. They are rarely converted into cash (although conversion is possible) and are therefore listed last under current assets.

Fixed Assets. The next major asset classification is fixed assets, which may also be called *plant assets*; *property, plant, and equipment*; or *tangible fixed assets*. Fixed assets are relatively long-lived assets that are held for use by the business in the production of goods or sale of goods or services. They are not acquired for resale in the ordinary course of business but must have a useful life of at least one year. The reported value of fixed assets is based on the amount it cost the company to acquire them, called the *historical* or *acquisition cost*. Items in this category include the following:

- *Land*: On which the company may have already constructed buildings

- *Buildings*: Office or plant locations used in routine business operations

- *Furniture and fixtures*: Desks, chairs, and similar furnishings used by company personnel

- *Equipment*: Office or production machines used by the company

Fixed assets other than land are assumed to have limited lives because time, obsolescence, and normal use eventually reduce their benefit to the business. Those assets are therefore called *depreciable assets.* The process of allocating the cost of these assets ratably to the accounting periods in which they are consumed and benefit the company is called *depreciation.*

Depreciation expense is taken each accounting period as an expense on the income statement and results from an attempt to allocate systematically the asset's acquisition cost over its anticipated useful life. The depreciation accumulated from all previous periods appears on the balance sheet as a reduction of the related fixed-asset account cost. This yields the presumed fixed-asset value to the company at the balance sheet date.

The useful life of an asset is an *estimate* and is subject to many uncontrollable external factors such as obsolescence, technological advancements, and unexpected wear and tear. Therefore, the balance sheet value of fixed assets does not necessarily represent the value a company would receive if the asset were to be sold at the balance sheet date.

Other Assets. Other assets, if reported at all, refers to miscellaneous assets difficult to classify as either fixed or current assets. Investments, long-term receivables, and goodwill are examples of assets that the company intends to hold for more than one year. Investments may include securities of other companies that the business has invested in or that the employer owns or controls. Long-term receivables may indicate the sale of expensive items for which payments are spread out over more than one year. Goodwill is associated with the price paid by one company to purchase another, which is often higher than the value of the net physical assets acquired. The excess amount paid is called *goodwill* and reflects the purchaser's belief in the company's potential to earn high profits.

Current Liabilities. Liabilities are claims of creditors against the assets of the business. Current debts or obligations that must be paid or otherwise settled within one year or the normal operating cycle of a business are called *current liabilities.* These are the company's most immediate obligations, and cash or other current assets are necessary to liquidate them. These claims are usually not against a specific asset of the company. Within the classification of current liabilities there are several subclasses.

- *Accounts payable*: This represents amounts owed to ordinary business creditors for unpaid bills for inventory and supplies. If the claim is evidenced by a note or other written document, it is usually segregated as a note payable.

- *Bank loan payable*: This represents money owed by the company to its bank. Because it is shown as a current liability, it implies that it is payable within one year.

- *Accrued wages and salaries payable*: This refers to amounts owed to employees of the business at the time the balance sheet was drawn up. An example of this is when employees are paid on a weekly basis and the balance sheet has been drawn up at a point during one of the pay periods. As a result, wages and salaries owed to employees but not yet paid to them are recorded as a liability.

- *Current portion of long-term debt*: This amount represents the portion of the long-term debt principal (not interest) payable within twelve months of the balance sheet date.

- *Taxes payable*: This amount is owed but not yet paid to the federal, state, or local government for taxes due on income, payroll, inventory, and so on.

- *Unearned revenues*: These are obligations to provide goods or services to customers who have made advance payments. For example, subscription receipts that have been received by a magazine publisher in advance of sending the magazine issues are unearned revenues. Rent that is received in advance by a landlord is another example of these types of liabilities.

Long-Term Liabilities. These claims against assets are due to be paid after the next twelve months. This category includes property mortgages payable, long-term loans payable, notes payable, and bonds or debentures payable. Unlike accounts payable, these liabilities tend to be evidenced by formal documents indicating a definite obligation to pay at some future time. Often long-term liabilities are a guaranteed claim against some specific assets, known as a *lien*. Any portion of long-term payables becoming due within one year from the balance sheet date should be included in the current-liabilities category. Any amount recorded here represents only the principal amount due.

These types of obligations usually have an interest payment associated with them. The interest due is not recorded on the balance sheet, however, because interest relates to the use of money or funds over time. Interest is not initially recorded until your company has had the use of someone else's funds for a certain period. Then the expense is recorded in the income statement and the payable recorded separately as a current liability.

Owners' Equity. The owners' equity section of the balance sheet represents claims made against the assets by the owners of the business and is simply the portion of the company not claimed by anyone else. It is also known as *book value* or *net worth.* The manner of reporting owners' equity on the balance sheet depends on the type of business for which the balance sheet is prepared; a business may be organized as a single proprietorship, a partnership, or a corporation.

The owners' equity section of Andrew Manufacturing Company, for example, indicates that it is organized as a corporation. Corporations are created under and regulated by state and federal laws. These laws require that a distinction be made between the amount invested in the corporation by its owners (the original shareholders) and the increase or decrease in owners' equity due to daily operations.

The amount invested by the owners, called *common stock* or *capital stock,* is entered on the balance sheet at its stated value, which might be the price paid for the stock, its par value, or some other figure agreed upon at the time the stock was issued or sold. Subsequently, there is no relationship between the recorded value and the market value of the stock. The increase or decrease in owners' equity due to daily operations, called *retained earnings,* reflects the earnings of the company from daily operations in prior years that have been left in the business and have not been paid out to the owners in the form of dividends.

The word *surplus* was used in place of *retained earnings* in the past but is not in current use today. Retained earnings or accumulated amounts of net income belong to and are a claim of the company's owners and are always shown *after* common stock in the owners' equity section of the balance sheet.

When a business is owned by one person, it is called a *sole proprietorship,* and the sole proprietor's equity may be reported on the balance sheet in either of the following two ways.

1. Ryan Andrew, capital   <u>$256,000</u>

2. Ryan Andrew, capital,
    January 1, 1995 $200,000
    Net Income for the year ended
      December 31, 1995 $323,000
    Withdrawals   <u>267,000</u>
    Excess of earnings over
      withdrawals   <u>56,000</u>

    Ryan Andrew, capital,
      December 31, 1995   <u>$256,000</u>

When two or more persons own a business as partners, changes in their equities resulting from earnings and withdrawals are normally shown in a supplementary financial statement entitled the "Statement of Partners' Equity." Only the amount of each partner's equity and the total equities are shown on the balance sheet itself.

Partners' Equity

Ryan Andrew, capital	$128,000
Daniel Andrew, capital	<u>128,000</u>
	<u>$256,000</u>

Thus in the owners' equity section of the balance sheet, capital (cash or assets) contributed by the owners of the company as well as earnings accumulated since the business began are accumulated as claims against assets.

Income Statement

A second type of financial statement, the *income statement,* presents the results of a company's operations for a given period — a month, three months, or a year. The last day of that period will be the date of the balance sheet information that accompanies the income statement. The income statement is also known as the *profit and loss report, P & L,* or *operating statement.*

    This statement presents sales, the cost of the specific goods or services sold, the other costs associated with selling the goods or services, and the resulting profit or loss (net income, bottom line, or net profit). Thus this statement shows all sources of revenue generated by the company's operations as well as all related expenses incurred to generate that revenue. The format and specific revenue and expense classifications will vary, but the income statement illustrated in this section is fairly typical.

Income Statement

Andrew Manufacturing Company
Income Statement
for the year ending December 31, 1993

Gross Sales		$3,600,000
Less Sales Returns, Allowances, and Discounts		250,000
Net Sales		3,350,000
Less Cost of Goods Sold		1,650,000
Gross Profit		1,700,000
Less Operating Expenses		
Selling, General, and Administrative Expenses		
Insurance	$ 12,000	
Office Salaries	311,000	
Selling Expense	175,000	
Heat, Light, and Power	23,000	
Advertising	165,000	
Telephone	57,000	
Office Supplies	17,000	
Automobile Expense	30,000	
Bad Debt Expense	97,500	
Travel Expense	133,000	
Depreciation Expense	20,000	
Miscellaneous Expense	53,500	
Total Selling, General and Administrative Expenses		1,094,000
Research and Development Costs		250,000
Other Operating Expenses		16,000
Total Operating Expenses		1,360,000
Operating Profit		340,000
Other Income and Expenses		
Interest Expense	100,000	
Interest Income	(73,000)	
Miscellaneous Income	(10,000)	
Total Other Income and Expenses		17,000
Profit Before Taxes		323,000
Provision for Corporate Income Taxes		147,000
Net Income		$ 176,000

Accounting Period

Income Statement Periods. For most businesses the official accounting period is one year. Income statements, however, called *interim statements,* usually are prepared for shorter periods as well. Most companies have income statements prepared on a monthly basis to report the operation of the business during the past month. Thus the accounting period covered in a monthly income statement is one month. The report is prepared from information accumulated in the accounts of the business. Information often must be reported to various government agencies and banks on a monthly or quarterly basis, so income statements are often generated for these reasons as well.

Common Accounting Periods. For most companies the accounting period is a *calendar* year, the year that ends on the last day of the calendar, December 31. Some companies, however, end their year at the end of their busy season. This is called a *fiscal year* end. For example, colleges and universities usually have a June 30 year end. Retailers often end their year at the end of January. Sports-related businesses end their year at the end of the month that their season ends. The accounting period for these businesses is the *natural* business year, not a calendar year.

The fact that accounting assigns events to a set period makes the problem of measuring revenue and expenses into that period one of the most difficult problems in accounting, but it does not affect the daily operations of the company. In rare instances an accounting period may extend beyond one year if the business activities of the company extend beyond twelve months from the time the transaction is initiated until it is completed. This situation occurs in companies dealing with long-term contracts or in those companies whose production processes are lengthy. If your company falls into this category, the accounting period and the income statement covered by it may extend beyond twelve months.

Income Statement Accounts

Sales. The first entry on the income statement is the *sales* for the period. It is customary to show gross sales revenue earned by the accrual method and then to deduct any returns, allowances, and discounts given during the period to arrive at net sales. By showing sales returns and allowances separately, attention is called to any unusual amounts (increase) shown in this category.

Sales revenues are inflows of cash and other assets received from others for goods exchanged or services performed. The result is an increase in total assets, a decrease in total liabilities, or a combination thereof. Terms such as *income, revenue earned,* and *received* preceded by a noun such as *rent, interest,* or *commissions* identify a revenue source. Revenues derived from sales to customers are often described as *sales revenue, fees earned,* or *commissions earned* in the income statement. Other revenues unrelated to customer sales include *commissions earned, dividends received, interest income,* and *rental revenue.*

Expenses. In accounting *expenses* are considered as the outflow of cash or other resources of the business during a specific period. The accrual principle is followed. Expenses relate to the consumption of assets or the incurrence of debt for goods or services consumed by the company to produce revenue. The common classifications of expenses are as follows:

- *Cost of goods sold:* This represents the cost of *purchasing goods for resale* as well as the cost incurred in *manufacturing products for sale* to customers. This category should include, to the extent possible, only the costs associated with goods sold during the *current* accounting period. In a manufacturing company such costs include raw materials, direct labor, and manufacturing overhead. Manufacturing overhead includes all allocated product-related costs other than raw material and direct labor, including indirect labor, fringe benefits, supervision costs, plant rent, insurance, freight, light and power, plant depreciation, quality assurance, shipping, and so on. The cost of any goods remaining on hand at the end of the period is shown as inventory in the current assets section of the balance sheet.

- *Gross profit:* This represents the amount of sales revenue realized in excess of the cost of goods sold. This amount must exceed the amount of all remaining expenses of operating the business if the business is to be profitable. Gross profit is also known as *gross margin.*

- *Operating expenses:* Operating expenses are incurred in the normal operations of the business. Operating expenses are not incurred in producing a product; rather, they are considered *costs of the period.* They are often subclassified by function, such as selling and distribution, research and development, and general and administration expenses.

Selling expenses include all expense incurred during the period to perform the sales activities of the firm. Such expenses include salaries paid to sales people, commissions, rental of sales facilities, depreciation on sales equipment, and advertising costs. *General and administrative expenses* are those incurred during the year in administering overall company activities. They often include office supplies, officers' salaries, depreciation of the office building and equipment, rental of office space, property taxes, legal fees, accounting fees, office employee salaries, and related fringe benefits. *Research and development (R & D) expenses* are incurred by the company in pursuit of further improvement of existing products or development of new products. These expenses include salaries of R & D personnel, facilities and equipment expense, and other like expenses incurred for research and development efforts.

- *Operating profit*: This represents profit earned from the normal business operations of the firm. It represents sales revenues minus the cost of goods sold and operating expenses. Operating profit also may be called *income from operations* or *net operating revenue.*

- *Other income and expense*: These are *nonoperating sources of revenues or expenses* not resulting from the daily operations of the business. They include items such as interest income from investments, interest expense on loans or other outstanding debts, profit or loss on the sale of fixed assets, and revenue from nonrelated business operations. They are listed separately to highlight their difference from other revenue and expenses related to the business' primary operations.

- *Profit before taxes*: This is the net difference between all revenues and expenses of the business and also may be called *income before taxes.*

- *Provision for corporate income taxes*: Included in this classification are all federal corporate income taxes. Local and state taxes are sometimes included here as well. If not, they are included with general and administrative expenses. If the company is a sole proprietorship or partnership, the business pays no taxes. Rather, the owners include their pro rata share of the business profit (or loss) on their personal tax returns and pay taxes on this profit individually.

- *Net income*: Also known as *net profit* or *"the bottom line,"* net income represents the amount of profit the company has earned for the period covered by the income statement.

Statement of Cash Flows

A third type of financial statement, illustrated on page 526, is the statement of cash flows. Although this financial statement is required by standards governing certified public accountants, it is not regularly used by management. The statement presents the sources and uses of cash and cash equivalents of a company for the same period covered by the income statement. This information helps inform its readers about events that have occurred within the company that affect cash balances but that are not reflected in the other two financial statements; that is, not related to the items a company owns at a specific time and not related to the results of operations for a certain period. This financial statement is also known as the *source and application of funds statement,* or the *"where got-where gone"* statement.

SYSTEMS AND PROCEDURES

Secretaries who are familiar with accounting as the language of business are better able to perform the many duties and functions they encounter. Included are activities related to handling cash, such as recording cash receipts and disbursements, controlling petty cash, and performing a bank reconciliation; recording investments in securities; and recording the acquisition of fixed assets. The various tasks a secretary undertakes may be handled manually or electronically. Often, the work involves a combination.

Accounting Systems

An accounting system consists of all the business papers, records, reports, and procedures used in recording and reporting transactions. An accounting system is really a data processing system that functions in one of the ways described in the following two sections.

Statement of Cash Flows

Andrew Manufacturing Company
Statement of Cash Flows
For the Year Ending December 31, 1993

Cash Balance, January 1, 1993 $ - 0 -

Cash Flows Generated (Used) from Operating Activities

Net Income for the Period	$ 176,000	
Depreciation	20,000	
Decrease in Marketable Securities	10,000	
Increase in Accounts Receivable	(30,000)	
Decrease in Inventories	19,000	
Increase in Prepaid Insurance	(3,000)	
Decrease in Accounts Payable	(30,000)	
Decrease in Accrued Salaries Payable	(2,000)	
Decrease in Taxes Payable	(2,000)	
Cash Flows Generated from Operating Activities		$158,000

Cash Flows Generated (Used) from Financing Activities

Increase in Mortgage Payable, net of repayments	$ 75,000	
Decrease in Bonds Payable	(77,000)	
Sale of Common Stock	50,000	
Cash Flows Generated from Financing Activities		48,000

Cash Flows Generated (Used) from Investing Activities

Purchases of Fixed Assets	$(153,000)	
Purchases of Long Term Investments	(43,000)	
Cash Flows (Used) from Investing Activities		(196,000)
Net Cash Generated (Used) for the Year Ending December 31, 1993		$ 10,000

Cash Balance, December 31, 1993 $ 10,000

Manual Data Processing   With a manual data processing system, the accounting work is performed by hand. This type of system may be used in some small businesses and for certain parts of the information process in medium- and large-sized businesses. In larger companies it is useful for discussing and illustrating the application of accounting concepts and principles as well as for explaining the accounting process. A manual writing-copying-posting procedure accomplishes its objectives but is often time-consuming and error-prone. Therefore, any procedure that reduces the number of times information is copied and recopied improves the system.

An example of a manual system is the one-write, or pegboard, system. It is designed to process all or a large portion of the data in a transaction with one writing. This can be done with payroll, sales, purchases, cash receipts, and cash disbursements. For payroll the paycheck, employee earnings record, and payroll register are all recorded simultaneously via a system of alignment of documents and carbon copies. Similarly, for credit sales the entry on the customer's month-end statement, the posting to his or her account, and the entry in the sales journal are all made at once.

Electronic Data Processing   With an electronic data processing (EDP) system, computers of varying sizes and sophistication (large mainframes to micro- and minicomputers) are used to process information accurately and rapidly. This equipment has a large capacity to store data and the capability to manipulate and recall data with great speed. Electronic data processing involves the use of hardware (the central processing unit and related peripherals), systems software (the computer programs that give instructions to the computer), applications software (such as a spreadsheet program), as well as other related items for system operations (such as training material).

The EDP equipment in use today performs many functions that accounting needs. It can handle arithmetic procedures (add, subtract, multiply, and divide), memory storage (file maintenance), memory recall, comparison of information, repetition of the same set of instructions, yes-no decisions, and "what-if" analyses. For more about system components, refer to Chapter 1.

Computers process data with speed and accuracy. Before a computer can do this, however, a human being must think through the procedures that the computer will use in processing the data, anticipate every processing exception, and then instruct the computer in great detail how to do the job. Although computers are a big help in the processing of accounting information, they are only as good as the people programming them and the correctness of the data being processed.

The Accounting Process

The basic accounting process is the same for all businesses, large and small. The purpose of an information processing system is to facilitate the accumulation of data needed to make decisions and to prepare financial statements. The basic components of that information processing system, whether manual or electronic, are the same (see the illustration in this section). The components of the system include the following:

COMPONENT	PURPOSE
General journals and special journals	For formally recording the data obtained from the analysis of individual transactions.
General ledger	For accumulating and summarizing the data recorded in the journals in terms of the dual-aspect concept for the balance sheet and income statement accounts. There is a separate account page for each general ledger account. See the illustration of general ledger accounts on pages 530–531.
Subsidiary ledgers	To provide a detailed analysis of the balance recorded in a specific general ledger account (accounts receivable, notes receivable, marketable securities, inventories, fixed assets, and notes payable).

When a company must record hundreds or thousands of similar transactions, such as credit sales or purchase of materials, the information-processing system must handle the transaction as efficiently as possible. This makes the use of special journals that record and summarize like transactions advantageous.

The Basic Accounting Record-Keeping System

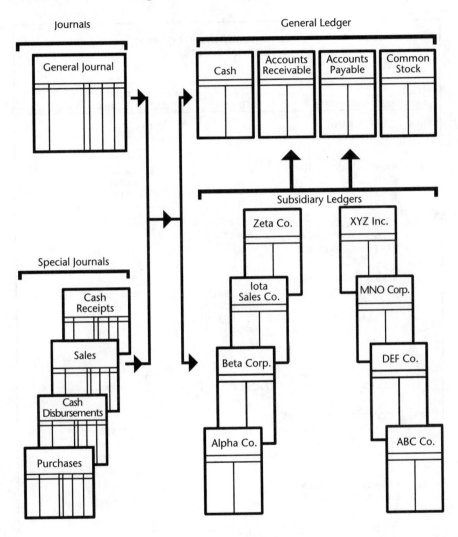

Transaction	Special Journal
Purchase of merchandise or raw materials on credit	Purchases journal
Cash payments	Cash disbursements journal
Credit (and sometimes cash) sales	Sales journal
Cash collections	Cash receipts journal

General Ledger

```
                    ANDREW MANUFACTURING COMPANY
                         GENERAL LEDGER

AS OF 12/31/93                                              PAGE 1
```

ACCT NO.	ACCOUNT NAME	FOLIO	BALANCE FORWARD	CURRENT PERIOD	BALANCE
1000	CASH IN BANK		.00		
	INV REG SUMMARY	IR		.00	
					.00
1001	CASH IN BANK - CHECKI		.00		
	CHECKS FOR PERIOD	CD1		3,704.00 –	
	RECEIPTS FOR PERIOD	CR1		9,191.00	
					5,487.00
1002	CASH IN BANK - SAVING		.00		
	CHECKS FOR PERIOD	CD2		.00	
	RECEIPTS FOR PERIOD	CR2		.00	
					.00
1100	ACCOUNTS RECEIVABLE -		.00		
	ALPHA COMPANY	CR1 12/04/93		730.00 –	
	ZETON W.	CR1 12/20/93		1,000.00 –	
	DELTA COMPANY	CR1 12/30/93		550.00 –	
	INV REG SUMMARY	IR		.00	
	INV REG SUMMARY	IR		.00	
					2,280.00 –
1200	MARKETABLE SECURITIES		.00		
	SALE OF MARKETABLE SECU	CR1 12/12/93		2,000.00 –	
					2,000.00 –
2000	ACCOUNTS PAYABLE - TR		.00		
	ABC COMPANY - NO. C370	CD1 #7031		1,313.00	
	MDSE PURCH SUMMARY	MP		.00	
	MDSE PURCH SUMMARY	MP		.00	
					1,313.00
2600	BANK LOAN PAYABLE		.00		
	BANK LOAN	CR1 12/21/93		4,500.00 –	
					4,500.00 –
3050	RETAINED EARNINGS		.00		
	PERIOD NET INCOME (CR) OR LOSS (DR)			1,980.00	
					1,980.00

The formats of special journals vary depending upon the needs of management. The two special journals discussed in detail are typical examples but may be modified to meet goals for cost and time savings.

Cash Receipts Journal   A cash receipts journal is used to record all cash receipts of the company. It is designed to handle not only pay-

General Ledger, continued

AS OF 12/31/93   PAGE 2

ACCT NO.	ACCOUNT NAME	FOLIO	BALANCE FORWARD	CURRENT PERIOD	BALANCE
4000	SALES - MATERIALS		.00		
	CASH SALE	CR1 12/07/93		471.00–	
	INV REG SUMMARY	IR		.00	
					471.00–
4010	SALES DISCOUNT		.00		
	ALPHA COMPANY	CR1 12/04/93		7.00	
	ZETON W.	CR1 12/20/93		27.00	
	DELTA COMPANY	CR1 12/30/93		26.00	
					60.00
5000	C/S - MATERIALS		.00		
	QRS COMPANY - NO. 11078	CD1 #7033		750.00	
	XYZ COMPANY - NO. KBQ3	CD1 #7036		125.00	
	MDSE PURCH SUMMARY	MP		.00	
					875.00
5010	PURCHASE DISCOUNT		.00		
	QRS COMPANY - NO. 11078	CD1 #7033		22.00–	
	XYZ COMPANY - NO. KBQ3	CD1 #7036		14.00–	
					36.00–
6100	INTEREST EXPENSE		.00		
	BANK LOAN INTEREST	CD1 #7034		300.00	
					300.00
6200	RENT EXPENSE		.00		
	R.W. WALP	CD1 #7032		1,100.00	
					1,100.00
6230	UTILITIES - WATER		.00		
	ACTON WATER DEPT.	CD1 #7035		152.00	
					152.00
9999	INCOME TRANSFER		.00		
	PERIOD NET INCOME (DR) OR LOSS (CR)			1,980.00–	
					1,980.00–
	TOTALS		.00	.00	.00

ments of credit and cash sales but also other revenue sources. The procedures to follow in recording cash receipts are performed daily. See the illustration of cash receipts entries on page 532. In this example the date and payor are entered first, followed by the general ledger account number and the subsidiary account number (if any). Following that is the amount as well as any discount amount, with the net recorded in the sixth column.

The columns in the cash receipts journal are totaled on a monthly basis, and the totals are recorded in the general ledger accounts. The total of the miscellaneous account column is not recorded in the general ledger since it represents the sum of amounts already recorded in several different accounts. Start a new page in the cash receipts journal each month and number each page sequentially.

Cash Receipts Journal

ANDREW MANUFACTURING COMPANY
CASH RECEIPTS
CASH IN BANK - CHECKING

AS OF 12/31/93   PAGE 1

DATE	PAYOR	G/L ACCT	SUB ACCT	DETAIL	NET AMT
12/04/93	ALPHA COMPANY	1100	C101	730.00	
		4010		7.00−	
					723.00
12/07/93	CASH SALE	4000			471.00
12/12/93	SALE OF MARKETABLE SECURITY	1200			2,000.00
12/20/93	ZETON W.	1100	C102	1,000.00	
		4010		27.00−	
					973.00
12/21/93	BANK LOAN	2600			4,500.00
12/30/93	DELTA COMPANY	1100	C103	550.00	
		4010		26.00−	
					524.00
	BATCH TOTAL				9,191.00
	TOTAL				9,191.00

Cash Disbursements Journal The cash disbursements journal is used to list all checks written during the period. A sample journal is illustrated below. In this example, the date, payee, and check number are entered first, followed by the general ledger account number and the subsidiary account number (if any). Following that is the amount as

Cash Disbursements Journal

ANDREW MANUFACTURING COMPANY
CASH DISBURSEMENTS
CASH IN BANK - CHECKING

AS OF 12/31/93   PAGE 1

DATE	PAYEE	CHECK NO.	G/L ACCT	SUB ACCT	DETAIL	NET AMT
12/12/93	ABC COMPANY - NO. C370	7031	2000			1,313.00
12/17/93	R.W. WALP	7032	6200			1,100.00
12/20/93	QRS COMPANY - NO. 1107	7033	5000		750.00	
			5010		22.00–	
						728.00
12/21/93	BANK LOAN INTEREST	7034	6100			300.00
12/27/93	ACTON WATER DEPT.	7035	6230			152.00
12/30/93	XYZ COMPANY - NO. KBQ3	7036	5000		125.00	
			5010		14.00–	
						111.00
	BATCH TOTAL					3,704.00
	TOTAL					3,704.00

well as any discount amount, with the net recorded in the seventh column.

The columns in the cash disbursements journal are totaled on a monthly basis, and the totals are recorded in the general ledger accounts. The total of the miscellaneous amount column is not recorded in the general ledger since it represents the sum of amounts already recorded to several different accounts. Start a new page in the cash disbursements journal each month and number each page sequentially.

Both cash receipts and cash disbursements records may be simplified for a small company or greatly expanded for a larger, more sophisticated accounting system. The system should be designed to meet the needs of the company's managers and owners.

Bank Reconciliations

The bank reconciliation is a comparison of the information contained in the bank's monthly statement with the company's own cash accounting records. A separate reconciliation should be prepared for each bank account, using your company's format or the form provided by the bank along with each monthly bank statement. It should be prepared promptly upon receipt of the bank statement and canceled checks included with the statement.

The canceled checks should be compared to the company's cash disbursements records to insure that the checks have been made payable to the proper person or company (payee) and have been written for the proper amounts. The bank's list of deposits should be compared to the company's cash receipts records and the company's copies of the bank deposit slips to verify that all cash receipts have been properly deposited.

Because of timing differences between the company's recording of cash receipts and disbursements and those reported in the bank's statement, the ending cash balance in the company's records and the cash balance reported in the bank statement will usually differ. The sources of these differences are called *reconciling items*. The purpose of the bank reconciliation is to identify the reconciling items and, by making the proper adjustments, to determine the correct cash balance. Generally, follow these steps:

- Gather the current month's bank statement and canceled checks, the prior month's reconciliation, the checkbook or check register listing checks written during the period and the cash balance at month end, and the record of deposits or the company's copy of the month's deposit slips.

- Trace all canceled checks and bank memorandums to the bank statement to insure that there are no differences.

- Put the canceled checks returned by the bank in numerical order.

- Compare the canceled checks to the prior month's outstanding check list and the current month's listing of checks written by the company.

- Make a list of outstanding checks at the end of the current month.

- List information from the bank memos for inclusion in the bank reconciliation.

- Compare deposits on the bank statement with the company's copy of the deposit slips or other listing of cash receipts. Note differences for inclusion as deposits in transit.

- Complete the bank reconciliation in a format used by your place of business or use the form provided by your bank.

- Correct or adjust the company's records as needed. Notify the bank of any errors they have made.

Petty Cash Fund

Many companies maintain small amounts of cash on their premises to cover small disbursements when it is impractical to write a check or when cash is needed immediately. These petty cash funds may cover the purchase of office supplies, postage, coffee, and so on. Also known as an *imprest fund,* the petty cash fund is normally established at an amount sufficient to cover two to four weeks of needs and is usually between $100 and $500. When the amount is determined, a check payable to "Petty Cash" is made out and cashed, and the cash is then placed in a locked box or drawer under the control of the secretary or other custodian having sole responsibility for the fund.

Using Petty Cash Vouchers   All expenditures from the petty cash fund should be made by the custodian, and adequate documentation should be maintained to support the payments. Often petty cash vouchers, purchased from any stationery or office-supply store, are used for such documentation (see illustration on page 536). Each voucher

Petty Cash Voucher

```
AMOUNT $ 50.00              NO. 43
        RECEIVED OF PETTY CASH
              March 13        19 95
  FOR Lunch Expenses - Guest
  CHARGE TO Editorial

  APPROVED BY            RECEIVED BY
  WAR                    A.Thd
  AICO FORM NO. 55-081          PRINTED IN U.S.A.
```

shows the date, purpose of the expenditure, the department or account to be charged, the signature of the person receiving the cash, the signature of the person disbursing the funds, the amount disbursed, and a sequential voucher number. This information may be maintained on a separate disbursement sheet rather than on petty cash vouchers, but that practice is less common.

Replenishing the Fund   At any time, the amount of cash on hand plus the amount of disbursements noted on the petty cash vouchers should equal the established amount of the petty cash fund. When the cash in the fund is low, it should be replenished by writing a check to "Petty Cash" for the amount needed to restore the fund to its authorized amount. The check is cashed and the proceeds are placed in the petty cash box. The fund is now back at its original amount and is ready for use once again.

In some offices the secretary must prepare a record of transactions (as recorded on the vouchers) before a new check can be cashed. This record should contain (1) the amount in the fund at the beginning of the period; (2) an itemized list of each expenditure (date, voucher number, to whom paid, for what paid, amount); and (3) the balance in the fund at the end of the period (after deducting all the expenditures from the beginning amount in the fund).

Some secretaries keep a handwritten or computer record *during* the period, so that a final copy can be quickly prepared at the end of the period. For a handwritten record, use a columnar-style accounting sheet. For a computer record set up columns like a table. In both cases use the items listed in the previous paragraph as headings (date, voucher number, and so on), and fill in the appropriate information in the columns below each heading.

Investment Transactions

Many organizations invest in stocks, bonds, and other assets to earn a return on excess funds. It is important to record all information related to these transactions properly, not only for the company's financial records but also to comply with governmental agency requirements. When handling security transactions, you should maintain the following documents or files:

- Keep a separate record for each security owned, and maintain the records in alphabetical order. Post all investment activity as it occurs. See the illustration "Record of Security Transactions."

- Compile an alphabetical list of all investments in securities owned and update it on a weekly, biweekly, or monthly basis, depending on the volume of investment activity. See the illustration "List of Securities Owned" on page 538.

Record of Security Transactions

Andrew Manufacturing Company
Record of Security Transactions

Security _____

Exchange Listed on _____

Broker _____

No. of Shares	Date	Purchase/ Sale	Price/Share	Broker's Commis.	Total Purchase Price Paid/Sales Price Rec'd

Cap. Gain or (Loss) on Sale		Bal.	
Short-term	Long-term	Shares Owned	Total Cost

List of Securities Owned

Andrew Manufacturing Company
List of Securities Owned
December 31, 1992

Number of Shares or Face Value	Security Name and Description	Total Cost	Current Market Value
Stocks:			
Bonds:			
Investment Funds:			
Other:		_____	_____
Totals:		$ _____	$ _____

- Keep a file of all brokers' trade advices. It is the basis for recording information in the individual security records. A *trade advice* lists the purchase or sale of a specific investment including the trade date, settlement date, purchase or sales price, broker's commission, and security being purchased or sold.

- Keep a file of monthly brokers' statements that are verified by tracing to the individual security records maintained by the company and noting agreement of month-end information.

- Keep a record of interest or dividend income received based on actual cash receipts and deposits into the cash account. See the illustration "Record of Interest and Dividend Income."

- Keep security certificates in a locked vault with access limited to a very few people. Access should never be permitted to fewer than two authorized persons accompanying each other.

Fixed-Assets Record

Records of plant assets having a productive or service life beyond one year must be maintained to insure the proper safeguarding of com-

Record of Interest and Dividend Income

Andrew Manufacturing Company

Record of Interest and Dividend Income
Period Covered _____

Interest Income (grouped by security)

Security	Date Received	Amount	Annual Total

Dividend Income (grouped by security)

Security	Date Received	Amount Received	Annual Total
	qtr 1		
	qtr 2		
	qtr 3		
	qtr 4		
	qtr 1		
	qtr 2		
	qtr 3		
	qtr 4		

pany-owned assets and to allocate properly the cost of the asset to the appropriate period the asset is benefiting (depreciation). Refer to the illustration on page 540 for a sample format.

The estimated life of a fixed asset is the period the asset is used in producing or selling other assets or services. This period varies by type of asset (buildings, equipment, furniture, or fixtures) but is usually standardized by company policy. *Salvage value* is that portion of the asset cost that is expected to be recovered at the end of the asset's productive life.

Allocating the cost of the asset over its service life (depreciation) can be done by many methods. Four common methods are straight line, units of production, declining balance, and sum of years digits.

- When the *straight line method* is used, the cost of the asset minus the estimated salvage value is divided by the asset's productive life in years or months. This method allocates an equal share of the asset's cost to each accounting period.

Fixed Assets Record

```
                    Andrew Manufacturing Company
                         Fixed Assets Record
Asset Description  _____
Purchase Date & Vendor  _____
Purchase Price (including freight and installation costs)  _____
_____
Asset Location  _____
Asset Identification Number  _____
Estimated Life  _____
Depreciation Method  _____
Annual/Monthly Depreciation (if applicable)  _____
_____
Estimated Salvage Value  _____
Disposition Date  _____
Sales Price When Sold  _____
```

Year	Original Cost	Depreciation Expense	Net Book Value	Sales Price	Gain or (Loss) Upon Disposition

- The *units of production method* divides the cost of an asset after deducting estimated salvage value by the estimated units of product that the asset will produce over its service life. This process gives depreciation per unit of product. Depreciation for the period is determined by multiplying the units produced in a period by the unit depreciation.

- Under the *declining balance method,* depreciation of up to twice the straight line rate, without considering salvage value, may be applied each year to the declining book value of a new plant asset having an estimated life of at least three years. If this method is followed and twice the straight line rate is used, the amount charged each year as depreciation expense is determined by (1) calculating a straight line depreciation rate (100 percent divided by the useful life in years) for the asset, (2) doubling this rate, and then (3) at the end of each year in the asset's life, applying the doubled rate to the asset's remaining book value.

- Under the *sum of years digits method* (*SYD*) the years in an asset's service life are added, and the sum is used as the denominator of a series of fractions used in allocating total depreciation to the periods in the asset's service life. The numerators of the fractions are the years in the asset's life in their reverse order. The following example shows the SYD method used to calculate the depreciation of an asset having a five-year life and a cost of $6,000:

Number of years for the denominator = $1 + 2 + 3 + 4 + 5 = 15$

YEAR	ANNUAL DEPRECIATION CALCULATION	ANNUAL DEPRECIATION EXPENSE
1	5/15 × $6,000	$2,000
2	4/15 × $6,000	1,600
3	3/15 × $6,000	1,200
4	2/15 × $6,000	800
5	1/15 × $6,000	400
		$6,000

BUSINESS LAW

Businesses of all types and sizes must perform their activities in compliance with the laws and regulations that affect them. All secretaries, whether or not they work in a law office, can therefore benefit from an understanding of legal concepts and basic terminology. Secretaries who are seeking certification, such as the Certified Professional Secretary standing, may even be tested on their knowledge in this area.

Familiarity with general principles of contract law, agency, and corporate law may help you to deal with various documents and issues more effectively and confidently. You should also be aware of a number of statutes and regulations generally applicable to the conduct of a business. In particular, you should learn to recognize common legal documents, such as a contract, and become familiar with the terminology used in them.

CONTRACTS

The law of contracts is basic to business law, since the negotiation, preparation, execution, and performance of contracts are the foundation for much of the conduct of business. An understanding of the elements of a valid contract and its legal formalities will help you when your office is involved in producing and executing such documents. (If your company executes a substantial number of similar contracts, such as an employment contract or an outside services contract, you may have a standard form on your computer with blanks or spaces in which you fill in the appropriate information.) An understanding of contracts may also be helpful in connection with aspects of office management in matters ranging from ordering supplies and purchasing equipment to dealing with personnel functions.

General Principles

A *contract* is an agreement that is legally enforceable. It can be created by an oral promise or a written document, or it can be implied when the circumstances indicate. It is not always necessary to have a formal, written agreement for a contract to exist. The factors necessary to create an enforceable agreement include *parties* who are competent to contract, an expression of the *terms* of the agreement, and *consideration* for the agreement. The object of the contract must not violate any public policy or statute.

Consideration *Consideration* for a contract most commonly consists of payment in exchange for services or goods or of a promise in exchange for another promise. Except in limited circumstances, if there is no consideration or if the consideration is regarded as inadequate, the contract will not be enforceable. The law considers that a promise not supported by consideration is a gift rather than a binding obligation, and the courts will not compel a party effectively to make a gift. In spite of this rule, a contract "under seal" is considered enforceable without regard to consideration. Furthermore, the courts will rarely look behind a statement in a contract that the parties believe the consideration is adequate.

Competency There are two issues relevant in determining whether a party is competent to create a contract: whether the party has any legal disability and whether the party has the proper authority to enter into the particular contract in question. The issue of authority to enter into the particular contract depends on the circumstances of the situation. An agreement made by an individual who is legally competent will be binding on the individual. Agreements made by corporations or other business entities will be binding if they are executed by officers, agents, or employees who have been authorized to bind the company, either under rules of agency or by specific corporate action. See the section "Agency" for a fuller discussion of this issue.

Terms of Agreement There are no specific rules on the expression of the terms of the agreement, although this criterion is often expressed as a requirement that there must have been a "meeting of the minds" to create a binding contract. That is, there must be sufficient evidence that the parties had reached an agreement even though all of the terms and conditions are not clearly defined. Although the parties' failure to express adequately the terms of their agreement can result in a finding that no contract exists, more often a court will attempt to reconstruct what the parties intended at the time they entered into the contract. This is especially true when one of the parties has performed or partially performed its part of the agreement.

In certain instances some of the terms of an agreement will be provided by statute if the parties have not expressed them. This is particularly true with regard to the sales of goods under the Uniform Commercial Code, discussed later. It is generally more satisfactory, however, if the terms of the agreement are clearly expressed by the parties. Such a statement need not be extensive. An offer by a merchant of a certain product for a specified price and an acceptance of that offer by a customer by tendering payment or submitting a purchase order will be sufficient expression of the terms of an agreement. More extensive provisions, however, will be necessary in more complicated relationships.

Formalities

A well-written agreement should follow certain rules of form, some of which relate to the elements described previously and some of which are simply good business practice. Many of the following suggestions about form can be varied to meet a particular situation or suit an individual's style and are intended to serve only as a general guide.

Introductory Clauses　The agreement should begin with an introductory clause that describes the agreement and identifies the parties. Some circumstances require inclusion of the full address of each of the parties, and even when such information is not required, it is good practice to include the information. The introductory clause also provides an opportunity to assign a short descriptive term to each of the parties, such as "Buyer" and "Seller," as a means of easy reference throughout the agreement. The date of the agreement also should be stated, either in this introductory clause or in the testimonium clause described later. The following example is a common form of introductory clause.

> This Agreement is made this third day of February 1995 by and between Hemingway Incorporated, a Delaware corporation with a usual place of business in Boston, Massachusetts (hereinafter called the "Company"), and Peter F. Trombley, of 123 Park Street, Newton, Massachusetts (hereinafter called the "Consultant").

The manner of identifying a party will vary depending on the legal status of the party. An individual should be identified by his or her name and, usually, residence address. If the individual is in business as a sole proprietor and the agreement relates to the business, the business address should be used.

A corporation should be identified by its registered name, state of incorporation, and principal place of business. The name of the corporate officer who will be signing on behalf of the corporation should *not* appear in the introductory clause. The description of the corporation can be in the form indicated in the preceding example, or a more formal approach may be used.

> . . . Hemingway Incorporated, a corporation duly organized and validly existing under the General Corporation Law of the State of Delaware and maintaining a usual place of business at 73 Tremont Street, Boston, Massachusetts . . .

Sometimes a corporation is organized under one name but conducts its business under a different name. The phrase "doing business as" is often abbreviated as *d/b/a.* If the information about the different name is available, it should be included as follows:

> . . . Hemingway Incorporated, a Delaware corporation doing business in California as Hemingway Business Forms, Inc., and maintaining a usual place of business at 1999 Wilshire Boulevard, Los Angeles, California . . .

Professional corporations should be identified by their corporate names in the same manner as business corporations.

General partnerships in most jurisdictions are not considered legal entities apart from the individual partners, and for purposes of bringing suit each of the general partners must be named. A general partnership usually conducts its business under a trade name, however, and may be referred to by such trade name for purposes of most agreements, especially when there are a large number of general partners. For example:

> . . . Thayer & Crispin, Attorneys-at-Law, a general partnership engaged in the practice of law . . .

It is also appropriate to identify each of the general partners. For example:

> . . . Jean G. Thayer and Sandra Crispin, general partners engaged in the practice of law under the name of Thayer & Crispin . . .

A *limited partnership* consists of one or more general partners who manage the business and can bind the partnership and one or more limited partners who have no managerial authority. The partnership must adopt a name that must be registered, usually with the secretary of state. The limited partnership should be identified by its registered name, and the state of registration should be stated.

Limited liability companies are another form of business organization. A limited liability company retains most of the simplicity of a partnership and limits liability for acts or omissions of the business.

There are a number of different types of trusts, including general trusts, business trusts, and realty trusts. Generally, a *trust* does not have a separate legal identity, and an agreement involving a trust should be made in the name of the trustee.

> . . . James P. Overmeyer, as trustee of the Adam Thomas Family Trust and not individually . . .

Similarly, when a contract is made by any other fiduciary, such as the guardian of a minor, the conservator of an incompetent, or the executor of a will, the fiduciary should be named as a party and clearly identified as acting in a fiduciary capacity.

Recitals   It is common practice to *recite* the background of an agreement, the relationship of the parties, or other facts that tend to clarify the basis for each party entering into the agreement. In addition, a recitation of the consideration for the agreement is often made, either as part of the preliminary recitals or in the body of the agreement (or both). Recitals generally take one of the two following forms, the first of which is the more traditional.

> WITNESSETH:
>
> WHEREAS, Seller has developed and markets a software program relating to legal time and billing that has been adapted for uses on the XYZ personal computer; and
>
> WHEREAS, Buyer is a law firm that has need for a legal time and billing program for use on its XYZ personal computer and desires to acquire a license to use Seller's program;
>
> NOW, THEREFORE, in consideration of the payment of the licensee fee by the Buyer to the Seller and of the mutual covenants and promises set forth herein, the parties agree as follows: . . .

Recitals

a. The Seller is in the business of manufacturing headsets for use with tape-recording equipment and has the capacity to produce in excess of 5,000 headsets per week.

b. The Buyer is in the business of marketing tape-recording equipment to the general public and has need for headsets that can be used with its equipment.

c. The Buyer desires to reserve the Seller's capacity to produce 5,000 headsets per week on the terms and conditions of this Agreement.

The Parties therefore agree as follows: . . .

Body   The body of the contract contains all the provisions relating to the actual terms of the agreement. There are no rules about format or style other than general rules applicable to all business documents. For more about the preparation of documents, see Chapters 6 and 11.

Testimonium

Common Forms. The *testimonium* is the clause that appears at the end of the body of the contract and before the signatures of the parties. Such a clause, in its various forms, serves to affirm that the parties are aware that they are entering into an agreement and that they intend to be bound by the terms of the written document they are signing. Common forms of testimonium clauses include:

IN WITNESS WHEREOF, the parties have hereunto set their hands and seals to this Agreement the date and year first set out above.

IN WITNESS WHEREOF, the parties have executed this Agreement in duplicate the 5th day of June 1995.

For business entities the following forms may be used:

IN WITNESS WHEREOF, the parties have caused this Agreement to be executed by their duly authorized officers on the 1st day of February 1995.

Joseph P. Smith, as trustee of the Smithfield Realty Trust, and George A. Grey, as President of George A. Grey Associates, Inc., have signed this Agreement this 3rd day of April 1995.

Corporate Seal. Frequently the testimonium clause will state that the parties have "set their hands and seals" or that the document is to have the effect of a "sealed" document. The concept of a sealed document derives from early common law, which provided that the presence of a seal eliminated the need to prove that there was consideration to support the contract.

The effect of a seal and its necessity under current law depend on the circumstances and the applicable law of the jurisdiction. Usually, a seal is used to prove corporate authority. Most jurisdictions provide by statute that a statement to the effect that a document is sealed is sufficient to give it the force of a sealed document, even if no seal is actually affixed.

Signatures   The agreement should be signed by an individual who is a party or who is authorized to bind a party. The signatory's name should be typed below the signature line, and except when an individual is signing on his or her own behalf, the authority of the person who is signing should be indicated. The following example is a proper form for execution of a document.

Hemingway Incorporated

By _____

James P. Jacobs, President

As a general rule an agreement on behalf of the following entities should be signed by a person who fills one of the indicated positions.

ENTITY	PERMISSIBLE SIGNATORY
Corporation (including professional corporations)	Corporate officer
Limited liability company	Officer
General partnerships	General partner
Limited partnerships	General partner
Trusts	All trustees, unless there is evidence of authority to act alone
Estates	Executor or administrator

If one person is a party to a contract in more than one capacity, the best practice is to have the person sign the document on separate lines for each capacity. The description under a single signature line should make it clear that the person is signing in more than one capacity.

Attestations   Although not always required, signatures are often attested by witnesses to the signing. This can be helpful if later there is some doubt about who actually signed or the circumstances under which the document was signed. An *attestation* can simply be the signature of the witness under the word *witness* or an attestation clause can recite any information that is relevant, such as the following:

Signed, sealed and delivered by the above-named Peter Gregory, in my presence, at Boston, Massachusetts, this 3rd day of June 1995.

Signatures of corporate officers are often attested by the corporate clerk or secretary to verify that the corporation has authorized the document to be signed. The attestation takes the following form, and the corporate seal is embossed over the attestation:

Attest: [*Corporate Seal*]

_____
Clerk/Secretary

Acknowledgments Some documents, most notably affidavits or documents dealing with real property, must be *acknowledged* before a public official such as a notary public or judicial officer qualified to administer oaths. An acknowledgment executed by a public official has the effect of verifying the facts stated in the acknowledgment, without the necessity to prove them by testimony. Frequently used forms of acknowledgment include the following:

State of _____ December_____, 19____
County of _____

Then personally appeared the above-named James P. Jacobs and acknowledged the foregoing to be his free act and deed, before me,

_____
Notary Public

State of _____ December_____, 19____
County of _____

Then personally appeared the above named James P. Jacobs, Vice President and General Manager of Hemingway Incorporated, and acknowledged the foregoing instrument to be the free act and deed of the corporation, before me,

_____
Notary Public

The form of acknowledgment for an affidavit or other statement of facts should appear substantially as follows:

State of _____
County of _____

The undersigned, Lynn F. Green, known to me and known to be the person who executed the foregoing document, personally appeared before me this _____ day of _____, 19_____, and stated that the facts stated therein are true to the best of her knowledge and belief.

_____
Notary Public

If the affidavit includes a statement by the affiant that the statements contained therein are true to the best of his or her knowledge and belief, it is sufficient to add just the notary jurat at the end of the document after the signature of the party offering the statement. This should include a statement of the venue (state and county) and the language, "Subscribed and sworn to before me," as well as the notary's signature and seal.

AGENCY

Businesses are regularly involved in arrangements with people or organizations that act in a capacity as agent or agency. The *law* of agency is concerned with a number of issues raised when an individual acts on behalf of another party. These issues should be of some concern to the secretary from at least two perspectives. First, contract law and business relationships raise a number of questions, such as who is able to bind a corporation contractually, that involve issues of agency. Second, an employee is considered for many purposes to be an agent of the employer, and, especially when he or she has administrative or managerial responsibilities, the secretary should be aware of the potential consequences of his or her actions as an agent of the employer.

Legal Principles

Agent-Principal Relationship   An *agent* is an individual authorized to act on behalf of another party. The party on whose behalf the agent acts is called the *principal*. The principal may be either an individual or a business entity. When a valid agency exists, the agent can bind the principal and the principal will be responsible for the acts of the agent that are within the scope of the agency or that occur while the agent is fulfilling his or her duties as agent.

In some forms of agency the principal's liability to third parties for the acts of an agent may extend to acts not directly related to the agency, such as when an employee is involved in an automobile accident while making a delivery for the employer, and to acts not expressly authorized by the principal, such as when a managerial employee refuses to hire an applicant because of the applicant's race.

Scope of Authority The scope of authority of an agent depends on the terms of the agency. In some cases the agent's authority is a legal consequence of the relationship of the parties. Hence corporate officers are agents of the corporation, and general partners are agents of their fellow general partners and of the limited partners in a limited partnership. In each of these cases the agent's authority to act for and bind the principal exists only to the extent that the agent is acting within his or her role as corporate officer or general partner, as the case may be.

Unfortunately, it is not always clear whether the agent is acting within this role, and that issue often leads to serious disputes. In other principal-agent relationships the scope of the agent's authority is created by an express agreement and is, consequently, more clearly defined. For example, a homeowner may retain a real estate broker to find a buyer for his or her house at a certain price. The broker is the agent of the homeowner only for that limited purpose and clearly is not authorized to otherwise act for the homeowner.

Authority to Bind a Principal. Generally, the agent is able to bind a principal contractually only to the extent that he or she acts within the scope of the agency. To some extent, third parties who deal with the agent do so at the risk that the agent is acting outside the scope of his or her agency.

When it is not clear from principles of agency that the agent is authorized to act as a consequence of his or her relationship to the principal, or when there is otherwise any question of authority, a third party will often require evidence of authority, such as a certificate signed and sealed by a corporate clerk certifying the adoption of a resolution by the board of directors that authorizes a specific corporate action or certifying that the officer signing an agreement is either generally or specifically authorized to do so.

There are some circumstances under which an agent can bind a principal even without express authority. The authority to do related acts may be implied from the express authority given to the agent, such as when an office manager's authority to hire a receptionist may imply the authority to fire the employee.

An apparent agency may exist when the circumstances lead a third party reasonably to believe that the apparent agent has the authority to act for another person who could but who does not do anything to deny the agency. In some situations a person will ratify the acts of another who purported to be his or her agent and thereby create an agency by ratification. In each of these cases the determination of whether an agency exists depends on the particular facts.

Principal's Liability. The extent of the principal's liability for the acts of an agent that are not within the scope of the agency depends in large part on the degree of control the principal exercises over the agent. The strictest agency relationship is commonly referred to as a *master-servant relationship.* It exists when the principal exercises significant control over the conduct of the agent, such as by setting hours of work, providing tools or equipment, and supervising the work performed. It generally applies to employer-employee relationships.

In a strict agency relationship, as a result of the high degree of control and close supervision, the employer is liable not only for authorized contractual commitments made by its employees on its behalf but also for accidents and personal injuries caused negligently or intentionally by them during their employment. The employee need not be actually performing work for the employer at the time he or she causes personal injuries or similar damage; as long as there is a reasonable link between the activity and the employment, the employer may be liable.

In other types of agency relationships when the principal exercises a lesser degree of control over the actual performance by the agent, such as those involving independent contractors, the scope of the principal's liability is correspondingly smaller. Even when the principal is liable to third parties for injuries caused by an agent, however, the agent is primarily liable to the injured party, or when the injured party recovers from the principal, the agent may be required to reimburse the principal.

Power of Attorney

Many agencies are created by the use of powers of attorney. A *power of attorney* is a written document by which another person is specifically authorized to act for the person signing the document. When a person is authorized to act for a definite and specified purpose, he or she is often referred to as an *attorney in fact* for such purpose.

There is no particular form that must be used to create a power of attorney, although certain governmental entities — most notably the Internal Revenue Service — have issued printed forms that they require to be used in connection with matters brought before them. Any document intended to serve as a power of attorney should contain a clear statement of the powers and duties of the attorney in fact.

In executing the power of attorney, the formalities required to complete the act effectively should be observed. For instance, if the attorney in fact is given the power to execute a deed, an act requiring an acknowledgment by an official, the power of attorney must be likewise acknowledged. It is always important to provide an attestation by witness, even though it may not be legally required, since it may avoid questions later concerning the signature of the principal granting the power of attorney.

Execution of Documents

Whenever an agent is acting for a principal in the execution of a document, whether under a power of attorney or other agency, it is important that the fact of the agency be expressed. If it is unclear whether the agent is acting for himself or herself or for a principal, the agent may be personally liable on the contract. It is also possible that the principal will not be liable at all, which may be to the detriment of both the agent and the third party. For more about the execution of contracts, refer to the previous discussion of contracts.

UNIFORM COMMERCIAL CODE

The Uniform Commercial Code (UCC), a collection of laws relating to commercial transactions, has been adopted in varying forms in all states. It is intended to provide for relatively consistent regulation of commercial transactions among the various jurisdictions. The discussion here focuses on two of the areas covered by the UCC, transactions involving sales of goods and secured transactions. These two are likely to be relevant in most business environments and hence are of the greatest interest to secretaries.

Sales

Article 2 of the UCC applies to transactions involving sales of goods and has two basic functions. Broadly, it establishes standards of fair dealing among buyers and sellers primarily by imposing an overriding obligation of good faith and commercial reasonableness in sales transactions. Article 2 also provides definitions of commonly used commercial terms that serve to clarify the expectations of the parties and standardize the usage of terms in the commercial world.

In addition to its general role, Article 2 has a more practical application. Although the law gives the parties wide freedom to set the terms of their agreement, it also recognizes that parties occasionally fail to provide for all contingencies. There are numerous situations when the UCC will come into play unless the parties otherwise agree.

Article 2, for instance, contains rules for determining, in the absence of an express agreement, whether an offer has been made and accepted, where the goods are to be delivered, what warranties are given or implied, the buyer's right to inspect and reject goods, the seller's right to withhold shipment, and remedies for breach by either party. Frequently, the parties will intentionally omit a provision in a contract knowing that the UCC will govern or will specifically refer to the relevant section of Article 2 and incorporate its provisions into the agreement.

Security Interests

When your business finances the purchase of office equipment or similar items, or if the company takes out a loan for other purposes, the lender will usually require a security interest in the items financed or in the assets of the corporation. Article 9 of the UCC governs the creation of security interests and provides for a filing procedure by which such interests are perfected.

Security Agreement   A security interest is created by the agreement of the parties. The agreement should be in writing and signed by the debtor. The parties are generally free to set the terms of the security agreement, although certain provisions of Article 9, primarily with respect to the rights of third parties, will override contradictory provisions in a written agreement.

Generally, a security interest gives the secured party the right to repossess the collateral if payments are not made or if the debtor is otherwise in default and to receive the proceeds if the collateral is sold. If the security interest is perfected, as explained below, the secured party can repossess the collateral even if it has been sold or transferred to a third party.

A security interest is enforceable against third parties only when it has been perfected. Except in very limited circumstances, a security interest is *perfected* by filing a financing statement with the appropriate governmental agency. The proper place of filing varies from state to state and may also depend on the type of collateral covered by the security agreement, so the statute in effect in the place where the collateral is located must be checked to ensure proper filing.

Financing Statement   Most states have adopted some version of a relatively standard financing statement, which is called a *Form UCC-1*. There are some variations for different states, and the requirements of your particular state should be checked. A completed UCC-1 relating to the purchase of office equipment is illustrated on page 556. If your company is frequently involved in UCC filings, there should be a form in your computer.

A financing statement must be signed by the debtor, unless the security agreement signed by the debtor is filed with the financing statement. It is often necessary to file the financing statement with more than one office, and a Form UCC-2 is designed for this purpose. It is a duplicate of the UCC-1 but has an extra sheet of carbon attached so that it can be placed over a UCC-1 and the form need only be typed once. There is also a form UCC-3, which may be used to continue, terminate, release, assign, or amend a previously filed UCC-1 financing statement.

REGULATION OF BUSINESS

Secretaries are concerned with anything that affects their work, and like all employees, they are affected by the statutes and regulations that govern the conduct of business in their companies. Business enterprises are subject to a variety of statutes and regulations that may affect the conduct of the business generally or may affect only specific aspects of operation.

There are statutes governing the creation of business corporations and providing rules for the basic structure and functioning of the corporation. The offering and issuance of securities are governed by

Uniform Commercial Code Financing Statement — UCC-1

Uniform Commercial Code — FINANCING STATEMENT — Form UCC-1

IMPORTANT — Read instructions on back before filling out form

This FINANCING STATEMENT is presented to a filing officer for filing pursuant to the Uniform Commercial Code.

4. ☐ Filed for record in the real estate records.	5. ☐ Debtor is a Transmitting Utility.	6. No. of Additional Sheets Presented:
1. Debtor(s) (Last Name First) and address(es)	2. Secured Party(ies) and address(es)	3. For Filing Officer (Date, Time, Number, and Filing Office)
Gorham Enterprises One Park Place Arlington, MA 01000	Smith Leasing Co. 155 Wagner Road Arlington, MA 01000	

7. This financing statement covers the following types (or items) of property:

Xerox Copier, Model 1045, Serial No. XPF6666666

☐ Products of Collateral are also covered.

Whichever is Applicable (See Instruction Number 9)	*Peter Gorham, President*	*John Smith*
	Signature(s) of Debtor (Or Assignor)	Signature(s) of Secured Party (Or Assignee)

Filing Officer Copy – Alphabetical
STANDARD FORM — UNIFORM COMMERCIAL CODE — FORM UCC-1   Rev. Jan. 1980   *Forms may be purchased from Hobbs & Warren, Inc., Boston, Mass. 02101*

another set of laws and regulations, and still other statutes regulate certain relationships between businesses. Every business with employees is also required to comply with a variety of laws and regulations relating to certain aspects of the employer-employee relationship, such as payment of wages, hours worked, discrimination, worker safety, and benefits for injured workers. In fact, two areas that are likely to be relevant in any business are the employment relationship and corporate law.

Some enterprises, however, are subject to regulation because of the nature of their business. The most prominent examples of this specialized regulation are telephone and utility companies and the insurance companies. Businesses dealing with consumers are generally subject to consumer protection statutes, and companies involved in hazardous operations may be required by law to follow extraordinary safety precautions. Secretaries should be especially familiar with the measures that affect their particular types of business.

Corporate Law

Corporations exist only if created in accordance with state law. Every state has enacted a statute that sets forth the requirements for establishing a corporation and maintaining its corporate existence. General rules relating to corporate functions such as issuance of stock and the holding of annual stockholder meetings are also found in the statute.

Often, much of the paperwork relating to the creation and continued existence of the corporation is done by the corporation's counsel. There are, however, certain forms and procedures that you may see in your work, and the following general explanation may help you understand these matters better.

Charter   The charter document for a corporation is often called a *Certificate of Incorporation, Articles of Organization,* or something similar. It usually contains the following information: the name of the corporation and its purposes, the address of its principal place of business, the type and number of shares of corporate stock authorized, any stock restrictions or special rules for the governing of the corporation, and the names of the initial officers and directors of the company.

The charter document must be filed with the proper state official, usually that of the secretary of state, and becomes effective upon approval. Amendments can be made by vote of the stockholders of the corporation and also must be filed and approved to become effective.

Bylaws   The corporate *bylaws* are the rules by which the corporation conducts its internal affairs. The bylaws, which must be consistent with state law, generally describe the relative functions and powers of the corporate officers, board of directors, and stockholders. Bylaws do not need to be filed and are effective upon adoption by the stockholders. They also can be amended by the stockholders or in some instances by the board of directors.

Organizational Structure   A corporation is organized in three tiers consisting of the stockholders, the board of directors, and the officers.

- The stockholders own the stock, elect the board of directors, and must approve certain corporate actions, such as authorization of additional stock, mergers, or sale of the corporate assets.

- The board of directors is responsible for overseeing the operation of the corporation at all levels and elects the corporate officers to handle the day-to-day affairs of the corporation.

- The officers, who generally include a president, one or more vice presidents, a treasurer, and a secretary or clerk, have duties given to them by the bylaws or the board of directors.

In a small company the stockholders, directors, and officers usually a few individuals. Large corporations may have a very complex organization of officers and directors and usually a large number of stockholders not otherwise involved in the business.

Securities Law   Although the corporate structure is established pursuant to state law, one important aspect of the corporate operation — the sale of securities — is regulated under two federal securities statutes as well as securities statutes known as *blue sky laws,* which are in effect in every state. As a general rule, the securities statutes require that stock either be registered with a regulating authority or specifically be exempt from registration under the statute. Under federal laws, stock that is not exempt must be registered with the Securities and Exchange Commission (SEC), and each state has identified a state agency that enforces its blue sky law.

Registration. Registration requires the preparation and filing of a statement and a prospectus that fully disclose pertinent facts about the history of the corporation, its financial and business affairs, and similar information. Once stock has been registered, the company must continually update the information that was provided in the statement filed upon initial registration. Properly registered stock may be publicly traded, which means that it may be offered for sale to the general public. All stock traded on the major stock exchanges or sold over the counter is registered stock.

Exemption. The federal securities law and most of the state blue sky laws exempt private offerings or limited offerings from the registration requirement. Strict statutory requirements must be met to qualify for this exemption. But most small corporations whose stock is owned by a few individuals and which do not offer their stock for sale to outside investors qualify for it. (References to *public corporations* means those corporations that have registered their stock for sale to the general public. Private corporations with only a few stockholders actively involved in the corporate enterprise are often referred to as *closely held corporations.*)

Employment Relationship

The rights and obligations of employers and employees to one another are governed in part by the express agreement of the parties; in part by statutory regulation by federal, state, and local governments; and in part by the common law. Although the agreement of the employer and employee generally establishes the terms and conditions of the employment relationship, that agreement may intentionally or inadvertently fail to address many of the issues that arise during the course of employment. It may also include provisions that are unenforceable because they violate public policy or a specific statute.

Employment Agreements   The agreement between the employer and the employee, like any contract, may be oral or written, simple or complex. It is important from the perspective of both parties that the agreement be as specific as possible with respect to the basic issues:

- What work is to be performed by the employee?

- Is there a formal performance review and evaluation?

- Is there a probationary period?

- What is the salary and when is it paid?

- Are there benefits such as medical and dental insurance, profit sharing or pension plans, and life insurance?

Within the limits of certain regulatory statutes, the foregoing are all issues that are open for negotiation, and it is a good idea to raise them early. The oral and written agreement of the parties with respect to these and similar terms and conditions of employment constitute the employment contract. If the employer has written employee policies, they, too, will be considered as part of the employment contract. *Caution*: You should be aware that if you are interviewing or hiring new employees, you are considered an agent of your employer, and what you say will be binding on the company.

In most instances the relationship between the employer and employee is considered a *contract at-will*. This means that it can be terminated by either party for almost any reason or for no reason. The agreement may require one or two weeks' notice, but generally no reason need be given to justify or explain the termination. Problems can arise upon termination by the employer, even in an at-will contract, when the reason for terminating is prohibited by law or public policy, such as when the employer terminates an employee to avoid paying a large commission that is about to become due.

Wages and Hours   An employee cannot waive the protections established by the federal wage and hour laws. The National Fair Labor Standards Act, applicable to most employers having fifteen or more employees and engaged in interstate commerce, establishes minimum wages for regular and overtime work. The statute is enforced by the Wage and Hour Division of the Department of Labor.

As a general rule, an employer must pay its employees not less than the minimum wage for the first forty hours of work per week. The employee must be compensated at one and one-half times his or her regular hourly rate for all hours worked in excess of forty hours for the week. In addition to the federal statute, there may be state and local laws that regulate the maximum number of hours a person can be required to work, whether work can be required on holidays or Sundays, under what conditions minors may work, and related issues.

Employment Discrimination   A number of federal and state laws prohibit discrimination in employment. The following are examples of important federal laws:

- *Title VII of the Civil Rights Act of 1964* applies to most employers having a least fifteen employees and makes it unlawful to base employment decisions on or to discriminate with respect to terms and conditions of employment because of an individual's race, color, religion, sex, or national origin.

- The *Age Discrimination in Employment Act (ADEA)* prohibits most employers with twenty or more employees from discriminating against employees between the ages of forty and seventy.

- The *Equal Pay Act* is part of the wage and hour law and makes it illegal to pay unequal wages to men and women who do substantially equal work.

- The *Americans with Disabilities Act of 1990* forbids businesses with fifteen or more employees from discriminating on the basis of disability and requires that places of business provide access for disabled persons.

In addition to the federal laws, many states have similar statutes prohibiting employment discrimination.

Enforcement Procedure. The federal Equal Employment Opportunity Commission (EEOC) monitors compliance with Title VII, ADEA, and the Equal Pay Act. Many states have local agencies or commissions responsible for enforcing the state discrimination statutes.

The procedure established under most discrimination statutes requires the employee to file a claim with the proper agency within a relatively short time of the incident claimed to constitute discrimination. Generally, the agency then has the option to investigate, attempt to conciliate, bring a legal action on behalf of the claimant, or authorize the individual to bring legal action. The filing of the claim within the period established by the applicable discrimination statute is almost always a prerequisite of later court action.

Employer Liability. When a supervisory employee is responsible for a discriminatory decision, the employer will be liable. The employer also will be liable for discriminatory acts by employees who are not in supervisory positions if the employer is or should be aware of the conduct and does nothing to correct the situation. An employer guilty of employment discrimination may be required to hire or reinstate the affected individual, to pay back wages, and in limited circumstances to pay compensatory damages.

Some forms of employment discrimination are more obvious than others. It is important to note that a pattern or practice that tends to affect any of the identified classifications can constitute prohibited discrimination, even if there was no overt discrimination against an individual. Sexual harassment is a form of sex discrimination and exists when there are sexual advances, requests for sexual favors, and other verbal or physical conduct of a sexual nature. Sexual harassment is illegal if it affects the terms and conditions of an individual's employment or if it creates a hostile or negative working environment. Refer to the discussion of sexual harassment in Chapter 3 for guidelines on steps that an employee may take to deal with this problem.

Workers' Compensation Workers' compensation laws have been enacted in every state. Although the statutes vary from state to state with respect to what kinds of employees are covered, how claims are administered, and what benefits are payable, they generally require that every employer maintain workers' compensation insurance to cover *compensable losses* of employees. Compensable losses can be very broadly defined as injuries from accidents or diseases resulting from an individual's employment.

Workers' Compensation Insurance. Businesses are required to cover most employees by workers' compensation insurance, whether employed by a private business or by a public agency. A few statutes exempt businesses with fewer than three employees and some permit corporate officers, working partners, and owners of the business to be excluded from coverage. An employer can face significant penalties for failing to provide workers' compensation insurance, including fines, imprisonment, inability to raise defenses to a claim, personal liability of owners or corporate officers, and increased levels of compensation.

If an employee is injured on the job or suffers injury or disease resulting from his or her employment, the employee is entitled to receive compensation for lost wages, medical expenses, and rehabilitation costs. With few and limited exceptions, a worker's exclusive remedy against the employer for work-related injury is the recovery of workers' compensation benefits. This means that the employee cannot bring a personal injury suit against the employer, even if the employer was negligent or otherwise at fault for the injury.

On the other hand, workers' compensation benefits are payable regardless of whether the employer was at fault. The theory underlying this system is that the employee is assured of a reasonable measure of compensation to be paid without delay, and the employer is relieved of the burden of defending personal injury suits in exchange for providing the insurance that pays the compensation benefits.

The amount of the benefits payable under workers' compensation is established by statute and depends primarily on the wage level of the injured employee but also may involve other factors including the type of injury, whether the employee is totally or partially disabled, and whether the disability is temporary or permanent. There is usually a ceiling on the amount recoverable for a single injury. Workers' compensation insurance is available from private insurance companies and, in a few states, from a public fund. In addition, many states permit self-insurance by large corporations or groups of smaller businesses.

State workers' compensation statutes are governed in most states by a board or commission and in a few states by the courts. The usual procedure is for an employee to file a claim with the employer and the employer to notify the insurance carrier. The administrative agency responsible for implementing the statute receives reports concerning claims and resolves disputes concerning the extent or duration of the injury and the amount of benefits payable.

Unemployment Insurance. The unemployment insurance system is part of the Social Security Act of 1935. Through this system unemployed persons are paid a weekly income for a specified period. All employers are required to contribute a certain portion of an employee's wages to this fund. The amount of money that an unemployed person can collect is determined by the amount that was paid into the person's account by the employer when the person was still employed.

INDEX